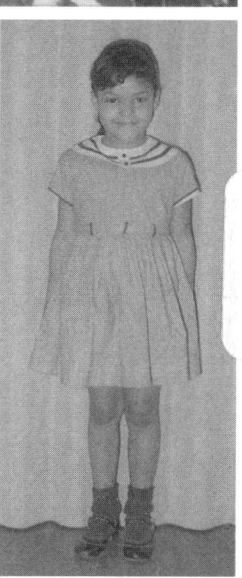

# PRAISE FOR *PLAIN JAYNE*

"A woman like no other finally shares her true journey. Jayne had no script to follow on the road to becoming one of the most recognizable women in entertainment. A true multi hyphenate, Jayne broke down seemingly impenetrable walls in daytime TV, late night, sports, variety shows, and even movies. Jayne was the girl next door America didn't know it wanted, but she did! Jayne's legacy lives and her words serve a timeless, empowering message to all women. Beautiful and brilliant!"

—Tamron Hall

"Jayne Kennedy is an icon. Her willingness to candidly share her struggles and triumphs is an inspiring reminder of the value of resilience and integrity. For those of us women who chose to pursue a career in sports, we are indebted to Jayne for fighting important battles that made our paths a little less rocky."

—Jemele Hill, author and sports journalist

"From small-town Ohio, to the glitz and glamor of '70s Hollywood, to the fast-paced newsroom of *The NFL Today*, Jayne Kennedy takes readers on a captivating journey through her remarkable life and career. Told with honesty, candor, and sharp insight, *Plain Jayne* is a once in a lifetime memoir by an extraordinary woman, who is one of the inspirations behind my own TV career."

—Deborah Roberts, *20/20* cohost and award-winning ABC News correspondent

"Despite the title of this moving memoir, there was nothing plain about Jayne. Not only was she young, beautiful, and talented, but she had humor and a real connection to the audience. I hope that all producers have a Jayne Kennedy in their résumé. . . . I'm sure glad she's in mine."

—George Schlatter, creator of *Rowan & Martin's Laugh-In*

"The courage it must have taken for Jayne to commit to paper this unflinchingly candid recollection of her private life and professional career is both inspiring and empowering. I am in awe of her resiliency and how she's overcome crippling obstacles. Despite having to navigate the land mines of Hollywood 'isms' and dodge the bricks of betrayal being lobbed at her personal life—including a very public scandal—she emerges triumphant as a history maker and way maker. This book demonstrates how Jayne cleared a path for every African American female entertainer and entrepreneur who has come after her. She shows us all that even with clipped wings, Black Swans can soar!"

—Sherri Shepherd

"When Jayne Kennedy joined *The NFL Today*, she was among the trailblazers for women and people of color who covered sports. The pressure and the often-cruel backlash Kennedy faced are part of the life story of a woman who has a hard-earned place in the history of sports television."
                                                                    —Bob Costas

"Jayne Kennedy is not who you thought she was, if you remember her from the early days of *The NFL Today* on CBS. Ridiculed as a Black beauty queen who didn't know sports, she was, in truth, a complex, compassionate woman who grew up captivated by Shirley Chisholm, the first Black woman elected to Congress. Jayne's heartfelt book takes the reader on Kennedy's voyage of growing up beautiful and ambitious and often unwelcome. Congresswoman Chisholm once said, 'If there isn't a seat at the table, pull up a folding chair.' That is exactly what Kennedy did."
          —Lesley Visser, Hall of Fame sportscaster, first woman to cover the NFL
     (*Boston Globe* 1976), first woman inducted into the Pro Football Hall of Fame (2006)

"The word *iconic* is grossly overused in our modern-day lexicon, but Jayne Kennedy has earned that distinction on so many fronts, in so many ways. What I love about Jayne is that unlike countless others, she was never seduced by her iconography. As she writes, 'Plain Jayne' is just fine. But plain is not to be confused with bland. I enjoyed reading every single sentence of this book, learning even more about the backstory of a boss woman like no other. I think you will too. Enjoy!"
                                —Tavis Smiley, broadcaster and bestselling author

"*Plain Jayne* is not just retracing the footsteps of a broadcasting pioneer. It is illuminating the often razor-thin line between professional excellence and personal pain. Its honesty is both refreshing and brutal, and its message of perseverance, faith, and forgiveness is timeless and inspiring."
                          —Ernie Johnson Jr., host of *Inside the NBA* and author of
                          *Unscripted: The Unpredictable Moments That Make Life Extraordinary*

"From her early childhood, to Hollywood, to cohost as the first woman of color on a national sports broadcast, to friendships with the likes of Muhammad Ali and Smokey Robinson, Jayne's courage and beauty, inside and out, shines throughout. Her story about family, success, heartbreak, and love is an inspirational read. The many women who have followed in her footsteps owe her a debt of gratitude."
                                —Robert Fishman, CBS Sports director (1975–2023)

# PLAIN JAYNE

A MEMOIR

# JAYNE KENNEDY

ANDSCAPE

LOS ANGELES   NEW YORK

First Edition, September 2025
10 9 8 7 6 5 4 3 2 1
FAC-004510-25170
Printed in the United States of America

This book is set in Avenir, Gotham, and Minion
Designed by Amy C. King

Library of Congress Control Number: 2024949421
ISBN 978-1-368-11095-2

Reinforced binding

The authorized representative in the EU for product safety and compliance is
Disney Trading B.V.
Asterweg 15S, 1031 HL
Amsterdam, The Netherlands
email: DCP.DL-EU.bookscontact@disney.com

www.AndscapeBooks.com

SUSTAINABLE FORESTRY INITIATIVE
Certified Sourcing
www.forests.org
SFI-01681

Logo Applies to Text Stock Only

*I dedicate* Plain Jayne *to my father,*
*Herbert H. Harrison Sr., who passed away April 28, 2014.*
*And to my incredible ninety-five year old mother,*
*Virginia Mary Thompson Harrison.*
*They are my soul . . . my air.*
*Through them I have learned everything I know about being a better*
*person in my family, in my career, and in my community. They have taught*
*me to be a better mom and a better wife.*
*My journey through this life began with them for a reason.*
*I chose them to show me the way!*

*To the spirits of my ancestors . . . thank you. I see you.*

*And to my steadfast husband, Bill Overton.*
*You have seen my love, my joy, my struggle, my pain, all of me.*
*You will always be my rock, and for that I will be eternally grateful.*
*"At a time in my life when I needed God most,*
*He sent me you."*

*And lastly, I dedicate my entire heart to my reasons for living,*
*my daughters: Cheyenne Maree, Savannah Ré, Kopper Joi, and Zaïre Ollyea.*
*You have given me a purpose far beyond anything that I have searched for*
*when I became your mom.*
*Of all the things I have done with my life,*
*I am most proud to be your mother.*

—JAYNE HARRISON KENNEDY OVERTON

# BLACK SWAN

Most of my life, people have thought that things always came easy for me because of my appearance. Or that they had to "take care" of me simply because I was such a nice person and would be taken advantage of by others. Or that the "poise and confidence" exhibited when I walked into a room was a message of control and self-assuredness. Or that because I had "made it" at a time when so few Black women had achieved that level of meteoric success I must have it all figured out and have all the answers. *Nothing could have been further from the truth.* And while there is much that *is* known about me . . . or should I say there is much that people *think* they know about me . . . I was the proverbial Black Swan gliding gracefully across the lake not causing so much as a ripple to the casual observer, with the sun reflecting off my black, water-glossed feathers—but underneath the waterline I was paddling furiously, as fast as I possibly could, just to stay afloat.

No one ever saw that.

What they did see was a young, ambitious woman who seemed coolly unflappable in the face of insurmountable odds. In reality, I was a somewhat naive nineteen-year-old Black girl from a very small Midwestern town who believed she could go to Hollywood in 1971 and become a star. Long before the existence of internet branding and social media platforms. Before exclusive haute couture and brand ambassadorship deals. And long before the #MeToo, #TimesUp, and BLM movements. No mentor. No team. No entourage. No significant public relations.

And still I paddled.

Today when I hear stories of gender and pay discrimination from women in sports broadcasting and entertainment, on one hand it breaks my heart, but on the other hand I think . . . you have NOOOO IDEA. In all honesty, I thought we'd be much further along as a society than we find ourselves in 2025, when my daughters have fewer freedoms and less agency over their bodies than I did at their age.

I recall several years ago while driving, I saw an LA city bus that was wrapped top to bottom with a photo of the beautiful Kerry Washington, promoting her hit television show *Scandal.* All I could do was pull over and cry. Tears of happiness for her in having achieved that level of success . . . but what I would have given to have had that kind of acceptance and support during my acting career.

It's been over fifty years since I arrived in LA.

Thirty years away from it all.

No one knows what I really went through.

They only saw the Black Swan.

# ONE MOMENT IN TIME

was on my second marriage and raising three amazing daughters. Endless days and nights on the road managing a bustling Hollywood career since 1971 had become a vision in my rearview mirror. It was 1992.

"Bill, let's take the kids to the beach," I said to my husband on a perfectly beautiful Sunday morning in Santa Monica, California. He immediately agreed. After working ten months at seven days a week, we finally had a day off and would be heading out on tour soon. But I didn't mind this time, because I would be touring with my entire family, much unlike those years and years of being on the road—alone. Our musical stage production *The Journey of the African American* was a rousing success, running almost a year in Los Angeles. Soon, we'd be heading out on a three-city tour . . . Bill, our young daughters, and me. I could not have been more excited.

"Girls, get your things together, we're having a beach day," I yelled.

That's all they needed to hear. My heart just bubbled over with pure joy as I watched them screaming and scrambling throughout the house to find their swimsuits, toys, and towels, giggling with each other while Bill and I packed up.

We chatted about the play we had produced together that had done phenomenally well, earning us a command performance invitation from Los Angeles mayor Tom Bradley when the city opened its arms to welcome Nelson Mandela on his first visit to LA after being released from a South African prison.

It was a particularly calm moment for Bill and me. I was accustomed to constantly being on the move since I had first left Ohio and come to Los Angeles. After crisscrossing the globe for work, living through a beautiful first marriage that ended in a stressful existence, divorcing my ex-husband, Leon, and even getting to a place of *forgiveness* with him, I had everything I could hope for and dream of. An amazing husband, a strong family, a fulfilling career, and most importantly—a future that was nothing but bright.

And then . . . the phone rang.

There are moments in your life when your future changes in an *instant*. You don't realize you're seeing someone for the last time. Or you find out you're pregnant. Or that you're not. Bob Hope smiles at you and tells you to pack your bags—you got the job. You lost the job. It goes on. Throughout our lives these moments shift our everything. And that one phone call shifted my entire being.

"Hello?" I answered the phone, still smiling at my girls.

"Jayne."

I instantly knew who it was, but something felt different. This was not a *casual* call.

We had been divorced for eight years, yet . . . I could still read him. The first thing I noticed—the very *first* thing that indicated to me this would be a life-changing call—was Leon's voice. His tone. It was his practiced radio DJ voice.

I instantly found myself taking a deep, deep breath.

"I need to talk with you," said Leon, his voice strong, yet shaky. "Right now."

I saw Bill looking over at me, a bit concerned, as my facial expression must have suggested something was amiss.

"Well, we're here now," I said. "You can come over anytime." I already knew beach day was off.

"I'm on my way."

I need to explain to you now, my reader, this book is *not* about a singular incident in my life some thirty-plus years ago. I'm simply finally taking my agency and control of *my true story*. A story that begins three thousand miles away from this phone call . . .

My actual story is one of family, love, ambition, hard work, pain, more hard work, faith, struggle, community, and so much more.

And yet, a not-so-insignificant part of my life hinged on this single call.

When I opened the door, Leon stood there. I noticed his pressed dress shirt was soaked with sweat from under his arms down to his waist. That was the second thing that let me know this was more serious than I could ever imagine.

I turned and said, "Girls, go to your rooms, please."

The girls made their way out of the living room, my firstborn, Savannah, throwing just a bit of side-eye in our direction as they all left.

I waved Leon to the couch, and he sat on the edge, back straight, hands on his knees, eyes directly on me.

"Do you need to speak privately?" Bill respectfully asked.

"No, Bill," Leon said. "I need to speak with *both* of you."

Bill, my rock, sat on the other couch, still and attentive. While I sat on the chair . . . all by myself . . . isolated on an island alone.

I was fortunately blessed to have a husband and an ex-husband who were friends from many, many years ago when Bill met Leon before he even met me. Which is why I knew Bill would be supportive of whatever *this* was going to be.

There was no small talk.

"Jayne, the tape is out."


And there it was. Just like that.

I was frozen . . . not even breathing, hearing little else he was saying. My mind was pounding with one question over and over and over again: *How did I get here?*

To understand me, nothing in the conversation that followed would help you.

To understand me, you would have to go back to 1951.

# CHAPTER TWO

# JANE HARRISON, A SAFE HAVEN

When I was four years old and living in Cleveland, Ohio, I had a little shorts set with painted palm trees. I don't know how I knew palm trees represented California, but I did. And I always wore sunglasses with pointed cat-eye frames decked out in rhinestones.

"I like your outfit, Jane," Aunt Pearl would say.

I'd flip off my glasses to give her a dramatic stare. And, as she says, I'd *switch* across the grass, tossing my hips and my hair from side to side and telling everyone, "I'm gonna be a movie star."

"Well okay then, Miss Jane," Pearl would say, laughing hysterically. Then my sister would try to stop me and Grandma Lois would say, "Leave Fancy Prancy alone, she can be a star if she wants to."

I told everyone I was going to be a movie star, though I had no idea how to make it happen. It didn't matter.

My recurring fantasy of flying off on a white-winged horse began a few years later when we moved to Wickliffe, Ohio, a suburb fourteen miles away. Every night I looked out the window, listening to the B&O train whistling along the shores of Lake Erie as it prepared to stop in downtown Cleveland and wondering where these people were going, where they came from. My family is scattered up and down the East Coast and we visited often, but it was family. I wanted to see everything there was to see in a world I imagined was a billion times bigger than their backyards. I dreamed that one day I'd finally go west of the Mississippi. Or as Dad would recite, "M-I-Crooked Letter, Crooked Letter-I-Crooked Letter, Crooked Letter-I-Humpback, Humpback-I."

I was born Jane Harrison at Freedmen's Hospital in Washington, DC, October 27, 1951, at 5:47 p.m. to Herbert and Virginia Harrison. Founded in 1862, Freedmen's was the first hospital in the US for former slaves and evolved to become the primary care facility in DC for African American families. Mom, Dad, Shirley (my older sister by fourteen months), and I lived on Thirteenth Street with Dad's cousin Marie.

When I was nine months old, Dad heard that there were better work opportunities up north. Like so many African Americans from 1910 until the 1970s during the Great Migration north, my young parents made the difficult decision to leave DC, where they had more family support, and ventured off to Ohio.

My dad's sister lived in Cleveland and he would stay with them while he looked for a job. Mom took us to her home in Danville, Virginia—awaiting the letter that would signal: *It's time to take the train to our new home up north.*

I absolutely recall this, even at that young age, as my very first memory: I vividly remember waiting on the train platform in Cleveland for Dad to pick us up, when all of a sudden . . . the train whistle blared as it prepared to leave. A massive cloud of white smoke erupted from the funnel. My entire body lurched in panic. I was terrorized by the deafening sound of this huge black train no farther than twenty feet away from me in my stroller with smoke pouring off its back as I screamed and screamed. Aside from the fact that I was so tiny by comparison, the train was also on an elevated platform, which made it appear even more ominous. I remember it was cold, and the picture in my head is, oddly, in black and white. I remember Mom grabbing me tight because I wouldn't stop screaming, and then Dad saw us and came running, swooping us up. He held me close and made me feel safe. Don't ask me how I remember all that at nine months, but I do.

Over the years our extended family grew and grew and was always close—whether it was the cousins, aunts, and uncles who lived in Ohio or the relatives who visited frequently from Pennsylvania, New York, New Jersey, DC, Virginia, or South Carolina, family was always around. Uncle John had just gotten out of the army and would come by all the time. As soon as he hit the front steps, he had chewing gum for all of us. My mom's sisters, Aunt Ruby and Aunt Cat (Catherine), came from Virginia to live with us until they settled in. Aunt Ruby was always a trip. Loud and flashy, with her hair dyed bright ruby red. She loved to dance, and she made sure everyone knew that—especially the men. Sometimes when we had parties and Aunt Ruby would start to dance, Mom would make us leave the room.

The loudest relative was Daddy's aunt Katie, Grandma's sister. She lived in DC, and occasionally came to visit. You could hear her coming from two blocks away. She was a big, husky woman with a voice to match, and every time that voice came within proximity of my house I would run and hide under the bed, trembling the whole time, and stay there until she left, or someone dragged me out kicking and screaming.

My favorite was Uncle Harold, who was married to Dad's sister Janet. At the time, they lived in Philadelphia, but they visited fairly often. I don't know why I liked Uncle Harold so much; maybe it was because of the bags of cat's-eye marbles he always gave me. But it was more than that. Uncle Harold held a special place in my heart until the day he passed recently. And I haven't owned a cat's-eye marble in fifty years.

It seemed that everybody in our family had some kind of nickname. Aunt Elizabeth was Aunt Fat. Then there was Po' Boy, Pootney, Spider, Buss, Bootsey, Black Gal, Whis, Snowball, Cat, Ducey, Big Man, Poot-Butt, Shugg,

Gip, and so many more. The relative who had the most influence on me was probably Aunt Ruth, Dad's sister—they called her White Rabbit.

White Rabbit lived in Cleveland, and she was an Avon lady. Well, need I say more? Every time Aunt Ruth came to visit, she would bring the old samples of lipstick, perfume, blush, shadow, creams, lotions, and dusting powders. Whenever Avon came out with anything new, I was in heaven. It wasn't because I got any of the *new* Avon products. I didn't need them, because I wasn't even ten years old. What mattered was that Aunt Ruth would bring precious little bottles and boxes of all the old stuff she didn't need anymore, all the testers and samples that never got used. Aunt Ruth would teach us how to be pretty young ladies with those tiny little tubes of pink, red, and orange, along with glass bottles of sweet, exotic smells, all no bigger than your thumb.

I remember our little preschool at one of the houses on the next street over from our home on Utica Avenue. We used to sit in a circle and listen to stories. Mom said I was always the leader of the group—well, *any* group. I was always sitting in the middle, telling stories, and telling them what to do.

I recall Mom walking us to school one particularly windy day, when the wind picked up the skirt of Mom's dress, tossing it around her waist. Mom had rushed us out of the house so fast that she had forgotten to put on her underwear, so since she had to hold our hands, we held her dress down, glued to her legs. We laughed about that one for years.

Friday nights Mom and Dad would give card parties and people would fill the house with smoke and drink, laughing and playing cards until the early-morning hours. The living room, dining room, and basement were filled with tables where men talked trash, drank too much, and patted the pretty ladies on the butt. I never understood the games they played (looking back, I'm sure it was bid whist and tonk), but it was just fascinating to watch the interactions of grown people laughing and having a great time after a week of hard work and disappointments. They rarely talked about their jobs. But they did dance. Dad always had all the best music of the times. Mom would cook and Dad outtalked them all. Of course, I was never supposed to be there, but I would lie at the top of the stairs and peek through the rails so I could see, defying sleep until I just passed out. Then when it was all over, Dad would pick me up in his big, strong arms and put me to bed.

We always went to church as a family. We had the prettiest little church dresses. Mom took great pride in having her girls look pretty as little dolls. On special occasions, she'd curl our hair into what she called "Shirley Temple curls." We loved to bounce our hair around our shoulders and pretend we were princesses.

But aside from those wonderful memories, the most vivid come from the Utica Avenue house, quite close to Hough Avenue, where I had the most horrible recurring nightmares the entire time we lived there. Not yet five, I couldn't read well, and every day I would look up at the outside of the building. Carved into the cement cornice high above was THE GOSS HOUSE. Being so young, I thought it said THE GHOST HOUSE. In my nightmare, I would hear the ghosts long before I ever saw them, an army of them marching down the boulevard that led to our street. They always made so much noise that my heart would stop, my body turning freezing cold, and I would shake so hard I thought I would break. Then I would hear them growing louder and louder as they turned the corner and headed to my front doorsteps. I would hide at the top of the bedroom stairs, staring out the front window and watching until I could see them march up the steps, across the porch, and through the front door. Every time we'd knock one down with the only weapon that seemed to work—our dish towels—another would come through the door. I was so terrified. Night after night I'd fall asleep in fear of the ghost brigade. I already had a very fertile imagination . . . a harbinger of things to come.

Mom and Dad eventually decided not to raise their girls in the rough-and-tumble inner city, so when I was five years old with two sisters, they bought a piece of land and built a house in Wickliffe. The contractors built the basic house, but Mom and Dad wanted to put on the finishing touches themselves. Every weekend we'd drive out to our new house and spend the days painting, varnishing, landscaping, and doing whatever was needed.

One weekend shortly before we were ready to move in, we had just dug up the front flowerbeds. I remember that the earth was so warm and soft.

It was getting dark, and we were really tired, so Mom and Dad made a bed in the dirt with some blankets and pillows while they finished up the final touches for the day. Exhausted, I fell asleep quickly, and my dream again turned into a nightmare. . . . I heard the ghost army coming. I panicked. I had thought that when we moved they would never be able to find me, and what I had thought was going to be my dream house was turning into my nightmare home, again. They got louder and louder as I heard them come down the avenue just north of our new house. The front steps divided the two flowerbeds, and we were in the one to the south, farthest away. I stuck my head up over the edge of the cold concrete, just barely peeking to see if they would find me. I prayed and hoped, hoped and prayed. If I squinted, I could see all the way down the street, around the bend, to where it met the avenue. Holding my breath, I saw them marching right . . . past . . . our street. Not one of the ghost brigade turned south toward us. Not one of them even looked in my direction; they just kept marching and clanging and singing. They didn't know where I was. I never had that dream again, because Mom and Dad had built me a safe haven.

# CHAPTER THREE

# A HARRISON GIRL

G rowing up in Wickliffe was the closest thing to a *perfect* childhood. We'd left the harsh concrete for the green, open landscape of the suburbs. Though the dead-end street we lived on had twenty or so older houses, most of the street had empty lots. However, as far as we kids were concerned, the lots were filled to the brim with fun. One lot spilled over onto the sidewalk with the sweetest, juiciest wild blackberries and strawberries. You couldn't just walk by and ignore them—they were covering the sidewalk, bursting up through the cracks, so you just *had* to pick one. Another lot had trees with the most succulent apples and black cherries that I had ever tasted.

At the end of the street was what we called "the woods," a most enticing and haunting place for a young girl to scout out. Around every bend was some kind of horrible bug or giant spiderweb, and every time you ducked to miss those, you were caught up on the briars and prickles of another blackberry patch. But the woods was *the* place to find peach trees, plum trees, pear trees, crab apple trees, and apple trees.

The town itself had an amazing rumor of being a station on the Underground Railroad, and in the late 1890s, the Rockefeller family had owned a summer home across the street from city hall on Johnnycake Ridge (Ridge Road) when that part of town was known as Millionaires' Row. Cleveland had become the fifth-largest city in the nation, with a booming industrial center. Many of these wealthy families made their summer homes in the suburb of Wickliffe.

Johnnycake Ridge spanned the length of Wickliffe, running east and west along the northern edge of the ridge overlooking the flats. We lived in the flats, which stretched out to the southern shores of Lake Erie. Many a day growing up, I would climb the hill behind the Presbyterian church at the end of our street and sit overlooking the flats, to the waters and beyond, dreaming of where life would someday take me. Though I never thought it would be possible that I would ever travel west of the Mississippi, I desperately wanted to see the world.

My dream of flying away on a white-winged horse was just as real to me as my ghost-house nightmares had previously been. But living in Wickliffe made me believe that something as wonderful as this could actually be possible . . . somehow.

Dad loved to "drive truck." He built a small moving company as a second job with his pickup truck and would do local moving and long-distance East Coast runs on the weekends with a larger truck body he built all by himself. When we girls were old enough, we earned our allowance as his *team*: packing, loading smaller boxes and items, reading maps, sidekicking as we drove late hours keeping him awake. He often moved people from Ohio to West Virginia and Kentucky. And every time I'd beg, "*Pleeeeeeeease* take me."

Most of the time he would take one, or maybe two, of us. It was so scary on those West Virginia trips because every house seemed to be on top of a steep hill with a long, winding Blue Ridge Mountain road. And there we were in a truck loaded with furniture, headed uphill, helping Dad navigate the hairpin turns and narrow roads so we didn't drive right off the side of the mountain.

The empty ride back was just as fun—tired, late nights with no sounds aside from the whirring engines of the approaching and passing vehicles. The air was so clean and dark. The smell was so fresh. And the bumping of a big empty truck (except for the mounds of moving pads that Dad had made into a bed) heading back home is one of the clearest memories of my childhood.

We also used the pickup truck as our *family* car. We rode in the back—even on the freeways. There were no mandatory-use seatbelt laws back then or prohibiting of riders in the truck bed. Dad made camper tops of all sorts that made riding in the back truly comfortable for all of us. Dad could build *anything*. He'd proudly say, "Why buy it if I can make it?"

Late nights again, all of us stretched out in the truck bed on big, fluffy moving pads, lights out, and there were those sounds again . . . the whirring engines, so beautifully peaceful, the oncoming whine of the approaching engines getting louder, the rush as they passed and then softly faded away, and then they were gone, then another one, and another one, over and over. I know for a fact that's when I got my first taste of the visceral *thrill* of travel.

"Herb," my uncle John would say, "you need to get a car for all those pretty girls in their pretty dresses."

Dad's response was always the same. "But, John," he'd say, "if I get a big pretty car, then my girls will all be in raggedy dresses. This truck makes money and *keeps* them looking pretty."

Dad also loved motorcycles. He taught me how to ride when I was only eleven or twelve. I would drive up and down our dead-end street with him sitting on the backseat. I loved the rush of the wind in my face. One time we hit a bump and Dad's shoe hit the street, came off, and flew up in the air, but I just kept gunning it. He was laughing and yelling, "GIRL! Go back and get my shoe!"

Dad's cousin George was a stunt motorcycle rider in exhibitions all around the country. During World War II, he was a tail gunner. His airplane was shot down and the tail section was cut off from the rest of the plane.

When they found him, he had been burned over most of his body. They were able to save him by grafting skin all over him. His face was a patchwork quilt. After that he feared nothing. At least, that's the way it seemed to me. Cousin George could do the most amazing stunts. Sometimes he'd let me ride on the back of his bike during a race; I'd sit backward, my arms outstretched behind me and wrapped around his waist, a spoon in my mouth and an egg in the spoon. Then he'd have to weave in and out of cones, laying the bike down as close as possible to the ground on the turns without touching it and without dropping the egg. I think I did great. But what do I know? I was a kid. We never broke the egg, though.

One late afternoon we kids were sitting at the dinner table, Mom standing by the kitchen window, and suddenly she started screaming, running to the door and out of the house. Of course, we all followed her. Dad was crawling up the driveway, bloodied head to toe. He'd been on his way home when he started to "round" a corner where a truck had spilled gravel. His bike hit the spill, and Dad went flying. When his body hit the street he skidded, sending tiny particles of gravel under his skin all over. That was the end of my love affair with motorcycles, and I haven't ridden one since.

In the summers, we often visited Mom's hometown of Danville, Virginia, where my uncles John Albert (J'nalbert), Alzonia (Zona), and William Edward (Wil' Ed) ran tobacco farms. Whenever we arrived, we leaped out of the pickup ready to take over any chores from our more-than-willing-to-relinquish-them cousins, Jean and Blue. And we loved it. While Mom always had her famously well-stocked vegetable garden at home in Ohio, this was so different. The tobacco smelled so sweet, and the leaves were nearly half as big as we were.

The house was a farmhouse up on a hill, with a wood-burning stove. The wood had to be cut down from the neighboring woods daily. The stove served the dual purpose of cooking and heating the house. There was an outhouse for a bathroom, which I hated, truly hated (for obvious reasons), and we took our baths in a big metal tub. Each morning, we filled it with water from the creek, and by evening, the water was warm as could be.

The arduous harvesting process was to bring the leaves from the field, hauled in by horses and off-loaded so that we could string them onto sticks and hand them to Uncle Kenny high in the two-story barn rafters above. The hanging of the tobacco started at the very top, laying the rods across the planks, filling up the barn until the entire barn smelled of the sweet, intoxicating fragrance of fresh-picked tobacco. It was a rich aroma that hung heavily in the air and became even more fragrant once the fires were started below. A warm flame burned in each barn at least eight days, curing the tobacco leaves. Once the now-golden leaves were taken down, they had to be sorted out into the different grades, then tied into bundles and hung on another stick. Finally, the leaves were loaded onto a flatbed truck and taken into Danville to be auctioned at market.

At the end of the day, the dishes were done, the small kids were bathed in the tub in the middle of the kitchen floor right next to the potbelly stove for warmth, the older children bathed in the bedroom tub, the hogs and chickens were fed, and the wood was brought in to dry for the next morning's fire. Then we'd sit on the porch, play games in the grass, catch lightning bugs in a jar, and collapse on our backs staring up at the stars. I never saw so many stars before in all my life. Without any other source of light, the night sky was black and filled with diamonds of every size. Gazing up at the stars, I would often wonder what beings were out there lying on their backs, looking back at me from some far-off, distant planet, and I wondered if I would ever get a chance to travel into space.

Oftentimes, there were barn parties with all twelve of Mom's brothers and sisters. Uncle Wil' Ed (who had at least fifteen kids himself) would dig a hole in the ground and roast a pig, while three or four other fires barbecued so much food we had enough to feed an army. And ohhh, yeah . . . there was a *lot* of drinking home brew and moonshine whiskey, with everyone having a *hi-ho* time.

And of course, music, music, and more music. Motown and Philly International records were playing loudly, and we were all doing the latest dance, called "the Fish." I loved the sounds of Motown, especially Smokey

Robinson and The Miracles singing "Shop Around" and the Supremes singing "Where Did Our Love Go." My sisters and I swooned over Smokey and loved singing along with Diana Ross. Back home we had practiced in our basement mirror, memorizing every word and every step to every song. And yes, I could "Temptation Walk" with the best of them. Oftentimes we'd even have a *show* and charge all the grown-ups a quarter to be entertained—my very first paying gig!

# CHAPTER FOUR

# GROWING UP JANE

The day we moved into our new house in Wickliffe, an old white man knocked on the door and then stood back.

"Can I help you?" my Dad said, still holding some moving boxes. I stood behind him peering out, staring at the strange man wearing aging suspenders and a much too big, old, tattered black coat.

"Wadda?"

"What?" Dad asked, a bit confused.

The man held out a large mason jar and pointed to the faucet on the side of our house.

"Wadda, side a house."

My dad's eyes followed to where the man was pointing his tiny, wrinkled finger.

"Oh. You want to get some water out of our faucet? Sure, lemme get ya some."

The man nodded his thanks and then pointed to himself—

"Tony."

"All right, Tony. I'm Big Herb."

\* \* \*

In 1868, John D. Rockefeller began building a summer home on Millionaires' Row, right outside of Cleveland. He wanted the finest carpenter in all of Italy to create the numerous intricate carvings on the structure. Rockefeller was informed that the man he wanted was Tony Turo. He sent for Tony to come to America, along with Tony's sister, who became Mr. Rockefeller's chef.

With a fiancée back home, Tony had ventured to America to also find a new beginning for the two of them. He saved enough money to start building their new home and he wrote to his fiancée to come to America to start their new life as husband and wife. But she broke their engagement and his heart when she told him she had found someone else.

Tony never finished *their* house and never married. He became the proverbial "town drunk" and was known as a loner.

By the time we moved in, no one associated much with Tony except for the local police, who were constantly called out to quiet him down. Tony's sister lived right next door to him on the other side. They never spoke to each other, except to yell obscenities in Italian over the wire fence between the two houses during the day. At night, he would go to the corner bar for a couple of hours and stumble home inebriated, singing Italian songs, and literally howling like a dog at the top of his lungs, which is usually why the police were called.

Tony had an extensive garden. He had the most incredible grapevines, cherry trees, and plum trees. He'd let us pick the fruit and Mom made the wine, always giving Tony the first bottles. He also had three goats and a lot of chickens that he used for milk and eggs. While his dog, Ruby, roamed the neighborhood freely, he kept his cat tied up.

Every holiday, Mom would fix him a plate of food and we would have to take it to him. But in all the years we did that, we never ever went up his stairs, never actually ventured into the house. That was too scary. We'd stand at the foot of the stairs and then we'd yell "Tony, Tony, Tony" and wait for him to come out. We weren't supposed to leave without making certain he got his plate. Sometimes we had to wait for a long time, since he was often sleeping off the booze. Then we'd finally just leave it on the steps.

Tony never let anyone on his property but us. He often invited my younger sisters and brother into the sheds in his backyard where he kept his display of military uniforms adorned with medals from when he fought in the "Italo War," often referred to by Ethiopians as the Italian Invasion.

He was a watchdog over our property. We'd come home and Tony would report, "Pretty lady in red car come. Man in brown truck come, knock three times, go in back, look around . . . go." Whenever we played outside, he'd watch. Then when Mom came out, he'd report in his broken English everything we did: "Gin, you got *good* kids."

One day he brought us a scrawny little weeping willow twig about a foot long and showed us how to plant and care for it. He wanted us to know how important it was to take care of our own things. Mom's garden was Mom's Garden; this was *ours*. He paced around our property trying to find the perfect spot to plant it.

What a sight we were: Tony—with his bent-over back, shuffling around in his oversize black pants, held up by worn suspenders, and his three-times-too-big old, tattered black coat—with a skinny little twig in his hands, mumbling about something or other in unintelligible broken English, and a trail of little Harrison Girls following his every step, fascinated as to where he was going to find the exact location and straining to understand every broken word. Finally, he stopped at the corner of the garage where we often played. As he dug a hole in the soft dirt with his dirty, trembling, stubby little finger, and delicately placed the roots inside and patted the soil firmly around the base of the stem, he smiled at us, and his red wine–drenched eyes twinkled. He pointed at us and said this tree would grow tall and strong and would be there to watch over us when he was long gone.

I was in my twenties and living in LA when Mom called and told me Tony had died. The huge, crooked roots of Tony's weeping willow tree had indeed branched out, looking exactly like his outstretched arthritic fingers, as he said they would. But when the roots began to break through the garage floor, Dad had to cut it down.

That day I cried for Tony . . . and the tree.

Tony Turo was a *huge* lesson in my young life. I watched how my parents loved and respected Tony because he was a lonely old man with a heart of gold. They taught us that everyone who teased and taunted him, who looked down on him because he dressed poorly, was cruel, and that it was wrong of them—that image wasn't everything. Through their example they showed us that what was *inside* was what truly mattered. That we must all look out for our neighbors, respect our elders, and care for those less fortunate. They never boastfully lifted up their efforts for anyone to see; they simply went about the everyday challenge of raising a family, never looking for anything in return, dealing with life's obstacles with grit and determination, never acknowledging that it was difficult at all.

# CHAPTER FIVE

# BLUE BOY AND GRANDMA JANE

The Harrison Family Reunion has taken place every two years since the first one in 1977 in Aunt Fat's backyard and has been named "one of the largest Black family reunions in the United States" by *Ebony* magazine. Each reunion averages nearly one thousand in attendance, and every reunion committee is responsible for the *Family Reunion Memory Book*. All new and newfound family members are added to the family tree, which now numbers well over seven thousand. Also included in the memory book is a copy of the original Bill of Sale of the slaves Harriett and her two children for $1,240 from the Edmunds Plantation in Virginia to the Harrison Plantation in Fairfield County, just outside of Columbia, South Carolina, on January 1, 1856. There, Harriet met and married Peter Harrison and had twelve children, including Chamberlain. Chamberlain then married Minnie Harris Harrison, and they had ten children, including Jane. Jane "Jannie" Harrison had ten children, including Herbert H. Harrison, my father.

A copy of the original Bill of Sale of my great-great-grandmother Harriet Edmunds and her two children from the Edmunds Plantation in Virginia to the Harrison Plantation in South Carolina. On page one, note the double asterisk near the bottom listing "Harriet & her two children by John Harrison for $1240.00" among the animals, supplies, wagons, grain, and more. Her mother's name was Rose. She never saw her again.

Herbert H. Harrison Sr., aka Blue Boy, was born in 1930 in Winnsboro, South Carolina. His mother had raised her children as a single mom. There are not many documents on the life of my grandfather, but according to my family's research, Dad's father was William K. Setzer, born around the 1870s in North Carolina. As far as I know he previously lived in Virginia with his former wife. Eventually he moved to Rion, South Carolina, where he met my grandmother. He was a night manager at the nearby Rutland Rock Quarry and was a lot older than Grandma.

My amazing dad, standing six foot three and at any time between 280 and 320 pounds, had a big, booming voice that struck fear in our hearts every time Mom would say "Just wait until Daddy gets home." He was also a master storyteller.

I remember spending hours listening to him talk about his childhood on the farm from 1930 to 1946. Many of the stories sounded like an entire library of Deep South, African American Brer Rabbit tales. Some were about the war; some were about *his* wars . . . fights at school, fights with his sisters (those we related to with ease). Then there were those stories he told about growing up on a farm during the Great Depression, about going to church and "Big Day Sunday." There was the story about the day his beautiful country home burned to the ground, the result of a smoldering ember cleared from the woodstove and left unnoticed in a cardboard box in the corner of the kitchen, and the stories about how Grandma used to feed the soldiers that traveled through during their army basic training at Camp Jackson. He'd talk about school and his teacher Ms. Lucinda Holokawinkle (and this spelling is truly a shot in the dark), whom they would teasingly call Lucinda Holla-Out-da-Winda.

When he told his stories, we were riveted, especially when he told the ones about ghosts . . . the ones he saw when he was a boy rounding up the cows at dusk, the ones that stood in the way of his horse as he attempted to cross the creek to take food to a sick neighbor, causing that horse to never again go near that creek. We loved them all.

But there are other stories, hidden stories. There are things that happen to our parents that ultimately shape us, even when we know nothing about them. I'd have to share those kinds of stories with my own children many years later, so I now know how my father felt when sharing with me what happened in 1940 when he was just ten years old.

He and his sisters were headed into the house after a long day out in the fields doing their chores on the Harrison farm in Winnsboro, South Carolina, when he heard shots ring out. Being the fastest sibling, he ran to the front door but couldn't get in; something on the floor was blocking the way. He then ran to the back of the house, with his sisters coming fast up the steps behind him. Dad was the first to get to his mother, lying in a pool of blood in their living room. He lifted his mother's head into his lap and saw where she had been shot in the neck, behind the ear, three times. The blood was gushing out and he could hear it gurgling inside her body. She died in his arms.

His mother was Jane. My namesake.

The man that killed my grandmother had come to the house with his sister. Apparently, it was initially a social visit but he and Jane had gotten into an argument, so he shot her . . . and ran. When his sister turned him in, he confessed and went to jail for her murder. Bob Boulware had not only murdered a woman, but he had also upended the lives of her ten children, forever. Three sons and seven daughters: John, Mae, Willie, Dorothy, Irene, Herbert, Elizabeth, Ruth, Janet, and Mable.

Jail was not a safe place for the man who killed Jane Harrison, the man who took my grandmother's life with her children at home, leaving a nine-month-old baby to grow up without a mother. He was severely and repeatedly beaten by the other inmates, and they eventually transferred him to a jail in another county for his safety.

Everyone who knew Grandma Jane had truly loved her. Despite struggling during the Depression, her farm survived selling potatoes to nearby Camp Jackson (which eventually became Fort Jackson), and Jane never turned away anyone who was hungry—friend or stranger. Most of Fairfield County knew Jane. Great-Uncle Pete, Grandma's brother, said hundreds participated in her walking funeral procession, which was over a mile long.

When Grandma Jane was murdered at the age of thirty-nine, Grandpa Setz was near seventy. This was the South, and in 1940 interracial marriages were forbidden and strictly against the law. Heartbroken, my white Irish German grandfather could not attend the funeral of his Black, beloved Jane. Instead, he sat in his car under a tree outside the church with his ten-year-old son, my father, as they watched and cried together. Soon after, my grandfather became ill and his white Virginia family came to "rescue" him, moving him away from Jane and their children forever.

The days that followed Grandma Jane's funeral were unimaginable. The children fought to keep the family together, even when some of the relatives were determined to tear them apart, and tried to weed out the vultures that moved in to take everything Jane had built, leaving her kids to scrounge for the leftovers. One of Dad's aunts moved in with her kids and immediately changed everything. She ran the house like Dad and his siblings were the outsiders in their own home. Her kids ate first, then Jane's. Her kids got new clothes, and then Jane's got the hand-me-downs. Jane's farm was a prize and Great-Aunt sought to take it all for herself.

That arrangement didn't last very long. Dad was his mother's son indeed. He quit school in fifth grade and forcibly threw her out and threatened anyone else who attempted to destroy his family, vowing to raise his siblings by himself if need be. . . . And he did, with the help of Great-Grandma Minnie. Even when her son told her, "Take all those kids and put them in a home, don't bother yourself with them." How could he say such a thing? Great-Grandma Minnie could cuss with the best and she never held back one second once those words came from her son's mouth. My father's little sister, Aunt Janet, stood there overhearing it all as it sent shots through her soul, telling me years later, "That kind of thing stays with you your entire life."

The next four years were hell for my father, trying to earn money to care for his siblings, but when Eleanor Roosevelt's Civilian Conservation Corps was hiring robust and hardy young men, Dad went to work building roads and highways across the state of South Carolina. It was torturous, backbreaking work for a now fourteen-year-old (who had lied that he was seventeen just to get the job)—but options were few and my father knew he had to provide for and support his siblings.

Aunt Janet eventually left the family home, moving to New Jersey to live with her older brother John and his wife. Dad promised she could come back home if she didn't like being there. Soon afterward, Janet called Dad to come and get her. When Dad called ahead to let his brother know he was on the way, John said she could not go home because she was needed to help his wife around the house. Janet insisted she did *not* want to stay, so Dad went to his aunt Katie in Washington, DC, and asked if he could borrow money to take the train to New Jersey to retrieve Janet.

Aunt Katie was the kind of person who loved to step in whenever *she* felt someone was being wronged, and this was one of those times. She jumped in her car and drove Dad to Jersey herself. They arrived around five a.m. and started banging on the door. Obviously, they were not met with welcoming arms, and immediately they all began to argue. Katie said, "The chile don't wanna stay, so she ain't gonna stay. She wonts to go home. And we com to take huh home."

Well, Uncle John's wife then let go with "You ain't takin' huh nowhare. And I heard you called me a hoe. If she goes anywhere, she sho ain't goin' wit you."

Turning to Uncle John, Aunt Katie began to preach, "I ain't called that hoe no hoe." And there it was, on and on.

She grabbed Janet by the arm and left, took Dad and Janet to the store, bought them both new clothes, took them to the train station, bought the tickets, stuffed cash into Janet's pockets, and sent them home: "And don't you git off dis train till you git home."

That was Great-Aunt Katie, my grandma's sister. The same Aunt Katie whose booming voice would make me hide under my bed in fear.

With lots of family in the DC area, Dad moved to Washington, DC, at age seventeen in hopes of finding better job opportunities so he could send more money back home. At eighteen, he met Mom, and by age nineteen, he had started a family of his own. At twenty-one, the army tried to draft Dad, so he told them how many dependents he was supporting, which at that time included most of his sisters, his new wife, *and* his two new kids. They told him that they were not concerned about his family. He'd still have to serve his country. He said, "Then I'm not going."

The sergeant, who didn't like to be told no, jumped to his feet and leaned over his desk declaratively. "Don't you want to go off and fight for your country?"

And Dad yelled back, meeting him nose to nose: "HELL NO. When you say that my sisters will be left out on the streets because you won't take care of them while I'm off riskin' my life, then this ain't my country."

The sergeant then thought he'd take another approach. He gave Dad some paperwork, saying "Take this" as he shoved the papers in Dad's face. "Have all your dependents, everybody ya gotta take care of, sign off here. They gotta write how you're responsible for each and every one of dem, and then report back to the draft board in DC by eight a.m. Monday morning."

Frustrated but not knowing what else to do, Dad jumped in his car at five p.m. on Friday and raced from Washington, DC, to South Carolina, to New Jersey, to Philadelphia, collecting signatures. Once in Philly he met a sergeant who took a look at the papers and wrote a letter, giving it to Dad and saying, "You tell this piece of shit that you need to stay at home and take care of your family. Give him this letter and if he has a problem with it, he can come to see me."

But still Dad had to be back at the draft board by eight a.m. Monday. He put the "pedal to the metal" so hard that the engine began to smoke, but he never stopped, not until a police officer pulled him over for speeding. When he found out that Dad was trying to make his draft board appointment, he gave him a warning and sent him on his way. But not without another warning: "That car is gonna catch on fire before you git there, boy." Dad rolled into the draft board office with the car literally falling apart in the street. The engine was totally gone. He gave the papers to the sergeant, who looked at him and said one thing: "You go home and buy yo wife, kids, and sisters some chocolate 'cause dey saved you, boy." Dad's only reply was "Hell no, I saved them."

My aunts all worshipped the ground Dad walked on. Years later his cousin Claudette, whom he had to also take care of as a baby, had a stroke and couldn't walk. She was hospitalized, couldn't talk for six months, and was basically medically unresponsive. Eventually it seemed her time was coming to an end, so Dad went to visit her. The very moment he walked into the room, she sat straight up in the bed and called out, "Blue Boy." Everyone was shocked. She smiled and sat listening to him all the while he visited. The next day when Aunt Irene visited her, she told Irene, "Don't worry about me. Blue Boy fixed my legs." A few days later she passed away with a smile on her face. Another cousin, Spider, had been sick for some time and was just barely hanging on. She was sleeping, when suddenly she woke up for only a moment and told her cousin, "Blue Boy just told me I could go. I'm ready." And she was gone.

More than ten hard, seemingly impossible, years after Grandma Jane had died, and Dad was now a husband and father of two and we were visiting family in South Carolina. While he was in town shopping, Dad ran into a warm old familiar face from years before. They stopped in the street and swapped tales about how everybody was doing, and Dad told her about his two kids, and she laughed, saying, "You just cain't stop takin' care o' folks, can you?"

Suddenly something caught her eye. She pointed her trembling finger at a man crossing the street. "Blue Boy, you know who dat is, right?" And Dad turned and saw a hunched-over old man, who was clearly in bad health. Though years had gone by, Dad instantly recognized the man who had made his life a living hell. The man who had taken away his youth, his joy, his future, and most importantly—his mother.

"Why you wanna do that, Miss Suzie? You know I know who that is. What you tellin' me? He's out?"

Miss Suzie answered, "I jus' thout you should know, das all, Blue Boy. He's dyin'."

My father quickly said goodbye to his old friend. With a jumble of clarity and anger racing through his mind, he dropped his family off at Aunt Lilly Belle's and went to pay this man a visit, parking his truck and walking up to the porch where the man who had murdered his mother was sitting calmly.

Agony and grief flooded over Dad as the memories of the hard years resurfaced . . . quitting school to take care of his sisters because his older brother was in the army and the other was nowhere to be found. Her killer just sat there, calm and peaceful in his rocking chair, smoking his pipe. This was too much. It was not right.

Dad approached the man, with a sense of impending terror clouding out any sensible thoughts that he might have had in his head, all the time thinking of the shotgun in the back of his truck. He managed to get out a calm "Hey. Are you Bob Boulware?"

The man never missed a beat, kept on rocking, and said, "That'd be me."

Anguish began to override reason. The memories that he could never quiet of the murder itself began to bubble up . . . flashbacks of his mother dying in his arms—a mere ten-year-old boy—her blood gushing, a smell he could never erase from his mind no matter how hard he tried; his sisters growing up without a mother or father, and how he had raised them; the endless nights of going to bed hungry, and of a commitment to never be separated; the endless crying of the nine-month-old baby Mable, who would never know the warmth of her mother's embrace. Pure rage welled up inside him, fanned by the indifference toward him by the man on the porch.

But Grandma Jane must have been watching over Dad that day, because suddenly he thought of his own two little girls (one of them being me), and how he didn't want them to know what it was like to grow up without a parent, as he had. And it was at that instant that lucidity won. He walked back to the truck and simply drove off.

My father has told many stories about everything imaginable, many with colorful, over-the-top exaggerations for added spice and entertainment value. Throughout the years we heard all of them more than once. Then there were the times we'd be with a new group of friends, and he'd get started and we'd say, "Oh no, here he goes again." He never just *told* the story. He'd have both arms flailing, with all the emotion of the event, and a loud animated voice. Standing up, pacing back and forth, and poking you in the arm to make sure you didn't miss what he was saying. Sometimes I'd think the whole neighborhood could hear him when he was on a roll and I'd imagine everyone collectively saying, *Oh no, there he goes again.*

But despite all the hundreds of stories, he never once told me about how his mother had died until I was almost fifty years old. I had gone home on vacation to the same house where I grew up. My kids were playing as Dad and

I sat at the kitchen table. He was in the seat that used to be mine, sadly the same seat where he was sitting when his heart finally stopped nearly a dozen years later. He told the story of his mother's murder as if it had just happened yesterday, with tears running down his ruggedly handsome face, the face I used to hold in my two little hands and cover with butterfly kisses.

"Dad, why have you never told me this before? Why have you held this in all these years? You talk about *everything*, why not this?"

Then he looked at me and said: "Because it hurts too much. He took away my mother. He took *any* joy that I could have had as a child. I spent all my life trying to make that memory go away, but I keep smelling the blood . . . every day. Every day when things get too hard, I can still smell the blood. I spent my whole life trying to be a man . . . the man she would have wanted me to be. But I didn't know what being a man was, so I had to make it up along the way. And talking about this all the time is not what a man would do."

"Daddy, you're the best man I know. From nothing . . . look what you made. I have had nothing but a blessed life due in great part to you. I love you, Dad."

We sat there for quite some time with my hands on top of his until our tears dried. Sitting across the table from him, my mind flashed back to the time I first cut my hair. As a child, I'd always had a long black ponytail. But when I cut my hair, he became outraged and angry. I was so confused. Sometime later I found out that his mother always wore her hair like mine. She had a long black ponytail across her shoulder when she died. I know now it was my long hair and my name that made Dad feel her presence was still with him in me, and I had unwittingly taken that away with that simple act. I never cut my hair again until well into my thirties, and then only once. Some of my critics have said that I wore my hair long just to show off, when actually, it was *only* for Dad . . . just for Dad.

Jane Harrison is buried at White Oak Baptist Church in Winnsboro, South Carolina. If you visited there today, you'd find a great number of the tombstones are Harrisons'. I visit my grandma Jane whenever I'm in South Carolina. I never knew her, but I truly wish I had. I feel her deep in my bones. I feel her spirit, in my blood, and I feel so much a part of her. I pray that I have done well by all of them; for Great-Grandpa Chamberlain and Great-Grandma Minnie, for Great-Great-Grandpa Peter and Great-Great-Grandma Harriet, and for Great-Great-Great-Grandma Rose.

In the summer of 2005, I went back to South Carolina for the fifteenth biannual Harrison Family Reunion. I had been looking for so many answers, and here I felt at home. At the close of the family reunion my cousin Oscar (the reunion committee president) said that he had prayed that morning for God to let him know what it was he would have him say in his closing remarks.

With a slight hesitation, standing before the audience, Oscar continued on: "He gave me three names. . . . Some of you may think I should say some-one else, but God gave me these three names. . . . He didn't tell me why . . . just that I should call them out."

One of them was mine. . . .

It would take many years for me to understand that this was God's message directly to me to have faith and stay on my path. When we say *Harrison Strong*, it's because it is true.

# CHAPTER SIX

# GINNY FROM VIRGINIA

Virginia Mary Thompson Harrison was born in Danville, Virginia, on a tobacco farm, in a family of thirteen children. She—along with her seven brothers, Alzonia, Willie Ed, John Albert, Richard, James, Kenny, and Percy; and five sisters, Leonia, Louzetta, Catherine, Ruby, and Pearl—had a very hard life. Tons of fun, but tobacco farming was no casual walk in the park.

I barely know where to begin to tell you about my mother, my friend, my teacher, my counselor, my *rock*. My mom, the one with the perfect skin, is one of the most beautiful women in the world. Whenever anyone would ask me where I got my looks, my skin, or whatever, I'd simply say it was a "gift" from Mom. She is the most full-of-life person I know. Always happy, always positive, and always supportive.

Whenever we'd come anywhere near the kitchen and Mom was cooking (and she always put her "foot" in it), we could hear her sing. Mom has a great voice, and she loves her country music. Not that country and western brand, but *soul country*, which is infused with early R&B and the blues.

She'd be standing at the kitchen window shakin' her hips, washin' the dishes, and singin' loud enough for all to hear. Yep . . . you guessed it, our entire household was loud, loud and full of life. She'd be swinging to something like "Johnny B. Goode" by Chuck Berry or one of her other favorites. I loved to watch her sing, while she tossed her head from side to side, rocking to the beat with a huge smile on her face. She also loved the song "Trouble in Mind," and would sing along about leaving your heart on the 2:19 rail line. After she was done singing, Mom would smile. No matter the song . . . Mom always smiled.

That love of music I know she got from her father, Percy George Washington Thompson, who everyone called Turk Thompson. He had a special gift of playing the piano like no one else. He was never taught; he just sat down and played—and many times he didn't even sit.

Turk liked to drink, and when he drank and played, his soul soared throughout his body to the tips of his fingers. He played for many churches in the Shockoe, Danville, and Chatham area and people would come from miles around just to hear him on the keyboards. When he finished at one church, he wouldn't wait for the sermon to be over; instead he packed up his three daughters (Aunt Ruby, Aunt Catherine, and Mom) and went off to another church. When he got to the next one it didn't matter if the pianist was in the middle of a song, Turk would just brush him to the side and take over. Mom and her sisters would then join in, sometimes doing solo work, but most of the time they were backing up Grandpa. Every Saturday morning, they'd rush to the radio station in Chatham, where they would perform on-air as Turk Thompson and the Thompson Girls—something I never knew until I began to write this book. I knew Mom, Ruby, and Cat could *sang* . . . but a radio show in the South in the late 1930s and early '40s that featured an African American family? That was pretty extraordinary.

What kind of man was Turk Thompson? Let me put it this way: One night he was performing and he saw a woman in the audience named Bootsey out there dancing and her skirt kept flying up around her waist. Turk couldn't decide whether to keep playing or dance with Bootsey. After a while he just jumped off the stage and caught her around the waist and they danced the night away. Needless to say, this was *not* at church. When he wasn't playing at church, he was performing in the local bars and nightclubs. All this on top of running a tobacco farm.

From my childhood, I have a vague memory of him on one of our visits to Virginia. The country house seemed huge, and all the walls were white—everything was white, whitewashed with a heavenly glow. I heard this loud, upbeat, pulsating, rockin' music inviting me in, and slowly I followed the sounds to a room where the door was halfway open. I was afraid to go in, afraid to interrupt, so I hid. For me Grandpa was fascinating, yet kind of intimidating. Peeping through the crack and the hinges, I could see a white upright piano shaking from him slamming on the keys. As I stood mes- merized with my back glued to the wall, I could barely lean around to peep through the front edge of the door, where I caught a sliver of him standing over the keyboard. I could hear the tapping of his feet and the pounding away on the keys as his fingers raced in a blur. The kick pleats in the vents of his black suit jumped up and down on his butt as he danced and played. I've often wondered where Jerry Lee Lewis got that schtick—no doubt from someone just like Turk. I have no idea how Grandpa kept his ever-present black derby hat from falling off his head. He was just mesmerizing.

Grandpa Turk had dark black skin with a rich red tint. I was told that his father was of the Blackfoot Nation mixed with Cherokee. His skin was dark, his cheeks were strong and high, and his hair was thick, silky, and curly. The black suit, the hat, and the music all seemed to merge in the heartbeat of the rhythm. I never went in. I just stood there, hiding, watching, and listening in complete awe.

Later that evening, I found Grandpa Turk sitting on the front porch as I peeked out the screen door. He saw me and waved me over, then picked me up to sit on his knee as we watched the stars poke through the pitch-black night sky. We didn't say much, just sat watching the fireflies dance, while high above the stars took their places in their own kind of twinkling symphony.

"Ya know how to fin' da North Star?" he asked.

I just shook my head no.

"See da Big Dippa . . . *riiiight* there? Well, if you look for the two stars at the end of da cup, see . . . right there . . . right there . . . yeah." Then he smiled. "Now try to see a line drawn tween the two from the bottom to the top, and den just keep goin' dat way, keep goin'." He pointed it all out, with me trying to line my eyesight along his arm to the tip of his finger. "There, da brightest one. Dat's the North Star." Then he put his hands to his face and played with the edge of his derby as if in thought. "My daddy taught me dat."

"I see it. Hey, Grandpa, I see it." I jumped up, twirling around to see if it would move or stay in the same spot. But then I got distracted when a lightning bug passed right in front of me. Grandpa quickly grabbed the mason jar, and I actually caught the bug. When I pulled the green glowing thing off the bug, he took it from my hand and stuck it on my earlobe.

"Now ya got earrangs," he said, and I was grinning ear to ear.

The only other time I remember seeing Grandpa Turk was at his funeral when I was maybe twelve. When he died, he had *fifty-nine* grandchildren. The church was packed with family and friends. People were crying, some were shouting, some were quiet, some were screaming. Aunt Louzetta screamed so much she passed out and had to be carried away.

Grandma Lois (Turk's wife), on the other hand, was the quietest person I ever knew. She had a very low whisper of a speaking voice and the most beautiful head of silver-gray hair. When I was about fourteen or fifteen Grandma had moved from Virginia to Ohio, and that afforded me the opportunity to actually get to know her. By then, her voice was but a wisp of air and it was hard to hear her. When I got married, she was holding my hand as if she never wanted to let go. She asked Mom, "Ginny, how can you just *give* your daughter away?" She had watched all her children leave and go their separate ways, but she had never stood publicly and done what she was watching her daughter do now. To actually stand as a mother and *give* me away was a concept that hurt her to her core. I didn't realize it at the time, but there was a bond developing between Grandma and me that I hadn't noticed before, but once I moved away, she was always in my thoughts. I seemed to carry her spirit within, even across the three thousand miles between Wickliffe and Los Angeles. When I bought my first home in Pasadena, I was completely shocked when she joined Mom, Dad, and my siblings on a cross-country road trip in a cramped station wagon to visit me. Chewing and spitting tobacco along the way.

A few years later my tall and usually strong grandma became very ill, and she spent her final days at her daughter Leonia's house in Virginia. A voice within kept nagging at me, *Go see your grandmother*. I called Mom and made plans to meet them in Virginia. Mom and Dad drove from Ohio with my young brother, Herbie. By the time we arrived, Grandma was in the hospital.

When people ask if I have any regrets, I'd have to say one of my biggest is that I left home too early, at nineteen. Not because of my age, but I still had a six-year-old brother and a ten-year-old sister at home who I never really got a chance to know. I missed sharing my brother's childhood. I'd always wanted a brother and when I got one . . . I left him. I wasn't there to watch him grow up. I didn't want to completely miss out on developing our brother-sister bond, so I would often go home just to catch his basketball or baseball games. He was handsome, tall, and very athletic and excelled in basketball, later playing on a full scholarship for Marquette University.

But this occasion was a real eye-opener. I had been on TV for some years by the time we traveled to see Grandma Lois, and my family back home was all very proud of me. I hadn't spent time with my Virginia family in at least six years, so there were a lot of people coming to visit the whole time I was there. Little did I know that while I was visiting, Little Herbie was "soliciting business" outside: "Hey, Jayne Kennedy's my sister. You want me to get an autograph for you?"

He would then go to the back of Dad's closed-in pickup truck, wait for a minute or two, and return with a torn sheet of paper with my name (in his writing, mind you) scrawled across. "She's inside trying to get some work done but she sent this out to you anyway. That'll be two dollars." When Dad busted up his little operation, he had to find everybody and return their money. Oh my gosh.

It was great to be with family but the time I spent with Grandma was very trying—she seemed so helpless. She was very frail and by now couldn't speak at all. Her hands and body trembled constantly as she looked at me with pleading eyes that I didn't understand. She tugged at my hands with her delicate fingers that were now so thin and silky they felt like the skin of a newborn baby, but with no flesh . . . seemingly translucent. She tried to move her lips, but to no avail. Still trembling, she slightly motioned to her legs, and I realized she couldn't move them at all. She was too weak to write, so she squeezed my hands tighter and motioned to her legs again. Her eyes were trying to tell me something, but I had no idea what. I stayed by her side as I talked, stroking her strikingly beautiful silver hair off her face again and again. She used to pay us a quarter to brush her hair when we were kids, but now I felt completely helpless. I asked Mom if anyone knew what Grandma was trying to say, but no one did. My last day there I said my goodbye and Dad drove me to the airport.

A few days after I got home, Mom called and said that Grandma had passed away. I was eternally grateful I had listened to that little inner voice because I had been able to share her last days with her, but I was also angry that I never knew what she tried to tell me. About a week later, Mom called to tell me that the autopsy had shown that Grandma had a fractured hip. Apparently, the night nurse had left the bed rail down, and Grandma had fallen out. The nurse returned Grandma to bed and never filed it in her notes.

I can't imagine the pain Grandma must have been in. She was trying so hard to get someone to do something, but she could never communicate what had happened. Since we couldn't do anything for her, God stepped in. For years, I hurt each time I recalled my anguish at having no idea what she was trying to say. The "if only" thoughts often filled my heart. I am so sorry to this day that I didn't understand. She had called out to me three thousand miles away, and though I heard her and rushed to her side, I couldn't help her with her discomfort. I only found solace in knowing she wasn't in pain any longer.

While Saturday nights belonged to Dad, when we would watch boxing and wrestling matches as we ate steak and white rice, Friday nights were all Mom's. We looked forward to Friday night with her all week long. Every Friday night she bought potato chips, corn chips, and cheese puffs, mixed them all together, and set up in front of the television with a six-pack of RC Cola to watch scary movies. For years it was our ritual. Sometimes we'd all cuddle under Mom, hiding our face at the worst parts, but most of the time we sat and laughed at Ghoulardi, the host of the Friday night *Shock Theater*. And any time there was a beauty pageant on, we would all gather and argue about who was going to win. Then the next day we would clip the winner's photo from the paper and add it to our little pageant photo album.

Mom was awesome—she was so much like one of us. She has always been there for me, as she was for all six of her children. She taught us about living life and believing in yourself. She believed her children could do *anything*. We were taught to strive for the best, that whatever we wanted we could attain, even if it meant that we had to fight for it. Growing up in a large family, Mom was a fighter herself and was never afraid to rumble. Learning how to fight like the best of them, she would often be recruited by her brothers to fight their battles. My aunt Pearl once told me that nobody messed with "Ginny from Virginia." She could definitely hold her own in nearly every situation.

Mom's a great cook, seamstress, mediator, and friend. She is the ultimate homemaker, putting every minute of every day into her children and her grandchildren, sacrificing any and all desires she may have ever had outside of our home. But then again Mom was never an outside kind of girl anyway. She never liked staying out in the sun since her childhood days in the tobacco fields, she hated the cold, and she was totally happy with all her indoor duties and hobbies. Mom never joined any clubs or groups; sewing was her thing, her passion. She taught all of us girls to sew well before the sixth grade. I recall in my seventh grade home economics class when our sewing project was to take three months, and I proudly handed mine in on the second day, to the amazement of my teacher.

On the other hand, Dad was *always* outside—building truck campers, working on the cars and trucks, expanding his moving company, working in the garden, shoveling snow . . . but there were also times when he would just go outside and take it all in. He'd even go out and sit in the snow. If it snowed just one inch, Dad would be out there shoveling. He couldn't stand to be inside. He'd dress up like he was going hunting, in all his thermal wear, gloves, hat, snowsuit, and overalls, and throw his scarf around his neck. He'd set out his fluorescent heat lamps and just sit there in the snow. Often, he'd light a wood fire in a giant barrel, and if anyone tried to entice him to come in to warm up, his answer was plain and simple: "I have my friend Jack Daniel's here to keep me warm."

Then Dad would always tease, "Mom. Come on outside and let the wind blow up your butt."

But not Mom. "No. I don't need to go nowhere. I go out to the garden, to feed the birds, to church, to the fabric store, across the driveway, and to the market. That's good enough for me. I don't like to be cold. If I died today, it won't be from pushin' no snow."

That's my momma. That's my dad. I *loved* watching them and how their relationship was such a gift. To see them laugh, dance, hug, kiss, and walk hand in hand was what I always dreamed being married would be like. Of course there were down days, no relationship is perfect, but the good ones when they are good . . . *solid gold.*

One important rule in our house growing up was that we were never, ever, allowed to fight each other, and when we did the consequence was that we had to kiss, hug, and make up afterward. That was worse than being mad, so we tried our best to always get along. The rule of no fighting was rooted in Mom's childhood sibling rivalries, which were intense. One day she had been provoked to hit her brother in the head with a two-by-four; unbeknownst to her there was a nail in the board that hit him dead center in the forehead, leaving blood gushing everywhere.

To hear Mom tell it: "I was kinda bad. . . . But it wasn't my fault. They always picked on me. Like the time with Richard, I had to close the door on Richard's finger, breaking it, just to get him to leave me alone. And then they'd dare me to do things because they knew I always would. Zona [Alzonia] told me that when Leoni [Leonia] came in the house, I should slam the door on her . . . so I did. Her face was covered in blood. Then they'd deny it to Momma. And there was the time we were playing croquet and John Albert wouldn't let me play, so I grabbed the wicket out of the ground and threw it at him. Lucky for him, it missed. Momma grabbed a switch, and I was running like mad, and did I love to run. I always ran fast and no one, no one, could ever catch me. But that meant I had to stay out in the onion field all day.

"I wasn't bad. I was just mischievous. We used to pick peas in the fields. Everybody had a personal bag to fill. I never picked much cuz I was playin' around all the time and Louzetta always picked the most peas. So, I'd take Louzetta's bag and pour it into mine. She'd get so mad. We fought all the time. We fought so hard that it got to the point where it didn't even hurt anymore. So, I grabbed her and threw her down and of course she started cryin' all over again and John Albert kept yelling, 'Hold her, Ginny. Just hold her down.' I should have never done that. Louzetta was my buddy. What a fool I was. That was the day I decided when I have kids, I'm never gonna let them fight."

There were so many kids in Mom's house growing up that the older girls helped to care for the younger ones while the others worked the fields. Mom loved to work, but she preferred working indoors. She made the babies love her so much that they wanted to only stay with her. Grandma Lois then worked the fields in her place.

The work on the farm was truly hard, and eventually it seemed to Mom that she was going nowhere. Exactly three months after she turned seventeen, Mom decided she would leave home. She wrote her aunt Carrie, who lived in Lynchburg, Virginia, a much larger town than Danville, and made plans to stay with her. Then she finally got up the nerve to ask Grandma if she could go. Grandma was always a woman of very few words. After a brief moment, Grandma simply said, "It's okay by me. You might be able to do better. There's nothing here for you."

While Grandma never told her not to go, Grandpa was very upset. Grandpa said, "Remember, you can't come back." Mom responded, "I'm never coming back here to live." She took the train and never looked back. She settled in and got a job, but she couldn't shake her father's last words. At the end of her first week, she sent him her entire paycheck of ten dollars, which she had earned as a live-in companion: making and serving meals, running errands, and assisting with personal needs such as bathing and dressing.

To her surprise, her daddy wrote her a thank-you letter, the first letter she had ever gotten from him, a gesture that said he supported her too.

She soon moved to Washington, DC, in 1948 to stay with her sister Leonual, and she got a live-in job with Mrs. Janet Farr, a very wealthy white socialite, as a helper. Mrs. Farr was married to the owner of the DC Franklin Simon department store and the Chevy Chase Land Company.

A lot of what happened to Mom in her early DC days impacted how she raised her Harrison Girls. She would often say, "I left home at seventeen years, three months. I knew nothing. I was green. I look back and remember the temptations and dangers that stood in my way, and I knew that there was nothing but God guiding me. I bought a gun and a switchblade knife because you couldn't walk the streets without the guys stopping you, even the bus drivers. That's why I was strict on all you girls, because beautiful women have a hard time in this world. You've got to stand your ground. You go anywhere and the men will stare, trust me. You *have* to be careful at all times."

Then she stopped as if deep in thought. "I always wanted you to dress beautifully, but real beauty comes from inside. Some of the most beautiful women in the world are filled with ugly." Through all the years that followed, I have never forgotten her words.

After a man on the bus followed Mom when she left work at Mrs. Farr's, Mr. Farr hired security on the street whenever Mom was to arrive or depart.

Mrs. Farr was one of the nicest people you would ever want to meet. She thought the world of Mom, and she made a huge impact on Mom as well. There hadn't been "high society" on the farms in Virginia, so Mom watched and learned. At Mrs. Farr's, the two Farr daughters, ages seven and ten, would walk down the stairs to eat breakfast always looking like little angels, with starched dresses and hair done in Shirley Temple curls. They went to school just like they were going to a party, and Mom decided right then and there that if she ever had girls, they'd look just like that. And she did, so every Easter the Harrison Girls were just like that; every school day, the Harrison Girls were at their very best.

Mrs. Farr and Mom remained friends long after Mom got married and moved to Ohio, through all the children, and until the day Mrs. Farr died in 1996. She had always given Mom advice on dating, clothing, and living in the big city, and on raising young ladies. It was a dream job. She never had Mom doing any of the hard work, and Mom thought she was so blessed to have met someone who treated her like a daughter.

About a month after Mom started working for Mrs. Farr, she met Dad. Vernell, a girlfriend from down home, had told Mom about her boyfriend's new best friend: He was about eighteen, and he was *so* good-looking. Mom wanted to know when she could meet him. Vernell told her that her boyfriend was always going over to his friend's uncle's house.

One day Mom and Vernell went to Uncle Tom's, and the new friend wasn't there. The next weekend they went to a party at Uncle Tom's cousin Marie's house, pretending to be visiting her, but waiting to see if the new friend showed up. The two girlfriends were sitting in the living room when Dad and one of his friends walked in.

Every time Mom tells this story, she still giggles like a teenager. "Blue was laughing and *skipping* around the room. There were a lot of people at Marie's. I was sitting over in the corner with my legs all crossed up, wearing a black dress. I knew I looked pretty good, and I knew he saw me. I was talking to a young girl that was maybe thirteen and had a lot of energy and personality, who seemed to know everybody there. So, I was telling her how fine I thought that guy across the room was. I had forgotten all about the fact that I came to meet Vernell's new friend. From time to time the little girl would be lost in the mix of people at the party, but then she would come back and talk to me. Pretty soon I noticed that she was going over quite often to talk to that handsome man I had my eye on. I had no idea that the conversation on the other side of the room was going something like 'Hey, Ruth. You see that fine, long-legged, brown-skinned gal over there, all crossed up? Go find out who she is.' And that's just what his little sister, Ruth, did. Everything I told her she ran back to repeat to her big brother."

They met, fell in love, and then a year later married on May 2, 1950.

When we were growing up, Mom never did drive a car, because she never wanted to get a license. So, if Dad wasn't there to drop us anywhere, we walked. At five foot eight Mom had the longest legs, and she always walked so fast that we'd have to run along behind her, trying desperately to catch up. When we went to the market, we took our little red wagon. It was quite a picture, Mom's long, chocolate-brown legs striding down the street, pulling a red wagon, with a bunch of kids behind running to keep up, looking like a line of little ducklings.

Once, when I was eight or so, we were at the market, and I was so tempted to take just *one* piece of candy from the loose candy display. I loved Brach's candy and my favorite was the pink-, brown-, and white-striped coconut bar. I wanted that one little piece. . . . I wanted it so bad. Every time we went to the market I would drool over that candy. I could taste the melting coconut sugars, and whenever I was lucky enough to get one, I would never pop the whole thing in my mouth all at once. I would take a million tiny baby bites to make each piece last longer. Sometimes I would eat it by the row, nibbling off each color one at a time. So that day . . . I just took it. I couldn't help it. I didn't dare eat it right there, because someone might see me. Worse yet, Mom might see me. I locked the candy in the palm of my hand with my fingers digging into my flesh, and I hid it in my pocket for a more appropriate time. I wouldn't take my hand out of my pocket for fear the candy would somehow fall out.

As we walked home from the market, I was pulling the wagon loaded with groceries with one hand, and my other hand was in my pocket, fingering my precious, sweet little secret. My stomach started to hurt, and my hands got sweatier with each step. After we got about halfway home, I couldn't take it anymore. My heart was trembling, and I couldn't breathe. That candy was "burning" a hole in my hand. I *had* to tell Mom what I had done. I didn't need to wait for her to say anything—her glaring look of disappointment was enough. I knew immediately what I had to do. I ran all the way back to the store to return the stolen property, where I also had to confess to the store owner. We shopped there *every* weekend, so he knew exactly who I was. I was so embarrassed, and I felt I had let Mom down. And she waited. I walked so slowly back to where I'd left Mom and my sisters and they were all standing there, waiting. I made a promise to myself: never again. Then Mom slowly turned around and we started the longest walk home of my life. She never spoke of it again. But it felt so much better to confess. There's no way to sugar-coat stealing a piece of candy. To this day, I still smile whenever I see that little pink-, brown-, and white-striped coconut bar in a store.

At mealtimes, we all had our spot at the table. I always sat at the corner by the kitchen door. For as long as I could remember, Mom never sat at a meal. She would stand leaning against the counter between the stove and the sink, with her plate perched in her left hand at her chest. Dad worked second shift a lot, so most of the time we ate long before he ever came home.

One night as we sat eating dinner, Mom had gone to the bathroom, and I heard a jiggle at the kitchen door. I turned to look and that's when I saw the doorknob, ever so slightly, turning left and then right. The door had a half window, and it was always curtained. I tried to look through the folds and the glass, but I couldn't see anything. By then the others had been drawn to the tiny little noises that signaled to us that someone was trying to break into our home. It was totally dark outside except for one streetlight. We all froze. The doorknob stopped rotating and there was dead silence for what seemed like five minutes. All of a sudden, the intruder jerked the knob and jiggled it hard back and forth in an attempt to break in.

We were all shocked and scared out of our minds. We all ran screaming to the bathroom, throwing open the door. "Mom, someone's breaking into the house."

Mom jumped up and ran straight to the bedroom, grabbing the pistol from the dresser drawer. She moved so quickly, next grabbing something from the other drawer, and loaded the gun. Then she grabbed an article of clothing, throwing it over the bright, shiny gold barrel of the gun to keep it from being seen. As she slipped down the hallway, we hid in the skirt of her dress, terrified and crying, not letting go of her legs, even as they were still a little dripping wet. But Mom kept saying, "*Shhhh.*" We ever so slowly crept down the hall and rounded the corner into the kitchen, where she flipped off the lights.

Mom leveled the gun and steadily approached the top of the three stairs that led down to the door. Quietly, she took off the safety and cocked the gun. In that slight motion, the drape covering the barrel shifted. The bright street-light that always flooded into the kitchen window caught the barrel, causing a glimmer to flash across the room.

"Hey. It's me. It's me. It's just me!" Dad screamed at the top of his voice. He'd only meant to play a little trick on us and scare us, which he surely did, but thank God the cloth slipped and he saw the reflection off the barrel.

What I remember most of all was that our brave mom never hesitated for a moment. There is no doubt in my mind that she would have pulled the trigger to protect her children. She was so angry at Dad. She unlocked the door, slammed the gun into his hands without saying a word, and went back to the bathroom . . . and Dad never played a trick like that on us ever again. He did, however, teach us all how to handle a gun. And a rifle and shotgun.

# CHAPTER SEVEN

# THE EDUCATION OF MISS JANE

"Jane? Do you want to dance?"

Cutie-pie Mark. Oh my gosh, I had crushed on him for years. He held out his hand and before I could think twice, he led me to the dance floor in the basement.

It was my first time going to a boy-girl blue-light basement party. I was only there because my older sister was invited, and my parents told her she *had* to bring me. I guess they thought if she had to keep an eye on me, she would also stay out of trouble.

I was expecting to sit there the entire night, watching the couples swaying, their bodies pressed together and sweaty, and just be content to hear all my favorite songs: "Since I Lost My Baby," "Under the Boardwalk," and my absolute favorite of all favorites, "Ooo Baby Baby" by Smokey Robinson and The Miracles.

"Are you nervous?" Mark asked.

I couldn't even respond. I just smiled.

While Little Anthony and the Imperials crooned "Goin' Out of My Head," Mark lifted my chin and leaned into my lips. He kissed me. A *real* kiss. A French kiss—not a peck. It was like a movie. My heart was thumping even after he pulled away. I couldn't even tell you how long we stayed at the party or how we got home. I was floating on air.

Until a few days later, while I was outside at recess with the other eighth graders, and something caught my ear. Someone's older sister was pregnant, and it was a scandal around the neighborhood.

I overheard someone say, "She was French-kissing this guy on our porch and *bam*—now she's pregnant." I stepped into the group.

"What do you mean? You can get pregnant from kissing?" I asked, my breathing becoming shallow.

"Of *course* you can," she said, looking at me like I was a toddler. "Don't you know anything?"

It hit me like one of those Mack Trucks Dad made on his job at White Motor Company. *I must be pregnant.*

They went back to giggling and clucking their tongues, while I felt like I was drowning underwater. In middle school and there I was—impregnated by Mark.

Now, you think that sounds insane that I would believe you could get pregnant by kissing. But you must remember, there was *zero* sex education in schools at that time. All we were told about sex—don't do it. And keep your legs closed.

So, here I was, panic-stricken. I had no idea what I was going to do. I was too afraid to tell even my sisters. And certainly not my closest friends. That kind of conversation would not have happened with them at all. I could only imagine how outraged my parents would be. Their thirteen-year-old child was going to be walking around with her belly poking out for the world to see?

There was a fourteen-year-old girl at our school who had gotten pregnant two years before and she was shunned. The parents were disgraced. And that cloud never ever went away. They were always known as The Family with the Pregnant Girl, and I never saw or heard of her again.

I didn't even know how my parents ended up with six kids. That was a *lot* of French-kissing.

I had taken great pride in being at the top of my class grade-wise and captain on the cheer squad so that I could just be near sports. But I started coming straight home from school, not doing my homework. Just sitting there, devastated, trying to figure out what to do. Mark and his big brother lived right down the street. Our families went to church together.

Every day, I pressed my stomach, and it felt the same as always. But I knew that wouldn't be for long. I had seen my mom and aunts with their pregnant bellies and knew what was coming after seeing them kiss their husbands.

I spent the next two months in personal disgrace and terrified out of my mind. I had always gotten straight As in school, but with all the inner turmoil surrounding my secret anguish, my math grade dropped to a C. What was I going to do?

I knew I'd be sent away, so I thought maybe I would run away from home. But I had no idea where or how far or how I was going to get any money.

There was only one "out" that kept resurfacing in the recesses of my mind, and I never wanted to admit that it was a consideration, but I felt I had no other choice. I kept pushing the idea back further and further until I almost gave in and seriously contemplated suicide.

The next month, I wondered why I wasn't showing, so I decided to do some research. I slipped into the library and looked up books on pregnancy.

Hold on. What?

I read a few lines and saw a few pictures and realized: I was *definitely* not pregnant. I was relieved but, at the same time, so angry that I had spent months in such anguish, thinking I'd gotten pregnant from a simple kiss. What if I had gone through with the suicide? What was I thinking? Then I got angry with everyone, including myself. How could I have been so . . . so stupid?

That was the exact moment when I decided to make something happen in my life. No way was I ever going to be a victim or in a predicament like that ever again. I was determined to reach my full potential, and I was ready to start *that* day. Sex was the last thing on my mind for years to come. My commitment was that school would always come first. By the time I got to high school, I was making serious moves to run the world—nothing was impossible!

And yet I still had to be a kid, a teenager who loved family parties, hunting with Dad, music, dancing, sports, designing clothes, modeling, painting, writing poetry, and dreaming.

I remember one day we went hunting, Dad and my sisters, and we got lost. I was so proud of myself that I had remembered the diminishing stars in the early-morning sun and I was able to backtrack and find our truck by following the sun. I was always a dreamer and the sky was my friend.

All my life I loved listening to the radio to stay on top of my favorite songs. We had stacks and stacks of 45s and practically wore them out. By the time I got to high school, music was life!

*You're listening to Leon the Lover from WJMO radio, up next,* R-E-S-P-E-C-T.

It was the late 1960s and the Civil Rights Movement was in full swing, the Voting Rights Act was signed by President Johnson in 1965, and the police attack on John Lewis and the marchers in Selma, Alabama, was the same year. I watched the news with a fearful heart, but I loved to lose myself in the innocence of radio. It was my MTV.

*Hi, Leon. This is Ellen from Cleveland. I love you and your show. Can you play "Fingertips" by Little Stevie Wonder?*

*I sure can. Thanks for calling in, Ellen.*

*Thank you, Leon.*

It was two different worlds; one where I could be a kid and enjoy the beauty in everything, including music. But I also was caught up in the acknowledgment that there was more going on in the world than just music and fun.

My friends and family were dying in rice fields in Vietnam and those at home were burning their draft cards. Women were burning their bras and demanding equality. Black people were demanding representation and respect—frustrated and angry, and many with nothing to burn but our own communities. Drugs and the culture that came with it were destroying lives. Civil rights seemed like they might never be attained. Black Power was now a bona fide social movement. Flower children were free—but free speech was not. I *had* to do something. I had to make my voice be heard.

After showing leadership skills throughout my community, I was so proud in my junior year to be nominated by my teachers for the Wickliffe chapter of the American Legion Auxiliary as one of the school's delegates to their annual mock student government program, Boys State and Girls State.

The two seperate conferences began in the late 1930s as a way to make sure young Americans understood the process of government and its importance. As a participant in the program, Wickliffe High School chose six girls and five boys and sent us off to college for two weeks to learn about the structure of our cities, counties, and state government. The girls—Pat Adkins, Dee Arndt, Jeane Moeller, Margaret Mohar, Jaye Vincent—and I were on the bus to Ohio University in Athens when my fellow students convinced me to run for governor. Sounded like a great idea.

I had been working for the May Company Teen Fashion Board as a model. One of the fashion shows I worked was for a luncheon at Cleveland's famous Terminal Tower, which was the tallest building in the world until 1953. The Beatles stayed at the Terminal Tower hotel on their US tour in 1966. While I was supposed to be strutting my stuff on the runway that day, I was busy being captivated by the keynote speaker, the incomparable and fascinating Congresswoman Shirley Chisholm, the first woman from one of the two major political parties to run for president of the United States, in 1972. She was so impressive, so committed. She was a Black woman doing something I had thought was reserved only for white men. And here she was . . . a woman . . . a Black woman . . . talking about change and equality in the turbulent 1960s. Not equality just for race, but for gender as well. And then she outlined what it was going to take to achieve our dreams. Not just her dreams but *our* dreams. And I believed her. She became my idol. She was the perfect role model. Meeting her backstage was a highlight of my life. Then and there I decided that if I ever got the chance to go to college it would be Columbia

University in New York to study political science, and modeling was going to help me pay for it. This was my first giant step.

I did not win for governor; however, something very special happened at the end of our two-week Ohio program. There were 1,282 students at Ohio Girls State that year. Every state sends two girls functioning as senators to Washington, DC, for the Girls Nation National Conference. The Ohio delegates had to vote on who would be their two state senators. The write-in votes had been cast earlier that day. We were all seated in the auditorium listening proudly to the recounting of our events of the past two weeks. It was such a warm feeling as we were exchanging phone numbers and making promises to stay in touch. And then the results were in—Jane Harrison was going to Girls Nation.

Oh my God! This was unbelievable. My team went crazy . . . and I did too. I'd only known these 1,282 delegates for fourteen days and all I could think about for the next month was Girls Nation. It was summer and I was seventeen. The day I left for Washington, DC, was my very first airplane trip; I tried not to think about falling out of the sky, but every bump found my hands white-knuckling the handrest. I knew I had to put that out of my head, because I had serious plans to make. I had already decided I was going to run for vice president of the United States at Girls Nation, which meant that I would be running the Senate . . . so that's what I focused on. I had my speeches all prepared and I knew in my heart that this time I was going to win.

Our first week on the campus of American University, we toured extensively: the Smithsonian museums, the White House, the Lincoln Memorial, the Capitol, the Pentagon, and Mount Vernon. Never having seen any of these places, I was so inspired. Even though I had been to Washington, DC, to visit family many times growing up, it was never as a tourist. I had never visited these important historical landmarks.

Although Girls Nation was symbolic, it meant everything to us—especially at this time. Our party's ticket was RoAnn Costin, the senator from Nahant, Massachusetts, for president and Jane Harrison, the senator from

Wickliffe, Ohio, for vice president. We hired a campaign manager, Cyd Payne, aka Grit, from . . . I think it was North Carolina. You should have heard our meetings. Cyd had the deepest Southern drawl, and RoAnn's Boston accent was thick as Southern molasses. By the end of the two weeks, I had picked up the strangest hybrid accent any Midwestern girl with no accent ever had. *No one* understood me when I got back home.

It was 1969, and the words of Dr. Martin Luther King Jr.'s 1963 "I Have a Dream" speech were still ringing in my ears and in my heart. The assassinations of President John F. Kennedy, Dr. King, and Senator Bobby Kennedy were weighing heavily on my soul. The images of the twenty-five-year-old John Lewis leading six hundred marchers across the Edmund Pettus Bridge in Selma, Alabama, in 1965 gave me strength.

When I delivered my final campaign speech, my heartbreak echoed in every word, representing the passion of our party name: InteraBang. *Intera*: ask questions. And *Bang*: come up with solutions. I couldn't stop talking. I was totally engulfed in my newfound purpose in life, 100 percent engaged in the awe of the revelation of what I could do about the national issues our country was facing at that time in our history. Knowing that the road would be twice as hard because I was a woman . . . three times as hard because I was Black . . . I was on fire to make a difference and *just do something*.

It paid off. Jane Harrison won the office of the vice president of the United States American Legion Auxiliary Girls Nation.

The next day I placed my left hand on the Bible with my right hand held high and was sworn into office as the vice president by then vice president of the United States, Spiro T. Agnew.

"For God and Country, I promise to give unselfish and constructive cooperation, to share with others the benefits of my experience as a senator of American Legion Auxiliary Girls Nation, to participate in the government of my country, state, and nation upon reaching my majority, and above all, to constantly exemplify the highest type of Americanism."

He then handed me the official gavel on the chamber floor of the United States Senate, which we were allowed to use while the senators were in recess.

As vice president, I was president of the Senate for the remainder of our two-week stay, and I also was honored to be selected to place the wreath at the gravesite of President John F. Kennedy and at the Tomb of the Unknown Soldier.

After the amazingly successful Girls State and Girls Nation experience at the end of summer leading into my senior year, I found I had been granted a lot of latitude to explore my options. I had earned a reputation for honesty, responsibility, and trustworthiness. I had participated in nearly everything: class president, president of the girls' athletic association, captain of the girls' basketball and volleyball champions, captain of the varsity cheerleaders, wrestling cheerleader, and track-and-field and cross-country statistician; as well as membership in student council, the scholarship club, the madrigal choir, the a capella choir, girls' glee club, the National Honor Society, the yearbook staff, drama club, and the International Thespian Society; plus Ohio delegate to the National Junior Achievement Conference (NAJAC), where I won Miss Junior Achievement in recognition of my leadership as president of my Junior Achievement Company, blue ribbon winner in the state girls ensemble choral competition, and president of the May Company Teen Fashion Board. Oh, and I worked in the athletic office during lunch selling game tickets.

It was all very impressive . . . until I walked out of the doors of my school. Because no matter how many honors I had achieved, no matter how many friends I had *in* school and related extracurricular activities, none of it mattered *outside* those walls. It was 1969 and the harsh reality of the *real* world was hitting me squarely in my face whether I liked it or not.


"Jayne. Are you really coming to my birthday party?"

"Of course I am. Thanks for inviting me."

She beamed. "I just thought, you know, you're one of the cool girls."

"Well, you are too." And we laughed. "See you there," I added as I turned and walked to class.

Every party back then was in the parents' basement, and this one was no different, except it was mostly white kids—and me. I'd been in all-white or nearly all-white spaces before and it was always fine . . . at least as far as I could tell. The color of their skin was not important to me. I'd been looking forward to a world where multinational cultures and color was the norm since my young dreams on the white-winged horse.

It was going great: party lights, lots of food, dancing, and laughing. And then the bright overhead lights suddenly came on and we all winced.

"HEY."

The birthday girl, and all of us, stopped and turned to see her father at the top of the basement steps.

He looked at the crowd, clearly swaying, as it appeared he'd had too much to drink. I think we were all hoping he'd just take a look around and turn back, but he just kept scanning the room and grunting.

"Hey," he said, pointing at me. "Who invited the nigger?"

I think everyone died a little inside in that moment. I knew the birthday girl did. She couldn't even look at me. These were my classmates. Most were my friends. But the party was now over. Without acknowledging the racist remark, everyone started making excuses about why they had to leave early. I didn't give my friend an excuse. I didn't need to. I just left.

It was as if, at that moment, we all stopped trying to believe that integration was normal and that we all cared for each other. I was never invited to another birthday party with my classmates again. And I was never asked out on a date.

Then it was back to school, and I thought things would be back to "normal" again. My friend JD was dating my friend Dee, and we all hung out together at school. One day at lunch he came to the athletic office as usual. His eyes were teary.

"You know my father is running for mayor, right?" he asked.

"Of course," I said. "Everyone knows."

He took a deep breath. "Well, he said we can't hang out together anymore."

"Wait. What?"

"He wants me to, as he put it, 'sever all ties with you.'"

"I understand," I said—though I didn't. I could see that he was hurting. It was the first time anyone had said anything like that to me. Sure, there was this one guy who called another friend who would walk me to school a "nigger lover." And my friend didn't even flinch. We just kept talking and walking . . . and naively I thought that was an isolated incident.

"What do you mean, you understand? I told him *no way* am I going to stop being your friend," JD said.

I flipped open the top of the ticket counter, and then I hugged him tight.

"But I don't want you to get in trouble," I said.

"It's gonna be fine."

Except it wasn't.

A few days later I saw him outside the gym while the wrestling team was practicing. He wasn't in uniform, and again, he looked upset.

"Why aren't you dressed?" I asked.

"I'm not on the team."

"What are you talking about? You're the captain."

"Not anymore I'm not."

"Your dad?"

"He pulled me off the team because I told him I was not going to 'sever any ties' with you. You've supported me more in my life through our friendship than he ever has. There's just no way I can do that."

"No," I said. "Just do whatever he says and get back on the team. The election will be over, and things will go back to normal."

He shook his head. "This world is never going back to normal."

That was true. There was nothing I could do but sit next to him on the floor in an awkward silence. Finally, as I was leaving, I reminded him, "We have a student council meeting tomorrow. I'll see ya there."

He just looked at me.

"Your dad pulled you off student council too?"

He nodded. He was right: The world would never be the same again.

But I still had hope. By that time, I had changed my name to Jayne (with a *y*) after a lifetime of "Where's Tarzan?" or "Where's Boy?" and "Did you forget your gorilla?" jokes. I had been toying with this idea since eighth grade as I'd wanted something different that would stand out. In 1967, in my tenth-grade year, actress Jayne Mansfield, Hollywood's bombshell vixen, died tragically in a car accident. I noticed in the newspaper how she spelled her name and decided to claim it for myself.

My senior year began with a huge surprise. My classmates had nominated me for the homecoming court, which meant I really had to get going on that sewing machine. Sewing had been a major part of my life. We made most of what we wore. Mom had taught us since we were barely able to sit in the chair. I designed and made my gown for the homecoming pep rally, a sleeveless, floor-length, slim-fit gown. The empire top was silver, and the bottom was white with a band of silver wrapping around and above the knee. The surprise was that under the silver band was a zipper that when undone left a mini dress. I also made a tan suit (jacket and skirt) for the homecoming parade. Now I just needed a date. It didn't have to be someone I was dating, since it was now obvious *that* wasn't going to be happening. Just more of an escort.

So . . . I asked Kevin, a friend and coworker from Great Lakes Mall. The May Company department store Teen Fashion Board where I worked on weekends as a model and sales clerk had branches throughout Cuyahoga County and all the satellite counties. Kevin worked for a men's boutique at the other end of the mall and went to a nearby high school. I liked Kevin a lot and we'd often have lunch together. He agreed with no hesitation, and I was truly relieved and very excited.

The night of the homecoming parade and bonfire, the cheerleaders were in one convertible, the football captain, Steve Diamond, in another, then came the school band, and so on, and all the homecoming queen candidates, each in their own convertible cars, followed by the class floats.

But when I was on my way, JD called to tell me that Kevin had been in a car accident and wouldn't be able to make it. I called the hospital hoping to get a chance to talk to him. He was groggy and incoherent and told me to go without him. I was going to skip the parade and check in on him, but he was clear—go to the parade.

I was so upset and worried, but I was expected to appear and to be all smiles, waving to the crowd. Somehow, miraculously, I pulled it off. Possibly foreshadowing many times in my adult life when I'd have to do the exact same thing—but on a much larger scale.

I was prepared to go to the dance alone that Saturday night as well. Even though now it's quite the thing to do, it was unheard of back then, especially for a homecoming princess.

But just before I left the house, Kevin suddenly appeared: He had sneaked out of the hospital. He was so drugged up and really should have been in bed, but he was determined to go. I took his keys and *I* drove. We lasted through the first dance, which was traditionally for the homecoming court, then I could tell he wasn't going to hold up much longer and I took him back to the hospital. I told him as soon as he was better we'd grab lunch together, and he agreed.

But he didn't return my calls. I didn't see him at work. He was just gone. It was so odd. A few weeks later, I learned what had happened.

He also ran cross-country and during a meet, people started whispering about how he took a Black girl to a homecoming dance. A competitor tripped him in the cinders while he was running and he ended up back in the hospital, bloodied head to toe. We never went out again.

# CHAPTER EIGHT

# JOY AND PAIN

M y last semester of high school was a period of extreme elation and extreme sadness, which began with spring break. Our school had several choirs, but madrigal was top level. The madrigal choir was scheduled to take its annual trip to New York City for a week with our music teacher, Mr. Lenenski, affectionately known as Mr. L. We were determined to have the time of our lives, going to see *Man of La Mancha* on Broadway, the Rockettes at Radio City Music Hall, and Rockefeller Center, dining in fine restaurants, and much, much more. The bus trip alone was going to be a riot. We had all been best friends for so many years. It was a great way to cap off our senior high school experience.

One of our group's friends, Paul, wasn't in madrigal choir, so he wasn't a part of the New York trip. For three years, I had sat with Paul at our alphabetized homeroom desks, so we were very close. We would chat about anything and everything. One morning Paul decided he was going to protest the tradition of roses being presented to the girls when we received our diplomas at graduation. He wanted a rose too. He had been assigned to be my partner when we walked down the aisle during the class procession. So I promised him that when they called my name, I was going to give him my rose, right there onstage. God, I was such a little rebel.

Paul decided to drive to Florida for spring break. He met those of us going to New York City at the school the morning we all left. As our bus pulled out of the driveway, headed east, his car pulled off to the south. We waved and yelled out the windows, "We'll meet right here in seven days."

New York was all we thought it would be: Night after night of theatre and dining was absolutely incredible. We even watched from our hotel window as a heroic NYC firefighter pulled a woman and child from the burning hotel next to ours to safety onto the ladder.

After an early-morning departure at the end of the week, we headed home to Ohio. I couldn't wait to get back to swap lies and stories with Paul. We unloaded our bags from the bus, kissed all the parents, and little by little the hubbub dwindled until there were only a few of us left in the school parking lot. We waited, but there was no sign of Paul. We thought he must have gotten delayed for some reason, so we finally decided to go home.

Later that day my friend Bill, who had been part of the madrigal trip, called. After pausing a long time, his voice cracked as he barely whispered, "Paul was in an accident. . . . He died." Then he simply hung up. I stood there with the phone in my hand, unable to comprehend what I had just heard, unable to think, to cry, to move. The happy, wild, jubilant, crazy memories of New York just a few hours before were suddenly a distant flicker. . . . Paul was dead.

The school's hallways were filled with the whispered hush of mourning teachers, administrators, friends, and classmates; everyone was in shock. Paul's funeral was held at Our Lady of Mount Carmel Catholic Church. I decided to walk to the services, solemnly reflecting on memories of Paul. It was my first funeral since Grandpa Turk had died, and those memories flooded back as well, in a mixture of sadness and happy times, one thought on top of another. The funeral was so foreign to me, so different from Grandpa's. It was my first time inside a Catholic church, at least *this* Catholic church, and I had never participated in a formal Catholic service. I had peered through their stained-glass windows for years. I had seen this church almost every day of my life but had never gone inside . . . and it was in my own backyard. In my mind, it was filled with hypocrisy. I had lived in this community most of my life, and I never understood how they could tell their members that they could not eat meat on Friday, but they could *not* tell them that they could *not* be racist. Filled with confusing thoughts, I sat quietly. I knew these parishioners would never understand. Quietly leaving at the first opportunity, I said my goodbye as I walked out the double doors and back into my own world outside. It was my last time there.

Graduation seemed to come quickly after Paul's funeral. In a respectful gesture of honoring him, I didn't want to walk down the aisle with another partner at the commencement ceremonies, but I was assigned to one anyway. Seems the new partner didn't want me either.

Mr. Patrick Penrod (my drama coach) was the commencement organizer and was in his classroom when my partner came to see him. It was quite obvious that he was struggling.

"Mr. Penrod, I need to ask you for a favor." He switched his weight back and forth with his hands in his pants pockets, obviously trying to find the words. "Mr. Penrod, my *grandparents* are going to be at the graduation. They are coming in from out of town."

"That's fantastic. Make sure you introduce them to me."

"No, you don't understand. I need you to assign me to a new partner." And then as he fidgeted some more, he blurted out, "My grandparents would not understand if I entered the hall with a Black girl."

All that stuff about my position in the class, cheerleading, homecoming, class president didn't mean a thing to *them*.

To them I was just Black, and that was enough; or perhaps more accurately, in their eyes, it wasn't enough. In reply, J. Patrick (as we lovingly called him) politely smiled and replied, "I'm sure *Jayne's* father would not want his daughter to walk into commencement with *you*. If your grandparents object to a Black girl, then that's their problem. Jayne's going to be just fine."

I was reassigned.

Last year the same student sent me a Facebook friend request. I declined. He should have stood up for me when he had the chance.

I sat on the stage at Severance Hall, where the Cleveland Orchestra makes its home. As the seniors were each called out in alphabetical order, we stood and filed one by one to accept our diplomas. As I waited for my turn in line, a pain literally stabbed my heart—for the first time since entering high school, I did not hear the name Gereby (Paul's last name) before I heard Harrison. I walked across the stage, fighting back the tears as I accepted my gold honor cord (indicative of my 3.89 GPA) and the long-stemmed bloodred rose, whispering, "This is for you, Paul."

As we exited Severance Hall, one of my best friends, Bill Floro, grabbed my arm and planted a giant kiss on my lips. "Now I don't have to listen to anyone tell me what I can and cannot do, and I've wanted to do that for a long time." Then we both smiled.

The night we graduated my best friend threw a party, but I wasn't invited. I had asked my dearest friend, Sam, to go with me to Paul's grave. I had something I needed to do. Sam had been my school crush since sixth grade and we did just about everything together: our academic classes, and drama club, and we were both on the May Company Teen Fashion Board, which meant we also worked together. We had spent countless days, months, and years in each other's company. But since he always had a girlfriend, he was just my best friend. He readily agreed to take me to the grave. Of course he did. . . .

Sam had this beat-up, but always reliable, yellow Volkswagen Beetle. He picked me up at home about ten p.m. and we drove to the cemetery where Paul had been buried only a few weeks before. Oddly, the huge wrought iron gates to the cemetery were wide open, so we simply drove in. That night, the sky was lit by a radiant moon, with no clouds, no wind, just a beautiful, clear evening with a sky full of stars.

Sam and I thought we'd have no problem finding the grave, but everything looked so different at night, so much so that we puttered around for some time, trying to remember where Paul had been buried. We finally got to where we thought the grave was, but it was hard to be sure because Paul's headstone had not yet been put into place. Sam turned the car around and left the motor running so that the headlights were shining toward the graves. We got out and stood in front of the car's low beams, held hands, and said a prayer for Paul. Then I reached beneath my jacket, pulled out my graduation rose, and, smiling through the tears, tossed the rose up as high as I could toward heaven in a symbolic gesture that I knew Paul would understand.

At that exact moment, the lights on the car went out, the motor died, and a bolt of lightning from that clear, cloudless sky lit up the entire cemetery, and we watched the rose fall to the ground, as if in slow motion.

Sam and I stood utterly frozen, but we weren't afraid at all. He squeezed my hand so hard I thought it would break, and then I whispered to Paul in heaven, "You're welcome."

I had kept my promise.

We slowly walked back to the car hand in hand and climbed in. The car started up with no problem, and Sam drove me home in a silence filled with wonder. As I got out of the car, he squeezed my hand again and we just stared at each other. Sam said, "See ya tomorrow," and we never talked about it again.

Some years later I returned to Wickliffe to initiate the Jayne Harrison Kennedy Scholarship Fund for the Arts. Pat Penrod and Mr. Lenenski were named the scholarship administrators. I also competed in many game shows in Hollywood, winning money for various charities, which helped to fund the scholarships. There was *Win, Lose or Draw* (sort of like Pictionary) hosted by Bert Convy, *Family Feud* hosted by Richard Dawson, and many others. I donated all my winnings to our Covenant Baptist Church Day Care Center, which was in threat of closing after losing funding. Wickliffe will forever and always have a warm place in my heart.

# CHAPTER NINE

# FORK IN THE ROAD

M y initial plans after high school graduation in 1970 were to somehow go to Kent State University for a year to get all my requirements out of the way. Kent State was potentially affordable and only forty miles southeast of Wickliffe. But on May 4 of my senior year, the eyes of the world were on Kent State. The Vietnam War protest on Kent State's campus left four students dead in its wake and that was not where my parents wanted me to be.

But in my mind, tragedy could be anywhere. As long as there is civil unrest and racial inequality, there is no running from it. The Hough Riots of 1966 left the streets of Cleveland suffering as much as the streets of Los Angeles after the Watts Riots of 1965 and of Detroit after the Detroit Riot of 1967. The Hough Avenue riots, caused by a quick decline in population and economic opportunity, found four African Americans killed and fifty injured. Two hundred and seventy-five people were arrested amid incidents of arson and firebombing. Hough Avenue was only fifteen minutes away. Where would I be safe?

I *had* planned to transfer to Columbia University in New York after Kent State, but the problem was I had absolutely no idea how to pay for any of it.

My guidance counselors basically told me that the only opportunities for me after graduation were to be a teacher, nurse, secretary, or housewife, all noble careers, but I was a girl who always thought outside the box. She never saw that. I'm quite sure she did not give that same advice to her students who were not Black. If someone in the guidance counselor's office who actually cared had taken just a few minutes of their day to review my accomplishments, I have no doubt that I would have qualified for a full scholarship, which would have definitely changed the trajectory of my life . . . or would it? Bottom line, I didn't have that option.

I don't remember anyone helping me to understand the process of student aid, scholarships, or anything about getting into college. I only remember taking the SAT, and I didn't understand the significance of that, other than it was a necessity to graduate and the score would be a barometer of me as a student. I don't even remember what I got on my SAT.

We were a big family, and my sister was already attending Cleveland Community College, and there wasn't enough money for two daughters in college at the same time. I had to figure a way to be creative, a way to find the money to further my education, but I didn't have the slightest idea how. My mom actually came up with a plan. She had seen an ad in the newspaper calling for applicants to the Miss Ohio pageant, and Mom thought it would be a good idea for both me and my sister to apply.

I had watched pageants all my life, in awe of the girls, the gowns, the crowns, and the money, but that was totally different from actually *entering* a beauty pageant. It didn't seem possible that there was ever a chance, ever even a remote possibility, to be a part of all that, but Mom always taught us to believe we could do anything, and she thought this would be fun. I thought: What the heck, it's an adventure. And I was a sucker for adventure. Ultimately, *she* sent in both of our applications.

To be eligible for Miss Ohio, you must have first won a "city crown." I was totally caught off guard when, because of Mom's application, I received a letter to say that I had been entered in the Miss Cleveland pageant, which would be held at David Blaushild's Chevrolet dealership. In all honesty,

I don't recall being all that excited; however, as it turned out, it was fine by me. I do recall the owner telling me before I went onstage, *You could win this whole thing if you used pumice stone on those tomboy knees.* I still won. The next step was to go buy some pumice stone . . . lots of pumice stone. From there I went on to compete as Miss Cleveland in the Miss Ohio pageant, which was held at the Great Lakes Mall, the very same mall where I worked on the weekends.

The first day I checked into the hotel for Miss Ohio, I saw another competitor with a drop-dead gorgeous, curvaceous, bronze-tanned body and blond hair. She had the perfect Florida look. Paulette Breen.

I just knew she was the winner, so the rest of the week I kicked back and enjoyed the experience. No frets, no nerves, no worries. At eighteen and as a senior at Wickliffe High, I was more concerned about missing that night's game fundraiser, which I had planned for our prom, than the Miss Ohio pageant. Senior boys riding donkeys on the basketball court trying to shoot buckets with animals that were not concerned at all about running up and down a court was pure comedy. This was one of our biggest fundraisers, and we were sold out.

The night of the pageant, my family, friends, and a few of my coworkers from the mall came to cheer me on because everybody else we knew was at the donkey basketball game. It all went smoothly as we finally arrived at the announcement.

All of the contestants were standing on the stage waiting for the runners-up and the crowning moment; there were no semifinalists. The emcee finally announced, "The first runner-up is Paulette Breen."

I was shocked. I couldn't believe it. Who could they have possibly chosen over her? I turned around to survey the remaining girls onstage, so I didn't hear the emcee announce, "And the new Miss Ohio 1970 is *Jayne Harrison*." My sister, seeing I wasn't responding to the announcement, grabbed me and yelled, "Jayne, you won!" I had no idea what she was talking about.

After seeing everyone's faces looking at me . . . it finally hit me. *I had won.* Dad walked up on the stage and held me as they presented the roses and sat the crown upon my head. Then all the family, including Grandma Lois, came to take pictures with the new Miss Ohio 1970 . . . a Harrison Girl.

Jim, another friend who had also defied his father's threats if he remained my friend, ran to the pay phone and called the gym, and the school made the announcement over the PA system during the basketball game: *Jayne Harrison from Wickliffe High School has just won the Miss Ohio Pageant.* The gymnasium erupted in shouts of excitement. I still didn't believe it. Everyone was so kind, so happy for me. I was overwhelmed and excited about the prospects of all that I was told would come next for me, as the new Miss Ohio.

However, I should have known better. There were no prizes, no money that a Miss Whoever might usually get. I remember watching pageants in our living room for years, watching these women walk away with college scholarships or cash prizes.

But each pageant, each city, each state has their own guidelines, and it all depends on their sponsors, donations, or supporters. I had no idea what a Miss Ohio winner had won in the past, but the only prize I received was a charm bracelet from a bank at the mall, the same one that they gave away to any new customers for opening up a hundred-dollar checking account.

I expected more. I had hoped for more. And I should have been devastated. But deep down inside I knew. . . . As a Black woman, there are parameters that always exist with a red flag that screams STOP! You do not belong here! Even at that young age, I had been climbing that mountain for many years. So yes! Of course. I expected this too. Another rung on the ladder that just made me stronger.

Carl Stokes was the mayor of Cleveland at that time. We loved Mayor Stokes; it seemed everybody loved Mayor Stokes, and I was lucky enough to live in Cleveland under his leadership. He was truly a Renaissance man. Elected in 1967 as the first Black mayor of a major city, he had served in the Ohio legislature and presided as a municipal judge. Eventually he went on to become the first Black anchor of a television news show in New York City and was the US ambassador to the Seychelles. Furthering his political power, his brother, Louis Stokes, served fifteen consecutive terms (thirty years) as a US congressman.

My first responsibilities as Miss Ohio were making personal appearances for Mayor Stokes's office, which was perfect for a young girl like me who wanted to go into politics. When Mayor Stokes presented me with the Key to the City, it was such an honor, and when his wife heard about what had happened with not receiving any prizes, including no money to finance or compete in Miami, she organized a group of politically and socially savvy Black wives, who solicited a group of stores that they frequented and *demanded* contributions.

The women, led by Mrs. Stokes, wanted me to have a complete wardrobe for the Miss USA pageant in Miami. I ultimately was given two dresses, two pairs of shoes, and two wigs. So funny . . . these Black women told me Miami would be humid and I would need wigs, so you better believe I packed them, just in case.

A mother of a former Miss Ohio gave me one of her daughter's gowns that her daughter hadn't used when she had gone to the nationals. The pageant officials made a little costume for the Parade of States portion of the pageant and told me my state costume was as an Indigenous woman from the Ohio River Valley. I think they believed that if I looked Native American, the pageant officials would forget that I was Black, and I might have a chance of winning.

That was April 1970. I was to be in Miami for the national pageant in one month. No time to plan. No time to prepare. No time to get sponsors. No time at all. And I was still a senior in high school; I had final exams and graduation coming up soon. To top it all off, the TV broadcast was the exact same night as my senior prom. I was going to miss the event that I had helped plan for three years, though in hindsight I guess it really didn't matter because I didn't have a date anyway. It was better to miss it because of the pageant than to miss it because nobody asked me to the dance. So, while the other girls at school were picking out their prom dresses, I was boarding the plane for Miami Beach, Florida.

Syd Freedman, the state pageant official, gave me my plane ticket that he paid for out of his own pocket, and sent me on my way, alone, and he arrived the next week. I had only been Miss Ohio for a month. Once there, things went really fast from the moment I walked into the lobby of the Fontainebleau Hotel. The meetings, the chaperones, the rehearsals, and MIAMI . . . WOW. This was all a dream come true. I couldn't believe it was really happening to me. After all those times hoping to one day go to Florida, I'd finally made it. Then I thought: What if I actually won?

It was unbelievable. We'd had such a short window of time before the Miss USA pageant, yet still, both my parents, my older sister, and a bunch of Harrisons and Thompsons did whatever it took to get to Miami to see the pageant live and in person.

I was so naive. The professional pageant competitors were everywhere; girls were there who had been in pageants since they were in kindergarten, while for me it had only been one month. Whenever I was asked whether I had dreamed of being a Miss Ohio or a Miss USA, my answer was aways, "Heck NO. I want to be Shirley Chisholm." But these girls had been raising all kinds of money, serious money, for this very moment. The outfits, the gowns, and the pageantry. The politics of it all were also very evident. I was overwhelmed and in way over my head. For comparison, I was still in high school, and many of the other contestants were already in their mid-twenties.

What saved me from being totally overwhelmed happened during the first meeting with our chaperones in the hotel lobby: There she was, Miss Virginia, walking in the door with the biggest green eyes, the most beautiful dark hair all the way down her back, the warmest, friendliest smile made up of perfect white teeth and perfectly shaped lips—and a perfectly tanned body. Jeez! My mouth just dropped wide open. I had done it again, I'd picked out the winner, and this time there was no doubt in my mind that I was right. The new Miss USA was definitely going to be Deborah Shelton, Miss Virginia.

The day the rehearsals began I started to hear rumors that Debbie Shelton *wouldn't* be the winner, because Virginia had won the previous year, and they wouldn't dare choose the same state back-to-back. Then there were two others who wouldn't win, Miss New Jersey and Miss Ohio, because . . . well, we were both Black. So once again, since I wasn't going to win, there was no stress, and I decided to just have fun and enjoy my Miami experience.

Debbie and I became good friends. It was Debbie who taught me how to do makeup, how all the other girls were wearing falsies (which was against the pageant rules), and all the other rules that were being broken while pageant officials were looking the other way. When there was a break in rehearsals, the press would barge in to do interviews with the contestants. As far as I know, no one tried to interview Debbie or me because we were already deemed "not winnables," so Debbie and I would lie down on the stage floor and laugh and just talk about anything—all during the rehearsals, the trips around Miami, meeting the city officials, filming the pretaped video packages, lying down just to watch the ocean, and meeting cool lifeguards.

Bob Barker was the host of the pageant. On the night of the live broadcast, we were instructed to say our names and hometowns at the show opening in the Parade of States.

One of the producers called me over as we finished our hair and makeup.

"Jayne, when it's your turn to introduce yourself, say you're from Cleveland."

"But I'm from Wickliffe, Ohio."

"Yes, but Cleveland is more familiar."

"I see, okay, no problem," I said.

And that's when I first discovered the power of live television.

There I was onstage in Miami at the Miss USA/Universe pageant, and all my friends were back in Wickliffe at my senior prom. The world was watching, including those attending my prom, because the committee had set up television sets and the pageant was running during the dance. The excitement backstage was electric as the live telecast opened and the Parade of States began. We danced and sang the theme song of all the states, which I can still remember to this day (and it has afforded me the unique ability to still name all fifty states in less than a minute).

Each of us took our turn to announce to the world who we were. I was up next, my heart pounding, trying to keep my legs from shaking as I walked barefoot in my Ohio River Valley Native American attire. Approaching the microphone, I proudly announced, "Jayne Harrison, *Wickliffe*."

I don't know what happened in the director's booth when I said Wickliffe instead of Cleveland, but I can tell you that everyone at the senior prom went wild. So what, I wasn't going to win anyway, right? But I was shocked yet again when Bob Barker announced shortly thereafter that I had made it into the top semifinalists.

The next phase of the competition, Bob individually introduced each of the top fifteen onstage for questions and answers. During pageant week the producers had pre-interviewed each of us to find out a little about our home life, and a lot about our dreams and aspirations. We were told that when Bob called our name, he would step to us in our little circle on the floor and there would be some casual icebreaker repartee, and then our competition question would follow. We were told to prepare for anything. Having been interested in politics and current events through my experiences at Girls State, Girls Nation, and then working with Mayor Stokes as Miss Ohio, I just knew I was ready for whatever question he could throw my way.

Bob called my name, stepped forward to meet me, and smiled. "Miss Ohio, I see here there are five girls in your family and one little boy. He must be spoiled."

"He is," I said. "The day he was born was the only time I've seen my dad cry."

"You mean he was sad?"

"No! He was happy he finally got a boy."

"Thank you, Miss Ohio."

I froze. Where was my question? There must be a misunderstanding. All the other girls were asked what plans lay ahead for them, what their goals were. An actual question that gives the audience and the judges a glimpse of their ability to perform the duties of Miss USA. Then I felt Bob gently place his hand on the small of my back as he ushered me off the little circle.

People in the audience started saying: "Where's her question? Miss Ohio didn't get a question." But it didn't matter—I wasn't given the opportunity to demonstrate my ability to think on my feet, and I was too young and inexperienced to ask for it.

The newly named semifinalists went backstage to prepare for the swimsuit competition. I was unbelievably excited to have made the cut, and I walked onstage in my bathing suit and heels with confidence; it went well. . . . I made the top ten swimsuit finalists. I could sense the crowd starting to come around in support of me, mostly because I could hear my family yelling at the top of their lungs . . . all five cousins, five aunts, a sister, and Mom and Dad.

For whatever reason, I did not go on to the top five. However, looking back on the show over the years, there were several things that stood out. I noticed I was the only candidate who didn't wear heels in the opening Parade of States. This is a very important "first look," and as the only barefoot contestant, it did not give my legs that long, shapely silhouette. And at five foot ten, I should have been able to capitalize on that. In addition, my costume wasn't fitted at all, so I didn't have a defined waistline, nor bustline, all being essential elements in a pageant—but what did I know? I had no time. I had no one to advise me before I left Ohio. I was essentially there on my own.

However, at that point I still had my mind set on modeling in New York to pay for Columbia, so I made a beeline to the famous Wilhelmina of the Wilhelmina Models in New York, who was one of the judges. She was so gracious in allowing me to speak with her and gave me sage advice along with her contact information. Bottom line was that she absolutely wanted me to come see her as soon as I arrived . . . but . . . "We will have to work on your thighs, they're just too big."

When they announced the top five and then finally the new Miss USA, Miss Virginia, Debbie Shelton, I couldn't have been happier if it had been me.

Mom and Dad along with extended family members partied seriously, and it was an amazing trip for the entire family. All of us returned to Cleveland the next day on the same flight. About three-fourths of the way home, the flight attendants started asking the passengers personal questions like "What is your home address?" I had no idea why.

As we approached the airport, I noticed fire engines lining the runway, but still did not know what the fuss was about. The plane pulled up to the gate and we all exited the jetway, where Uncle Leonard was waiting for us at the gate. He was a mess, and oddly he seemed too relieved to see all of us, but we soon learned why. As Uncle Leonard had watched our descent out the window of the coffee shop where he had shepherded all the family members who had come to greet us, he was horrified to see the tail of our airplane was on fire. We had had no idea while flying that there was a problem, but it explained the odd questions by the flight attendants along the way. That was the last time my family flew together. Dad and Mom vowed never to fly on the same plane ever again.

Coming back to school after the pageant was one big roller-coaster ride of emotions. Everyone was so excited I had done so well, and no one cared, not even me, that I didn't win. Close was good enough. My yearbook summer supplement posted on its back cover my Miss Ohio picture. When my summer supplement arrived in the mail someone had written a caption: *She won Miss Ohio, and we couldn't even make her our homecoming queen.*

Shortly before venturing to Miami, the local newspaper, the Cleveland *Plain Dealer*, wanted an interview. The reporter, John J. Murphey, came to my home and interviewed me in our living room and I thought it went well. We talked about the pageant, winning Miss Ohio, and my plans for the future. My parents were there for support and I was proud of how I carried myself. But he was abrupt and brusque. So much so that he didn't even say goodbye. He finished taking notes, stood up, and walked out of the house without even saying a thank-you, nothing. Mom, Dad, and I were shocked. But the photographer said, "Don't take it personally, he's always this rude."

Then the story came out and—"Negro Miss Ohio Sees Self as Symbol" was the headline. Then it went on to say: "Jayne does not live in the black ghetto of Cleveland, but she identifies herself with the people of the ghetto.

Most of her friends are white, she has no friends in the Cleveland ghetto. She can remember the resentment of other black children in her first school years at Glenville High in Cleveland because of her relatively fair skin and fine textured hair."

I was shocked! First, I never went to Glenville High, which also negated the "She can remember" blah-blah-blah. His second headline on the following page was "*Wickliffe High* Beauty Is Miss Ohio." What was he thinking? Is it Glenville High, or is it Wickliffe High? He obviously had his own agenda and issues, with the "ghetto" comments. Ironically, this reporter was a *Black* man.

The full story was even worse. He implied that I thought I was better than other Black girls because I had light skin and long hair. He criticized my parents for moving out of the inner city and into an all-white suburb. And on and on. It was not at all what we spoke about at our home. He took every quote I gave them and twisted it sideways.

I was only eighteen years old; it was devastating to be attacked for what I had thought was a significant accomplishment. My mom canceled her subscription to the paper the very next day, and they have never purchased the *Plain Dealer* since.

I learned a very valuable lesson from that first major exposure to the media, combined with my experiences in Miami. An interview could merely be an opportunity to vent a reporter's preconceived ideas. It was unprofessional to crush the spirit of an eighteen-year-old and exploit her with no regard to her feelings whatsoever, or the effect such an attack might have on her family. Yet, when I look back, some fifty-plus years later, it seems little has changed as the media has grown exponentially, with social media platforms now being the primary source of information for far too many people. Mis- and disinformation that can be sent around the world at the click of a computer key or a simple tap on a cell phone. Moreover, people are emboldened by the anonymity of social media and in many cases do not bother to consider the source of the information or fact-check it for themselves. I sometimes marvel at how I was able to navigate the media during those days when my life was a total blur and wonder how I would have managed in today's

24-7, TMZ-fueled landscape where clickbait rules, and facts oftentimes come secondary. To that point, I now have a great team that ensures that my interviews are with reputable journalists, but it has been yet another hard lesson to learn.

Soon after the *Plain Dealer* interview fiasco, I got a call from a man named Isaac Sutton, who said he was a photographer with *Jet* magazine. *Jet* was a weekly periodical covering all things relevant to the Black community. I had seen many issues over the years with Dr. Martin Luther King Jr., Diana Ross, and other major African American celebrities and notables, not only on the cover but profiled on the pages within. *Jet* was *the* primary source of national news for Black households and was known to be on nearly every coffee table in African American homes since its first issue in 1951—including ours.

Isaac went on to say that *Jet* was featuring my picture as Miss Ohio on its next cover, but they also wanted to do a photo shoot of me in a bikini for the *Jet* centerfold "Beauty of the Week." I thought it was amazing that *Jet* wanted to photograph me, so I eagerly said YES . . . but just as eagerly, Dad said no. After I pleaded with Dad that *Jet* would be different than the *Plain Dealer*, he called Isaac back himself. After almost an hour of grilling the photographer, my father finally gave in, with certain conditions, including that he had to be present during the entire shoot.

The very next day, the three of us were in downtown Cleveland—my dad, photographer Isaac "Ike" Sutton, and me. I had picked out a cute bikini, nothing sexy, nothing revealing. As Ike ran through a roll of film, Dad was standing just off camera with a gigantic white sheet. Every time there was a break in the shoot, Dad would hold up the sheet to cover me up. Then Ike would give a signal that he was ready to begin again and down went the sheet.

By the end of the shoot, the three of us were laughing so hard about this silly routine that I don't even know how we got the photos done. But what developed was far more than five rolls of film. In retrospect, it was the beginning of a lifelong friendship. *Jet* magazine, John Johnson, Bob Johnson, Isaac Sutton, Moneta Sleet, and *Ebony* magazine were what I called my silent partners throughout my career. It was because of them that Jayne Kennedy became a household name.

As for participating in Miss Ohio and Miss USA? Make no mistake about it, being in the pageants was absolutely exciting, but it never did anything special for me. There were never any fringe benefits, college scholarships, money, or jobs. If anything, when I first started going out on interviews in Los Angeles, I found that when anyone saw "Miss Ohio" on my résumé, the reaction was always the same: I must be some cute bimbo who thought she could get by on her looks and her pageant title. Instead of fighting the stereotype, I just took it off my résumé altogether.

When people ask me about entering pageants, I always give the same advice: "Yes, do it for the fun and the experience of doing something different. Or do it for a scholarship if your pageant offers one, mine did not. But most importantly . . . don't make anything more of it. It's not life or death."

In retrospect, it may not have done anything for me personally, but it was a landmark: the first African American to ever win the title of Miss Ohio. I was a pioneer. The stage had been set.

Ironically, no matter what I have done since the pageant, I have constantly been introduced as Jayne Kennedy, the first Black woman to win Miss Ohio. It seems to be more important to people now because of the historical impact it has had than when I actually won.

Representation matters.

Ever since I was seventeen and first met Congresswoman Shirley Chisholm in Cleveland, Ohio, my heart held fast to the idea that anything was possible—because I *saw* it. It was because of the congresswoman, and that one moment in my life back in the late 1960s, that I became stronger myself. She reinforced the values my mother had already instilled in me that anything was, in fact, possible . . . that I could do anything . . . that I could *be* anything. She inspired me to dare. She inspired me to be bold. Shirley Chisholm's voice was constantly in the back of my mind for decades to come.

When years later Secretary Hillary Rodham Clinton won the Democratic nomination for president of the United States, so many thoughts ran through my mind. At long last a woman had become the Democratic Party's nominee for president of the United States. And on day four of the 2016 Democratic National Convention, I could imagine what was going through the minds of all the little girls watching that night when Secretary Clinton accepted the nomination: Dreaming. Being inspired to dare. Never ever again believing that they were forever *meant* to be second.

In an interview the next day, Secretary Clinton shared that when she heard she was the Democratic candidate, one of her first thoughts went back to watching Dean Martin's Ding-A-Ling Sisters singing "I Am Woman" back in the early 1970s . . . and it inspired her, touching her soul. Well, I could not stop smiling and crying all at the same moment. That was me. When I became the first Black woman to become a Ding-A-Ling Sister on *The Dean Martin Show*, I had been asked to perform Helen Reddy's hit "I Am Woman" as my featured solo. It became a signature song for me because of the strength in the lyrics. Apparently, that hit home for Hillary as well.

With this one simple sentence from the United States presidential nominee, I became a small but significant part of the first woman's nomination to the highest office in America.

# CHAPTER TEN

# JAYNE, LEON, AND HOPE STREET

O*nce again, you're listening to Leon the Lover. And I have a letter from Latisha, who has a pretty interesting situation. Stay tuned. . . . But first let's hear "The Love You Save" by the Jackson Five.*

With high school now firmly in my rearview mirror, I spent my spare time listening to all my favorite radio shows, writing poetry, and getting ready to set the world on fire. In my mind, there were no boundaries that I couldn't cross, no hurdles that I couldn't jump . . . *if I believed.*

The summer of 1970 found me focused on my career, fulfilling my minimal obligations as Miss Ohio, making appearances for Mayor Stokes and the Cleveland Browns as a motivational speaker for local youth groups. I "graduated" from the May Company Teen Fashion Board to a professional modeling career with Pat Perry Modeling Agency. I was quickly signed as a spokeswoman for the Cleveland-based Bonne Bell cosmetics, appeared in a few local television commercials, and modeled frequently at local conventions, car shows, and ski shows. My career in entertainment had begun in earnest, with my eye still on the idea that this would pay my way to enrollment at Columbia.

One of those radio shows I listened to was WJMO's *Leon's Lover's Lane*. Leon had just returned to Cleveland after stints in Houston, Detroit, and Washington, DC. One day he happened to see me in a local TV commercial and asked his younger brother, John:

"*Who is she?*"

"Oh, that's that new Miss Ohio chick."

"Do you know her?"

"Nah, but I know someone who does. I'll get the digits."

His mom had been plotting all the while and had clipped a picture of me from the newspaper, showing it to her son and saying, "This is the kind of girl you should be with." So, John had his marching orders, and he actually came through. He got my number from one of his friends who was my coworker at the May Company, and then passed it on to Leon.

Leon grew up in a suburb of Cleveland known as the "elite" Shaker Heights. And to be clear for those who thought Leon took *my* name (a very common misperception), Kennedy is indeed Leon's surname. Not only was Kennedy Leon's last name, but he was born Leon Robert Kennedy III. His birth father, Leon Robert Kennedy Jr., in his efforts to make money while putting himself through medical school had become a professional boxer. He fought out of the famous Joe Louis camp, sometimes even training with and sparring with Joe when he needed a middleweight who challenged an opponent with more speed than a heavyweight.

When Leon was born and his mother was still in the hospital, a tragedy occurred that changed the trajectory of their lives instantly. His father had been training in Central Park for an upcoming bout when she got a call that her handsome, athletic husband had dropped dead while jogging. . . . He was twenty-seven.

Leon was only three days old.

Three years later, his mother remarried. John Isaac, who legally adopted Leon, raised him, and was the only father Leon ever knew. So, he always used the name Leon Isaac. He made a promise to his grandmother Cara Kennedy that whenever he did marry, he would use the surname Kennedy, continuing the Kennedy family legacy. But it got complicated. He had made the promise, but he also couldn't hurt John Isaac. He was an Isaac as much as he was a Kennedy. The solution was that he would legally change his name to Leon Isaac Kennedy.

The Kennedy family was a highly educated African American family out of Knoxville, Tennessee, and Leon was greatly influenced by his grandmother Cara Kennedy and the Kennedy family's lifelong love for education, theatre and the arts, boxing, and all aspects of their African lineage, which continued to be nurtured in Leon throughout his life.

Leon's father's brother, Dr. James Scott Kennedy, was a professor emeritus of theatre arts at Fordham University as well as the International University in Nairobi and London. His uncle Dr. Joseph C. Kennedy cofounded Africare, the largest and oldest African American–founded international NGO with an exclusive focus on the continent of Africa. One aunt, Janie Sykes-Kennedy, was an actress traveling the world with her husband and teaching theatre in the US, Australia, and Africa. Another aunt, Dr. Lillian Kennedy Beam, was named Kenya's first woman vice chancellor to the president of Kenya. In 1993, her work was so celebrated that a library was opened and dedicated as the Dr. Lillian Kennedy Beam Library.

And as recently as 2023, the play *Ohio State Murders* starring six-time Tony Award winner Audra McDonald, written by another aunt, Adrienne Kennedy, opened on Broadway. For her performance, Ms. McDonald was nominated for a Tony Award for best actress. The ninety-one-year-old Adrienne Kennedy received the Gold Medal for Drama from the American Academy of Arts and Letters. This was a true honor, as some of the other recipients have been Eugene O'Neill, Maxwell Anderson, Arthur Miller, Lillian Hellman, Edward Albee, and Tennessee Williams. Aunt Adrienne was only the second woman and the only African American, thus far, to receive this prestigious award.

I never really got to fully know the Isaac side of his family.

Leon's mother, June Kennedy Isaac Dawson, who was married three times, was a career woman—a social worker and teacher—and was always described as avant-garde when it came to trends and fashions.

Perhaps because his father (Leon Kennedy Jr.) and his grandfather (Leon Kennedy Sr.) had both died at the age of twenty-seven from a heart attack, Leon's sense of urgency and self-empowerment from day one was steeped in his DNA. His driven heart lay in the field of entertainment, and all things show business.

At the young age of fifteen, Leon became a local radio disc jockey. It was then that he met Smokey Robinson at a concert, and immediately they bonded as *soul brothers* . . . truly. Claudette Robinson, Smokey's wife and my best friend, vividly remembers the day they met:

"The Miracles were performing in Cleveland and at the end of the first show, this kid with a backstage pass shows up at the dressing room door begging the security to allow him to meet Smokey. I thought, 'Wow, he's too young to be at this nightclub,' but even though the guard turned him away, Leon showed up again the next night . . . and the next night . . . and the next. Finally, after our last show, there he was once again, waving his arms trying to get Smokey's attention. This time, Smokey said, 'Hey, man, just let the kid in. He's got guts coming back here every show.'"

Claudette remembers laughing and thinking: We were all just kids too when we started The Miracles.

Smokey's and Leon's lives were interwoven into a gifted and complex relationship spanning the decades. When Leon moved to Detroit, he became friends with most of the others in the Motown family as well, including Claudette, Marvin Gaye, Berry Gordy, the Supremes, Martha Reeves and the Vandellas, the Temptations, the Four Tops, and Stevie Wonder, just to name a few.

Leon's radio show, *Lover's Lane*, had quickly become a huge hit. Introducing letters sent in by listeners pleading for advice on their love lives, he would respond in prose or poetry in a soothing melodic tone, accompanied by the perfect song to capture the sentiment or mood of the listener's letter.

During the segment, Leon would take on-air callers, and everyone would talk about their related love problems as well, which of course were never-ending. Leon received *thousands* of letters per week. Leon was young, attractive, and a local celebrity, and many young women were vying to be a part of Leon's *real-life* lover's lane.

But behind the on-air flash, Leon was always an astute businessman. Eventually, he successfully syndicated his radio show in Cleveland, Detroit, Houston, and Washington, DC. During his time in DC, he enrolled at Howard University, he was a daily on-air radio personality, and he also was the host of the hit TV show *Teenarama* (the early prototype for *Soul Train*), which aired daily at five p.m., catching the youth audience as they came home from school.

In 1969, while in Houston, with his eyes already channeled on a career in television, he began to develop a TV show with his former Cleveland radio DJ "partner in crime," Mike Payne. The show, *Outta Sight with Leon and Mike*, written and produced by Leon, was sold to a local Houston TV affiliate. Debbie Allen, who was then an up-and-coming local talent in Houston, was recruited as a dancer and to choreograph the show.

The team continued to work on *Outta Sight*, selling it to the local DC affiliate. Although *Outta Sight* became a hit with the collegiate market there, Leon yearned to return to Cleveland. *Outta Sight* was now a bona fide syndicated TV show, albeit at that time only in two markets—it eventually aired in twenty-two markets. Keep in mind, this was *before* Don Cornelius syndicated *Soul Train* in December of 1970. Thus, *Outta Sight* was the nation's first Black syndicated TV show, and Leon was only twenty-one years old.

Once back in Cleveland, he began investing his time in securing a home for *Outta Sight* at WUAB-TV in Lorain, Ohio, just southwest of Cleveland. The station was new, having its first airdate September 15, 1968. Even at a young age, Leon understood the business of production. His self-confidence was always evident in negotiating with the studio owners and executives, which was no easy task. When he initially pitched *Outta Sight* to WUAB-TV, twice, the owner said, "No. I don't like it at all."

Leon responded, "You don't have to like it. This show's target audience is fourteen to twenty-nine."

Then the owner retorted, "Well . . . we don't have a budget to produce this show."

"I will get the funds to produce it. All *you* have to do is air it," Leon insisted. "I'll be back."

Leon knew that with a fledgling company, they only needed to be prodded, and if it didn't cost them anything, they would be happy to air a product that would generate advertising dollars. Even when a large portion of those dollars would go into the production, it was a great opportunity for two-year-old WUAB-TV Channel 43. And *Outta Sight* would have a home.

He went to several local businesses selling commercial airtime and shooting station promos himself in the streets. So not only was the show self-financed, but it also had on-air promos for the station to run as well, at the time a very novel and innovative business strategy (and one that television mogul Byron Allen employed to start his own media empire several decades later). And *Outta Sight* made it on the air. The only problem now was the time slot. The show was airing on Saturday mornings at eleven a.m., not ideally conducive to reaching the show's target demographics and certainly not the upper end of the age group. But the audience found it nonetheless, and the ratings quickly continued to grow, making it a success. And the owner now loved it. So much so that he slated it to run *twice* on Saturday, both at eleven a.m. and eight p.m.

That's when Leon decided it was time to bring in the reigning Miss Ohio to join the *Outta Sight* family.

I still remember that first phone call from Leon.

"Hello, this is Leon Isaac from WJMO radio" . . . using his best practiced disc jockey broadcast voice.

I was so excited. I had been among the throngs of fans of his radio show, and I would tune in every day. Dad was standing there right next to me, listening to every word as we shared the phone.

"I'm producing a TV show that I'd like to talk to you about."

"Wow, I'd love to talk about—"

That's when Dad snatched the phone. But I pressed my ear to the handset as they continued the conversation.

"Mr. Harrison," said Leon, "I'm sure you are most interested in protecting your daughter, but this is a legitimate TV show that will be aired weekly from the WUAB studios on the west side. I have secured sponsors, and we have a contract for the run of the show. I've been producing this show in two other cities, so there's no need to worry about Jayne. I will also remain on the air as a DJ here at WJMO."

"What are you expecting from Jayne?"

"She will be part of the skits and will only be required to show up at the studio when we shoot. That's it. You have my word."

After several other questions, I was actually surprised Dad said yes. He was always so extremely protective of us. He didn't trust anyone with his five daughters. He knew firsthand how treacherous men could be. The painful memory that one of "those men" had killed his mother still haunted him. As a father he was the guardian to ensure none of the devastating incidents he experienced as a teenager himself protecting his younger sisters ever happened to his daughters.

"Thank you so much, Dad," I said. "I promise I'll be extra careful, and you won't have to worry about me."

I could see a tear forming in his eyes, and I hugged him so he wouldn't think that I saw him cry.

Within a month I was a regular on WUAB-TV Channel 43's *Outta Sight with Leon and Mike*, billed as "with special guest appearances by Debbie Allen and the *new* Miss Ohio 1970, Jayne Harrison." It was the next logical step for my career, which had suddenly shifted from politics to an interest in entertainment.

Within three weeks, I had an almost-new career—and an almost boyfriend. It all happened so fast. Leon had this powerful spirit. I knew he was going places. But the true wonder is that he looked at *me* and saw the same thing.

"I can tell," Leon said in one of our early intense conversations, "you are not staying in Ohio."

"You're right," I said. "I've been dreaming of where I would end up nearly all my life."

We both laughed and then shared our dreams: film, television, being entrepreneurs. He had well-thought-out plans that went far beyond *Outta Sight*. And within that framework I saw how my career would spin off into its own direction. We truly worked well together.

When I met Leon, it expanded my horizon as to the possibilities that could lie ahead. Possibilities I had only dreamed of before. Of course, another three weeks later, after we began to date, I was infatuated not only with the beginning of a romance but with our conversations, his vision for the show, and his vision as to how he saw my potential—and how these visions coincided with my own dreams.

Within a few weeks, I wasn't just talent; Leon was asking *my* thoughts on production (which I knew well from five years codirecting and working behind the scenes in drama club). He wanted to know how to improve ALL aspects. What visions I had that could be incorporated within the show. He respected my ideas and began to include me more and more. I was no longer just Miss Ohio. I've always been a physically and visually creative person. Artistry is in my blood. This I was truly enjoying.

Time was now racing full speed ahead. Everything was happening so quickly. Even though Leon knew when he called Smokey after our very first date and said, "I met her. She's the one," I had no idea. I had no reference point. But I did know that this was special. For me, life was now viewed through grown-up eyes.

I loved the feeling of new discoveries. My dreams of flying off to exotic places on a white stallion were somehow coming true. I had always wanted to soar, and he made me feel that the heavens had opened, and I had no tethers at all . . . once I got past Dad.

When I met Leon, I had never had a romantic relationship with anyone. I had mad crushes, but never a relationship. For an eighteen-year-old small-town girl in 1970s Ohio, this new thing called love was very potent.

I fell head over heels in love with the first man I was seriously interested in, who was also seriously interested in me. Leon was exciting and so different from anyone I had known. I think that was a major part of falling in love with him. Being with him was a fulfillment of so many of the things I had always dreamed about—dating and romance, music, showbiz, and travel. I'm not saying that I married him to get all of those things, but I am saying that he *was* all of those things, and that was part of what I loved about him.

I first spoke with Leon in July. Mind you, I had just graduated high school in June. By August, I was on the show. By September, we were dating. It was on our first date that he met Dad. We were sitting in the living room and Dad was just coming home from a long day of hunting. Leon was sitting in the chair next to the kitchen, so when he turned to see Dad coming into the living room, he saw Dad's shadow first: the shadow of a six-foot-three, three-hundred-pound man in hunting gear with a rifle in his hand. And as Dad closed into the living room, the shadow on the living room wall grew even larger. When he stepped up to Leon, towering over him by five inches, he said a hello and then immediately: "Jayne has to be home by midnight."

"I'll have her home by eleven thirty, sir."

And he did.

If I lived in my dad's house, his rules were to be followed with no questions asked. Whenever Leon asked for a date, I had to ask Dad first. Whenever I was on a date, I had to be home on time. I was still working at the May Company on weekends at this point, so sometimes Leon drove the twenty-five miles to the Great Lakes Mall to join me for lunch. Sometimes we'd sit on the shores of Lake Erie. We talked about his family, and I talked about mine. We shared our dreams. We shared our disappointments. Sometimes he even invited me to a concert.

I had never been to a Motown Revue or a concert at the Cleveland Civic Center. But Leon, as a disc jockey, would often DJ the shows. He knew so many of the artists I admired, and it was fun to hear about their crazy back-stories. It was warming to hear how close he was with Claudette and Smokey Robinson. I got to see the Jackson Five, Sly and the Family Stone, and The Miracles . . . *twice.* The second time was when my family visited our cousins in Philadelphia and The Miracles were playing at the Uptown Theater; Leon got tickets for me, my sisters, AND our cousins.

When Leon asked me to marry him after only three months of dating, he proposed with a ring inside a giant red Russian nesting box, the box that has endless boxes one inside of the next until finally there was that tiny little ring box. It was Christmas Eve.

I had three words: "I'd be honored."

Years later, he told me that when I said *that* it was so much better than saying yes. It was a validation as to who he was and who he always aspired to be.

I often think, Jayne, you were so young. You didn't even know yourself yet. But in retrospect, in 1970, it was quite common to get married right out of high school or right out of college. Many of my friends did and are still married to this day, having married their high school sweethearts. So, this was not unusual at all. Mom and Dad had married and had two children by the time they were twenty-one. I had not seen that as my path. I had no interest in getting married at all for some time. But I fell head over heels in love and that changed my trajectory. For this new adventure, I was willing to leave my family behind. I gave up my dream of politics and embraced the idea of Hollywood and all it had to offer. I often wonder if it hadn't been so difficult to "just" date, perhaps I wouldn't have gotten married so early. But what did I know? I had zero dating experience. It felt like the right thing to do.

After announcing our engagement to Mom and Dad, I thought that they would be a bit more lenient with me dating. But that was not happening. There was a huge show coming to Cleveland and Leon was the DJ/host. After I had Dad's permission, Mom and I went shopping for the perfect attire. I spent the day washing my hair, putting it in beer can rollers, sitting under the hair dryer for hours, and stylizing my makeup and wardrobe. When Leon rang the doorbell, I passed Dad in the living room. He immediately asked, "Where are you going?"

"That's Leon, and we're going to the concert."

"No, you're not."

I stopped in my tracks. "But I asked you two weeks ago, and Mom even went with me to buy my outfit."

"I said you're not going. And don't let him in the house either. Don't open that door."

"But he already drove all this way."

"Tell him you're not going."

"How am I supposed to tell him I can't go if I can't open the door?"

"Tell him through the screen door."

I was so embarrassed. I was angry. I was confused. My Dad was definitely having second thoughts about my engagement. But I was determined, even if he kept me home until my wedding day. So, there we stood, at the kitchen door with our palms pressed against the screen, and of course I was crying.

Soon after the concert, Leon's mother threw a wedding shower for me at her home in Shaker Heights. I was very excited to attend until Dad shut it down, again.

"It's not proper for a single girl to be seen at a boyfriend's home before the wedding."

"But Dad, we're engaged. It's a *shower* for my *wedding*."

Dad didn't budge. He had five daughters, and he didn't play.

It was obvious Dad did not want me to leave. I honestly believe his second thoughts were a result of flashbacks to what he had faced raising his younger sisters. How he had to fight everyone and everything to raise them to be good people with a valuable life. His commitment to perhaps honor the dreams his mother would have had for her daughters suddenly became overwhelming when he thought of the lifestyle of a DJ—the concerts, the drugs, that environment, the type of men I'd run into—and he just got scared.

But I had to focus on my wedding gown and all that comes with wedding planning.

I was determined to use the sewing skills Mom had taught us from an early age beginning with Barbie clothes. She could sew anything. Her entire basement could double for a clothing store. It was not uncommon to visit our house to see three sewing machines going all at once. With five girls and an average income, we made a lot of our own clothing. I remember Mom always asking Dad for money to go to all the fabric sales. We'd come home with bolts of florals, prints, solids, plaids, denims, corduroys, woolens, cottons, knits. You name it, we'd sew it.

We had dresser drawers full of patterns. Literally boxes full of buttons and zippers; racks full of threads, polyester, silks, and cottons. We had so many clothes that everybody thought we were rich. Every summer we'd make skirts, dresses, and tops for the new school year. It wasn't until I got a job in eleventh grade that I started buying most of my clothes. But I never gave up sewing until I had my own children at thirty-four and ran out of time.

So, I designed and made my wedding gown, my veil, and all the bridesmaids' gowns as well. Mom and I sat up endless hours for nights on end sewing on seed pearls, crystals, and lace appliqués. Bless her heart. I made my entire wedding ensemble for ninety-seven dollars. I had it initially appraised at nine hundred dollars. Many years later it appraised at two thousand five hundred dollars. Pretty good for a small-town job.


"I've got an idea," Leon said, a few weeks before the wedding.

"Sure."

"We should have a parade."

"A *what*?" I said.

"A parade to celebrate the joining of Miss Ohio and Cleveland's number one DJ and TV host."

"Leon, are you serious?"

"Absolutely, we can get sponsors and the radio station to fund it."

"You're serious!"

"I already spoke to—"

"Leon, this wedding will be canceled before we do that. Weddings are sacred, not an event to be exploited."

"It's not being exploited. We're *sharing* our love."

"Leon, at some point we're going to Los Angeles, to Hollywood. But I need you to know now. I have to draw a line. There's a limit to just how Hollywood I'm willing to be."

Leon regretfully nodded. "I understand."


We began dating in September.

Within three months we were engaged.

Within nine months, on June 26, 1971, Leon and I were married.

Leon was twenty-three. I was nineteen.

We had a big wedding at Covenant Baptist Church, my family church in Wickliffe. Leon had asked Smokey Robinson to be his best man, Pete Moore from The Miracles was to be a groomsman, and Claudette Robinson, also of the original Miracles and dubbed "The First Lady of Motown" by Berry Gordy, would be in attendance as well. When the word got out that The Miracles were going to be there, the wedding got even bigger.

Then my sister Brenda, who was only eleven at the time, decided on her own to concoct a story and tell everyone that Michael Jackson was singing the wedding song. I was ready to pull my hair out . . . or hers.

Mind you, you can drive through the entire city of Wickliffe in five minutes. I know I said we had a big wedding, but that was relative. Our church was small, with the entire west wall made of glass. There were dozens of people standing outside the windows peeking in to get a glimpse of Michael Jackson and Smokey Robinson. At least they saw Smokey, and half of The Miracles in the wedding party, along with newlyweds "Leon the Lover" and "Miss Ohio."

Harrisons and Thompsons came from all along the East Coast. And the gifts were amazing, everyone was so generous. The presents had been pouring in for weeks—our entire basement was full of boxes, large and small. Dad's uncle Pete had driven his brand-new Cadillac from DC to Cleveland just so we could drive away in style.

I don't remember much of the reception, but I do recall that I stood in the receiving line for nearly two hours. We had made all these elaborate plans for a prestigious country-club reception, thinking nothing could possibly go wrong with all their experience in events such as this. As it turned out, the caterers set the food out well in advance of our guests' arrival, and by the time they did arrive, half of the food and drink was gone; the country-club guests had unbelievably helped themselves to our spread. My family members scurried frantically to get additional food and drinks.

Everyone wanted pictures, and I never did get the candid pictures that *I* wanted. But I did get the most important one . . . the dance with my father. The emotion behind the tears he shed was the best part of the entire night.

It was when everyone was leaving that Smokey and Claudette realized they had left their airplane tickets at the hotel. They had planned to depart straight from the reception to the airport, so Leon and I had to take them back to their hotel and then to the airport. They missed their flight and there were no rooms available at the hotel, so we gave them our hotel's honeymoon suite and we ended up staying at Mom and Dad's on our wedding night.

Initially, we had planned to live in Cleveland after we married. We had found a beautiful high-rise apartment at the Americana Gardens right on the shores of Lake Erie. By then, the acting bug had dug its fangs into me and my dreams of attending Columbia University had flown out the high-rise window. Working on *Outta Sight* had rejuvenated my love for drama that began when I was in seventh grade. I loved the theatre. I loved exploring parts of me that I had never shown to anyone, but actors can create realities far above who they actually are and live those fantasies out on a stage, free to explore thoughts and circumstances way beyond their wildest dreams. I've always believed that as an actor, you must be willing to rip open your chest and lay your heart on the floor and invite the world to stomp all over it, then pick it up and gently tuck it back in. That was the power of the arts once you fell in love with it. A grip that would never go away.

Unfortunately, because Wickliffe High was predominantly white, there were never any roles for a Black girl in the plays we did (and it certainly didn't help that I was always taller than most of the boys in drama club). So over the years I became very familiar with every aspect of production, with my favorite role being that of the director. I shadowed my eighth-grade drama coach religiously as I learned from him the nuances of directing. By my senior year, under the tutelage of Mr. Patrick Penrod, I loved *all* things theatre. I was the only drama club member who had earned enough points to become a member of the International Thespian Society, ironically without *ever* uttering a word onstage as an actor.

Back at WUAB-TV, the phone calls had been pouring in from across the country: "We want to buy your show. What would it take to buy *Outta Sight*?"

One of those calls was from the one and only Dick Clark in Hollywood. Yes, *the* Dick Clark from *American Bandstand*. But Leon had built a great relationship with WUAB, who he respected, and he knew that selling the show to Dick Clark at that time would mean that he no longer had a product. And this was when the lightbulb in his head flashed. *Time to go to Hollywood.*

With the love of the stage in our blood, Leon and I changed our minds about the high-rise apartment and decided to strike out west before we got too settled in Cleveland. We realized that with both our families in Cleveland, we might never decide to take the big plunge and try our luck in Hollywood. So, we gave up the lease on the apartment, packed up our bags, and within two weeks, we were headed to California. We thought it would be a great idea to take our time driving across the country and make it a part of our honeymoon as well.

"This is going to be amazing," I said. "A monthlong honeymoon that ends in Los Angeles."

"Right," said Leon. "And since we're on the road, I figured I'd approach a few television stations along the way. . . ."

"Hmm." After a deep breath, I reluctantly said, "Okay. Great idea."

"Right. And since we'll be selling the show, it's probably best for my partner, Mike, to come along."

"Wait, what? On our monthlong cross-country road-trip honeymoon? Bad idea."

"No, really. It makes sense. If we're selling the show they will want to see the two hosts," Leon said. "And Mike's wife can come along too."

Oh my God! I sighed an even deeper breath. I didn't even know her. His first step was the wrong step. Leon's partner, Mike, and his wife were traveling along with us? The four of us . . . in one car . . . driving across the country . . . for one month . . . on *my honeymoon*? What could go wrong?

I was dreading telling my mother about our plans to move to Los Angeles. I had put off saying anything, until the time came that I finally had to tell her. I'll never forget that moment. Mom and I were standing at the kitchen sink doing the dishes and she was singing as usual, and I blurted out our plans.

"Mom . . . we've decided that we're moving to Los Angeles. We're not going to take the apartment in Cleveland."

I couldn't look at her. I continued rinsing and drying while she washed. "Oh. And we'll be leaving next week."

She turned to me and said: "It's okay, Jayne. I know that you were meant to do something special . . . and it's not here. I knew that you were never going to be a secretary or anything like that. Ever since you were little, you always said you were going to be a movie star. You'll be just fine."

And that's when she gave me the most powerful advice I have ever received, to which I have clung many times over the years: "Just remember, you can never please everybody. The only ones you have to please are yourself and God."

She smiled as I added, "And you."

I had expected to run up against a brick wall—and I hadn't. Even Dad didn't object, which was *quite* surprising since he wouldn't even let me go to Leon's house to visit until *after* we were married. But it meant so much to me that I had both their blessings; otherwise I don't think I would have gone.

I had been staying at home since the wedding. The night before I left, the Harrison household was solemn and quiet. My little brother, Herbie, who was six years old at the time, was sitting on the steps that went from the kitchen to the side door. I sat next to him. After a while, he asked me to go with him for a walk. He tucked his tiny little hand into mine as we walked to the woods at the end of our dead-end street, both lost in our own thoughts.

I was remembering all the times I had walked to the end of this very street with my bike and then had taken off performing fantastical stunts, riding down the hill doing headstands on the seat, going as fast as I could; the days we spent learning to knit and crochet doilies from Mrs. Clark, who lived in the last house on the street right next to the woods; swimming in our friends Chris and Mary's backyard four houses down after a freak hailstorm and torrential rains had turned their concave yard into a literal pond; and making clothes that our neighbors across the street, Micheal, Danny, and Joey, had designed for all our dolls. Remembering how I would always take the heads off my dolls and switch the Black doll heads onto the white dolls and vice versa. I wanted multicultural dolls. So many memories. And no more time.

Finally, Herbie looked up at me and my heart ached. We didn't say anything for quite a while as we just stood there together. We finally were about to turn around and head back home when Herbie quietly said, "I want you to have this."

And with the greatest of care, he placed a penny in my hand, a brand-new, shiny copper penny. He gently closed my fingers around it and held my fist in his tiny hands, closing it tighter, and turned that precious little face up at me.

"I want you to always keep this so you will never go broke when you get to Hollywood."

Unable to hold back the tears any longer, he started to cry, and I scooped him up in my arms and held him tightly as he sobbed into my shoulder.

All I could think of at that moment was that I might never see my little brother again. What if something happened? And even if it didn't, how was I ever going to make it on my own, without my family? Even though Leon and I were now married, I had only known him for nine months. How was I going to leave everybody I loved and trusted? How was I going to be able to make a living? How was I going to find myself, and what was it I really wanted to do?

Would I ever go to college? Would I ever come back home? WAS I CRAZY? Everything had happened so quickly; I didn't really have time to think about any of this. Holding Herbie in my arms made me think of all the reasons *not* to go, the most important of which was that I would never watch my only brother grow up.

I couldn't stop thinking about the day he was born, especially Dad rushing Mom to the hospital, and then calling to tell us, "It's a boy." After five girls, he finally had his boy. I remembered Dad crying, and how he couldn't cook to save his soul, so while Mom was in the hospital Dad brought home tons of cold cuts, chocolate coconut bars, and all sorts of donuts. We thought it was great. We always wanted Mom to have lots of babies, because each time she was in the hospital, we got sandwiches and donuts. But I remember on the day Herbie was born how happy we *all* were that it was finally a boy.

For years I had wanted a brother so, so, so very badly. Now I had one, and I was leaving him. It all seemed impossible, but I knew I had to go. I set Herbie down and we finished our walk home in silence, then sat on the kitchen steps in stillness for an hour, just holding each other. All I could think about was that these were the very same steps that I had tripped on while holding him in my arms when he was barely a year old, and we both went flying through the glass in the door at the top of the landing. As I was lying in a pool of blood on the driveway with him still in my arms, Mom came screaming, "Give me my baby!" But it wasn't him that was bleeding. I had wrapped my arms around him so tight as we flew through the air that it was me who took on the glass and ended up in the hospital with sixty-five stitches, and I almost lost my hand. . . . So many memories.

The next morning at sunrise, Leon pulled up to the house, and everyone was helping me pack my bags, again in silence. Neither of us had furniture. Neither of us had much luggage. But we did have all those wedding gifts, which we decided to leave in Dad's garage until we found an apartment in LA. Mom had packed snacks for the journey. We must have hugged a million times. My sisters, my brother, and Mom and Dad waved goodbye as we backed out of the driveway.

And I left.

We had one more stop before we hit the freeway, picking up Mike and his wife. Sharing our honeymoon trip was not my idea of fun. I didn't know Mike well; heck, I didn't know Leon that well . . . and I certainly didn't know Mike's wife at all, and when I *did* get to know her, I didn't like her. The doubts continued to echo in my mind during the long drive west. . . . What had I done? Was this a tremendous mistake? This was not what a honeymoon was supposed to be. Why had I agreed to this idea? Yes, I'm an adventurer, but this was *crazy*.

There were frightening moments throughout the trip: getting caught in a tornado in Evanston (or was it Evansville?), Indiana. A scary midnight drive through a cemetery in Missouri during a thunderstorm with the most incredible lightning I'd ever seen. Then there was the time we were so tired, we pulled over to the roadside to sleep. We woke up the next morning in the heart of Texas, looking into the faces of a couple of very suspicious characters. That was the last time I *ever* slept in a car on the side of the road.

Looking back, I think we went through a ghost town in Texas one night. It was an old town, like the kind of Wild West town you see in the movies: one general store, one coffee shop. There was no noticeable color at all. Even though it was well into dusk, there should have been some color, but everything was gray, all different shades of gray. And everything seemed to be covered in layers of dust. It wasn't so late that you'd expect *everyone* to be in bed, yet this town had not a single person in sight. But it did have cats, lots of cats walking around like they owned the place, like they were the only residents, like this was *their* town. It was so creepy, almost as if the townspeople had turned into cats at sundown. It wasn't just my imagination; we all looked at each other as if to say, *Do you see what I'm seeing?* so we just kept on driving. This would definitely not be a place to spend the night.

It wasn't all scary. There were lighter moments as well. One day while we were driving through New Mexico, the guys had to relieve themselves. We were in the middle of nowhere, with no other cars on the road, just flat, reddish and pinkish dust, and brush as far as you could see. I had been driving, so I pulled over and waited in the car while the guys took their little hike.

Pretty soon I saw a cloud of dust in the distance that seemed to be moving in the direction of the car. I couldn't see anything else, just a cloud of red dust, and I could barely hear faint yelling that was getting louder and louder. Suddenly, I saw the figures of Leon and Mike out in front of the dust, and they were on a full-speed dead run to the car, shouting, "Open the door! Open the door!"

*Then* I heard a snorting sound, and realized a huge wild boar was chasing after them—it was right on their heels. They barely got to the car, diving in headfirst, when the boar caught up with them and stopped *just* short of the car. All I could think of was: This would be a great piece of tape to put on *Outta Sight*. I didn't drive away, I couldn't. I was laughing too hard. They could barely breathe, and they were covered in red dust, but I couldn't stop laughing. They didn't think it was funny, at least not for another hour or so. So, we checked into a motel and spent the night.

We finally arrived in Los Angeles the last week of July 1971. I was asleep in the backseat. Mike was driving, and he whispered, "Hey. Wake up, everybody. We're here." We pulled up on the off-ramp into downtown Los Angeles at about five a.m. I remember opening my eyes and looking at a beautiful waterfall cascading down a wall and over a sign right next to my window as we stopped at a red light. Then I saw the street sign: HOPE STREET. Was I dreaming? Hope Street? Really? For a young woman with a heart full of dreams, and a heart full of hope. From growing up literally and figuratively on a *dead-end street . . . to Hope Street*. A single tear started to form, and I just smiled. I did it. We did it. We were in LA.

We had planned to stay with Leon's aunt Rheba and uncle Henry in Pasadena, as they were the only family we had in California. They were the only people we knew in LA, period. Leon and Mike knew entertainers in the music business, but most of them lived in Detroit, DC, or Houston, not LA.

I was truly blessed to have Uncle Hank and Aunt Rhe there for me. Growing up in a very close and strict family and finding myself three thousand miles away from anyone and anything that was familiar, I was taken in by Leon's aunt and uncle as if I were their own daughter. Their real daughters,

Sherri and Linda, also welcomed me into their home as if I were their sister. Before arriving, I didn't know what they were going to be like, or what issues they might have, but God had his hand in this decision. I trusted him and he gave me a second family, just like the one I had left behind.

Uncle Hank worked in Century City managing a parking garage. Our first week in LA, he talked to one of the tenants of the building and they hired me as a receptionist for their law firm, Grobe, Rhinestein & Katz. I would start the following month (September) at seventy-five dollars a week. Step one accomplished . . . I had a job.

Hank and Rhe's house sat at the foot of the San Gabriel Mountains, right above the Rose Bowl. There was this huge mountain right out our back window, and I didn't even see it the entire first week we were there. Where did the mountains come from? Leon laughed at my innocence, saying, "Hollywood's a trip. They put mountains up overnight." In truth, there had been so much smog the week we arrived that I hadn't been able to see the city's skyline at all.

Leon and I only had one car, and Century City was a good hour's drive from our place in Pasadena, especially in rush hour traffic, so I went to work every morning with Uncle Hank. He had to be there at six a.m. to open the garage, but I didn't have to be at work until eight thirty. Every morning, Uncle Hank would wake me up ten minutes before he left. I'd roll out of bed only half-awake and fall into his backseat and sleep all the way there. When we got to the garage, Uncle Hank would let me sleep, then wake me again at eight a.m., and I'd go upstairs to the restrooms and dress for work. When I got off at five p.m., again I went to sleep in Uncle Hank's car and stayed there until he left at six p.m. unless Leon could pick me up, and we drove the hour's ride, getting home at seven p.m. for dinner.

Every night as I said grace, I thanked God that I didn't get sick from breathing in all that carbon monoxide from sleeping in the garage.

Our second week in Los Angeles, Mike had made plans for us to attend the 5th Dimension concert at the Hollywood Bowl. We were to meet them backstage, get the tickets, and then hang out with them after the show. The 5th Dimension was one of my favorite groups. When I was a senior, they had just topped the charts with "Aquarius/Let the Sunshine In," "One Less Bell to Answer," and "Wedding Bell Blues," the latter with the lyrics *Marry me, Bill* (now one of my favorite songs ever for obvious reasons), plus our teacher Mr. L. had us perform "Aquarius" at the spring concert. Now, only one year later, here I was going to see them perform live at the Hollywood Bowl . . . in Los Angeles.

I had seen the famous Hollywood sign off the Santa Monica freeway, but when we were driving north on the Hollywood Freeway and approached the Vine Street exit, I looked to the right where high above it all was a giant white cross up in the hills. It was plain, simple, and illuminated from within. I was thinking, Hollywood can't be so bad.

We went backstage before the show and Billy Davis Jr. was the first in the group I met, then I met Lamonte McLemore (who would eventually become the big brother that I had always wanted). He was always so warm and open, with the friendliest smile. They had a routine where each member of the group would go into the audience and bring someone up on the stage to dance with during the "Aquarius" encore to close the show. Lamonte looked at my ticket seat assignment and told me that he was going to come get *me* for the finale. I was so excited. . . . I was going to dance on the stage of the Hollywood Bowl.

I had been in my seat anxiously awaiting the start of the show for maybe fifteen minutes when I noticed this woman sitting in the box next to me who was drop-dead gorgeous. I thought I had never seen anyone so beautiful and perfect in all my life. If this was going to be my competition in show business, I was in trouble. She had a long skirt with a split up the side and a backless halter top. Her perfect skin was dark and glowing. Her hair was long, black, and shiny with just the right amount of wave. Just perfect. She was a diva indeed. Then the show started, and my attention turned back to the concert. I was in awe. Here I was, with one of my favorite music groups in an open-air concert in HOLLYWOOD. Somehow it all felt like it was part of my destiny; it all seemed to come so easily.

When the show was ending and the finale started, the lights began to dance, and Marilyn McCoo began singing "Aquarius/Let the Sunshine In."

I truly felt like I was in a "New Age." I would be twenty in less than three months, and I could not even begin to fathom what would lie ahead for me. Then the song was coming to the part where they ran into the audience, and I saw Lamonte running toward me. I stretched out my hand and was ready to go, but when he reached out, extending his hand to me . . . Miss Diva reached over me and grabbed his hand instead. *What?* Before I knew it, they ran back to the stage, singing and dancing, never stopping, and she gave him a big fat kiss as they finished the song and closed the show.

When I got backstage I learned she was *the* Sir Lady Java, quite a famous trans celebrity in Hollywood and a pioneer in her own right. But all I knew was that she was stunningly *beautiful*. And that was my welcome to Hollywood: Hope Street, the giant lighted cross in the sky above the Hollywood Freeway (that has long since been removed), the 5th Dimension, the smog, and *Sir Lady Java*. LA was now officially my home, and Wickliffe might as well have been on another planet.

A couple of weeks later, Lamonte called and gave me the name of the choreographer for the hit TV show *Rowan & Martin's Laugh-In*: Byron Gilliam, whom I was to meet at NBC Studios during his lunch break. Making it to Burbank from Century City, taking a meeting, and then getting back to work over a lunch hour was going to be pretty much impossible, but I went anyway. The cast was in rehearsal and pretaping a few segments when I arrived, so I sat in one of the empty audience seats waiting for Byron, waiting and watching as Dan Rowan, Dick Martin, and Sammy Davis Jr. rehearsed. I tried not to show how much I was freaking out at that very moment. Not even a year ago I was watching this show on my living room television and now I was on an NBC soundstage watching stars that I could actually reach out and touch. My heart was racing.

Caught up in my thoughts, I didn't notice a big, bearded guy walking over to me until he asked, "Can you dance?"

The thoughts that flashed through my mind were almost humorous: Not once in my entire life had I ever stepped inside the confines of a professional dance studio. Not once had my body ached from the endless hours of responding to the repetitive *and 5, 6, 7, 8* . . . , finding the beat, first in the music and then in your soul, or the stretching and stretching and stretching again, even in your sleep. Rubdowns in liniment, bandaged and bloodied feet that ached day and night, and tired aching thighs wrapped in plastic were never part of my world. Never. Yet I didn't skip a beat, and immediately replied, "Yes, I can."

What was I thinking? I wasn't thinking. However, "Yes, I can" was the correct answer. Besides, I hadn't lied. He hadn't asked if I had danced professionally; he had merely asked, "Can you dance?"

All my life, I had danced in front of a mirror in the basement. Getting on camera to shake my booty was surely not going to be a challenge when all I had to do was dance like Goldie Hawn, because I certainly had more booty to shake than she did.

"Yes, I can dance."

I had just learned the number one rule in show business: No matter what, if anyone asks if you can do something, the right answer is always "Yes, I can," and then you go home to figure it out.

But the guy then literally grabbed me out of the chair right on the spot. "GREAT. Go over there. When the music starts . . . dance. When the music stops . . . turn to that camera with the red light, look right into the lens, and just say this . . ."

He shoved a script in front of me, and there I was on the craziest psychedelic TV show in the world, *Laugh-In*, dancing my butt off, in my *business work clothes*.

The guy then came out of the director's booth. "That's great. Can you come back next week? We'll have more for you to do."

"Yes, I can."

"Oh, what's your name?"

"Jayne Harri—Jayne Kennedy. I'm Jayne Kennedy."

"Okay, Jayne Kennedy. You're hired for the season."

I couldn't believe it. Here was this big guy, with a big voice, a big smile, and a great big laugh, George Schlatter, the producer of the show. And that's how I got my very first job in Hollywood, dancing on *Rowan & Martin's Laugh-In* as a season regular.

George and I have remained friends for all these years. I never did meet Byron the choreographer that time. I quit my job at the law firm the next day and set out full-time on my quest to become an actress.

I was so looking forward to saying hello to Teresa Graves, since she had been one of the judges in my Miss USA pageant, but she had already left the show, to star in her own primetime show, *Get Christie Love!*

Goldie Hawn had left too, but Sammy Davis Jr. and Johnny Brown were still a part of the show, as were Dan Rowan and Dick Martin, of course. I had only been in Los Angeles for two months, and I already had a job on a huge network show. A job that not only was good for my career, but enabled Leon and me to move out of Uncle Hank and Aunt Rhe's and have our own place as husband and wife. We appreciated their support so much, but it was nice to have our own space. We quickly found an apartment in South Pasadena, and our new life began in our two-bedroom apartment with no furniture except for a bed for an entire year.

Then Leon got a call from the TV station in Cleveland, and he and Mike had to go back for a week. Mike asked if his wife could stay with me while they were gone and of course I agreed. She and I would drive into town together for work, then back home at the end of the day. So one day, I picked her up after work and as I entered the freeway interchange I quickly glanced over my left shoulder for oncoming traffic and she screamed, "YOU CAN'T TAKE YOUR EYES OFF THE ROAD! WHAT ARE MIRRORS FOR?" I tried to calm her down as I attempted to maneuver the busy freeway interchange, but she kept screaming. THEN SHE PULLED A BIG-ASS KNIFE out of her purse! Oh my God. My suspicions were true . . . she's crazy, I'm trying to drive in rush hour traffic in downtown LA, and she's threatening to stab me? Quickly I wiggled the wheel and said, "Oh no no no, we got a flat." And I pulled over to the side of the freeway and asked her to take a look. As soon as she was out of the car I took off.

I'm sorry to have left a woman on the side of the highway, but in my mind, this was life or death. I went to Uncle Hank's and I never went back to my apartment until Leon and Mike returned to LA. I was not raised around people like this. I was nineteen and had only left home two months ago. I was not ready for anything like this. What an eye-opener. Welcome to the real world, Jayne.

After I finished the season with *Laugh-In*, Leon and I started developing a plan as to what else we could do to meet people in LA. By now it seemed obvious to us that networking was the key to getting anywhere. Neither one of us had an agent, nor did we have any influential friends who knew the right people to meet and see. We had Leon's Motown connections, but Motown was still headquartered in Detroit. We decided we had to go to everything we could to be in the right place at the right time; the more places we went, the more people we would meet, and that would translate into more job opportunities. Since this was Hollywood, we thought that we might be noticed as an attractive couple, which could open more doors.

One morning I heard a radio DJ announce that they were looking for contestants for their Beautiful Hair Contest and that the winner not only would get a supply of product for a year but would have breakfast at the station. I sent in my photo and was shocked when I got the call that I had won. I went down to the high-rise at Sunset and Vine, took the elevator to the penthouse, and stepped into Simply Blues, the chic restaurant at the top. I'll never forget it; the panoramic view was the first time I had seen *all* of Hollywood. I was surprised: BIG, BAD HOLLYWOOD didn't look so big after all, and I thought, We can do this. We can really do this.

In October, I heard of another contest on KTLA Channel 5, an annual pageant to crown the "Queen of Hollywood," and I entered that too. Johnny Grant, the legendary honorary Mayor of Hollywood, was running the event. Johnny and KTLA were part of Gary Berwin's infamous Artists & Models Ball, which was a popular Halloween costume ball. Somehow, I was a winner again and was asked to attend the ball to receive my trophy.

Not having any kind of costume that would be appropriate for such an event, I went to Western Costume Company, a facility that rents costumes to the TV and film industry. It was truly amazing. I had never seen such a collection. So many costumes from so many huge movies. I think I saw Olivia de Havilland's wardrobe from the 1939 classic *Gone with the Wind*, Elizabeth Taylor's wardrobe from the 1963 *Cleopatra*, Errol Flynn's wardrobe from the 1938 *The Adventures of Robin Hood*, and so many more. I picked a beautiful red-and-gold velvet English gown that was from the movie *Camelot*. It had a matching headpiece, and a matching gentleman's costume for Leon.

The night of the ball I donned my corset, draped my gown, caught up my tresses, and tied on my hat. I found these cute velvet slippers, and when I put them on, I felt like Cinderella at the ball. The floor-length gown had long sleeves that billowed to the elbow. The only part of me that wasn't covered was my chest; my breasts were pressed so tight they popped up at the top, a look I never did like. All we needed was a horse and golden carriage, but since there was not one to be seen, we took off in our gold Pontiac LeMans instead.

We drove into Hollywood, parked, and entered the ball. OH MY GOD. What was this? I couldn't believe my eyes. There were *thousands* of people there, and I think Leon and I were the only two who were fully clothed. Everyone else was in loincloths, G-strings, and feathers, with jewels, baubles, beads, and glitter covering whatever the G-strings missed.

Then there was a contest for best costume. I swear I had never seen anything like it in all my life. This had to be an early version of what is now known as the West Hollywood Pride Festival.

We were so totally and completely overdressed. I just couldn't keep my jaw from dropping. Each costume was even more incredible than the next. So this was Hollywood . . . larger than life. I felt so small, and I thought, There's no way I can do this. It was obvious I didn't know the rules. I didn't know the protocols, and I stood out as the Midwestern girl from Ohio that I was.

It seemed like the more people we met in Hollywood, the more people there were to meet, and everyone was so beautiful. Johnny Grant quickly became my good friend, which was the best thing that came from the Queen of Hollywood Contest. I guess he felt badly for me that I was in total shock at the Artists & Models Ball, so in November he invited me to ride in the Hollywood Christmas Parade, which was second only to Macy's, and KTLA always went all-out with the pre-parade reception before everyone lined up to get in their assigned cars for the parade down Sunset Boulevard, on to Hollywood Boulevard, and then south back to the KTLA studios.

When they called my name, I found I was following the legendary actor Cesar Romero. I kept thinking how I wished Mom were with me, she *loved* Cesar Romero and his beautiful, shiny, silver-gray hair, and there I was, in the car right behind his. *Yes, I can do this. . . . I can make it in Hollywood.*

The second key to keeping the momentum going in Hollywood was to continue going out on auditions. Ultimately, it was a numbers game, and the more you went out, the more chances you had of booking a gig. I let everyone I knew in LA know that I would sincerely appreciate any help they could offer.

Johnny Grant and Lamonte both told me about the auditions for the Hollywood Deb Stars, a group of girls who were to travel on the 1971 Bob Hope USO Christmas show, "Bases Around the World." I made it to the audition in Burbank, but I was turned down. I had already been in LA long enough to know that it could have been for any one of a hundred reasons: I was too tall, not tall enough, too light, too dark, breasts were too large, breasts were too small, hair was too curly, hair was too straight. Who knew? You quickly learned not to take it personally; you just let it go and moved on to the next audition.

Smokey was considering moving to Los Angeles around this time and had been commuting back and forth from Detroit to LA quite often. He had lived on the road almost his entire life, and he truly appreciated any opportunity for some home cooking. Over the years I had learned how to cook from watching Mom, but it was Uncle Hank and Lamonte McLemore who taught me to *cook*. Whenever Smokey arrived in LA, he'd call, I'd pick him up, and I'd make a great home-cooked dinner just for him. Although our furniture was still back in Cleveland in storage, we did have pots and pans.

One night in early December, Smokey was booked on *The Bob Hope Christmas Special*, which was rehearsing at the NBC Studios in Burbank. When we arrived at the studio, I sat in the audience seats during the rehearsal while Leon was in Smokey's dressing room.

Next thing I knew, Bob Hope came over to me and asked, "You're from Ohio, right?"

"Yes, I am. From Wickliffe." A little puzzled, I thought . . . how did he know?

"Would you like to go on my USO tour?"

"Really? I just auditioned last week, and I was turned down."

As soon as the words were out of my mouth, I could have kicked myself for being so stupid. Why had I told him of my previous failure to make the cut? Bob smiled and leaned in close. "Let me say it a different way. . . . *I'd like for you to go on my Christmas tour. Can you?*"

Oh my God, I must have looked like an idiot. But then I said those three little magic words, "Yes, I can."

Bob then took me over to his manager. "Put her on the tour as one of the Hollywood Deb Stars." Then he turned back to me. "Young lady, we leave in two weeks."

I was in shock!

I found out later that when Bob walked onto the set, Leon yelled out to him, "Hey, Packy East." And Bob immediately turned around.

Back in 1919, when Bob Hope lived in Cleveland as then Leslie Townes Hope, he had started boxing at the age of sixteen under the name Packy East, using the name of his hero, Packey McFarland, and his high school, East High.

Bob was a boxer at Cleveland's Moose Hall and ended his career with a record of 4–1. Leon knew this because he loved all things Hollywood, and knew everything about the Hollywood legends, especially the ones who came from Cleveland. So, when Bob heard Packy East, that was it; he was captivated that anyone still knew that.

"So, you know Packy East?" Bob said to Leon.

"That's right," Leon said, shaking his hand. "I just moved to LA four months ago. See the girl over there in the audience seats? That's my wife, the former Miss Ohio. We just arrived from your hometown, Cleveland."

Bob looked at me, decided to walk over, and suddenly I was on the Bob Hope USO tour—just like that. I know this all sounds like the far-fetched stories you hear about young girls coming to Hollywood, hoping to make it big in the bright lights, and suddenly being "discovered," but it really did happen just like that for me.

Rehearsals started the next day, and before I knew it, I was packing my bag for a two-week trip around the world with Bob Hope. I was leaving the week before Christmas, my first Christmas with my new husband. We hadn't even been married six months, and I was leaving. We were both torn. I was wondering if I was doing the right thing, literally feeling like my heart was breaking, and feeling scared at the same time. I had just turned twenty in October. All this was so overwhelming. The night before I left, I almost called the production office and quit.

Instead, Leon and I hugged and cried. We knew Christmas could wait. We came up with this silly little plan where we promised each other that no matter where we were in the world we would call each other at midnight at the end of each month and say "Rabbit, Rabbit, Rabbit." Yeah, it was silly, but it kept us bonded. And sometimes that's all the time we had, just a few seconds to say "Rabbit, Rabbit, Rabbit."

The next morning, I left out of Van Nuys Airport on a C-141 military cargo plane. I was on my way to Vietnam. I know it is no way near the same, but I had prayed every night for years that my brother would never be drafted and ironically, I was the one who got that notice.

## CHAPTER ELEVEN

# TOUR OF DUTY

I was on my way to the other side of the world, and there was that word again—*hope*. Things had happened so fast and so easily. I often had the feeling that so much of my life was predestined, and I was right on track. I didn't have to think about it—I just had to be willing to go along with the flow, to follow the stars, and I did.

There were no commercial seats on the C-141, only parachute jump seats lining both walls of the huge, cold, and empty interior—empty except for us, and of course thousands of pounds of cue cards (the large cards placed next to a camera with the written dialogue for the talent to read). I've never seen so many cue cards in all the years of being in this business. They were stacked to the very ceiling of the plane. (Today, it is so much easier with the advent of digital technology.) I kept thinking, We're traveling all the way around the world in this? But I didn't realize how quickly I would get used to this new mode of travel with none of the usual conveniences.

Our first stop on the Bob Hope USO Christmas show, "Bases Around the World," was Hawaii, for a formal reception and send-off. There were twelve girls that made up the song-and-dance group called Bob's Hollywood Deb Stars. Bob referred to us as "twelve of the most beautiful and talented dancers in Hollywood." Most had been nominated by Hollywood makeup artists and hairstylists, and then had been selected for their dance abilities. It was the 1970s, so of course our costumes included short shorts and white go-go boots. We were booked along with a group called Sunday's Child, actor Jim "Gomer Pyle" Nabors, country western singer Charley Pride, astronaut Neil Armstrong, Hawaiian superstar Don Ho, baseball legend Hank Aaron, and a host of others.

After performances at Camp Eagle in Waikiki, Hawaii, we went on to Wake Island, to Guam, and then to Okinawa, Japan, before going on to Da Nang and Long Binh, Vietnam. Vietnam in 1971 was not exactly where I had ever imagined I would be. Like many of my generation, I felt Vietnam was an unjust war—that war was never about bettering the lives of people like you and me. War has been, and always will be, about power and wealth.

I could never imagine what it was like for our troops, many of them younger than me. I would never want to ever experience the horrors they lived through. To this day, I can never understand man's inhumanity to man. If the brief time I spent there would make it easier for just one of my fellow countrymen, then I was determined to do my best.

We were told that North Vietnamese had threatened to destroy the USO troupe if we came for the holidays, so schedules were highly susceptible to last-minute changes. In previous years, the troupe had stayed on the bases in Vietnam; however, because of the threats we had to stay in Bangkok, Thailand, and fly to the different Vietnamese bases via helicopters. For most of the shows we had makeshift dressing rooms allowing for costume changes. This also gave us an opportunity to speak with the soldiers before leaving and returning to Bangkok.

In Bangkok, I was struck by two things: One, the large number of golden Buddhas in all parts of the city and countryside. And two, the intense poverty in the inner regions of the city. I will never forget how polluted the river was, with babies and animals bathing in the same waters that were used for food and washing clothes. While we didn't spend much time there, the city made an indelible impression on me as I began to understand the world through a different set of eyes. It made me rethink everything I thought I knew about being an American. It made me eager to learn more. This was far greater of an education than I ever thought possible when I dreamed of traveling as a child. I was determined to see and discover all I could.

Our next two shows were in Thailand, at U-Tapao and U-Ban. Then we arrived at "Freedom Hill" in Da Nang. The stage was in the middle of a huge bowl-shaped field. The hilltop perimeter surrounding the bowl was lined with army tanks and armed guards at the ready. Because of the threat against Da Nang specifically, the troops were sitting there in the tanks waiting to defend us at the first sight of any issues, large or small. There had been a typical Vietnamese rainstorm before our arrival. It had been raining buckets nonstop for forty-eight hours. Due to the poor visibility, we were delayed, again, but the soldiers had been sitting there, waiting for us for six hours, in mud up to their waists.

We were not allowed to land at Da Nang. Instead, three helicopters filled with the performers hovered above the stage. When the time came for an act to go on, a chopper would set down, let the talent off, then return to its hover position. After the act was done, the next helicopter would land, load the talent, and lift off. Next. And this rotating procedure continued until the show was over. Looking back, it reminds me of the same scenario from the Francis Ford Coppola film *Apocalypse Now*.

When the Hollywood Deb Stars came onstage, it hurt me so much to see our boys so desperate to go home. They would call out their hometown, and if you came from anywhere near them, they would throw you their hats so that some part of them would make it back Stateside. I wanted to cry but knew I couldn't.

We did our numbers and went back up to the helicopter to hover until the finale, when the entire troupe came onstage to sing "White Christmas." Normally for the finale, we would change into long, white chiffon gowns with big green ribbons at the empire waist, but that day at Da Nang there was no time for a costume change. There was only time to live in that moment, as performers and soldiers alike all cried together singing the Bing Crosby classic, dreaming of home.

Our next stop was to be onboard the USS *Coral Sea* in the Gulf of Tonkin, but due to the heavy rain and poor visibility we couldn't land on the carrier. Four thousand troops sat eagerly waiting for us, and we had to cancel. It was so disappointing, but it gave us a chance to do an impromptu pickup show at Camp Eagle in the ancient city in Vientiane, Laos.

Next it was on to Long Binh for our biggest show yet, on Christmas Day, when all the surrounding bases joined together, taking advantage of the twenty-four-hour Christmas truce. But there was not much time to celebrate, because we had a fifteen-hour flight ahead of us. After the show ended, the troupe loaded up and headed to our next destination.

Our original flight plan called for us to fly over India, but at the last minute, India refused to allow us into their airspace due to their civil unrest. Having to fly around the southern tip of India meant that we would need to refuel, and that was not an option.

Everyone in the troupe was asleep but me as the crew tried to figure out a new flight plan. I looked up and saw Bob wave me up to the cockpit.

"Pretty exciting, right, Jayne?"

"Very. But I've been nervous too."

"We all are."

"Even you, Bob?"

"Of course. Always remember that those butterflies in your stomach mean you care. You care that you do well. You care that it makes a difference. You care that you can positively impact another one's life. And when you stop caring—you need to quit."

It was amazing to be sitting next to *the* Mr. Bob Hope. Then he pointed out the windows to our fighter jet escorts, two on each wing.

"Those are the Screaming Eagles of the 101st Airborne escorting us. We're thirty thousand feet in the air above the Gobi Desert begging for a place to land." And then came that famous laugh. That famous smile.

"Looking desperately for a gas station up here is no easy task," I replied. And then we both laughed.

We finally convinced the Shah of Iran to grant us permission to land in

Tehran, with heavy military presence. We were allowed to disembark onto the terminal only to stretch our legs. What little I experienced in the Tehran airport was incredible. The allure of the aromas and fragrances that hung heavily in the air, the woolen coats and alpaca vests, and the unique patterns and the bright, rich colors of everything they sold in the gift shops all seemed magical. I had never traveled abroad before this trip. . . . Heck, my first time ever on an airplane was only two and a half years earlier to DC for Girls Nation.

The next scheduled stop was at Vicenza in northern Italy, home of the 173rd Airborne Brigade Combat Team, and that also had to be canceled due to weather conditions. So, we made our way on to Naval Station Rota and Torrejón Air Base in Spain, just outside of Madrid.

Before we left Los Angeles, the USO office had asked all of us if we had any family and friends in the armed forces. A few of my friends from high school were in bases around the world. One such friend was Bill Bokelman, who often drove me to school in the fresh morning snow. He was stationed in Portugal. When I got to Torrejón, I was told to report to the BEQ (bachelor enlisted quarters); I had no idea what for. I sat in this huge empty room for quite some time and no one ever came in to tell me why I was there. It was extremely off-putting, being in a foreign country without any indication why I had been "brought to the principal's office." Then suddenly the door opened and there stood my old friend Bill. They had flown him in from Portugal as a surprise for not only me but him as well. We spent the next hour catching up and then he had to return, and I did too, as we were only in Madrid one day.

Another surprise awaited me in Cuba, which by the way has *the* clearest, bluest deep water I have ever seen. From the dock, I could see clear down to the bottom of the ocean. Guantánamo Bay, now known mostly for its troubled history, was one of the most beautiful beaches I had ever seen. By then I had become used to the GIs throwing their hats and yelling out hometown names. But then, out in the crowd, making his way to the stage was the brother of another high school classmate. There he was, running up to the stage and screaming like we were old friends, just like that scene in *Forrest Gump*. For him, it was a familiar face so far from home. Everyone was saying how that probably made his day. Humph, it made *my* day.

Guantánamo Bay, Cuba, was our final show.

We were heading home, but not before making one final stop in Colorado Springs at the Air Force Academy for a special tribute to General Emmett "Rosie" O'Donnell Jr., who had just passed away on December 26. General O'Donnell was a United States four-star general who had served as commander in chief of the Pacific Air Forces from 1959 to 1963. He was a dear friend to the USO, and a close friend of Bob Hope's. The tribute was highly emotional and did justice to the amazing commander, but none of the tour experiences touched me as much as that day we had spent in Da Nang. It has been fifty-four years, and I can still see the armed tanks sitting on the perimeter, the thousands of troops sitting in the mud with expressions of hope on their faces . . . *men* younger than me. And I wonder . . . how many made it home?

# CHAPTER TWELVE

# DEAN MARTIN'S DING-A-LING SISTERS

When we returned to Los Angeles, one of the cue card guys from the Bob Hope tour gave me a phone number and suggested I give Greg Garrison a call. Greg was the executive producer of NBC's hit *The Dean Martin Show* and they were looking for singer/dancers for The Golddiggers. In the late 1960s and early '70s, The Golddiggers had become very popular for their song-and-dance routines with Dean, so popular that they were given their own half-hour TV show. Then Greg decided to come up with another girl group for Dean's show. The performers in Golddiggers were constantly being dropped and replaced, but Greg took two of the best and made a second group, the Ding-A-Ling Sisters.

At the exact time Greg was casting for other Golddiggers, I had auditioned and was hired—until Greg told me what the job entailed. The group was touring relentlessly and taping their show the rest of the year. As he described all that was involved, I had to tell him that it would be a pass for me. I had only been married less than a year, and I wasn't interested in leaving for such extended periods of time. Greg was not happy; he almost always got his way. But I felt good about my decision.

The very next day Greg called back. This time, he said that the Ding-A-Lings needed two new girls and he'd like me to be one of them. He wanted to make it a multiethnic group by adding an Asian dancer, Helen Funai, and me. Being a part of the Ding-A-Lings would only require travel for approximately three months of the year. We'd be taping Dean's show at the NBC Studios in Burbank for the whole season and wouldn't be sent out on the road until after the season. The show would start in autumn of 1972, which meant that I wouldn't have to leave until spring '73. Now *that* was much more appealing.

When I went to the studio to sign my contract, I was told that the other requirements of joining the group were that I was never allowed to mention or publicly acknowledge in any way that I was married, including not being allowed to wear my wedding ring, and my husband was never to be seen or to be on set at NBC. In addition, I would never be allowed to give interviews on my own. The group was just that, a group, so any publicity had to always be handled by NBC as a group.

In Greg's mind, we were nothing but sex symbols whose primary role was to always give the impression of being available. All the costumes were skimpy little nothings consisting of bare midriffs and deep décolletage–cut dresses and pantsuits. Many of the songs and skits were filled with not-so-subtle sexual innuendo. I told Greg we needed to talk before I could officially take the job.

"First, with all due respect, I would never pretend not to be married. And my husband can be anywhere I am. . . ."

"The issue is—"

I stopped Greg. "And I'll be interviewed by any legitimate reporter who wants to talk to me."

"Well, we have to—"

"No, no, no. I'm in this business to get ahead. And with the name Ding-A-Ling I already have one strike against me. If any of this doesn't work, I'm sure you can replace me."

The next day, Greg called back and said I was hired. We never talked about the conditions again.

Now several months into having a steady income, and with Leon hired as a writer on comedian Scoey Mitchell's late-night talk show on NBC, we finally were able to ship our belongings from my parents' garage in Ohio, moving from our empty home in South Pasadena to a two-bedroom at the Oakwood Gardens apartments near the NBC studios.

I became a Ding-A-Ling Sister along with Tara Leigh, Lynne Latham, and Helen Funai. Tara and Lynne had come from The Golddiggers and were already part of the Ding-A-Lings. Helen and I were the new kids on the block and became roommates when we traveled. We have remained good friends to this day.

It soon became apparent that the idea of not having to travel until spring was an empty promise. We were often sent out to do a show at some small lodge or club, only to return to an immediate rehearsal or taping. The routine was to rehearse Mondays and Tuesdays; show it to the director on Wednesdays; camera block on Thursdays; prerecord the songs Thursday nights; and shoot two shows on Fridays, one at five p.m. with one audience, and one at eight p.m. with another audience. After that, we would have reshoots on anything that might have gone wrong.

My very first day on the set of *The Dean Martin Show*, I was standing backstage waiting to go on camera. Someone came from behind and tapped my elbows.

It was Nipsey Russell.

Pointing to my elbow, he said, "You're showing your color," slang for dry and ashy skin. "We have to look out for each other," he said with a wink. I laughed and rushed back to the dressing room and doused my elbows in lotion. No one else on the set would have noticed that—but every Black person in America would have when the show aired.

In all the time I worked the show, I would never see Dean Martin until Fridays at taping. We only did songs with Dean that he already knew. The real job of the Ding-A-Lings was to stand shoulder to shoulder with Dean and gently nudge him, guiding him to all his camera marks on the floor. Dean had been doing the show for as long as I could remember, and he now worked as little as possible. We did the show openings, filled in for the little sketches, did intros into Dean's songs to set him up, and performed our two production numbers and the show closing. Not being a professional dancer, every Monday morning I was scared to death that I would not be able to do a certain routine and I'd be found out. But I was a quick study and by showtime at the end of the week I always had it down pat.

The roadwork for the Ding-A-Lings usually entailed one-nighters. Once we did an entire month of one-nighters and never left the state of Texas. We performed at a broad spectrum of venues, from rundown joints to really nice private supper clubs. . . . We never knew what kind of gig was next. Most of the time we did two shows a night, and sometimes even three. Some of the one-nighters even included doing the first show in one town, then driving to another town to do the second show. After we finished at about one in the morning, it took a while to wind down, and that's when our road manager would drive us to the next town. We slept in the afternoon and started all over again the following night.

When there were rare times where we had the opportunity to stay in one place for more than three days, I would rent a sewing machine and make my clothes. I always traveled with one suitcase full of materials, patterns, and sewing notions. For the most part, I lived in jeans, tank tops, and sweaters, because I was never a clotheshorse and never really liked shopping. I also did any necessary repair work on my costumes as well as for the other girls in the group.

All this for the glamorous television job that paid a whopping three hundred dollars a week, from which we paid for our own food and sometimes even had to pay for our own hotel. By the time we got back to LA, there wasn't much money left. But whatever I did have, I saved for a house.

I didn't eat much on the road either. I was 142 pounds at five foot ten and a half. Even though I was skin and bones, I was always dieting and exercising—all of us were. Lynne used to wrap her thighs in Saran Wrap and put on plastic dance pants to sweat. Then she'd bang her thighs against anything hard, like the floors or walls, to break down the tissue. Though I never tried that, I did wear the plastic pants.

The Thursday before taping a show, I wouldn't eat for fear that my stomach would poke out. I never had an eating disorder, but it was just that all our costumes had low-cut waists and dipped at the navel, and I was determined to have a flat belly. Plus, it was hard to dance on a full stomach anyway.

A lot of times we ate in our hotel rooms because it was convenient. And most of the small-town restaurants were not open when our shows were over at twelve, one, or two a.m. Snacks saved us—sardines, sausages, crackers, hard boiled eggs, and grilled cheese sandwiches were routine. But we often ate in our rooms out of another kind of necessity. Many of the truck stops and cafés were not too keen on serving Blacks. Our road manager (who did all the driving) would pull into a truck stop around two a.m. after a show. I recall many times having to stay in the car while he and the other girls went in to order the food. And the truck stops were not too keen on serving a bunch of women in stage makeup either. Once, when we tried to get served, the customers got out of hand, calling us prostitutes, and began to get rowdy. We left promptly without even getting our order.

Racism in the early 1970s raised its ugly head more often than not. After a show in Atlanta, I was shopping at a convenience store. We were all laughing and picking out the simple little items we were going to snack on during our drive to the next show. I finished my shopping first and put my basket on the counter. We were all talking as the other girls finished and paid for their items. Finally, when the clerk hadn't rung up my items, I put the basket in front of her and mentioned that I was done.

"We don't sell to Blacks."

"Oh, okay, then I guess mine is FREE?"

No response from the clerk. I picked up my items and strutted out of the store.

Helen, my Asian roomie, told me about when she danced in the road company for the Broadway show *Flower Drum Song*. She was traveling in the South when the bus pulled over for a rest stop. When she got to the restroom and saw the two signs, WHITES and COLORED, she was so fearful and confused not knowing which one she should use that she just got back on the bus and decided to wait.

In Texas, we had just finished a show in Houston and were scheduled to appear at the Petroleum Club in Beaumont, a short drive away. My sister was living in Houston at the time, so I invited her to come see the shows.

While I was in the dressing room (which was usually a small space just off the kitchen), I got a note: *Hi Jayne, I'm sorry. Can't stay for the show.*

I ran out to see if I could catch her, and she was still outside the club.

"What's wrong? Are you okay?"

"I'm fine. We just have to go."

She was angry and had tears in her eyes, so I pressed, "Please tell me what's going on."

"They don't allow Black people here."

I was shocked. Shocked . . . It was 1973 . . . and they still had a "Whites Only" policy. In my lifetime. Not something that I read in a history book. But in *my* lifetime.

I asked her, "Did you tell them your sister is *in* the show?"

"Yeah. Doesn't matter. Whites only."

"You wait right here," I said.

Back in the theatre, I told our road manager I was not performing as I began to take off my costume. "They don't allow Blacks, then they don't allow me. I'm going home."

The road manager called our office in Los Angeles and Greg called the club manager, who threatened to sue. By now I had put on my street clothes. The guests in the club were getting upset because they weren't being served. The kitchen staff, who were right next door to us and were all Black, had overheard the rumble and stopped working. We all just sat there.

The club manager was arguing with our manager, and he was arguing with me. I didn't say a word. I, along with my Ding-A-Ling Sisters, just sat there fuming. Then the club manager went over to Tara and asked her what happened if one of us was sick . . . pointing out that we surely had a backup plan where the three remaining girls could still do the show.

Tara, who was the last one of the group I expected to speak up, looked at him and said point-blank, "We're the Ding-A-Ling *Sisters*. If one of us doesn't go on, then none of us go on." She didn't bat an eye, and she didn't hesitate a moment. None of the girls budged an inch. Then they began to remove their costumes.

Finally, the club acquiesced, and my sister was allowed to watch the show. The kitchen staff went back to work, and we went onstage. After the show I found out she had been seated behind a pole, but we still broke a social barrier, and she did sit and watch the show at the Beaumont Petroleum Club among an astounded white audience . . . that eventually did get fed. I just knew back in LA Greg would hit the ceiling and I'd probably lose my job when we returned. But he never uttered a word.

Every now and then, we did glamour gigs, like Vegas, Miami, Puerto Rico, or Hawaii. When we did Caesars Palace and I saw our names on the marquee, you could have knocked me over with a feather. The first day on the night we were to open at Caesars was spent in rehearsals and sound checks. I was unabashedly excited. The main showroom was huge. It was hard to believe that I was actually going to be on that stage, that very night. My life was whizzing by, and it was like I was watching all the events of my life flash right before me. It was as if there were two different people—Jayne *Harrison*, just two years out of high school, and Jayne *Kennedy*, working at Caesars Palace in Las Vegas.

I knew that I had some time after the rehearsal before I had to go to my room and prepare for the show, so I chose to wander through the casino and take in the sights. After all—it was my first time in Vegas. As I glided down the main staircase headed straight to the blackjack tables I was stopped by this big guy. He asked, "Are you working tonight?"

And with all the energy I could muster, I proudly answered with the biggest smile, "YES. Yes I am." And he handed me his room key.

*UGGGGGGGGHHHH.* I have never been more embarrassed in all my life. I shyly stepped back and informed him that I didn't do *that* kind of work. I ran directly to my hotel room, and I didn't come out other than to perform.

I have always had a difficult time being on the road. I'm not kidding when I say I didn't come out of my room. Whenever I went down to the restaurant to eat a meal, I would be seen as a lone woman who wanted company or more than that. When the truth was, I just wanted to be by myself. Being on the road with a group was so much different than the times when I was on the road by myself. With a group at least there was someone to talk to. When I was on my own there was never anyone to talk to. A chance conversation with any man often led to "Hey, do you think you and me could . . . ?" All they saw was a pretty woman with no man around, so she must be on the make. I hated that. It was so much easier to just stay in the room, order room service, and catch a movie on television.

Being sequestered in the room is not the way to spend your life.

After a while all the hotel rooms begin to look alike. The airports begin to look the same, and the cities always look the same, with one exception: New York. I always knew when I was in New York from the moment I got off the plane. New York has a vibe that smacks you in the face the moment you step through the airport terminal doors to venture outside. Good and bad, the impact of the city is unforgettable. You could be sleepwalking and still know you are in New York.

But I gotta say, the funniest thing happened to me with one particular cabdriver many years later. I was coming out of the hotel one cold, windy November afternoon. Everybody was looking to hail a cab. This driver ran right past several people and came to pick me up. I jumped into the backseat and before we could get out of the driveway, he caught my glance in his rearview mirror. "Hello, Miss Kennedy," he exclaimed excitedly with a very thick foreign accent. "I am one of your biggest fans. I love your work, especially on the football. I have watched you from the time you were a little one. I will never forget you when you were standing at your father's grave with your hand up in that little salute."

I . . . I didn't know what to say. He was obviously very touched, but I knew that if I said something he would be thoroughly embarrassed. So, I just said thank you and smiled.

I have often wondered how people could think that I was one of the Massachusetts Kennedy clan, which unbelievably happened quite often. I was always being called Jackie Kennedy for some odd reason. I still don't get that one.

When we were on the set and the other girls were not allowed to bring their boyfriends or husbands around, Leon came whenever he wanted. Leon was working as a writer on NBC's *The Scoey Mitchell Show* just down the hall, so he was already on the lot. Greg never said a word. *Sepia* magazine did a full-blown eight-page cover story on me, and Greg never said anything . . . even when I brought the magazine into his office and placed it on his desk. He looked at it for a second, then returned to his work. I'm guessing that he respected me standing up for my principles. I could be wrong, but that's what I'd like to believe.

Then there was the time we performed in Hawaii as the opening act for singer Freda Payne. I was awestruck that I was sharing the stage with one of my idols. One morning my high school friend Jim called and said he was in Honolulu and wanted to come to the show. What a great surprise! So first we went to Diamond Head Beach with Helen. We decided to go snorkeling. Unfortunately, I made a huge mistake by wearing my hair down. While in deep water, I got caught in a strong undertow and my hair got tangled in my goggles, making it impossible to see. I'd gasp for air whenever I was tossed topside, then I was back in the rumble. I knew I was going to die. There was NO ONE there. Jim had swum in ahead of me. The beach had been empty when we arrived . . . so there would be no help. But suddenly a man appeared next to me from nowhere and saved me. He took me to a giant boulder not far from where I was struggling to stay alive to catch my breath. Then, holding my hand, he guided me to shore. Once I felt the ground under my feet, I stood and turned back to take in what could have been the end of me. As soon as I turned around . . . he was gone. It had only been a few seconds, but he had disappeared. The beach was huge and there was no one else there but my friends, who sat far away. How could this man just disappear?

That night I called Mom, and she said he was my angel—it was not my time. My purpose was yet to be realized.

After two years on the show, April 5, 1974, was the last episode of *The Dean Martin Show* and an end to the Ding-A-Ling Sisters. All the shows had been taped but Greg wanted us back on the road again. I was done, so I turned in my resignation letter to Greg. He was not pleased. Leon and I had saved enough money to buy a house, and I was so proud that I had bought my first house at the age of twenty-two. I have never been the type to put my business in the street and I had never talked about buying a house. This would be a great opportunity to stay at home . . . a real home. I had envisioned how much fun it would be to redesign and decorate.

As soon as Greg read the letter, he picked up the phone and called Leon.

"How can Jayne quit—you just bought a house, and you need Jayne's paycheck."

How disrespectful! Greg hated that he couldn't control us and that he couldn't stop Leon from being on the set. Greg often said things to Leon like "Oh my, is that a new suit you're wearing since Jayne just got paid?"

He'd been this way the entire time, and just thinking about his behavior made me grateful for being rid of him.

Once when my parents visited the set, he greeted them with "Hey, you two should put yourselves out for stud service." No hello. Just walk up to a Black man and his wife whom you have never met before and say something as racist and disrespectful as that. He'd always walk around patting women on their butts. I couldn't wait to leave the show.

When he died in 2005 and the obituary was lauding his career and saying flowery things about him, my only thought was . . . I guess that's what obituaries are for.

And I didn't go to the funeral.


My family was having a blast with my being on TV—Dad loved it when the guys at work called him Daddy Ding-A-Ling. Every Thursday night, my family got to see me on TV, right there in their living room in Wickliffe, Ohio, and whenever we performed anywhere near Ohio, they made sure they would come to see the show with Grandma Lois in tow. I got to see this country and meet all kinds of people. I matured, being on my own for the first time. I got to frolic on beaches in San Juan, and Honolulu, and do nothing but soak up the sun. I met up with Lamonte in Miami, where we were both performing, and he showed me what Miami was really like outside of the beauty pageant. And I made friends that have lasted a lifetime; Michelle DellaFave, Helen Funai, Lindsay Bloom, and I recently celebrated our fiftieth Ding-A-Ling Sisters friendship anniversary.

In retrospect, being a Ding-A-Ling Sister was a critical stepping stone for my experience in front of the camera and onstage. At only twenty-two years old I had already worked with Dean Martin, Frank Sinatra, Sammy Davis Jr., Mike Connors, Nancy Sinatra, Glen Campbell, Tom Bosley, Paul Lynde, Norm Crosby, Jonathan Winters, Eva Gabor—and literally every other star of the era. With all of the negative, it was definitely a net positive in the end.

## CHAPTER THIRTEEN

# PRIDE AND JOY

I worked so hard those first two years on the road as a Ding-A-Ling, saving enough money to buy a house. I didn't buy clothes or a car. I made sacrifices because Leon and I had set a goal. Leon worked relentlessly on *The Scoey Mitchell Show* and spent hours and hours expanding our contact list. Buying a house would be a major achievement that we could check off on our ten-year plan and a measure of success.

When we first decided to make a ten-year plan for becoming Hollywood notables, our intention was to first have an endgame, then lay out a yearly plan of what achieving each step would look like. Much like a business model. Although we enjoyed working as actors, we knew the power to control our destiny would lie in the root of the business plan, ownership and production. Eventually, we would build our own studio. But the ten-year plan was to first be known as highly capable and commercially marketable talent.

The prestige of owning my own home was rooted in my childhood. When I was growing up, there were two adults and six kids in a small three-bedroom house, and the only place I could assure myself of privacy was the bathroom. I would sit on the floor, just contemplating my life and planning my attack on the next day. Mom always said one of the best things we had going for us was living in a small house, because it forced us to get along, a skill that would pay off later in life, but I still wanted to have my own place, my own space.

I was in heaven in our first house. It was huge, a one-story ranch with four massive bedrooms, two and a half baths, and a step-down living room with vaulted ceilings. It had a fireplace with skylights on either side, a large gourmet kitchen, a recreation room and dining room with sliding glass doors, a *formal* dining room with sliding glass doors, and a primary bedroom with— you guessed it—sliding glass doors. The best part of the house was a ravine in the backyard with a small creek running through it. The house sat on almost two acres of land—*two acres*. That's almost unheard of in Los Angeles. It was high in the mountains above Pasadena with a view that was incredible on a clear day (which was very rare).

The house needed some work when we bought it, but it was a welcome challenge for a Harrison Girl who could do anything. Leon was not handy at home repair . . . at all. For years, I painted, hammered, sewed, and had a blast making it our home. Even though I was performing constantly, the pay was a joke. So, at the piecemeal completion of each project, I had to wait until we could afford the next decorating step.

Leon had found the house when I was on the road with the Ding-A-Lings. We had been looking to buy a house for some time and in this very neighborhood. We had seen a house down the road from there, but when we went to make an offer, the broker and owners made us wait outside in our car when they saw that we were Black. So, we waited and waited. After an hour or so, another car came up and a white couple got out and went inside. They made an offer, and it was accepted on the spot. The broker then came out to our car and said, "Sorry, somebody else beat you to it." We started to file a racial discrimination complaint, but then Leon found this house.

Leon knew this was the perfect house for us, so he started the paperwork before I even came home. After picking me up at the airport, he drove me up to the house blindfolded. It was a long way up to the end of the road. Then we drove through a gate and made a left, and there it was on the right— it was perfect.

At a selling price of $57,000 (equivalent to $411,000 today), we had no idea how we were going to pay for it. The monthly mortgage payment was $347, and I had just quit *The Dean Martin Show*. Leon was still working, and we trusted that our financial needs would be met, and somehow, they were. We lived in that beautiful house nine years.

Our home was an hour from anywhere we needed to go in LA. Everyone teased Leon, saying he moved me way out there so that he didn't have to worry about anyone coming unannounced to see me. For the first few years we had just the bare minimum in furniture. Leon had struck a deal with one of the Cleveland advertisers on *Outta Sight* before we left Cleveland and they gave us a bedroom set, so we had that.

We had the boxes and boxes of wedding gifts that we had stored back home in Ohio shipped out to us at Oakwood, but the rest of the house was bare except for this huge built-in wall unit that separated the dining room from the brick walkway to the formal dining room and living room on the other side. It was handmade of solid oak, and it was my pride and joy. I kept that thing polished and loaded with so many wonderful wedding gifts that had been boxed up for two years, desperately waiting to sparkle and shine. I had begun to collect different items and art pieces from my various trips around the world. Many of them were displayed, along with my wedding announcement engraved into a gold-and-enamel tray, on this two-sided unit that became the focal point of my home.

Our first official welcome to the neighborhood was a banana nut bread loaf anonymously left in our mailbox. So good.

Our second official welcome the very next morning was a *burning cross* on the front lawn.

It was a neighborhood that could offer good times and bad, and we had to decide which it would be for us. I decided that no matter what, I would never let them take away my pride in the fact that I had bought my first home at age twenty-two. They would not run me away. But I must also admit that there were many lonely nights that I lay awake afraid. Afraid of the noises in the woods. Afraid of the many sliding glass doors. Afraid that there were no neighbors near enough if something did happen. Afraid that the neighbors who were close could have been the ones who left that nice "welcome to the neighborhood present" on our front lawn. Leon, on the other hand, decided to give them a reason to be afraid.

We were out walking one morning when our next-door neighbor walked right up to us and said: "How do *you* people at such a young age afford to buy this house?"

Leon and I looked at each other. She had a lot of nerve.

Leon replied with the straightest of faces, "We sell drugs."

She clutched her bag and her dog and darted off at warp speed and never bothered us again.

## CHAPTER FOURTEEN

# WELCOME TO HOLLYWOOD: 101

The very first movie I did was a low budget comedy in 1972 called *Group Marriage*. I had a very small part and honestly, I don't remember much about it because I only worked one day, but I do recall how exciting it was to be on a movie set and to see how all the seemingly disparate parts magically came together . . . or in this case maybe not so much. However, my second film in 1972 was one that you may have heard of called *Lady Sings the Blues*. Of course, this was the big leagues . . . Berry Gordy and Motown's very first foray into theatrical film.

I would be working with Billy Dee Williams and the amazing Miss Diana Ross, who was one of my childhood idols (still is, for that matter). I thought I had died and gone to heaven.

My role was Billy Dee's girlfriend before he met Diana Ross. We had many scenes together establishing our relationship and who Billy Dee's character was and his backstory, just as they did scenes setting up Diana's backstory leading up to their eventual fateful meeting.

Then came the scene when Diana first saw Billy in the nightclub in Harlem, when she went to the club owner looking for a job. In that scene, the club owner proceeded to tell her that she didn't have what it took: "To be a showgirl, you gotta have something to uhm, to show. No amount of slinky or makeup is gonna change you into a female that makes you look something like . . . like THAT."

He then pointed to me as I walked down the stairs in a sexy, skintight red satin spaghetti-strap evening dress and a black fur walking just ahead of Louis (Billy Dee). Well, Diana never saw me. All she saw was Billy Dee, and she immediately fell in love in that sensational close-up shot of her where she literally slid down the wall (along with every other woman in America who remembers that scene). One of the most iconic character introduction shots in the history of Hollywood . . . Billy Dee Williams was the finest thing God ever made.

So, the months went by in postproduction, and I could envision my Hollywood star rising. I was so eager to see the film's rough cut. I knew I had done well, and I was confident that, with the way I was shot and looked in that scene, I would finally be on the map.

When the day came for the special cast-and-crew screening, I drove the forty-five minutes from our home in Pasadena on pins and needles to the Paramount Studios lot on Melrose Avenue. I had also invited some close friends, and there were some Black Hollywood heavyweights in attendance as well. As we all sat there in the private screening theatre waiting for the movie to start, the anticipation was electric. I just knew this was going to be a turning point in my life. After tonight's film, I'd walk out of this screening room a newly discovered talent.

Shows what I knew.

The movie opened. There was Diana. The movie went on and on and oddly no Billy . . . and no me. We were supposed to be in the opening. Then came that nightclub scene. It's a pivotal point in the story. I thought to myself, Okay . . . well, this is it—I have to be here.

Then came those words. . . . I hung on. "Uhhh . . . you gotta look something like . . . like THAT."

The cut went to me coming down the staircase with barely enough room to see my head due to the second-floor stairwell that blocked my face—which was only seen for roughly two seconds. But that dress from my neck to my hips and that fur delivered the intended message: just my boobs. They looked great in that red satin, but they could have been anybody's boobs. That was it. Never once in the film did anyone ever see my face for more than those two seconds. I wasn't even listed in the credits until many years later. I was cut out of the film almost entirely.

I was told later that once they got into postproduction and saw the footage, Berry Gordy knew he had the opportunity to make Billy Dee Williams into a Black Clark Gable. Remember when Clark Gable first appeared in *Gone with the Wind* and that classic close-up shot of him when Scarlett first saw him? . . . That's exactly what Berry wanted. Not only was the female lead completely smitten but more importantly the audience was as well. And that shot with Billy Dee was critical to the film. . . . Berry wanted everybody to see "Rhett Butler" when they saw Louis.

Berry told Billy Dee, "When Jayne came into the shot it just took too many eyes away from Louis, it ruined the effect. We had to cut her out of the film."

Smokey was the one who told me about that conversation that Berry had with Billy Dee . . . and you know what? It made complete sense, and I would have made the exact same decision had I been in Berry's shoes. Rationally and creatively I totally understood it—but it still didn't take away the sting.

Class is in session: Welcome to Hollywood: 101, kid.

Despite my not being in the movie, I too fell in love with Billy Dee Williams right there along with Diana and all the other millions of women in America. Years later when Billy and I were cohosting a show in Chicago and laughing about me being cut, he pulled me in close with those soft, warm, velvety eyes of his and slowly whispered into my ear, "That's okay, Jayne. They couldn't stop you. You were gonna make it anyway."

## CHAPTER FIFTEEN

# POTS, PANS, AND GREASE

As a fledgling in the acting business, you are perpetually unemployed. After I left the Ding-A-Lings, I attempted to find work wherever there was an opportunity. When there wasn't any, I would stand in line at the Hollywood unemployment office. I saw a lot of Hollywood celebs there, but everyone was so embarrassed to be there that no one would speak to anybody else. They just gave understanding nods of acknowledgment.

In between jobs, I would take a class in drama or dance, along with my twice-weekly voice lessons in Hollywood with Giuseppe Balistreri. I caught a break soon after leaving the Ding-A-Lings. NFL legend John Mackey and his wife, Sylvia, lived near us in Pasadena, and Leon and I had met them at a party a few months earlier. No one lived in faraway Pasadena, so when we found out we lived only five minutes apart we immediately became friends. Sylvia was a prominent model in LA and she graciously made a call on my behalf to Holly Mitchell, a fashion show producer.

Holly's bookings were not standard fashion shows but productions, with singers and dancers intertwined with high fashion—fabulous presentations that allowed me to model, dance, and sing. Since there were always a slew of charity events and luncheons in Hollywood and Beverly Hills, work for her agency was fairly regular. The pay wasn't bad for the time—sixty-five dollars per show, which included a wardrobe fitting. I booked an average of two shows a month; sometimes, we'd do a show in Vegas or Disney World, then it was back to the unemployment line the next week.

Working for Holly I learned all the ins and outs of the various hotels, along with a slight hint of what the fashion world entailed. With my job as a Ding-A-Ling, I had already become accustomed to dressing rooms that hung off the corner of kitchens, small innocuous spaces that most people never see—dressing rooms that barely held the clothes let alone the models, oftentimes both men and women. There was no such thing as being shy backstage; you changed clothes as quickly as you could and never thought twice about being exposed.

Though I was grateful for the work from Holly, I needed to do more than work a few bookings a month. It was important for me to capitalize on my recent success traveling with Bob Hope and being on *The Dean Martin Show*. Leon and I were sure we could complete our ten-year plan, but it was imperative to have a bold, aggressive overall strategy.

We were partners working diligently on both our careers, and this was our "company." We had so many ideas, assuming if we threw enough things up against the wall, one of them just might stick. We tried to go to every event we could get into, just so we could meet people. Initially, we didn't know anyone in LA, so that in and of itself at times seemed almost impossible, but we felt it was the only way to move ahead. Hollywood was then, and still is now, all about having the right contacts. It was also important to have the acting credentials that gave you "legitimacy" in the eyes of the agents.

In the 1970s for TV and film, there were two acting unions: the Screen Actors Guild, or SAG, and the American Federation of Television and Radio Artists, or AFTRA. (In 2012, the two unions merged into one union,

SAG-AFTRA.) SAG was a union for those appearing in film, and AFTRA was for those in television and radio. The vicious cycle of not being able to get a job unless you were in the union, and not being able to get into the union unless you had a union job was a big hurdle for actors to overcome. Agents didn't want to work with anyone who wasn't in the union because it was more difficult to get them auditions for union jobs. I was a member of AFTRA because of my work on *Laugh-In*, but I needed my SAG card too.

Leon and I made a point of using unusual tactics to try to get to know as many people as it would take to get a job that would break the union cycle problem. We assumed that one of the right places to be was at the Oscars. But it was nearly impossible to get a ticket to the actual show, especially since we didn't have the money to buy a ticket even if we could. But that wasn't where the mingling happened anyway—the real place to be discovered was at the after-parties, or so we thought.

Leon came up with a plan to crash one of them. But I didn't have a dress, and we didn't have money for me to buy a dress. So I whipped out my trusty sewing machine and made a gown from a baby blue tie-dyed jersey knit that clung to every curve.

I jazzed it up with silver piping and rhinestones around the plunging V-neck and contrasted it with the same design at the top of the side slit that ran up the side to the top of my thigh. Accented with four-inch silver heels and a bouffant wig, I was armed and ready to rock.

The after-party was being held at the Beverly Hilton. We drove up to the hotel, parked in the garage, and were going to try to get in without a ticket. I knew the Beverly Hilton ballroom like the back of my hand because I had worked there many times as a model with Holly Mitchell Productions. As models, we knew the kitchen and the wings of the kitchen that we used for dressing rooms. We never entered or exited through the main ballroom, so I knew exactly where we should go. Leon and I entered the hotel through the back door and made our way to the kitchen. But between where we were and where we needed to be, there was a barrier I hadn't anticipated—the kitchen floor.

One step in and I thought I would die before I actually got to the other side to enter the ballroom. The floor was so slippery in my four-inch heels that I literally skated across as Leon steadied and dragged me through. My feet were sliding everywhere, and I was trying to take baby steps for fear of breaking my neck. With each one, I had a vision of my feet flying up in the air and me lying under a pile of pots, pans, and pasta with makeup running down my face. It was wild and way too funny. I thought we'd be able to sneak through the kitchen, but it was hard not to notice me struggling to keep my balance. I swore that was going to be the *last* harebrained idea of Leon's that I would ever listen to.

After we finally crossed the floor, we entered the after-party ballroom so gracefully that no one ever noticed. After a trip to the restroom to refresh from the crazy entrance, we proceeded to mingle as if not having a ticket was the last thing on our minds. Then we met some of the executives who we already knew, and they invited us to their table, and we met even more people. The night turned out to be a huge success and we were being seen by all the *right* people in town.

Leon and I had often sought to expand our network since it was obvious that networking was the key to success. I had first met Sammy Davis Jr. on *Rowan & Martin's Laugh-In.* Sammy quickly became a very good friend, along with his wife, Altovise. Leon and I were always invited to the Friday night movies and Sunday dinners at their beautiful home in Beverly Hills. The guest list always included many of the cream of the Hollywood crop. So many of the friends we made there remained friends for many years to come. I always found the barbed wire fencing and patrolling of the military-like armed security guards surrounding his house quite intimidating. But inside . . . we always had an absolute blast. After we divorced, Leon and Sammy did a film together that Leon wrote and produced called *Knights of the City.* Leon and Sammy were great friends until the day Sammy passed away in 1990.

## CHAPTER SIXTEEN

# MUHAMMAD ALI AND ME

June 10, 2016—the day my dear friend was sadly laid to rest. My heart had been hurting all week. I had already written and thought a lot about this amazing man during this writing process, but on this day, I could not comprehend that he was no longer with us . . . no longer among the living. My heart and head pounded in unison.

This was the day when the world said goodbye to the GOAT.

I had known this day would come sooner rather than later. The last time I saw Ali had been in Hollywood on the Sunset Strip outside a nightclub in the late 1990s. In my excitement, I ran to give him a big hug as he walked up the sidewalk . . . and he had absolutely no idea who I was. Mind you, ours was a friendship of more than fifteen years as Leon and I traveled the globe with him to both exotic and remote locations. On these exploits he would teach, and we would listen. His words were always far more profound for me than anything he ever accomplished in the ring.

Yes, I had said goodbye to my friend years before. But my headache on this day would not go away. I know my heartache *never* will.

The first time I met the phenomenon that was Muhammad Ali was February 1974 at the NATPE (National Association of Television Program Executives) convention in Los Angeles. NATPE is a huge business forum for programmers, distributors, and buyers from around the world. More importantly, NATPE is a must-attend event for anyone looking to propel their career forward. And even though it had started only ten years prior, it was the most important and influential conference of its kind. However, it was still somewhat intimate and personal back then with just over 1,100 or so attendees.

For Leon and me, NATPE was the business event that would provide us with important networking contacts in the television industry. It was one of our many excursions to gain access to Hollywood's small, insular world of show business.

We were browsing the distributors on the main floor, and we heard from someone that Muhammad Ali was upstairs in one of the presentation suites. We headed to his suite, walked through the door, and went to stand in the back of the press-filled room, with everyone clamoring to get even just an inch closer to Ali, who was holding court while sitting on top of a dresser. As soon as we entered the room, Ali looked over at us and yelled at the top of his lungs, "Hey! There's that Ding-A-Ling girl!" and pointed to me.

All heads turned in our direction as my jaw pretty much dropped to the floor. He then invited me to come sit next to him on his perch atop the dresser. I looked over at Leon, who was just as surprised. It was thrilling and surreal to be sitting next to Muhammad Ali in front of the press, laughing and joking together. We had thought that attending NATPE would be important to our careers, but little did we know that the best thing that would come from that convention was meeting Ali.

I can't explain it but from the day of that conference Ali, Leon, and I became the best of friends. He had so many real friends and the other kind of "friends," so what was it about us? We were so close that Muhammad invited us to his infamous fight with Joe Frazier in the Philippines known as the "Thrilla in Manila." My jaw dropped again. It was October 1, 1975, just twenty-six days before my twenty-fourth birthday, and the two champions were having their third and final encounter. The entire world was watching, and we had front-row seats.

We set out on the seventeen-hour flight from San Francisco to Manila. The entire first-class cabin was filled with Ali's entourage (which somehow now included us). We had a layover in Hawaii, where we picked up one passenger, Ali's second wife, Belinda, and the atmosphere on the plane suddenly intensified. She was angry and everyone knew why. At five foot ten she was big and bold, and her personality equaled her imposing stature. I had heard that it took several bodyguards to literally keep her off Ken Norton the night he broke Muhammad's jaw during the second round of their 1973 bout in San Diego.

"Who are you?" she asked me as she boarded the plane.

"I'm Jayne," I said quickly.

"Where's Veronica?" she asked.

Everyone was silent.

Ali had referred to Veronica as his wife to the press. And she would indeed become the third Mrs. Ali. But at that moment, Belinda was his wife, and when she became aware of what was in the press she decided to join the flight to Manila, go straight to the hotel, and give Muhammad a piece of her mind.

A few hours later, she was on the first flight back to Chicago. Some say she must have been really upset, but anger doesn't make you do that. Love makes you do that. Love makes you cast all reason to the wind and just follow your heart. I truly admired Belinda for that loving act of strength and courage.

I eventually became good friends with Belinda, who had changed her name to Khalilah. She and I are the same height and we both commanded attention with our presence. Many times, during my career, I would meet all kinds of people who said they looked just like me. Most of them didn't—not even remotely. But Belinda and I could have been sisters.

Many years later there was a tribute to Muhammad Ali at the Forum in Los Angeles. Everybody who was anybody was there. Ed Bell, who had been my attorney from Detroit for a number of years, had flown into town and we were going together.

Ed and I pulled up at the artists' entrance in a long stretch limo. The traffic was staggering, and it was almost impossible to get to the VIP entrance. Ed called out to one of the parking attendants and motioned to me, indicating he had Mrs. Muhammad Ali in the car and we needed to get in ASAP. The attendant peeped in the window, took a quick look at me, and we were in just like that.

But in Manila, I constantly had to pinch myself. I couldn't believe we were part of the official Muhammad Ali entourage, and it was clear when we arrived in Manila that we were to be treated like royalty.

Many events were staged around the upcoming fight, and the Philippine government made sure the press was aware that no expense was to be spared in entertaining Muhammad's friends from America.

Everything was on the grandest of scales. We were introduced to many of the social and political elites of the islands and were invited to their opulent homes. Enrique Zobel was an extremely well-to-do, prominent, and powerful member of the prestigious Zobel de Ayala family, who had built and modernized the central city of Makati. He invited Leon and me to join him on a wildlife safari. Enrique had his limousine pick us up and chauffeur us to Punta Baluarte, his resort in Calatagan, Batangas, in Luzon, the second richest province in the Philippines. It was a completely self-sustaining resort. All the two hundred members of his staff lived there, and he owned it all. It was like how you might imagine *Fantasy Island* to be, but larger and even more extravagant in every way.

After a delicious and bountiful lunch, Enrique's helicopter picked us up, and we flew on a photo safari, discovering the beauty of the Philippine islands. Every moment just kept getting more and more scenic, as if we were turning the pages of *National Geographic*. Exotic birds of every kind, herd after herd of gazelles running across the prairies—just beautiful.

The next day we were taken whitewater rafting at Pagsanjan Falls in Laguna, and we lunched in the cave behind the falls. The third day, we were invited to dine with the Philippine "royal family," President Ferdinand and his wife, Imelda Marcos (and no, I did not see her infamous shoe collection), in their home at Malacañang Palace.

For all the splendor of the wonderful events, these were just the appetizers. The real event, the main dish, was the fight. Muhammad had invited us to attend the prefight weigh-in, and that's when I discovered that Muhammad was a notorious *prankster*. He kept telling everyone that I was Belinda and that "we" were back together. I didn't think it was so funny, but Muhammad did, and he loved messing with your head. Sensing an opportunity for even more press exposure, Leon played along and kept saying it was true. Most of the foreign media were duped, and soon enough there were pictures in all the international papers of Ali and me. Considering Ali's girlfriend, Veronica, had accompanied him to the Philippines, it was a well-played practical joke, but I'm fairly certain she didn't think it was humorous at all.

The "Thrilla in Manila" heavyweight championship of the world bout took place at the Araneta Coliseum in Cubao, Quezon City. It was to begin at ten a.m. to accommodate the time differential in America and the live broadcast over HBO's first ever pay-per-view boxing event. The excitement in the air was so overpowering you could literally feel it. The palpable aura in the arena that morning has lingered with me ever since. There were so many people from all over the world, a veritable melting pot of languages and faces. Everybody was dressed up to the nines for the fight. There were elegant gowns and tuxedos. Outlandish fashion fads in clothing, makeup, and hair, and super-glamorous people in all types of cultural motifs. I couldn't stop looking at the thousands of faces that had come from every corner of the globe to see Muhammad Ali exchange blows with his nemesis, Joe Frazier. It reminded me of the Romans coming to watch the Christians fight the lions. Two gladiators standing toe to toe in the fight of their lives, with the crowd cheering them on . . . me included.

I was one of Muhammad's biggest fans. Not only was he physically gorgeous, but he was also a man in the best sense, someone whom I admired for standing up for his convictions and beliefs. Muhammad wasn't afraid of any-one or anything. In my eyes, he was an unflinching, unapologetic, and fearless Black man at a time when the world was in turmoil. Similar traits to what I saw in my father. As the Cleveland riots and the Kent State University massa-cre happened, he was the hero that I had hoped for coming out of the turbu-lent era of the 1960s when racial strife and the desire for liberation was being felt by Black women and men, not only in America but around the world.

When he entered the ring, I could see that sense of purpose and determi-nation on his face—this was the biggest fight of his life.

I sat ringside in Muhammad's corner. I had my little Sony eight-millimeter camera, determined to get my own "home movie" of the most exciting event of my life. I'm sure this was the night that I truly fell in love with boxing.

Although, when I was a kid, I would watch boxing on television with my father, cheering on Sugar Ray Robinson and Floyd Patterson. And later when I was nineteen, Leon and I had bought tickets to watch Ali and Joe Frazier fight "The Fight of the Century" (their first of the three) on the very first closed-circuit broadcast, on March 8, 1971.

For Ali, that 1971 fight was his third fight, aside from two comeback fights against Jerry Quarry and Oscar Bonavena, after having his title stripped for his anti-Vietnam stance and his refusal to be drafted, leading to the US government exiling him from the ring for three years during his prime. For Frazier, the fight made him a pro-war symbol for conservatives. For fans across America, it was way more than a heavyweight championship title bout.

Unfortunately, they had oversold the tickets, and there were hundreds of angry fans still outside the doors who weren't having it. Leon and I ended up being pushed through a glass wall and escaped by jumping a barbed wire fence, and then we went to another venue where "he knew a guy" . . . and were secretly ushered through a back door. In total, a record *three hundred million viewers* around the globe watched breathlessly . . . including yours truly.

And yet incredibly, here I was, just four years later, literally sitting ring-side, eight thousand miles away from home at the very center of the fight universe, and I couldn't wait to tell Dad about every single minute of it.

During the entire fight, I screamed until I couldn't scream any more. I gasped and cried with each blow that did the slightest damage to my hero . . . my champion. My heart soared when he danced, and I smiled at what would become his patented "rope-a-dope."

But I wasn't the only one—everyone was screaming in so many different languages—it was insane. Then, from out of nowhere, someone would start the chant, "Ali. Ali. Ali. Ali," and magically all the languages in unison would unite, "Ali. Ali. Ali." Thousands and thousands at the top of their lungs: "Ali. Ali. Ali." And I could see him briefly look out and acknowledge the crowd . . . and he would begin to dance. He was so beautiful to watch.

At the end of the fourteenth round, Ali was victorious. He had narrowly defeated Joe Frazier by a "technical knockout," when the fight was called by Frazier's trainer, Eddie Futch.

I could finally breathe, and tears of joy flooded down my face as Ali's gloved hand was held up in victory. Ali, now the undisputed heavyweight champion of the world, walked back to his corner as he gasped, one deep breath after another.

He was begging his trainer, Angelo Dundee, to cut his gloves off just before he turned to sit on the stool. As I wiped away the tears from my eyes, I then saw Ali's knees buckle. My heart stopped. Drew Bundini Brown, Ali's brother Rahman, and Ferdie Pacheco caught him and sat him down on the stool. He had given every last drop of himself that he had to give.

Odd that I never heard anyone ever mention that last step to the stool, but I know what I saw. The Champ had held on as long as it took to win, and that's why he was such an awe-inspiring, internationally adored warrior. He just never ever gave up.

Muhammad remained friends with me and Leon, and we shared many wonderful times together in the years that followed. The year after that bout, he invited us to his training camp in Deer Lake, Pennsylvania. We were flying in his private jet along with Howard Bingham (known for some of the most iconic photos of Ali ever taken), his cornerman Brown, Lloyd C. A. Wells (a close confidant of Ali's), and Rahman.

The weather got quite bumpy about a half hour out of Chicago. It was obvious that a few of us were nervous. Muhammad reassured us, "Hey. Don't worry, this used to be Elijah Muhammad's plane. It's been blessed by the Honorable Elijah Muhammad. It will never crash."

Then the very next instant the plane suddenly dropped several hundred feet, and everybody just stared at each other. But there was not a word. Then it dropped again, and Ali blurted out, "Is this thang fallin'?" and he bugged his eyes to get a reaction.

Leon laughed uneasily and said, "How could it fall? You said it's been blessed." Everyone chuckled half-heartedly.

Just then Leon turned to me jokingly and said, "Just my luck, if I die in a plane crash with Ali . . . no one will ever mention *my* name." That comment was so Leon.

The camp at Deer Lake was just that: a camp. It was serene and beautifully rustic, and a real home away from home, with log cabins scattered every-where. Pathways took you where you needed to go, and the land was uneven, giving it a wilderness vibe. Everyone made us feel welcomed, just like family. And his aunt, the chef, was incredible. I could easily see why Ali loved it there.

It was totally different hanging out with Muhammad privately. He was so quiet, introspective, and spiritual, and always so easy to talk to. Some days, he would hold "sessions" with the fans that came to visit. He would sit on a rock or a pile of logs, inviting me to sit with him and just talk. He would take pic-tures with the fans, answering all their questions about anything. Muhammad loved people. He loved teaching people. He loved being around people. As I sat there on the logs next to him, I was a sponge just soaking in all of his wisdom.

As I've mentioned, Muhammad had an incredible sense of humor and a very quick wit. He loved practical jokes and would often sneak up behind me and rub his fingers against his thumb right at my ear, making the sound of a cricket, which would invariably make me jump. He would do it with everybody and then with that warm, devilish, and disarming smile of his say, "You're the *real* champ."

When it was time to leave Deer Lake, Muhammad came to our cabin at about six a.m. and personally delivered our wake-up call. I still laugh at that. After we had breakfast, he grabbed *all* of our bags, all at once, throwing them under his arms and carrying the others in his hands. Muhammad loaded just the two of us onto his huge bus, he jumped in the driver's seat, and we headed toward the airport in a drive that took about an hour. We laughed at him all the way to the airport, and if that wasn't enough, he jumped out of the bus and loaded our bags onto the plane . . . just like he was our porter. . . . Muhammad Ali, the heavyweight champion of the world, chauffeuring us around, as if *we* were royalty.

But away from Deer Lake, you would find him as the Ali the public knew. The only time I ever saw him speechless was when I introduced him to my mom. He bear-hugged her and teasingly asked, "Who's the greatest of all time?" to which she proudly replied, "My husband." That did it. . . . He had no response for that sassy Ginny from Virginia.

Whenever we walked in public, he would walk behind Veronica and me, telling Leon, "Wait, wait, we'll just walk back a few paces. Look at them. Ain't they pretty? Just look at everybody looking at our women."

We were invited to his third wedding, when he married Veronica in 1977, and he even agreed to guest star in the movie *Body and Soul*, which Leon and I produced in 1981.

One day I was at the airport returning to Los Angeles. I didn't have any checked luggage, so I went straight to the curb awaiting my car service. As I exited the airport doors, there was Muhammad sitting on the hood of his shining Rolls-Royce parked at the curb, signing autographs. It was indeed a pretty unusual sight, seeing the most loved and recognized man in the world in public by himself—without his entourage.

When I asked him where he was off to, he casually said, "Nowhere." So, I asked, "Well, where are you coming from?" Again, Muhammad and his mind games . . . he said, "Nowhere." Then he gave me a big smile and said in his most genuine voice, "I was just sitting at home and decided to come out and sign some autographs. When I get tired, I'll go home." By then I figured he was fine, so I asked him if he needed anything. He said "Nope," and my car arrived shortly thereafter, and I went home.

And that's the way I will always remember my brother and close friend, Muhammad Ali, "The People's Champ."

Sitting on top of a dresser . . . or a pile of logs . . . or a Rolls-Royce . . . or on top of the world . . . just being himself and holding court.

## CHAPTER SEVENTEEN

# ADVENTURES IN PARADISE

I had made a conscious decision once we departed Cleveland for Hollywood that I would never allow myself to become anyone other than that home-spun girl from Ohio. I decided that if I had to inherently change who I was in order to achieve success, then it would not be worth it. Wickliffe would always be my home base, my safe haven. My plan was to go home as often as possible so that I could remain grounded. The best part about traveling so much back then was that I could always book a flight with a long layover in Cleveland and my parents would come to the airport to join me for lunch. Way before the intense security in airports today, people could actually walk through the airport without a ticket and even meet you at your arrival gate.

Whenever things got a little rough, I would go home, even if only for a few days. As it had always been in the past . . . my safety net was my family. I always thought, How could anyone ever make it in Hollywood without that? It takes incredible fortitude to maintain one's self-esteem in this business, and I always found strength in my family and in my husband.

I can't imagine being young, all alone, on my own, at audition after audition. Having to hear over and over how I was lacking: too tall, too short, too young, too old, too light, too dark, too much shape, not enough shape, hair too curly, not curly enough, lips not big enough, voice not right, too Black, not Black enough. It's no wonder that so many young, hopeful actresses become self-destructive in one way or another when they are continually being told day in and day out how they are not good enough—except to take to bed.

However, having my husband's and family's support did not mean I was immune to the darker side of Hollywood. The entertainment industry has a legendary and scandalous history full of sharks: males in power who sought and often demanded sexual favors for consideration or advancement. Most recently we've seen that this behavior is unfortunately not some relic of the past, with the likes of Harvey Weinstein, Matt Lauer, Bill Cosby, Charlie Rose, Russell Simmons, Sean "Diddy" Combs, and so many other powerful men who appear to have taken advantage of their positions within the patriarchal, male-dominated hierarchy of the industry.

Unfortunately, I (like all of the women of my era) did not have the #MeToo and #TimesUp movements to advocate on my behalf. It was still every woman for herself, and the men who held our careers in their hands knew all too well that we were easy prey and that for every one of us who stood up for ourselves (many times at a huge sacrifice), there were literally thousands of others who did not . . . so it was a pure numbers game to these predators, and the odds were *always* in their favor.

But because I had been fortunate enough to quickly book three major jobs when I first arrived in LA—*Rowan & Martin's Laugh-In*, *The Dean Martin Show*, and the Bob Hope USO Christmas show, "Bases Around the World," plus three other Bob Hope specials—I hadn't yet been exposed to that underbelly of the business. It wasn't long, however, before I witnessed firsthand what every young actor most fears about Tinseltown and its dirty little secrets.

In the summer of 1975, I had been asked to audition for a weather-girl role at a news station, even though I had no meteorological experience whatsoever.

It was just the producer and me in the news studio standing in front of the weather green screen. The camera was there as if set up for an audition, but no technician.

Producer: "We're going in a different direction for the afternoon weather slot."

Me: "Okay, and what would that be?"

Producer: "Well . . ." And then he looked at my boobs.

I immediately knew what was up. The approach he was interested in certainly had something to do with fronts—but nothing to do with the weather front. I walked out.

But I must also mention that I had an option to walk out. I had a husband. Many young actresses who did not have that support and backup, sadly, had to endure more demeaning treatment simply because there was no other option for them.

Soon after, I went to an audition for a movie at a hotel in Beverly Hills. The director was from Europe and had rented out a suite for the auditions, which was quite common at that time and from what I understand still was until recently, when new guidelines were put into place by the Producers Guild of America that established restrictions on where auditions can be held.

There were supposed to be other girls there, as well as the film's producer and casting director. When I walked in and the producer was the only one there, I instantly became cautious. He said I was a little early, so I should just wait. There were trays of refreshments around the room, and it was set up like a makeshift office, but something was wrong. Then he said that his neck was stiff from the long flight, and could I massage it for him? Reluctantly, I said yes, and before I knew it, he was trying to grab my leg. I walked out of that "audition" too.

There were so many of these stories that it was routine to expect that a problem would occur. But I will never forget what happened in 1976. British film producer John Marshall had somehow come into the rights to produce the life story of Muhammad Ali. Everyone was talking about this film set to star major Hollywood talent: Ali as himself, Ernest Borgnine, Robert Duvall, James Earl Jones, Roger E. Mosley, Paul Winfield, and many others.

Beverly McDermott was the casting director, and whoever landed the part of Belinda Ali (Ali's wife) would have the chance to make her mark in Hollywood. For six months or more, people were talking about the auditions before they even began. But John was an arrogant, bitter, racist, and vindictive man, and the word was out that he seemed determined to use this project to get into bed with as many Black actresses as he could, including me.

I'd known John long before and he had already made advances more than a few times and had gotten nowhere. I didn't expect to be asked to read for the part of Belinda Ali, even though everyone thought I should be cast as her because of our striking resemblance. Even Muhammad and Belinda both requested that I be given the part. Surprisingly, I did finally get an appointment to come in and read. I was cautiously optimistic, even given my contentious history with John.

The auditions were held at Columbia studios. When I arrived, there were two other actresses waiting to go in, and I knew them both (like I said, Black Hollywood was very small back then, and since there were so few lead roles for Black females we were always up for the same parts). One was Vonetta McGee. Vonetta had done several films with major Hollywood stars and was well-known for starring in *Thomasine & Bushrod*, directed by Gordon Parks Jr., along with her then husband, Max Julien (who also wrote the film for Columbia Pictures). Max and Vonetta were Black Hollywood royalty. Max was a writer/producer/actor, and he had just written *Cleopatra Jones* for Vonetta to star in, although the studio ultimately chose Tamara Dobson instead. However, they both had paid their dues and had some clout, given Hollywood's caste system for Black actors.

I liked Vonetta and Max a lot. I admired how they worked together and how down-to-earth they both were—they never put on "airs." I loved how unpredictable Max was, and how strong and self-assured Vonetta was. The only thing they both wanted was to be allowed to do the best work they possibly could, but Hollywood was not ready for such a young forward-thinking

Black couple with progressive ideas about filmmaking, so like most Blacks of that day in Hollywood their leverage was always conditional.

Vonetta went in to read before me. I was sitting in the waiting room getting more nervous by the second. I knew I was going to have trouble with John. He *knew* I didn't like him, on top of the fact that I always hated auditions to begin with.

Pretty soon I heard Vonetta's voice, loud and angry, but I couldn't make out what she was saying. I thought perhaps she had different sides (scenes) to read than I did.

I didn't think anything else about it until I saw Vonetta flying out of the room fuming. Then there was dead silence. No one moved. You could hear a pin drop. About two minutes went by and the next thing I knew, Max appeared through the door, and he was on the rampage. He stormed into John's office and exploded with fury. Anyone in their right mind knew that you didn't make Max mad. But apparently John, being a Brit, not living in Hollywood, and most importantly not knowing Max's reputation as a firebrand, didn't—and that made me so happy. John deserved exactly whatever Max was giving him. There was no sense of me staying around after that, and I just left.

A couple of weeks later, Leon and I were at a black-tie event at the swanky Century Plaza Hotel in Century City, and John came right up to the both of us, looked Leon directly in the eye, and then said to me, "This job could have been yours, if you'd sleep with me instead of him."

Even though I already knew he was unbearable, this was so much worse. I was outraged and abruptly interceded before Leon could say anything. "How dare you say that to me in front of my husband?" I couldn't believe his arrogance and gall. I couldn't resist and said, "You are so not worth it," and then I turned and walked away.

"That's what you say now," he called after me. "They all say that. 'I never want to see you again' . . . that is, until they need me."

I heard later that Lonette McKee got the part, but a couple of days into filming she walked off the set. She was a friend of ours and called Leon to get his advice regarding her stance. She had been made several promises, including a certain type of dressing room. When she got to the set it was not at all what she had expected, and she walked off the set until they honored the clauses in her contract. So, Leon asked her, "How many days have you shot?"

"None yet."

"Yeah, you kinda f—d up. If you had days in the can, they would have to listen to you, but now you have nothing to prevent them from just replacing you."

And that's exactly what they did. Annazette Chase ended up playing Belinda Ali opposite the real Muhammad Ali in the studio film *The Greatest*. I don't know how Lonette and Annazette managed to get the role without dealing with Marshall's harassment, but I never heard that either of them had any trouble with him.

After the Century City incident, I thought my problems with John Marshall were over, but again, Hollywood is small. Everywhere you go, you run into the same people, so I shouldn't have been surprised when I clashed with John yet again.

I was asked to audition for an NBC television series pilot called *Cover Girls*. It was right around the time of the huge hit ABC television series *Charlie's Angels*, for which I had also been considered as a replacement for Kate Jackson in the third season, when she left after disputes with the show's producers over scheduling.

I had heard that after I became a finalist they, not surprisingly, decided they couldn't risk casting a Black woman in Kate's slot for fear of losing the precious Southern affiliate TV stations.

*Cover Girls* was about two girls posing as international models who were undercover agents for the CIA. Their "boss" would be a then little-known actor by the name of Don Johnson, and their photographer, also working undercover, was Ellen Travolta (John Travolta's older sister). David Gerber (the show's producer) and Columbia studios had created *Cover Girls* with the hopes that it would have the same success as *Charlie's Angels*. That was a very common practice in Hollywood at the time (and still is to some extent); quicker than you could blink, copycat ideas of hit shows were already in production.

I was in the shower on the morning I got the call that one of the two leads on *Cover Girls* was being cast Black. It was 1977 and *Charlie's Angels* was ruling the airwaves. All the networks were rushing to find and feature sexy young women in action-related roles. This would be huge. A Black woman in the lead of a dramatic TV series had only been done twice: once with *Get Christie Love!* with Teresa Graves, and once with *Julia* starring Diahann Carroll.

My agent said I had to get over to the studio for an audition ASAP. No way could I get dressed in character like a model and still be there on time, so I raced to the interview with my hair still dripping wet and no makeup except for lipstick, which I also used for blush and eye shadow, hurriedly applied while driving erratically down the Ventura Freeway. Some look for an international model, right? The only saving grace was that I would hopefully be remembered, because certainly nobody else was going to come to an audition looking like this.

A couple days later, my agent called with the news that I had gotten a callback. They were very interested. The callback went well, and then I was asked to come in again . . . and again . . . and again. In fact, I lost count of the number of times I came in to "read," which was not typical. They called me back so many times they had to start paying me to audition, per SAG union rules.

But it was for a good reason. The producers were seriously interested in me for the role, but they just couldn't find the right "blond" to pair me up with. I thought Susan Anton would have been perfect. We knew each other already and had worked together a few times. She was smart, beautiful, blond, established, fabulously talented . . . and also five foot ten like me. But as much as I begged, they wouldn't call her in. On top of her talents, at the time she was dating Dudley Moore, who was soaring off the success of his film *10*, and I thought it would be amazing if they cast all three of us. Dudley, at less than five foot three, as the head of the agency with his two five-foot-ten model / CIA talents—Susan and me. . . . I would have still been receiving residuals to this day!

The producers had narrowed the search down to two African American women and three white women to screen test. The other Black actress was Tracy Reed of *Car Wash* fame. Interesting fact: People often asked me if I was the girl from *Car Wash*, her big hit film. Tracy and I were somewhat similar in our looks, and surprise . . . we were friends, like most of the young Black actresses in town, but I really, really wanted this part. This could very well be my "big break"—or hers—yet again.

Then there was the ever-present question: "She's so tall, who can we cast as her boyfriend?" When I heard this, I immediately called six-foot-three actor Bill Overton, who had just finished filming the TV version of *Guess Who's Coming to Dinner*, and I said, "Have your agent call Columbia . . . now!" We had already worked together on a modeling assignment cover shoot for a new magazine called *TWO* and I knew this would work. It was only a small part in the pilot, but if the series got picked up, he would be a regular on the show.

The day of the screen test came. We had all been in hair and makeup and were waiting our turn on the set. Lunchtime came around, so Tracy and I decided to go to the commissary to eat there instead of in our trailers. I put electric rollers in my hair to keep the set in for the screen test and we took off.

We were halfway through our lunch when none other than John Marshall came over to our table. He instantly became enraged, shouting, flailing his arms, saying to me, "How dare you come in here with your hair in rollers. You have no honor for your craft. What are you wearing—a robe? Who the hell do you think you are?" His ranting went on and on: "If it's the last thing I do, I will see to it that you *never* get this part."

With that, he stormed off, headed for David Gerber's office. I was furious—actors in wardrobe in the commissary was very common—but Tracy kept telling me not to let it get in my head or I wouldn't be able to do the scene later. I figured that was exactly what John was trying to do, so I just settled down. I decided to rethink my approach to the scene and use my anger to round out my character for the screen test.

Later that day after production had shut down, David came to me and said that John had indeed paid him a visit after seeing me at the commissary. He had proceeded to tell David all kinds of lies about me, making it sound like I was an absolute tramp, and flat out said that if I were hired, Columbia would have trouble with me because of the "morals clause" in the contract.

Thank God David already knew me—we had worked together several times before. Most prominently on the television series *Police Story* with David Janssen, as well as *Police Woman* with Angie Dickinson. I had made a positive impression on David on the set of *Police Woman*, where I played the part of a prison inmate dealing drugs.

After seeing the first day's dailies (clips of footage shot that day) on *Police Woman*, David had walked all the way across the lot and pulled me aside and said, "Jayne, you are so unlike most of the beautiful women that come through the gates here at Columbia. I admired the way you pulled your hair up in a ponytail and went without makeup in an ugly prison uniform to allow us to see the character. Remember this, when you are onstage, it's not you, it is the character you create that you want the audience to see." He went on to say how much he admired my overall character and my talent.

So, John Marshall's over-the-top ranting fell on deaf ears because David Gerber already knew me and respected my work.

Even though I was then officially cast for *Cover Girls*, they still were having no luck finding my partner. Finally, on a flight to New York to interview more girls, David saw an in-flight movie featuring Cornelia Sharpe. She had small parts in a few films, including *Serpico* starring Al Pacino, and he decided she was to be my other half. Despite David's belief in our costarring in the television pilot, Cornelia and I were very different. Not only did we lack on-screen chemistry together, but the pilot ended up airing opposite the NBA playoffs on CBS, and ABC aired back-to-back episodes of *Charlie's Angels* as counterprogramming. We didn't stand a chance. The *Cover Girls* pilot died a ratings nightmare and did not get picked up for the first season.

Of course I was disappointed that *Cover Girls* didn't go anywhere, but my determination to make it in the business never wavered. Every experience in front of the camera brought me closer to my goal. I was going to do this, it was only a matter of time—and at just twenty-five years of age, I knew I had all the time in the world.

Our lives were expanding so quickly. We had become accustomed to the pace of the ups and downs, but it never deterred us—it would simply mean, What's next?

Whenever our dear friend Reverend Ike came to town, we'd meet him at his home high on the bluffs above the Pacific Ocean in Palos Verdes and head out to some fabulous restaurant for dinner in one of his Bentleys. We had the regular Friday night movie screenings and Sunday dinners with Sammy Davis Jr. and his wife, Altovise. Leon was welcomed at the Playboy Mansion whenever he wanted, and we went to many of Hef's star-studded parties.

Smokey and Claudette Robinson were always invited to shows and concerts, and we'd often go along. The four of us were constantly popping up anywhere and everywhere. Living in Pasadena was a real challenge in terms of the many meetings we had in town and the distance and time it took to go back and forth, so Claudette's became the hangout. By then, Leon owned various nightclubs, so we were welcomed at all the other clubs in town; having something to do was never a problem. And if we didn't feel like a night of hanging out, we'd just go over to Lamonte's and play backgammon until three in the morning, then fall asleep in what he eventually called Leon and Jayne's room.

Some days we'd play poolside at Richard Pryor's house in Encino, laughing nonstop at his crazy self. One of Richard's great ambitions was to produce and star as the character Cyrano de Bergerac in a movie, but the industry never took him seriously. Richard wanted me to play Roxanne, his love. After many meetings on developing a script, Richard's whole life changed when he was accidentally burned, and the Cyrano project vanished.

Then it would be back to Los Angeles for a party at Berry Gordy's home in the hills of Bel Air, or Diana Ross's in Beverly Hills, or Johnny Mathis's with his indoor swimming pool in the Hollywood Hills. Or maybe we'd hang out with Dick Van Patten and his family and play a little tennis. Or maybe it was tennis with Marilyn McCoo and Billy Davis Jr. It was never-ending.

Leon and I loved all the benefits of being up-and-coming celebrities because it meant we were getting closer and closer to closing the deal on our ten-year plan, and life was really very good. Happily married, we were enjoying the benefits of success, and for us there was no end in sight. We worked hard, played hard, and, having an uncanny business savvy, were always looking for ways to have a leg up on our competition. Being a celebrity was never my endgame, but it certainly had its rewards.

# CHAPTER EIGHTEEN

# IT'S JAYNE OR NOBODY

Sports was in my blood. It was practically a family tradition. With my Dad having had five daughters before he finally had a son, he often treated his daughters like sons. Dad was an amazing catcher on his company baseball team and our church team, and every game he traveled with his own personal cheer team piled in the back of his pickup as we watched him point to the outfield just like Babe Ruth and slug in the winning home run. Or we'd watch him literally take out the runner who dared to withstand his trash talk and attempt coming into home base, only to be flipped over Dad's shoulder.

Every Saturday night we'd watch the wrestling matches with him: Bobo Brazil and his famous "Coco Butt" knockout maneuver, and Haystacks Muldoon, who only had to sit on you to win. During football season we cheered on the Cleveland Browns and the mighty Jim Brown—that's what got me hooked on football. How could you live in Cleveland during the 1960s and not be a Browns fan? Then there was the "crosstown" rivalry with the Pittsburgh Steelers that started back in the 1950s. That was hard for me in the 1970s, because I loved the Steel Curtain. And of course I couldn't forget the Dallas Cowboys. I became a Cowboys fan because my cousin's boyfriend, who played for the Cowboys, bought me a banana ice-cream cone one day that was so good. Little did he know that on that day he had bought a fan for life.

Growing up, even though there was no Title IX for girls to participate in sports back then, I participated in the Junior Olympics in the standing broad jump and softball throw. In fifth grade I was the softball throw champion. In middle school I wanted to be anywhere near football, so I became a cheerleader. In high school I recruited and captained the girls' basketball champions and the girls' volleyball champs. When I fell through a glass door in eighth grade, landing in a pile of glass on the driveway that nearly cut off my left hand, leaving me with sixty-five stitches and a cast, the only thing I was worried about was whether I would be cut from the cheer squad tryouts. Instead, I was made captain.

In high school, I served as captain of the varsity football and basketball cheerleaders, the wrestling team cheer squad, and the JV football and basketball cheerleaders. And in the spring, since there were no cheerleaders for track and field, I became their statistician just so I could ride the bus to the meets. I just needed to be near the sport. Yeah, that was me. Every fall I'd take a deep breath, smell the changing of the leaves, feel the crisp wind blowing in my hair, and let the words out slowly: "*Aaahhhhhhh*, football weather."

It was spring 1978, and I was only eight years out of high school. Word was out that there was an opening on the desk of CBS's *The NFL Today* for a female co-anchor when Phyllis George left to be the host for a brief stint on the *People* magazine show. I knew that job was for me, that if I could get it, it could, in fact, be the turning point for my career. How many times had I said that before? But here, this time, if I managed to pull this off, my name would be instantly marketable.

I immediately contacted my agent at International Creative Management (ICM) to get me in for an audition. He turned me down, saying they were only submitting journalists. I had seen the list, and I knew that was a lie. I told him I knew I could do the job, but there was no talking him into it. He said that there was no way CBS would ever consider a Black woman.

ICM did submit a long list of talent, but there was no mention of Jayne Kennedy. When no one on ICM's first list was selected, a second list was compiled. Again, I asked to be put on the list. Again, I was turned down. After the third list did not include me, nor did any of their submissions get selected, I decided that the only way I was going to get an audition was to find someone else with a connection to CBS myself.

Leon and I came up with a plan to reach out to our friend Jay Bernstein, who was managing Farrah Fawcett at the time and would often offer us advice. Jay was sure I'd be a major star, but being a co-anchor on *The NFL Today* didn't fit into his star-maker formula. He was also concerned because I had such a squeaky-clean reputation that I was "too boring" to book any press or major magazine covers. He told me he was really swamped, and that while he could see me on *The NFL Today* desk, he was just too busy to pursue CBS on my behalf.

Then Leon called his friend Jim Brown, and Jim suggested I speak with CBS sports producer Bob Stenner, which I did. Bob set up a meeting for me to meet with George Wallach, who was managing the 1976 Olympic decathlon gold medalist Caitlyn Jenner. When I arrived, he was immediately sold on the idea of me auditioning for *The NFL Today* and called Linda Sutter, head of talent for CBS Sports, on the spot. She said she was coming from New York to Los Angeles the very next week and we could meet at George's Century City office. George and I agreed that if I landed the job, then he would officially be my manager. Now I had one foot in the door.

My meeting with George and Linda went exceedingly well, and Linda arranged for me to come to New York for the on-camera audition with Brent Musburger on *The NFL Today* set.

I had been in the entertainment business for eight years at that point, and I was completely aware that auditions were very unpredictable. It could be a long, drawn-out showcase where you would really get a chance to make your mark, or it could be a total bust: "Hi. I'm Jayne Kennedy." And they'd say, "Thank you very much." Wham-bam, thank-you-ma'am, and you're out the door.

It just so happened that Don King and Caesars Palace were throwing the International Sportsman Ball on June 8, 1978, the day before the Ken Norton versus Larry Holmes fight in Las Vegas and the Thursday night before my Sunday CBS audition. Leon and I were going to the ball, and I planned to leave for New York after the fight Friday night. So, we decided this was a perfect opportunity to gather some interview footage. Once we arrived, we borrowed a camera and crew from our friend Jim Hill, a CBS Sports anchor in Los Angeles, so that I could record some interview footage to take along with me to the audition. (Remember this was 1978—VCRs, camcorders, and cell phones were a thing of the future. Even in the early 1980s, people were only just beginning to have personal camcorders.)

I first asked Don King if he would be willing to be interviewed for my audition. I knew Don from many years back, and I had even assisted him in landing an interview with the press from Hong Kong at the "Thrilla in Manila." I had no doubt that his answer would be "Of course." Then I saw Julius Erving, and he also said yes. The great Minnesota Fats was sitting behind me at the ball, and I asked him for an interview as well, and when he agreed I was three-for-three. Jim Hill, Leon, and I put together the quickest interviews that you could ever imagine, and after the fight I raced to the airport and jumped onto the red-eye to New York with my unedited interviews tucked under my arm.

When I arrived at the Essex House Hotel in New York, there was a package of instructions and information for the audition, which would take place on Sunday at the CBS Studios on Fifty-Seventh Street. I spent the day researching and reviewing the packet outlining the process. The audition would be in three parts: some on-camera repartee with Brent, a segment reading teleprompter copy, and an in-studio interview with an NFL player TBD. CBS decided to give all the women who were auditioning equal time and access in preparation for the interview, so they didn't reveal the name of the player we would be interviewing until late Saturday night.

When I got my interview pack, it had a name, a position, a team, and a sentence that said something about the player working with children with disabilities in the off-season. That was pretty much it—a few statistics, but not much to do an interview. Libraries were closed on Saturday night, and this was long before the internet or Google for doing any last-minute research, so there were zero resources whatsoever.

My NFL player interviewee was Clyde Powers, a strong safety who I did not know. All during dinner, which I ate in my room, I kept going back to the feature I had just seen on life in the NFL trenches—the kill-or-be-killed war mentality required to do the job well. I decided to make that the focus of our interview: How did he balance his game head with his desire to help people with disabilities?

Just before I went to bed, I called my friend ex-NBA player Ron Allen. I asked him what he thought were my best qualities. He never hesitated: "Jayne, everybody I know always talks about how unassuming and unpretentious you are. You're so easy to talk to. You make people feel like they can open up to you without being threatened. However, when they first see you, they see your beauty and they are intimidated, but then you speak and you're so warm, with your feet on the ground. That's why guys like talking to you. They don't expect it because of the way you look, and then when you smile, it's like the smile of an old friend. It doesn't matter who you are interviewing or what the interview is about, if you can make that person tomorrow feel like that, then you've got it made."

I thought about that all night. I had never realized *any* of that before, and the information helped to calm me down quite a bit, even though it all came as quite a surprise.

Sunday morning, I walked into the CBS Studios fully prepared to do my best, and if I didn't get a chance to do just that, I still had the taped Vegas interviews in hand. I felt very good about this whole thing, even though I still hated auditions. This was my dream job, and I was ready.

As soon as I walked into the conference room, all my hopes and dreams went down the toilet. There were about fifteen other girls there for the audition and they *all* had blond hair. There was no way CBS was seriously considering *me*. Here I was again, the token Black girl.

I didn't know what to do. It seemed like such a waste of time and energy. But since I was there, I decided to just relax and have fun with the day and chalk it up to another one for the books. All that morning the girls were racing around furiously, trying to get their act together for their scheduled appearance on the set. I sat and watched. It was Miami all over again—Miss Ohio sitting on the sidelines because the Black girl's not going to win. I ate some potato chips, which I never do before I go on camera, but I wasn't worried, because I was not going to get the job. When the three guys scheduled to be interviewed walked into the makeup room, they were swarmed like bees to honey, everybody trying to get a tidbit of secret information. Each of us would have a chance at one of the three. I sat back and watched, amused.

When all the girls left the makeup room headed for their dressing rooms, only the guys were left, waiting for their turn in the makeup chairs. Ever since I started in the industry, I almost always did my own makeup, so I was already done. I kept thinking about what Ron had told me the night before, to just be myself and make a friend. Earlier, I happened to see a backgammon board in the corner of the room, so I introduced myself to my interviewee and asked him if he played backgammon, and his eyes lit up. "Yes, I do," he said.

The question wasn't as odd as it sounds. At that time, everyone was hyped about playing backgammon. There was even a very ritzy dinner/dance club in Beverly Hills called PIPS where the Hollywood elite played backgammon every night. It was a private club, so Marc Gordon, then manager for the 5th Dimension and my very first manager, would often take Leon and me, and we would play for hours while we networked. On any given night when Lamonte was in town, you could find Leon and me playing backgammon at Lamonte's estate high up in the hills of Encino, often until five o'clock in the morning.

I knew I'd be comfortable playing with this guy while we waited, comfortable enough to make a friend. By the time we got to the set, we were old friends, and we had a blast finally getting a chance to talk about football, about maintaining your dignity, about the fine line professional athletes walk in the struggle to realize the important battles in life. At least that's what I remember . . . and it all went great.

I was almost the last girl to be interviewed. I had completed my teleprompter reading, and my interview with Brent, and now I had just ended my interview with Clyde. I remember Brent immediately standing up and leaving when I finished, and then I left the studio.

I went back to LA pleased that I had performed well, and I was so hoping and praying that I would land the job, though never actually believing I would. I was truly shocked when I got the call from CBS a month later.

Leon and I were standing in our dining room with the phone held between the two of us, struggling to hear every word. We jumped up and down laughing, hugging, and crying like little kids who just won the peewee league playoffs. This was huge, and we both knew it. We had crossed another important barrier. It was meant to be. I remember it was July 11. 7/11. Lucky me.

I heard later when Brent got up immediately after my interview he declared, "It's Jayne or nobody." He never finished auditioning the other girls after me, and I don't think anyone ever looked at my Las Vegas interview tape that I had left with the producer and director. Brent had decided right there on the spot. Apparently, he was impressed with my knowledge of the game and how I had actually listened to the athlete. The fact that here was someone who could master an interview for the profile segments that the show thrived on was a hands-down done deal in Brent's mind.

Later I found out that it wasn't an easy task for CBS to hire me. When Brent decided he wanted me on the desk with him, the producer, Mike Pearl, agreed that I was the right choice. The director, Bob Fishman; the director of program development, Kevin O'Malley; and the president of CBS Sports, Frank Smith, also agreed on my selection.

In 2022, Rich Podolsky, who had been a writer on *The NFL Today*, authored the book *You Are Looking Live! How* The NFL Today *Revolutionized*

*Sports Broadcasting*. In it he quotes Kevin O'Malley as saying, "It was unanimous. And I remember Fishman saying, 'You couldn't make her look any more gorgeous if you tried.'"

Then CBS brought me back to New York to take me to dinner.

Rich went on to write, "That night they took her to Quo Vadis, where Jackie Kennedy and other celebrities often dined. It was commonly referred to as the last bastion of *grande luxe* dining in New York. 'Jayne was wearing a clinging silver lamé pants suit and looked beyond stunning,' recalled O'Malley. 'When we walked into the dining room, conversation stopped everywhere, and every man in the room dropped his jaw.' She thought the job was hers."

However, with me added to the desk, the set would become a white man front and center with a Black person on either side. And with two Blacks and one white, that would present a problem with the Southern affiliate television stations.

My audition tape was sent out for the Southern affiliates to review, and they all decided I was their choice but they would have to try to work something out to keep me on board. To change the racial dynamics, Jimmy "the Greek" Snyder was added to the anchor desk. Jimmy had been with the show, but not on the anchor desk. Problem solved: one Black, one white, one Black, and one white—me, Brent Musburger, Irv Cross, and Jimmy—with Jack Whitaker covering special features.

According to Rich Podolsky's book, when Van Gordon Sauter (who had replaced Frank Smith as president of CBS Sports) was asked if he was aware of the challenges I faced in my hiring process, he said, "'It would hardly surprise me that forty-two years ago a confidential poll of the Southern affiliates, or confidential poll within the CBS Broadcast Group on West 52nd Street, would reflect a general resistance to a 2-1 Black/white talent ratio." Podolsky then went on to say, "Race was an issue in the urban markets. Representation was critical. And that could be arcane. But I think a strong case could be made at that time, in Sports, for a Black male anchor, a Black female co-anchor and a white co-anchor."

\* \* \*

When I was hired to co-anchor the Emmy Award–winning CBS *The NFL Today* in 1978, I became the first African American female broadcaster on the first live nationally broadcast pregame show. And there have only been two women to hold that position in its half-century history. It was groundbreaking, and the press had a field day: lots of positive but so much more negative. I am eternally thankful that this was a predigital news-cycle era—no platforms such as Instagram, Facebook, X, or the myriad of other online resources. Journalists resented the idea that a woman held that spot, but what was worse to them was that it was a Black woman. I often wonder what the full impact was when I appeared on the set that first day.

It was initially only a six-week contract. They were extremely concerned that the Southern television affiliates would pull out of the show because it was another Black person (as well as a Black *woman*) on the desk, and they already had a Black person on the set with Irv Cross. At that time, having two Black people on at once was considered a huge risk, even though Brent Musburger (who was white) was on the team as well. I knew immediately that I had to prove I was worthy. I was to remain living in LA and fly in to do the show every weekend. If I worked out, then I would be picked up for one year.

My second week at CBS I overheard a very heated conversation at the *Sports Spectacular* desk between the producers and the CBS business affairs team:

"What are we supposed to run if we don't get that video in time?"

"Then we run a different segment."

"We're talking about Ali versus Spinks at the Superdome . . . and we're the network with no post-fight interview? That can't happen. We'll all be on the unemployment line."

"But they're asking too much, and that's outside of what we are prepared to pay."

I gathered that there was something going on with Ali's lawyers, and the producers couldn't secure an interview. Well, this is when knowing someone matters.

"Excuse me," I said as I put my hand up.

The producers looked at me like they'd never seen me before.

"Are you talking about Ali?"

"Maybe. Who are you? And why do you want to know?"

"I can get you the interview."

They all turned to look at me quizzically from head to toe.

"If you send me to New Orleans with a crew, I will have an Ali interview by showtime tomorrow."

I let them take that in as they scratched their heads.

"Do you want the Ali interview . . . or not?"

After they huddled together in a mini town hall meeting, they agreed—but only because they were desperate.

To this day I have no idea why they believed me. But when I asked them to give me a private jet and a crew and said I'd come back with the interview on Saturday morning in time for their *Sports Spectacular* afternoon show, they dropped everything and made it happen.

I left New York for New Orleans Friday afternoon on CBS's private jet as the only passenger on board. I would meet my crew in New Orleans. I had called Ali ahead of time and asked if he could make this happen. He said he would leave the key to his suite at the front desk and told me to have the crew set up and ready to shoot before he went to the official post-fight press conference. He'd come to the suite immediately after the fight for just a few minutes and grant me the interview. Of course, my adrenaline was running at 500 percent. My mind was racing as we sat in the suite waiting for his grand entrance: Was this really going to happen? Did I miss any signals? Would some attorney suddenly appear and crash the whole thing? But Ali had always been a gentleman and a man of his word to *me*. I took a deep breath and waited, mulling over my short list of questions. We would only have five precious minutes of his time.

Winning the fight in the fifteenth round on a unanimous decision, Muhammad sure enough walked into his suite just as he'd promised, exhausted but in good humor. He entered through the door—looking dizzy and tired, his hands sore—and walked directly up to our camera as if he were about to punch the lens out and said, "I'd *only* do this for my friend Jayne." And as we went into the interview, he said to me, *"I'm only granting you something special because you are the greatest just like I am the greatest."*

We got the interview wrapped up and then he was quickly whisked away to the real post-fight interviews.

I jumped back onboard the jet and flew straight to New York. It was edited in the morning and by their afternoon show . . . there was Muhammad Ali on *CBS Sports Spectacular*. They were gracious enough to cut a companion piece of the interview exclusively for my segment on *The NFL Today*. Now mind you, I didn't even work for them; I was hired to work the desk of *The NFL Today*. *Sports Spectacular* services were not a part of my contract. I had zero obligations to them. But I knew if I pulled this off, they would no longer be asking "Who are you?"

I flew back to Los Angeles on the Sunday night nine p.m. flight exhausted, and passed out.

By the time I woke up Monday morning, my six-week contract had been extended and picked up for the remainder of the year.

CHAPTER NINETEEN

# LA NIGHTLIFE
# AND THE CIRCUS

When I landed the job on *The NFL Today*, Leon and I had been building a string of nightclubs for several years. That same year, we opened a new nightclub in Hollywood. In the early years, everything we did we planned together, and that was no different with this club. We converted a warehouse into a very high-tech space with trapeze artists and other circus features. I named it Circus Disco.

I researched and designed the entire club, creating all the layouts, and Leon with his partners, Gene and Eddy, carried it all off spectacularly—Gene was brilliant in that capacity. The four of us made a perfect partnership and turned Circus Disco into one of the premier discos in LA.

The public relations and promotions were my responsibility as well. Many times, you could catch me in any nearby parking lot placing flyers, which I had designed myself, on the windshields of every single car. I never really enjoyed hanging out at nightclubs, so it was a rare occasion that you would actually find me there.

By the time I met Leon, even though he was only twenty-two years old, he was already a full-blown entrepreneur. As we got to know each other, I realized that part of his philosophy was that a "big-time disc jockey" should make four times whatever their salary was from outside activities leveraged from their fame. Today's celebrities, such as the Kardashians, being paid to show up for appearances is nothing new. Leon was doing this way back in the late 1960s: being paid for personal appearances and events at supermarkets, car dealerships, birthdays, special anniversaries, and state fairs. When I saw that in him, I realized we were both on the same path. After Miss Ohio, I was leveraging my name awareness as well.

For Leon, another source of lucrative income was "record hops," playing records at different venues, with fans showing up to see him spin and do his Leon-isms—an early version of rapping or talking over the beat as the record plays. This evolved into having special nights at specific nightclubs. Whether he was in Detroit, Washington, DC, or Houston, there were long lines of fans to hear him "do his thing" over the records while they danced. It was like the big band era, only in this case there was no big band and no singer—and people loved it!

When we were married and moved to Los Angeles, it was a natural evolution for Leon to continue this trend. Our first nightclub was Disco 1985 in the heart of Hollywood. It was 1972 and our ten-year plan was just starting to take shape. The club was not glamorous at all. But once you stepped inside, the music took you away.

Long before the infamous Viper Room or, on a larger scale, New York's legendary Studio 54, Disco 1985 became LA's celebrity nightspot. It was written up in *Jet*, *Soul*, and many other publications as the *must-see* spot to visit. On any given night, among the beautiful people, you would see Richard Roundtree (hot from starring in *Shaft*), heavyweight champion Ken Norton, The 5th Dimension, Smokey Robinson, Freda and Scherrie Payne, The Supremes' Mary Wilson and Cindy Birdsong, Marvin Gaye, Stevie Wonder, Claudette Robinson, and so many more.

Looking back, we accomplished so many firsts, and this venue was the very first Black nightclub in Hollywood. That sounds great, but there was tremendous pushback from the local authorities—mainly, the police department, the fire department, and the chamber of commerce. The racial prejudice in LA was so rampant that they did not want Blacks congregating in Hollywood, whether they were award-winning celebrities or not.

Initially, we wondered why there was so much negative attention; it seemed like every other week the fire department showed up to see if there were any violations, threatening to shut it down. We couldn't understand why it felt like the police were constantly harassing Leon, the other club owners, and our patrons, for absolutely nothing... and in some cases, fabricated nothings. It became so constant that it appeared we were going to be closed down. It was then that we decided to enhance our friendships with the only two Black LA city council members: Councilman David Cunningham and Councilman Robert Farrell. I can't count the number of times that Leon would have to call them in the middle of a Friday or Saturday night exclaiming, "Robert, the fire department is here, threatening to throw everybody out and close down the club." These great friends would immediately rush to the club to talk with the police chief or the fire chief to prevent the shutdown.

It was then that we figured out that we'd have to be political and make inroads with whoever was in power. We knew many in city hall and the mayor's office, but you don't call them to run down in the middle of the night. So we would meet certain politicians and form alliances and friendships in order to grow our business and counter the various obstacles.

You may be wondering why I'm focusing on the clubs as part of my memoir journey, but if you probe a little deeper, it highlights another important layer of my life. From the day we married, there was never any separation (i.e., *my* career or *his* projects). It was always *us*. From day one, Leon was involved and assisted in everything I did or was aspiring to do ... and vice versa. Even back with Leon's TV show *Outta Sight*, we used to build the sets together. Leon would be the first to say that I was much more artistic than he was.

In retrospect, the nightclub business brought in income that gave us the financial freedom to pursue our careers. We were never starving would-be artists. We had our ten-year plan, and the clubs gave us the financial clout to fuel our goals and ambitions.

We thought the timing would be perfect to announce my CBS job and the opening of Circus Disco with my twenty-seventh birthday party held at the club. We pulled out all the stops. Mom and Dad flew in from Cleveland, and the A-list guests went on forever, with media and celebrities—even Brent Musburger came. The morning of the party, I went to the camera store down the hill to pick up some film. When I came out, I saw a small trail of smoke at the top of the mountain to the east, but I didn't think anything about it. Being from Ohio, I was totally unfamiliar with California's history of wildfires.

By the afternoon the whole top of the mountain was on fire. By five p.m. the fire department was knocking on doors, putting us on notice for a potential evacuation. The party was starting at seven p.m. What were we going to do? I called Uncle Hank, and he raced over with his pickup truck. We started loading our personal and irreplaceable items into his truck as the fire was coming down the mountain.

By six p.m. Uncle Hank had climbed on top of the roof and started watering down the house with one of our hoses. I grabbed the other hose and climbed on top of the roof with Uncle Hank and told everyone else to go with Leon, we'd be there soon. There was no way I was going to let my home go up in flames. I could have another birthday party the next year.

By nine p.m. Hank and I were exhausted. The fire seemed to have shifted direction, so we gave in. He drove home, with the back of his truck still loaded to the brim with everything we held dear. I went inside, changed, and drove to the party. By the time I arrived all the prearranged media had left, along with many of the guests. But everyone who was still there partied into the wee hours of the morning. I didn't know what we would drive home to see, but I couldn't do anything about it anymore. When we pulled through the gates to our driveway, the house was still standing.

I quietly thanked God.

## CHAPTER TWENTY

# ALL THAT GLITTERS IS NOT GOLD

My typical week while I worked on *The NFL Today* was incredibly hectic. On Monday, I was home in Pasadena. I got up late and tried to catch up on other aspects of my life—husband, home, and other work. Tuesday, I spent preparing for the NFL Films interviews I did week to week. Because most of them were on the other side of the Mississippi, I normally flew out on Tuesday, did the interview Wednesday, and flew back home Wednesday night. Thursday was scheduled with interviews, publicity, meetings, and so on, and then Friday was filled with collecting information for that week's game. I flew to New York every Friday night on the United red-eye with Brent. He was living in LA then and was working the five p.m. news anchor desk for KNXT (now KCBS), the local CBS station.

The Boeing 747 was fairly new then and passengers were unaware that it was available as a lounge. Most of the time the upper deck was empty, so the flight attendants would save it for us. Eventually it was converted to first-class seating. I could stretch out and sleep all the way to New York, arrive about six thirty a.m., taxi into Manhattan, check into my hotel room, and crash. Originally CBS always booked me at the Essex House, which was not my cup of tea. Eventually I convinced them to put me up at the UN Plaza Hotel, my favorite. I would sleep late, get up, pore over information, and make phone calls for the show the next day.

Saturday nights, I did the "glam" thing with hair, nails, wardrobe, and one-hour bubble baths; grabbed dinner from room service; and then studied into the night under the hair dryer. I would get to bed about two a.m., then get up early on Sunday and go to the studio, into makeup and hair, and finally go on set by eleven thirty a.m. for our first *live* show at twelve thirty p.m.

The challenge with *The NFL Today* was in the logistics of broadcasting a live national show, not in doing the actual sports broadcast. Covering the sports aspect would be much easier if you did not have to concern yourself with the challenges of time zone changes. When you're sitting in your living room watching your favorite game of the week, you don't realize the myriad complexities that go into making that show look like a nice, friendly, and smooth update. Behind the scenes it was anything but.

On air, there were four people on the desk in a semi-unscripted half-hour show. Everyone had to be aware of not talking over each other and not hogging the mic. I wore my earpiece in my right ear, listening to everything that went on in the director's booth as he called out instructions to the crew and the talent, particularly the countdowns. All while chatting with my on-air cohosts.

There were huge banks of wall monitors to the right that showed all the games in progress across the country, all with their own start times, greatly influenced by what time zone the games were in. East coast games typically came first, with maybe three locations covered. By the time halftime came, we were now covering the start of games across mid-America. There was also the monitor at my desk, where I watched replays and highlights as they were broadcast within our show. The statisticians were behind us, collecting information. From time to time they would hand notes to me from behind or under the desk, behind the chair, or wherever they could, while still off camera.

We did not have the joy of digital technology. Everything was done by handwritten notes. During all of this activity, I had to be prepared for the countdown in my ear from the director for any segment I was involved in. After some light banter with Brent, I would read my scripted intro to the NFL Films segments done earlier in the week, and whatever else came up, all while chatting with the other cohosts in front of the millions of people in the television audience—with some no doubt just waiting for me to screw up.

They almost got their chance right out of the gate. My very first show, my very first interview, my very first live intro to tape—and there was no tape. The director was talking to the tape room, and at the same time talking to me in my earpiece:

"Jayne, you're gonna have to wing it. The tape machine just ate up your tape."

I could see the countdown . . . 6, 5, 4, 3 . . .

UGGGGGGGHHHHH.

"Coming to youuu . . . *NOW*."

The camera light lit up and I went on cool and calm. No problem.

Thank God my first interview was with the head coach of the Cleveland Browns, my home team. I swallowed hard, smiled, turned to Brent, and talked about Coach Sam Rutigliano's approach for the Cleveland Browns in the upcoming season. Sam's a great guy, and I loved the Browns, so I already had lots of info in my head to fill up the time. I didn't break a sweat.

While viewers may watch one or two games on any given Sunday, we covered almost all of them. At twelve thirty p.m., we had the live pregame show for the East Coast games. An hour later, we had the one thirty p.m. show for the games that were starting in the central time zone. By then it was time to do halftime commentary for the East Coast games, though they rarely were occurring at the same time, which meant we could end up doing several halftime shows with some of them overlapping. Then came the halftime reports for the central time zone games, while simultaneously prepping pregame shows for the Pacific coast games while also starting the cycle of East Coast *post*game shows. I'm simplifying it greatly, but you get the idea—it was like herding cats with no way to predict the timing—*and it was all live.*

When Brent Musburger would say "You are looking live," it was truly a *big deal* in the world of sports broadcasting. The concept of live pregame shows with real-time updates and footage was brand-new. *The NFL Today* was changing the trajectory of how sports shows would be made forever. And back then we were doing it all in a half hour.

After the broadcast, Brent and I would rush to catch our flight back to LA, arriving home at LAX in the wee hours of the morning, then I would jump into the limo for the one-hour ride to Pasadena.

I wanted to be successful as a co-anchor, and I begged CBS for an instructor to properly train me for this process. The network said no. I begged for a small apartment in NYC, so I wouldn't have to drag all my things back and forth between New York and LA every week. The network said no. Being on national television, it was important to look my best, so I begged for a wardrobe allowance. The network said no. My salary wasn't enough to rent my own apartment, but I took the initiative to go to a small Black-owned clothier in New York called Zagobi Boutique.

It didn't take much to convince the wonderful owner to provide me with a wardrobe each Sunday for the studio portion of the show. In fact, they were honored; they were very proud that a Black woman had such an opportunity. Each Saturday morning when I arrived at my New York hotel, there was a garment bag hanging at the front desk with a choice of three complete outfits. The one thing CBS *did* agree to was including end credits on the show: *Jayne Kennedy's wardrobe provided by Zagobi Boutique.*

But *The NFL Today* changed my life in so many wonderful ways. The best part was working with the *real* stars—the guys playing on the field. Being a celebrity was never my reason for doing what I did; I just loved the work. I loved it more than any other job I could ever imagine. But there were also the trappings that went along with being in the limelight. It became nearly impossible to go anywhere without someone asking about the show, with the most common question being "So what do you think about the game this week?" As it turned out, it was merely a prelude for them to let me know what *they* thought of the game that week. When I went to the gym, I could never get through one piece of equipment without the owner cornering me with his version of the "lowdown" on the touchdowns. In the restroom, at the airport, and even at church, I was constantly approached about football and the show. One of my pet peeves was when someone asked for an autograph at church. I always replied, "This is the Lord's day, not mine." Even years after, when I no longer worked on *The NFL Today* and I was being wheeled into the labor and delivery room with my first child, one of the nurses tapped me on the shoulder between contractions, asking, "So what do you think about Chicago?"

The second-most common question was invariably "What's Jimmy 'the Greek' really like?"

I can't say what Jimmy was really like, because I didn't know him all that well; I only worked with him on Sundays for six months a year for two years. But from my experiences I'd have to describe Jimmy as a big, angry teddy bear, a roughneck guy who was a bit spoiled. I don't think he would have agreed with me, but that's the way I saw him. All his life he got to play. His private life was very challenging for reasons I didn't know at first—he dedicated much of his joy to his ailing daughter. Three of his children had cystic fibrosis. He loved and believed in what he did. Jimmy always seemed to be on the edge, so eager to express his opinions, but he didn't really like it when I expressed mine. Let me give you a perfect example.

There were a few guys in the league who I would call to get a sense of what was happening inside the different ball clubs. It helped to get an understanding of the players—they became real friends, who just happened to become excellent sources of information. What I always tried to bring to *The NFL Today* was . . . who's the *real* person behind the number on the jersey?

One such player was Tampa Bay's quarterback, Doug Williams. Doug, an All-America quarterback from Grambling State, was an amazing athlete who destroyed the myth that Blacks could not be NFL quarterbacks. I first met Doug in Baton Rouge in 1978 at a nightclub. He had been drafted that year by

Tampa Bay, and when we met, his jaw was wired shut after being crushed in a mid-season game. A year later when we met again and quickly became good friends, he had gone from rookie to starting quarterback for the Buccaneers.

Tampa Bay was a fairly new club (having joined the NFL in 1976) when they found themselves in the divisional playoffs for the first time, playing against the Philadelphia Eagles. Everybody was picking Philadelphia to win. The week leading up to the playoffs, everyone was filled with excitement about the upcoming game, including me. So, when Doug called and invited me to dinner at his house with some of his teammates, I decided I would do the cooking. Tight end Jimmie Giles picked me up and took me to the market to get everything needed for the meal. I even remember my menu: trout with wild rice stuffing sprinkled with slivered almonds, with a side of broccoli in butter sauce. There must have been maybe ten guys there, and we laughed so hard and had a great time, giving me an opportunity to get to know the players much better.

Game day, the whole town was on fire. Tampa Bay was truly pumped for its first-ever divisional playoff game. I was on the set, which was built into the stands in the end zone—the back wall opened up to the field. The fans were clamoring around the set yelling behind us, and the energy at Tampa Stadium was frenetic.

We were in the middle of the pregame show when Brent asked me about my cooking dinner for the team the night before, and then he asked me who my pick was for the game. I hadn't expected to be asked, but I gave my opinion without hesitation: Although I really liked the Philadelphia Eagles and Coach Dick Vermeil, I picked the Tampa Bay Buccaneers. I said I thought Tampa Bay was coming into the game very underrated and that key members of the offensive line who had been out sick and injured would be returning that day. That meant there would be more pass protection for Doug, who was totally psyched for the game. I brought up a few other reasons why I believed Tampa Bay had a shot at winning. When I finished my analysis, they all laughed at me, and Jimmy clearly gave me a dismissive smirk, because everyone else had picked the Eagles to win.

Tampa Bay won.

After the game Jimmy came over to me and grabbed my arm, seething. "Don't you *ever* make predictions on this show again." Then he stormed away.

After the game Brent, Irv, and I were at the airport gates ready to head home when we heard someone yelling "Jayne!" calling after me to stop. We turned around and it was Doug Williams, sprinting through the airport like the old OJ commercial. He had dressed immediately after the game and raced to the airport in an effort to catch me before I left. He grabbed both my arms, hugged me tight, and, with the biggest smile on his face, said, "Thank you. Thanks for believing in us. The guys just want to say thank you." And that was it. Brent was laughing so hard. He couldn't believe how much that had meant to these guys. He kept saying, "Jayne. What'd you do to these guys? Are you cooking for them next week?"

When the Buccaneers beat the Eagles, they advanced to play against the Los Angeles Rams the next week with a home game in Tampa. I again arrived at the Tampa airport a few days early. The driver said, "Welcome to Tampa, Ms. Kennedy. Tampa Bay loves you. . . . I'm not going to take the freeway, because I want you to see something." All along the route I saw signs: TO HELL WITH COSELL. WE'VE GOT JAYNE. And: WE'VE GOT THE ORIGINAL MRS. BROWN, an apparent reference to Phyllis George Brown—who was now Kentucky governor John Y. Brown's wife—and to my skin color. When I got to the set before the game there were fans all over me with gifts of flowers, candy, plaques, silver mugs, buttons, ribbons, and cards. Unfortunately for them, the Rams won and were headed to Super Bowl XIV.

I will never forget the first time I met Jim Brown, though it was only for a brief moment. I'd seen Jim play in Cleveland, of course, and in the movies, but he was something else in person. I was at a gathering in Los Angeles years before *The NFL Today*, and I accidentally bumped into Jim. He had on a black fitted T-shirt with the arms cut out, and all I noticed was this incredible set of the hardest, biggest biceps I had ever seen—stone.

Once, I interviewed Sam Huff, and he told me a story about the first time he played against Jim. Sam had to psych himself up, willing himself to beat Jim on every play. The first play, Sam knocked Jim down, and he growled in Jim's face, "You stink." The next play, Sam knocked Jim down and he growled, "You really stink." The third play, Jim went wide, right past Sam, running all the way down the field for the touchdown, leaving Sam in the mud. As he crossed the goal line, Jim turned around and yelled back, "Hey, Sam. How do I smell from over here?"

Then there was Harry Carson of the New York Giants. I was told that Harry kept a life-size poster of me in his locker. The film crew at NFL Films in Philadelphia called to book an interview with him, and they wanted me to do the interview in the locker room (not after the game, mind you) next to the poster. When the film crew couldn't coordinate being in New York when Harry was available, he drove from New York to Philadelphia just to do the interview with me.

The first year I was on *The NFL Today* was the beginning of the controversy regarding women sports journalists having equal access to men's locker rooms, when sports reporter Melissa Ludtke filed a landmark lawsuit in New York federal court under the equal protection clause of the Fourteenth Amendment.

She challenged the New York Yankees' enforcement of the MLB policy that did not allow women the right to equal access to the team's locker room post-game, arguing that as a female sports reporter she was at an unfair disadvantage to her male counterparts by not being permitted to interview the players in the locker rooms immediately after the game, based solely on her gender. She won.

I have always believed in equal access to a story, but I have also always felt that *all* media should be barred entry to the locker rooms, and that there should be another area for the interviews. There is absolutely no reason why any reporter—male *or* female—should be in a locker room where men are showering; I believe it's an invasion of privacy.

There's no problem with putting off a shower for ten minutes while the media have access to the players. Sure, we might miss someone getting doused with champagne, but that's a small concession for treating the players and the reporters with respect. I've seen interviews where there are players in the background who did not know they were on camera, and they were butt naked. One guy had no idea he was on camera until he got the message from his wife. How was that fair?

Another favorite memory is my interview with Ottis O. J. Anderson. CBS wanted to interview him in St. Louis on a Monday, which was his day off, so he turned it down. When they told him that I was conducting the interview, he immediately changed his mind. The interview was staged in the team's public relations office. It was a dry setting, and the interview was going nowhere. I had heard him say that he wanted to get out in time to get dinner started. Apparently, every Monday night he cooked for the team at his apartment. I stopped the camera and checked with my field producer, Louis Schmidt, then turned to Ottis and asked if it would be okay to show up at his home to tape him baking his famous apple pies, and he agreed.

There was a complete turnaround on the interview. While cooking, Ottis talked about his philosophy that the number on your jersey affected the way you played—you didn't see a quarterback burdened down with a big, heavy number like 58; a defensive lineman didn't tiptoe around with featherweight numbers like 7; and only the fastest of the fast could wear a 32. The interview was a bit unusual, but the apple pie was amazing. After the interview, he jumped in his sports car and raced us to the airport, waving goodbye as he pulled away from the curb. Other unusual profiles included the Hannah brothers and their hundreds of chickens at their chicken farm. There was Lloyd Mumphrey and his shrimp farm. Joe Namath and his nightclub/restaurant. Tony Dorsett, Thomas "Hollywood" Henderson, Danny White, Lynn Swann, and so many more.

But there was some darkness during the light of this amazing new job. I traveled a lot, and I learned that my husband had been keeping busy with more than just nightclubs and films.

First, there was his former girlfriend from his days as a young man—we'll call her Denise. Two years before *The NFL Today*, we had produced a film with Smokey as executive producer entitled *Big Time*, starring Chris Joy, Roger E. Mosley, Tobar Mayo, and me. Producing movies starring Black actors in the 1970s was one thing, getting them distributed was another, so we self-booked the theatres (known as four-walling) and did all of the advance work ourselves.

It was when we went on the road to promote and distribute the film in Philadelphia that I noticed something was wrong. Leon, as the advance man, had gone a couple of days ahead of Smokey and me as usual to set up at the theatre for our arrival—typically we opened the show in one city as Leon went ahead to the next city—but on this trip he just seemed overly nervous.

I understood that. It was important that this film go well, not just for our careers but for Smokey, who had funded the film as executive producer. There was no way that we would do anything but our best to prevent him from suffering a loss. So, we went all out promoting the film, including convincing John Johnson to run a cover story in *Jet* magazine. But it was obvious to me that Leon's tension was due to something else. That's when I found out he was traveling with his former girlfriend as part of our advance team. I was stunned.

After we finished promoting *Big Time* and returned to Los Angeles, he moved Denise *and* her son to Los Angeles, leased her a car in my name, put the insurance in my name, and set her up in an apartment.

Every time I heard something new over the next year, I was filled with so much anxiety that I thought I would never make it through each day. I had no idea how to cope with this. I hurt from sunup until sundown and every second in between. I lost a lot of weight and was always a nervous wreck.

And just when I really thought it couldn't be worse . . .

"Denise is moving in with us," he said one morning.

"Excuse me?"—as I spewed my drink across the table. I almost had to laugh through the pain.

"I just feel like you can't give me the amount of love I deserve."

"You know what, Leon, that's fine," I said. "Then leave."

"No, I want you both . . . here."

"Are you out of your mind?"

"I think you and her would get along. She can be my second wife."

"No. Hell no."

I didn't leave. She didn't move in, but they were openly together.

The sheer audacity hit me like a punch in my chest. Indiscreet cheating I probably could have understood, but this? Wow. And now he was setting her up in LA. It was unacceptable. And her *child*?

However, I had so much to focus on that I had to lean into my career. Leon and his girlfriend and her son . . . and the apartment . . . and my car . . . would have to wait.

And wait and wait.

Yes, we all know that celebrities are human too, but we forget. We have no idea what is going on in their personal lives when they show up on the TV, in movies, or on the field or on the court. It's one of the reasons I try to stay away from the hype of Hollywood life . . . the facade is not the whole story.

So, in 1980 when I found myself with all this background running through my mind heading to Super Bowl XIV between National Football Conference champion the Los Angeles Rams and American Football Conference champion the Pittsburgh Steelers, the only thing that kept me sane was that old sports adage "Keep your eye on the ball." I couldn't afford to be distracted. I didn't want to be distracted. No matter what was happening, good or bad, Jayne Harrison, the daughter of Blue Boy and Ginny from Virginia, was going to the Super Bowl.

Of course, every NFL sports broadcaster dreams of someday working the Super Bowl, and I was no different. From the first moment I started with CBS, I couldn't wait to be a part of the granddaddy of all football games. Far beyond the fantastic career opportunity to be seen by more than 60 million people worldwide (it now routinely garners well in excess of 110 million), I was going to be a part of the most watched show on television. Me, Jayne Harrison, from a little Midwestern town in Ohio, who never thought she was even going to make it west of the Mississippi. I had come to Hollywood nine years earlier and there was no way I could have ever imagined this. Mom was right—anything was possible.

My first Super Bowl, Leon and I went as spectators for Super Bowl XIII in Miami between the Pittsburgh Steelers and the Dallas Cowboys on January 21, 1979. I could not believe the absolute spectacle of the event. Outlandish parties were part of the pregame festivities. The NFL had rented out a whole terminal at Miami International Airport just for a big bash the night before the game. At each boarding gate, there was an array of foods from a different country. The halftime show was "Carnival: A Salute to the Caribbean," and the entire field was covered to resemble water and islands. The Steelers beat the Cowboys in a close game, 35–31. And there I was sitting only ten rows back behind the Steelers bench. I was in heaven.

The following year CBS had the rights to Super Bowl XIV in Los Angeles. That meant that I was working the game at home with my home team. How lucky can a girl get? I remember watching the very first Super Bowl back home in 1967 in our living room with Dad. It was played in the Los Angeles Memorial Coliseum, where the Green Bay Packers beat the Kansas City Chiefs 35–10. I remember Dad and me jumping up and down when Bart Starr's quarterback sneak sealed the game *and* him the MVP.

I could not believe that there I was only thirteen years later, and I was one of the first female sports broadcasters to anchor the Super Bowl pregame. I kept thinking: I wish Dad was here.

I should have flown him out but literally everything was happening so fast. However, the two sets of Super Bowl tickets I did receive from NFL/CBS Leon and I decided we should give to Sammy Davis Jr. and Hugh Hefner as an act of gratitude for believing in us since day one.

I had been stationed in LA two weeks before the game to pretape a variety of interviews. I had all the pieces on the Rams, and Irv covered the Steelers. I'd been up until about four a.m. with all the late-night Super Bowl events around town, but this day I was ready. This day, game day, my assignment was to be in a helicopter offering a bird's-eye view of all that led up to the game. We were to start with a look at the Los Angeles Memorial Coliseum and what was potentially the future home of the Oakland Raiders, since the Rams had moved to Anaheim. So naturally we would take a look at Anaheim before heading back to the Rose Bowl for the game broadcast. I was prepared to do all my lead-ins to the pretaped interview packages I had done earlier that week from the chopper. And as a side note . . . I love helicopters, so I was doubly excited.

*The NFL Today* was never truly scripted; it was just outlined with time allotments and breaks. Some lead-ins were, however, scripted. I was in the helicopter following my outline—first flying over the Coliseum—then the director told me to throw it to Paul Hornung. Paul, who was in Beverly Hills at the restaurant of Carroll O'Connor (Archie Bunker), the Ginger Man, and was interviewing . . . Phyllis George?

What? I couldn't figure out why was she there. I had no idea she was to be a part of the pregame coverage. After that, there were other times when I was preempted by a live cutaway back to Phyllis George Brown with her husband, Governor Brown of Kentucky.

An angry burn started within—what the hell does the governor of Kentucky have to do with the Super Bowl in Los Angeles between the Rams and the Steelers? I was livid. I was being effectively minimized within the show—live broadcasts and taped interviews—while I was stuck hovering above the game on a local KCBS LA News chopper, with no way of doing anything about any of it.

At the beginning of the game broadcast, they finally did cut to the camera on board the helicopter, shooting out the nose at the approach to the stadium. The shot from the helicopter rose high in the air, then practically did a nose-dive, appearing to go right through the front door of the Rose Bowl stadium. I have to admit, that part was pretty spectacular, but my being in the helicopter didn't have anything to do with the effect. Then the show cut to Brent in the booth and the opening kickoff. The *NFL Today* pregame show had minimized my presence in the coverage and there was nothing I could do. After all, it was live television.

When I landed, dropping down behind the stands, I was beyond my boiling point. Irv Cross was right there waiting for me.

"Jayne, it's done. It's too late."

"What's done? What the hell is happening here? Irv, you have got to tell me."

"It's done is all I can say."

If he hadn't held on to me and calmed me down, I don't know what I would have done. I froze. I don't remember ever making it to the broadcast booth. I don't even remember doing the halftime show, but I was there. I do remember saying to Brent as we went into commercial, "Don't pull any more surprises on me."

I'd been ambushed, and it had certainly thrown me off. But I kept my cool. I stayed calm. But like the Black Swan, I was paddling furiously underneath.

People always ask me—what did your team do when all this was happening? But I had no team of people. Just me, Leon, and my manager, Rudy—in shock.

I should have known what was coming. . . .

Apparently, everyone else did.

According to Rich Podolsky, "Phyllis George's agent, Los Angeles attorney Ed Hookstratten, who had Johnny Carson and Elvis Presley as clients, had notified CBS that Phyllis would consider returning if there was an expanded role for her at CBS. In fact, a handshake deal had already been agreed to before CBS landed in LA. Jayne, through no fault of her own, was out. Unfortunately, no one told Jayne."

he first time I met Bill Overton was at a photo shoot for Lamonte McLemore. Lamonte had created
new magazine that featured images and stories about couples, aptly named *TWO*, and he chose us for
s first cover. THIS is my favorite. Zaïre says, "How many people can say they have a photo of the first
y their parents met?"

The magic of Lamonte McLemore, 1970s and '80s.

In junior high, my first job was delivering weekly newspapers on my bike. My third job, in grades ten through twelve, was as a model for the May Company department store Teen Fashion Board.

Look how many women made careers in sports broadcasting after I opened *that* door.

The first Black Miss Ohio and a panel of judges, including supermodel-turned-agent Wilhelmina and TV star Teresa Graves of *Get Christie Love!*

Official wedding photo of Leon and me. I am wearing the gown and veil I made for our special moment.

The dance with my father. Every year on his birthday, I listen to that Luther Vandross song over and over again.

Leon being pushed into the chapel by comedian Bill Murray, and Pete Moore and Smokey Robinson from The Miracles.

My very first photo shoot in Los Angeles. I'd only been in LA one month. Lamonte called and the rest is history. I was only nineteen. Over fifty-five years, Lamonte has continued to be my number one photographer, and best friend.

Lamonte and I thought this would be a great poster, but when we pitched it to Pro Arts, the company that produced the Farrah Fawcett poster, they turned it down, telling us that "Black people don't buy posters."

On the road with the Ding-A-Ling Sisters, circa 1974, when we were finally able to show our belly buttons. Just a few years earlier, NBC had not allowed Barbara Eden to show hers in *I Dream of Jeannie*.

All these years later, and *Laugh-In* producer George Schlatter is still my number one fan. He thought it would be funny to show me *Playboy* in braille.

Celebrity Long Beach Grand Prix. I was the first female non-professional celebrity to ever race in this event. Circa 1979.

On the set of *227* with Billy Dee Williams, and this time I wasn't cut out of the show. 1986.

With Muhammad Ali in Washington, DC, for the Jimmy Young fight at the Capital Centre. Who knew that two years later he would help me land a spot on *The NFL Today*?

When the call came from CBS that I had won the spot on *The NFL Today*, we couldn't have been more excited. We had pulled off what *everyone* said was *impossible*.

Receiving the NAACP Image Award for Best Performance by an Actress in a Motion Picture for my performance in *Body and Soul*, along with Louis Gossett Jr., who won Best Performance by an Actor in a Motion Picture for his role in *An Officer and a Gentleman*, in 1982.

Finally, my long-lost Image Award found its home again. The awards committee surprised me and regifted me a trophy in 2024. I cried.

Receiving the 2018 *Black Enterprise* Women of Power Summit's Legacy Award. Earl "Butch" Graves Jr. (president and CEO of *Black Enterprise*) insisted I bring my daughters to witness the accolade.

Elected vice president of the United States at Girls Nation (American Legion Auxiliary) with RoAnn Costin as president.

I first met Bill in 1973. On May 25, 1985, we married in Bermuda. My whole life changed.

And fifty-two years later, we are still here!

My favorite photo with Mom and Dad.

My extended blended family is priceless.

üre.

Savannah, Jacques, and Jaris.

Kopper and Khanh.

Overton ladies with Bill's mother, Hessie.

Aunt Katie and Grandma Jane.

Grandpa William Setzer.

Grandpa Turk Thompson

Great-Grandfather Chamberlain Harrison and
Great-Grandmother Minnie Harrison.

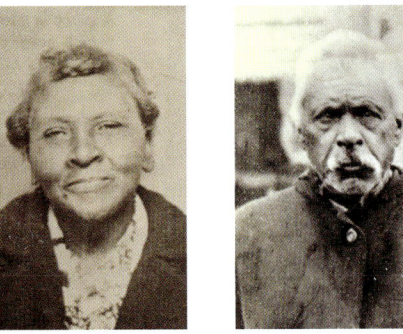

Great-Great-
Grandfather Peter
Harrison.

Great-Great-
Grandmother Harri
Edmunds Harrison.

Grandma Lois Thompson.

I guess you could say I first began to write *Plain Jayn*
at the age of five. Learning to type was the first task.
I named my first company Jane Books. Check out th
vintage Royal typewriter.

# CHAPTER TWENTY-ONE

# THE NFL TODAY– FIRED

There is no doubt that being on *The NFL Today* made me a household name. But there was a much larger perspective that even I hadn't considered at the time. It is only in retrospect that I realized the significance of my profile and the impact it had on Black communities all across America, and even abroad as African American troops cheered me on while they fought in a war for a country that hadn't fulfilled its promises to them.

There, on American television, was this poised, intelligent, confident Black woman who gave them all hope and something to aspire to. Black parents sitting with their young daughters in front of the television beaming with pride every Sunday, whether they followed football or not.

*Look at this Black woman. She is doing something that probably everyone told her she couldn't do. No matter what you choose in life, remember her, and know that you can do whatever you want.*

Oprah once told me that she and Gayle King would sit in front of the television and when I came on, they'd jump up and down shouting, "Colored people on TV! Colored people on TV!" Whenever they saw me on *The NFL Today*, they would say to each other, "If she can do it, we can too." And that all-too-familiar refrain has echoed through every Black household in America since the 1978.

Their dreams of seeing themselves as upwardly mobile, mainstream Americans and not the "others" were finally being realized, if only for brief interludes on the otherwise predominately white programmed broadcast networks. I was beginning to get courted by major publications to be included in their magazine pages, but encountered reluctance, as if the only audience I could ever appeal to was African Americans . . . and for the most part, advertisers didn't want or value that association with their products and brands anyway.

The indelible landmark made by my sitting at *The NFL Today* desk changed the conversation. The shift into the 1980s had begun a decade that would birth a new art form called hip-hop, born of self-empowerment and revolutionizing American pop culture with its Afrocentric sound and messages of Black pride and the calling out of racism—eventually redefining pop music all over the world.

Professionally, despite having acted for seven years in LA prior to *The NFL Today*, many in the industry considered me an "overnight success" and thought that my career began because of that job on CBS. It was so strange when I would go into an audition and the director would ask, "Have you ever done any acting before?" as if I'd just set foot in tinsletown.

My commitment to *The NFL Today* only spanned roughly six months per season, from mid-August to the first week of February, and I was determined to make it possible to work in sports and continue pursuing acting or other gigs for the remainder of the year. There was no way I was going to give up acting. . . . Acting was in my soul. I approached Frank Smith, the president of CBS Sports, and asked for permission to speak with CBS Entertainment in LA, with the thought of striking an overall deal with the network. It was quite common to be a series regular on one show, but during hiatus appear on other network shows. The cross-promotion was good for the network, and the opportunities to be seen on multiple shows was good for the talent. An overall deal with CBS Sports and CBS Entertainment would be a no-brainer;

after all, I was an actress who had become a sports journalist, and not the other way around. He told me to reach out to Bob Daly, then president at CBS Entertainment.

When I met with Mr. Daly, he told me that because of the previous television failure the network had had with my predecessor, Phyllis George, CBS Entertainment would not be interested in investing any money into another "sports personality." The irony of that reasoning was not lost on me—I had gone from being seen as an actress who wasn't qualified to be a sports personality to a sports personality who was no longer qualified to be an actress.

So, I went back to Frank Smith and asked for his permission to reach out to the other two networks (there were only three major networks at the time). He approved. In the spring of 1980, I was offered a job on NBC to cohost *Speak Up, America*, created by my old friend and *Laugh-In* producer George Schlatter.

It was an intriguing concept.

*Speak Up, America* was truly ahead of its time. A blend of news and entertainment, the show profiled current events of interest in America in pretaped video packages, then solicited America's man-on-the-street opinions on those subjects. We would present the video to a live studio audience as we got their reaction as well as those of the audience at home using a new interactive technology called CUBE-TV—we would ask the at-home television audience to electronically voice their opinions by casting votes in real time using the CUBE boxes in their homes.

At the end of the show, we tallied the votes and revealed what America thought. *Speak Up, America* was one of the early seeds that birthed the interconnectivity of the internet and social media as we know it today.

I brought my NBC offer back to CBS, as was the industry protocol, and Frank Smith told me he thought it would be "a tremendous opportunity for *The NFL Today* to get some prime-time exposure," and that I was free to sign the contract. I convinced George Schlatter to include that CBS had "right of first refusal" in my contract, so that legally my professional commitment to CBS would always hold priority over my commitment to NBC.

*Speak Up, America* was to be shot live on Friday nights in the NBC studios in Burbank, California. After the show I'd take my normal red-eye to New York for the Sunday football show. The field interviews for *Speak Up, America* were stacked over the summer, and I would be free during the fall to tape the weekly CBS NFL field interviews. Then I got CBS to sign off, giving me *written* approval to do the show while simultaneously appearing on *The NFL Today*.

In July 1980, I had been booked to host the Miss Universe beauty pageant for CBS in Seoul, South Korea. I was literally climbing into the limo at six a.m., headed to LAX, when a messenger service pulled into the driveway behind me.

The message was a formal notification that I had been *fired* from *The NFL Today*.

In that moment, there was absolutely nothing I could do. I had to be on the plane to Seoul in two hours, which the executives at CBS knew full well since CBS was broadcasting the pageant. I spent the entire eleven-hour flight to Seoul wondering what had gone wrong.

I didn't have the luxury to follow up when I landed, because I had to go directly to rehearsal. I walked on the stage and immediately one of the cue-card guys, who had been a friend of mine through the years, quickly approached me.

"Jayne, the producers were given instructions from CBS headquarters last night to minimize your participation in the broadcast. It's all hush-hush, no one is really saying anything about what happened. That's all I know."

"I don't understand." I stood there onstage with my hands on my hips while running all the possibilities through my mind and I still had no idea what was happening. I was so angry, embarrassed, and nervous. I felt nauseous.

"Jayne, this is huge," he said. "I've been up all night rewriting cue cards."

After rehearsal, where I basically stood around and did nothing, I went back to the hotel and finally got a chance to call home.

"I can't believe this, Leon," I said through tears. "I just don't know what went wrong."

He was really upset, but not with CBS.

"Well, I know one thing that's wrong. You wasted money to call international long-distance." And then he hung up on me.

I just sat there on the bedside . . . with the phone in my hand . . . alone and confused on the other side of the world.

I knew two things: One, I would not let this firing hold me back. And two, when your husband hangs up on you after you share an awful event, time to take stock.

The third thing, I did not know. . . . Who was *she* this time?

I was mentally, physically, and emotionally exhausted. A mixture of panic and pain started to well up inside my chest. I had no one to turn to. No one. Everything seemed to be collapsing around me. My marriage had been falling apart for quite some time now, primarily because of Leon's ongoing and not-so-covert affairs, and now my job was gone too.

For most of the pageant, I was relegated to "standing in the wings." I literally could have phoned in my part—but then maybe that would have cost too much too.

I just wanted to go home to my family in Ohio—my safe haven. I wanted to curl up on the sofa with Mom and have her tell me it would be all right. But I couldn't go home yet, as I had another work assignment.

At the end of the pageant, I was to meet up with the segment producer for *Speak Up, America*. Since I was already in Korea, we had planned to shoot a piece on the soldiers in the demilitarized zone (DMZ) that separates North Korea from South Korea. I was only authorized to enter the DMZ as a member of the USO.

The arrangements and instructions were strict, and I was only allowed to bring one other person with me. My field producer had to become my entire crew—sound, camera, and lights.

We interviewed many of the troops that were rotating the very stressful "Zone" duty, after which I was awarded their unit crest and was made an honorary member of the First Battalion, Thirty-First Infantry. It was truly a remarkable and memorable experience, for which I was later submitted as a nominee for an Emmy Award.

As soon as I got home, I called the Office of Business Affairs at CBS and was told that I had been fired for signing with their competitor, NBC.

*WHAT?* I explained the entire process of what led up to my working for NBC. "That's not true. I have written permission from our president, Frank Smith." And I gave them the letter.

A few days later I was hired back. I breathed a sigh of relief—there was no way I was ready to leave CBS and my dream job.

Within a week, I got a second notice of termination for a different reason.

And, yet again, within a few days I was hired back. Another week went by, and unbelievably, I got a *third letter of termination*, and this time there was no rehiring.

Of course, what I didn't know throughout all of this was that they had already made the decision to bring Phyllis back.

Soon, the media was reporting that I had breached my contract with CBS and that I had walked away from *The NFL Today* . . . and everyone believed it.

Black publications were saying I should have done whatever had to be done to keep that job even if I had to kiss ass, because being there kept the door open for other African Americans. No one knew that it wasn't me who had said goodbye, and there was no social media then for me to plead my case and engender support from my fans.

I then hired a little-known LA attorney by the name of Gloria Allred, who was beginning to make a name for herself, and we filed a wrongful termination lawsuit against the network. It was then that we learned CBS was claiming there was no way that I could do my job on *The NFL Today* and *Speak Up, America* at the same time. Yet Brent Musburger, my co-anchor, was doing *exactly* the same thing. I believe they just wanted an excuse to bring Phyllis back, and often wonder if it was a setup.

Brent had moved to Los Angeles and was working as co-anchor on the evening news desk with Connie Chung on KNXT-TV five nights a week and then in New York at the *NFL Today* desk on Sunday. I would have been working my *Speak Up, America* interviews during the summer, in the fall would be NFL interviews two days during the week, live in-studio at NBC on Friday nights with *Speak Up, America*, and the *NFL Today* desk on Sunday.

We both flew the same flights to New York and the same flights back to LA. But for some reason he could handle the pressure of that kind of schedule, and I couldn't. Really? CBS actually said in response to the suit that I would be too "taxed" and that no one could possibly handle my schedule, but they couldn't tell us why it was impossible for a woman . . . but totally acceptable for a man.

We reached a settlement with CBS that I was satisfied with. Unfortunately, the days of *The NFL Today* were forever behind me.

At the time I was fired, my salary on *The NFL Today* was a whopping $40,000 (equivalent to about $190,000 today) a year. But it was still peanuts in comparison to what others—including the men on my own set at *The NFL Today*— were making, well into the six and seven figures.

I don't remember the publication, but there was a newspaper article profiling me and several other female anchors and hosts years ago. They asked me during the interview if I could talk about my salary since that was one of the primary issues of the article. I declined to speak on that. But when the piece came out, it talked about women who were on the forefront of shaking up the industry as far as hosting TV shows. In all, there was Phyllis George, Lauren Hutton, Cybill Shepherd, and five others, of which I was the only Black woman. So naturally they assumed I was in the same salary ballpark as the others, who were listed in the high six figures on up into the millions. No one would have ever believed that I was only making $40,000. And from that paltry amount, I had to pay my agent 10 percent (the same agent who had refused to submit me for the job in the first place). Then, because I had to find someone who would submit me, I ended up with a manager who I had to pay 15 percent. Then there was my press agent, who got 5 percent. Do the math. And after Uncle Sam got his cut there wasn't much left for me . . . and I was a co-anchor on a major broadcast network for the richest sport in the world every Sunday.

It's not much consolation, but even Oprah tells the story of her male cohost making $50,000 a year while she was barely making $22,000 in 1980. When she confronted her boss with this disparity, she was asked, "Why should you make that much money? He has kids, do you have kids? He has to put his kids through college. He has a house payment. Do you have a house? So, tell me why I should pay you that much." She told him, "Because we're doing the same damn job." And her boss replied, "I don't think so."

And it's not just on the journalistic side either. In 2018 CNN posted a list of the one hundred highest-paid athletes in the world and not a single woman was included. It's hard enough as a woman fighting for equity, but as a Black woman it's nearly impossible.

Whether you supported women doing sports broadcasting or not, it was still groundbreaking at the time. I had done so well with the show, generating a huge fan base (both with viewers and athletes alike) that was growing each and every day.

But despite all the success, I never attempted to renegotiate my contract like I should have done. I signed in good faith for two years and I was going to keep my word. I had given CBS absolutely everything that I had to give. I was even working for them for *CBS Sports Spectacular* for free from time to time, all just to appease the network. I could not figure out why it suddenly went so terribly wrong. I had held up my end of the bargain, but that clearly wasn't enough. There were simply too many outside forces beyond my control working against my success.

After I was fired, the owner of the Pittsburgh Steelers, Art Rooney (with whom I had previously shot an interview segment), wrote to CBS in my support, as did many of the players and fans, but in the end it didn't matter. I initially had heard that CBS was afraid I was becoming too popular and would begin demanding too much money. That reasoning was as ridiculous as my not being able to keep the same work schedule as Brent.

You don't fire someone because of what you think the person might ask for; you wait and handle the situation as it arises. And the only reason I would be in a position in the first place to ask for more money would be if I were doing a great job—and I absolutely was. Ratings were at an all-time high for the show versus the previous year's broadcast numbers, and the 1980 Super Bowl broadcast was watched by one hundred million viewers.

I also heard that CBS executives wanted Phyllis George back on *The NFL Today*. The rumor was that they were getting rid of me to make room for her again because she had just married the governor of Kentucky, who had very close affiliations with the Kentucky Derby. CBS had held the rights to the Kentucky Derby since its first television broadcast in 1952. In 1975, ABC acquired the broadcasting rights away from CBS, and the extremely lucrative advertising revenue that came from the event. CBS badly wanted to get back the broadcasting rights and the prestige that came along with it. If Phyllis were rehired, the rumored theory was that CBS would have a powerful personal connection to get its foot in the door for those Kentucky Derby broadcast rights.

Whatever the reason, they rehired Phyllis George and replaced me on *The NFL Today*, but she left once again midway through the 1983 season on maternity leave and never returned to the show. And there hasn't been another woman on *The NFL Today* Sunday pregame desk since.

I'll never know if the rumors about the Kentucky Derby connection were true, but if so, the plan failed. ABC held on to the broadcast rights to the Kentucky Derby another twenty-one years, until the Churchill Downs race moved in 2001 to NBC, where it remains today.

In the wake of the turmoil at CBS the year I was fired, Frank Smith, president of CBS Sports, was let go, as well as several others, including Linda Sutter, who was head of talent and the one who was responsible for giving me my shot.

I loved working on *The NFL Today*. I had no reason to quit. It was my dream job in so many ways—until it sadly became my nightmare.

# CHAPTER TWENTY-TWO

# THE AFTERMATH

After returning in July from cohosting the Miss Universe pageant in South Korea and the USO piece in Korea's DMZ, I continued working for *Speak Up, America*. I taped more than ten stories, including the Magic Johnson interview when I was able to arrange for him to become a "special features by" correspondent. We finally went on-air live in September 1980, and I hosted three live shows. But the NBC News department was not going to have us infringing on their territory, so they fought us every step of the way. We were canceled. One of the weekly segments on the show featured satirical cartoonist Sergio Aragonés. On our final broadcast in late September, he drew a cartoon of the three hosts—Rhonda Bates, Marjoe Gortner, and me—lassoed and tied up by NBC News.

Later on in the fall of that same year, I sat alone in my home above the Rose Bowl stadium and dejectedly watched Phyllis George Brown at my desk on *The NFL Today*. Eight months before, I had watched the Super Bowl as a co-anchor, hovering above the Rose Bowl stadium in a helicopter, never realizing at the time that my tenure on the show had already ended. I was on top of the world then, so excited about my dual career roles on *The NFL Today* and *Speak Up, America*. How quickly things change in this business.

On top of all that, my marriage was totally falling apart. Often during those dark days, the thoughts of what happened at CBS kept going over and over in my mind. It would be another forty-two years before I found my answers as to what had actually happened that ended my tenure on *The NFL Today*.

While any firing was painful, being released from *The NFL Today* was devastating for more than professional reasons. As much as I loved my job, I regretted being on the road so much, even remarking to one of my sisters, "I missed having children. I can never be able to offer anything to a daughter or son, because I am never home."

She looked at me for a moment, the impact and hidden sadness of my admission sinking in, and she thanked me. I didn't understand what she meant at first, but then she said, "Thank you for being a role model for my daughter. How would you measure your contribution to the world, being a symbol and making a difference for thousands of little daughters, or for just one little girl of your own?"

The words struck home hard, and the tears streamed down my face.

I often thought about what my sister had said that day. But her words were more poignant because of the firing from CBS. Only Leon and I knew just how high a price we had paid—I had paid—for this job, just how much we had given up for it. Telling no one, I had quietly undergone an emotionally devastating abortion in the name of my career.

It was never said out loud, but I implicitly understood that my job on *The NFL Today* would be in serious jeopardy if I were to get pregnant. You have to remember, it wasn't until the late 1970s that there were women sports anchors, and certainly no Black female sports anchors, and a lot of people wanted to keep it that way. Many people wanted to see me fail, and a pregnancy would have been the easiest way to ease me out the door. The prejudices against being a woman on-air were already strong enough. I heard it all the time: "She got the job because she's beautiful, because she's eye candy."

The seasonal change to fall after the abortion was the most difficult emotionally. That fall was the first time that I felt abandoned with the change of colors. Where I had always welcomed the season with such anticipation, this year I truly felt alone. It was not the ideal situation for heading out on the road again. Leon and I never talked about it once it was done. I knew I was facing months and months of loneliness. I was horrified with the overwhelming sense of isolation that no one knew. No one would be my confidant. No one knew why I was lonely at all. The process itself, while emotionally heartbreaking, was relatively simple. Our decision was practical.

I also knew that I was relieved that we had not had children. It was one of those scabs that never healed, one of those things that I never spoke of. And as the years went on and there were those who were not supporters of my career choices for other reasons, this would only have given them more ammunition to expand the list. But I cannot ignore the price of having a career: the unfair plight and the collateral damage of being a woman within a male-dominated industry. Fortunately, today women have more choices and there are actual laws on the books that prevent job termination due to pregnancy, but back then . . . women did not have those protections. And I fear that with legislation currently being passed in many states within our country today, women's rights are sadly sliding backward.

# CHAPTER TWENTY-THREE

# I LOVE YOU, BUT NOT AS MUCH AS I LOVE MYSELF

Leon was an avid movie buff of the Golden Age of Hollywood, and we had stacks and stacks of coffee table books on the glamour days of Old Hollywood. He would often refer to us as the Black Douglas Fairbanks and Mary Pickford. Not because of any resemblance, but because as a power couple, they owned their own production company and their own studio. That was his dream, and we were actually on the way to achieving it. Even years later, when he referred to how people saw the two of us, he'd claim that we were much like Lucille Ball and Desi Arnaz or more contemporaneously Mary Tyler Moore and her then husband Grant Tinker, who ran MTM Enterprises in the 1970s and '80s.

Trying to capitalize on the success of his starring role in the film *Penitentiary* (released in November 1979), Leon approached Menahem Golan and Yoram Globus, known in Hollywood circles as the "Go-Go Boys," who ran Cannon Films, with the idea of remaking the 1947 John Garfield classic *Body and Soul,* with him as the star. They loved the idea, but then Leon added the caveat: only if they allowed him to write the script. After he produced a litany of properties he had written, they finally agreed, but with four demands: lots of sex, lots of blood, lots of violence, and a *strong* R rating.

Then came the biggest hurdle. Leon was demanding they allow him to produce the film. Well, that did not sit well with them . . . until they heard the rest of his offer.

"I will forgo my acting fee to put toward the production if I am named as the producer." Leon was always willing to gamble on himself to advance our careers.

After scratching their heads, first to assess the offer, second to assess whether he was deranged or not, they said, "Ahh, what the hell." They put the project in his hands and welcomed him aboard.

Then, as he was preparing to walk out the door, he turned and said, "Oh, and my wife will costar."

At first, they had no idea who I was and were insisting on casting Pam Grier, Vonetta McGee, or Annazette Chase, each a leading Black actress with big hits in their résumés. But then he flashed my picture and the Cannon execs green-lit the film. We were set to start preproduction in October 1980, with filming to begin that December. The timing worked out perfectly for me since my last appearance on *Speak Up, America* was late September.

I wanted to be home for as much of the preproduction as I could in my role as both coproducer and lead actress of *Body and Soul.* This was the first time since my television "fame" that people would see me in a film. It had been an extremely difficult year, and I knew I needed to rest before jumping into a major commitment like production on a film.

That summer, I had been asked by Muhammad Ali Professional Sports (MAPS) to do color commentary for a series of ten boxing matches around the country with boxing champion Carlos Palomino as the play-by-play analyst. The job was going to shoot in October through the end of December, just before the filming was to begin on *Body and Soul.* I turned it down. As much as I loved being considered, I knew our upcoming movie production would need me to be ready. However, Leon saw this as an opportunity to diversify my portfolio since no woman had ever done this before. He felt that with CBS replacing me with Phyllis, this would validate my stature as an in-demand sports anchor.

I had come home from a television assignment when I got a call from MAPS.

"Hi, it's Casey. I'm booking your travel."

"My what?"

"The ten boxing matches? You're starting in Miami and then you're going straight to Dallas, and you *might* be able to come back to LA for a day or two before you head to—"

"Casey? Is that your name? I am so sorry, but you've been misinformed. I'm not doing MAPS."

"No, ma'am. I'm looking at your contract right here."

"Can't be me, I didn't sign it."

"It looks like the contract is with your production company. Signed by Leon Isaac Kennedy."

Yes, it was a great opportunity, but I had made my choice. I desperately wanted to be hands-on as a producer. I desperately wanted to be my all-time best in the role of Julie Winters. Not only was this an amazing career opportunity, but it was a passion project that helped to minimize the still-lurking sting of being fired by CBS.

Now I found myself having to go back on the road in a week. I was furious that Leon had signed that contract. We had formed a production company together, and since both of our services were provided under that company, we each had the right to enter any contract for each other's services on behalf of our company.

He had broken the trust. The end of our marriage was not *written* on the wall; it was now *plastered* all over the wall in the form of that contract. There would be no turning back—it was just a matter of time.

After the girlfriend with the car in my name who Leon had moved to LA a few years before, we had reconciled. With the success of *Penitentiary* and *The NFL Today*, things were looking very bright. But then in late 1980, our relationship began to collapse so deeply I didn't think it could get any worse—but it did. I had never ever felt such heartache or anything so devastating like that before. And there had been other women, many other women.

This one was different. This one seemed to be a constant.

*Body and Soul* was a vehicle for Leon, of course. He had scripted the ultimate fantasy of his life while all the time giving the executive producers, the Go-Go Boys, exactly what they had demanded: sex, action, and violence. We were supposed to be writing the script together, but my being on the road with MAPS interfered with any kind of equal collaboration. Each time I read his new scenes, I wondered how much of what he wrote was fantasy, and how much of it was reality. We argued nearly every single day.

In December 1980, after I returned home from my MAPS commitment, we began filming. Leon and I were barely speaking to each other except for doing the work. Things came to a head New Year's Eve. We were on a location shoot at a hotel in the town of Carson, south of downtown LA, filming a scene that was to resemble an after-fight party with celebrities in every corner. Magic Johnson and our other celebrity friends were all on set. During part of that night's scene, Julie (me) was looking for Leon (Leon), and she walked into their hotel room, only to find him in bed with three women in the middle of having sex.

This was not the best thing for me to be experiencing right then, in a movie where he played a character named Leon. All this was a little too close to our life to be coincidental. By then everyone knew Leon and I were having trouble, so our director, George Bowers, only asked me to shoot entering the room once, and then I was sent home.

I had known about Leon's girlfriends for several years. We had fought about it many, many times. He even hired his current girlfriend to work in the *Body and Soul* production office, and the set we used in the film as my home was totally furnished with pieces from *her* house. I had been desperately trying to hold myself together to get through shooting the film, but on this day, shooting this scene, my anger finally broke through.

I abruptly said goodbye to Magic and George, and without a word to Leon, I got into my car, one of our matching his-and-hers Cadillacs, and raced to the South Bay.

I was scheduled to arrive backstage at the Rose Parade grounds at four thirty a.m. because I was hosting KTLA's *Rose Parade* with Bob Eubanks that morning. But instead, I went to visit a friend, and we spent a few hours together. Even if it was just for the moment—or so I thought—I didn't want to go home. And I still had to be on set at four thirty a.m.

That New Year's Eve my head was hurting, and my heart was aching from the flood of memories creeping through the recesses of my mind during the long drive home from the South Bay. I pulled into our driveway and raced into the house, trying to shift my focus to the important job at hand. For the previous two weeks I had been visiting the construction site for many of the Rose Parade floats, and I had a lot of interviews, research, and study to do in preparation for the broadcast. Ironically, I guess it turned out to be one of my best television appearances, since it later won me an Emmy.

On the way home from the parade, I couldn't help but think about my marriage, wondering how things had gone from being so in love, to ending up on a set location with my husband simulating sex with three other women in a film he wrote, produced, and was starring in. And how did I end up breaking my wedding vows?

The first few years of our marriage had been great, albeit difficult. We were making a lot of headway in entertainment, and even though we were separated a lot, it was all part of our ten-year plan. We knew what the sacrifices would be and we agreed that we would make it work. I was traveling and spent many nights on the road waiting to return home, and Leon waited for me to return . . . in the beginning.

Then Leon was building his nightclub base, so when I was home the nights were often spent alone waiting for Leon to come in at about four or five a.m.

In the beginning, I would go to the clubs with him, but I was never the nightclub type. The club thing was working well for Leon, and soon he outgrew the space and moved to a larger and better location, expanding again. He was becoming known around town for having a great place to hang out, no matter where it was. Our marriage was filled with his being in one club after another, one long night after another, and my waiting for him to come home, just as he had waited for me to come home.

We had seemed to have worked out our problems by the time I auditioned for *The NFL Today* in 1978. I remember how happy we both were that we had successfully pulled it off. Then once I started traveling again, I noticed some of the same old recurring behaviors. Like one day I bought a pair of black pants. I was packing for my trip to New York, and I had left them on the bed in the guest room. I was going to wear them when I returned in two days. But when I got back, they were gone, and I never saw them again.

Whenever I was on the road, I would clean the house, top to bottom, and leave the kitchen stocked with dinners prepared, as Leon wasn't a good cook. When I'd get back, the place was a mess, the food was gone, and the kitchen looked like it hadn't been cleaned in weeks, with food all over the walls. His excuse was always that he wasn't good at housework.

What I heard years later was that there were always several women staying with him at our home while I was away traveling to New York every week. And his somewhat dubious male friends . . . OMG. They would play games in the kitchen, throwing food against the wall, trying to rebound it into the trash can.

In 1980, months before filming *Body and Soul*, we were in a repeat performance of 1976, but with a different woman—probably someone he had met at the club . . . or so I thought. We'll call her Evil Spirit. What he didn't know was that she had plotted to break up our marriage from day one. A longtime family friend who had just moved from Wickliffe to LA and who also went to our church, Mount Zion Missionary Baptist, had gone into the restroom, when Evil Spirit entered with a friend. They began to talk about me and not in a pleasant way, so my friend pulled up her feet and tucked herself away in the stall. Then she heard this woman say, "I'm gonna take Jayne Kennedy's husband if it's the last thing I do."

She was more than a decade older than he was and looked just like his mother. Evil Spirit had multiple children of her own, and *he* wanted her to join our family and again insisted he wanted her to be his second wife.

Leon was so hung up on the idea that men needed two wives that he called our friend Minister Farrakhan and talked long-distance for two hours trying to get him to talk me into allowing Leon the same rights as the men of the Nation of Islam. Minister Farrakhan said, "Leon, you're not Muslim. The principles don't apply."

We belonged to a Bible study group that was organized to give celebrities and notables a private haven in which to worship. There were so many of us in this group that it became very popular, along with our annual Christian retreat in the San Bernardino Mountains. Typically, the retreats lasted four days, from Thursday through Sunday. I had always come away from the experience refreshed and spiritually uplifted. That year, the retreat was to be a welcome blessing after the turmoil I had been experiencing for the past year. I had to work and was not able to join the group until Friday. The sessions had already begun when I walked in the door after I had driven the three-hour trip from LAX.

Just as I entered, I could detect a shift in the topic of discussion, and the theme of the speaker suddenly focused on me.

"Divorce is not the way to go," the minister said, as everyone looked at me coming in the door. "As it says in the Bible, you must stand by your husband no matter what."

I looked around to find my husband and he was standing in the front holding hands in a circle with Evil Spirit. And *her* husband. And the minister who was *our* marriage counselor.

All of them standing in the front of the group session, holding hands. And they were all talking about how we were all going to work this out.

I was done. I had had it—church group or not.

As I was leaving the building, Dwight, a friend of mine from Chicago, rushed out the door after me.

"Jayne."

I turned around but I said nothing.

"You don't owe these people *anything*. You only have to answer to yourself and God. Everyone here who is telling you you can't get divorced is already on his or her second marriage."

"Thank you, Dwight." I gave him a big hug. I straightened up my shoulders and immediately drove the three hours back to LA.

This was supposed to be my last safety net, the church. This was supposed to be the place where I could go to keep my feet on the ground. And they wanted me to pray with *them*?

I had enough of praying. Leon wanted me to pray with him and her so that I would understand how we could all live together. He brought her to our home, *my home*, and wanted us all to *hold hands* and pray for understanding, for me to accept her into my family. I prayed to make my marriage work. I had been raised to believe that marriage was forever and all you had to do was overcome the challenges. I just thought it was my job to make it work but, ultimately, I was the only one making any attempt to hold the marriage together at all.


On the day of the Rose Parade, I only remember getting ready in the dressing room and talking to my publicist, Sue Patricola. I honestly don't remember any of the show. I think it's so strange that the jobs where I seemed to do my best work are jobs that I don't remember at all and were in the midst of a lot of personal conflict.

I had only recently hired Sue. Over the years I had hired several different public relations firms, all with minimal success. Even though they were some of the top names in the public relations business—Dick Guttman of Guttman & Pam, who represented names such as Barbra Streisand and Jay Leno; Paul

Bloch of Rogers & Cowan, who represented the likes of Tom Cruise and John Travolta—it seemed almost impossible to get the top-rank publicity for me, and it was impossible to get a coveted magazine cover, like *Harper's*, *Cosmopolitan*, *Vogue*, or even *TV Guide*. Even in 1980, the publishers were all adamant that they didn't put Black people on the cover of their magazines because "Black people don't sell magazines." We tried convincing them that my tenure on CBS would support my being on a cover since I had developed a crossover fan base. They were not interested: No Black people on the cover, period.

I had been on the cover of *Jet* more times than I could remember thanks to my longtime friendships with Isaac Sutton and Bob Johnson and had been on the cover of *Ebony* for many great stories. I had been included in *People*, *Us*, *Harper's*, *Vogue*, and many others, but never appeared on the cover. That year I had anchored the NFL, the Super Bowl, and hosted the Rose Parade and the Miss USA and the Miss Universe pageants, and cohosted the Mother's Day special (with Ed McMahon) and the Collegiate Cheerleading Championship (with superstars Lee Majors and Magic Johnson), some of the highest-rated shows of the entire year. I had been selected as one of the women with "The Most Hypnotic Eyes in the World" along with Princess Grace, Cristina Ferrare, and Sophia Loren . . . and I *still* could not get a cover on a major mainstream magazine.

Rudy Tellez had been my manager since my early days at CBS, though people often mistakenly thought Leon was, something that I was never comfortable with. When Rudy first introduced me to Sue, she made a deal: "I will get three covers for you within thirty days, or you don't owe me anything, and we go our separate ways."

I took her on under those conditions. Within the month, as promised, I had done three magazine cover shoots: *TV Guide*, *Total Health*, and *Mahogany*. Even if they weren't *Vogue* or *Cosmopolitan* covers, it was a start that eventually, over the next few years, led to *Good Housekeeping*, *American Baby*, and inside features in *Us*, *Shape*, *People*, and *Harper's*.

# CHAPTER TWENTY-FOUR

# PHOENIX RISING FROM THE ASHES

Professionally speaking, 1981 was beginning to look like it was going to be a great year—even after the heartache of being fired from *The NFL Today*—starting with my Emmy win for my Rose Parade coverage. Personally, it was a very difficult, roller-coaster year.

Like so many African Americans, I have always felt the need to know more about my cultural heritage, about my lineage and my family's connection to Africa. I wanted to know about the villages that my ancestors inhabited. I wanted to feel their blood running through my veins. I never expected to find any of that when I headed to France for the 1981 Cannes Film Festival (held that year May 13–27), where Leon and I would promote *Body and Soul*. Finally, my years of high school French were going to come in handy. The film festival takes place along the southern coast of France on the magnificent Mediterranean Sea and is known to be one of the most significant festival events in the entertainment industry, attracting the best films from around the world.

Celebrities, studios, and film executives flock to the festival hoping for the notability, publicity, and awards promised to the most significant films produced that year. Of course, the deals made were unreal; careers could be launched overnight. The festival is filled with dozens of screenings, each entry vying for the award for the best film at Cannes: the Palme d'Or. There are also many smaller independent films that may not enter the competition but hope to garner worldwide distribution deals. And for that reason, it was an important event for *Body and Soul* . . . and for Leon and me.

It did not go well.

It was glaringly obvious at that time that our marriage was not working. Leon spent a great deal of time in our production office on the phone with his girlfriend back in LA. I spent a great deal of time walking the beach.

Ahead of the festival, Leon and I had scheduled an extended stay in Monte Carlo, Egypt, Rome, and Athens, after our time in France, to try to salvage what was left of our marriage. If we had known how disastrous Cannes would be, we would have done better to save our money. But I had never spent any significant time in Europe and had never visited Africa, so I was looking forward to this trip, for many reasons. However, it was going to be odd traveling together, knowing about his current relationship with the other woman. Most of the traveling I had done in my life where I was on my own was for professional reasons. Once, Leon and I had worked together on a film shoot in the Philippines, and of course we were there again for the Ali fight, but I believe we had only taken one true vacation that wasn't work related in our entire ten-year marriage.

The drive to Monte Carlo from Cannes was beautiful. On the first day, we visited a small farming community and ate dinner with a local family that rented out a room in the back of their house. We arrived in Monte Carlo the next day. It was incredible to be there, but even more so because the Monte Carlo Grand Prix was just beginning. We had to walk a long way to the event, along with thousands and thousands of people in the streets.

As I was walking down the hill in the midst of the crowds of foreigners, I suddenly heard someone scream my name: "Jayne, Jayne Kennedy!" I was shocked. There was no way that anyone here in Monte Carlo, halfway around the world, knew who I was. I was wrong. It turned out that there were quite a few soldiers from several US Army bases who had come to the Grand Prix, and they had watched me every Sunday on *The NFL Today*. It took me totally by surprise, but a very pleasant surprise. I just never thought about a fan base *outside* of the continental US.

Two days later we headed for Cairo, Egypt. I *had* to go to Egypt. All my life, I had fantasized about visiting the Great Pyramid. I wanted to see it with my own two eyes.

My second year on *The Dean Martin Show* I had received a phone call from a woman that strengthened my resolve to see the pyramids. She claimed to be a "researcher" of ancient Egyptian culture and said that she had friends who had excavated many of the tombs, and from time to time she had joined them. Her specialty was in hypnotic regressions. She had watched me on *The Dean Martin Show* for weeks, when, suddenly, she had an image that flashed across her eyes. The image, she claimed, was of me as an Egyptian handmaiden to a high princess. Before the princess died, she gave me all her jewels to wear into the next life.

According to her research, I had been buried alive with the princess, fully adorned. This lady went on to explain that her friends had discovered a new tomb right next to a site where they had been digging for years. She knew this to be the site where I was buried. She wanted my permission to enter the tomb and retrieve the valuables. She said I was to have them, and as soon as I saw them, I would recognize them. She described me in her vision as wearing a snake bracelet with ruby eyes. The body of the snake was encrusted in emeralds. She said there were jewels on my head and much gold around my waist. She was adamant that I would recognize the pieces—she insisted that we meet.

I was quite hesitant at first. Her story seemed pretty far-fetched, and when you are on television you can attract people who may mean well but who are not always mentally stable. But there was something in her tone and manner that intrigued me, so I decided to meet her. I drove out to the San Fernando

Valley to a small, nondescript house on a very normal street. She was so sweet, and it seemed like I'd known her forever.

She looked into my eyes, and she said she knew then and there that she was right all along. She wanted my permission to hypnotize me and do a regression, and she promised that she would never regress me to relive my death—she just wanted more information about my life and the tomb.

Hypnosis had always fascinated me. This opportunity, I had to admit, was appealing, but I was afraid. I was afraid that something would happen to her while I was under, and I'd be lost forever. I had heard, whether it was true or not, that the only one who could bring you out of hypnosis was the one who put you under. I wasn't willing to put my life into the hands of a total stranger. Then there was the nagging thought in my mind that this wasn't right with God. I graciously thanked her for the offer and left. But I never forgot about all those jewels. Many decades later, I found a snake bracelet that was exactly like she described. . . . Of course I had to buy it.

Every minute of that night I kept thinking about all that she had said. I wondered what it would be like if I were to join her on the expedition, and if there even was an actual expedition. Regardless, I wanted to go to Egypt and see this tomb. What would happen?

Two days later, I was in a copy store on Hollywood Boulevard. I went there often, and I knew the owner. I was walking down the aisle when I noticed a man staring at me. When I looked at him, he glanced the other way. Then I went down the other aisle and there he was in front of me, with a piercing stare. He was looking directly in my eyes. Quite frankly, it scared me. I went to the owner and asked if I could wait in his office for a while until this guy left. I didn't want him following me to my car. We visited for about a half hour, and I left.

When I got to my car I found a note on the windshield: *I'm sorry to have frightened you. I was just so amazed. I have seen you before, but not here, not in this life. Here is my card. Please call. I am a doctor of parapsychology and I want to talk to you about your past life. I saw in your eyes your life in Egypt. If you're interested in regression hypnosis, please call.* How did he know which car was mine? Why had he approached me? Two different days. Two completely different people, in different parts of town, with basically the identical message. What was it that I was supposed to hear or learn? I never called him. I never found out.

That was in 1973, and this was 1981. I was headed to Egypt, and the thoughts of those distant experiences resurfaced. It was late in the evening when the plane landed in Cairo. I was dreading the chore of going through customs. I was too tired to be excited. It was too dark to see anything, so I saved my adventurous ambitions for the next morning.

The plane parked a short distance from the airport, and Leon and I had to walk down the rolled-out stairs, across the tarmac, and into the terminal. I had my carry-on in my arm and exited the aircraft, half asleep. I took care walking down the wobbly stairs, mindful of my fatigue, and when my foot touched the ground, the dirt, the earth, I felt as if roots sprang from my feet and went deep into the ground.

Suddenly, I felt totally energized—I felt alive like I had never felt before and haven't felt since. I felt like I had raced back centuries in time. For the first time in my life, I felt that I totally belonged somewhere. I had to stop and catch my breath. The spiritual experience was overwhelming. There were no words to describe it, so I kept it to myself and didn't share it with Leon as he walked into the airport ahead of me.

I was in Africa. I was home. It didn't matter that Leon and I weren't talking. I felt uplifted, I felt I had found myself, I felt like I no longer needed to be validated by anyone else. I set out to enjoy every moment and treasure it deep in my soul.

Early the next morning, I was awakened by the sounds of what seemed like the entire city singing. I was a little disoriented and jet-lagged, but I made my way to the window. It was nearing sunrise, and the streets were full of people praying to the east. The Fajr salah is the first of the five daily prayers and it is absolutely breathtaking and incredibly spiritual. The early-morning sun gave a golden wash to everything below. The tops of the temples and mosques were poking up over the city in every direction. The smells and sounds were so inviting I couldn't wait to get started.

We spent the day walking the streets of Cairo, visiting the museums, and viewing the King Tut exhibit: the full-fledged exhibit, not the show I'd seen that traveled America, which—as awesome as it was—didn't compare. We visited the marketplace, and suddenly the jet lag hit me, so we headed back to the hotel to take a nap before going out to dinner.

Oddly, my arm was aching from people pinching me on the elbow during the entire day. Each time, I'd feel this stinging pinch that hurt like crazy, and by the time I'd turn around I could never catch anyone. The streets were very crowded, and many of the women were dressed in black burqas and niqabs, some with their faces covered. What was with this pinching? I was getting annoyed.

I mentioned it to the taxi driver, and he told me that they pinched me because I had offended them. I looked Egyptian, but because I was dressed in a backless summer tank top and soft cotton wraparound skirt, they were expressing their anger with me for not dressing in the traditional attire for Egyptian women. Though the pinching itself hurt, the idea that so many women thought I was Egyptian was reassuring that I was where I belonged.

The next day we signed up for two tours that would change my life. The first was the Pyramids of Giza. It saddened me to see how ravaged the pyramids were. The smooth surface I had always pictured in my mind was gone from years and years of being picked at by tourists. The alabaster that had covered the blocks that built the pyramids had been stripped many years ago, to use in the tops of the temples throughout the city, and to keep as souvenirs.

The famous Great Sphinx of Giza sat outside the pyramids. It's so hard to believe that it was covered by sand for hundreds of years, because it's so huge. We mounted camels and rode around the base of the pyramids, and I eagerly learned all that I could from the guides. Then I looked out across the vast Sahara and realized how truly insignificant I was.

One of the most beautiful temples in the city, I wish I could remember the name, was made wholly out of alabaster. When the Egyptian sun was high, it shone right through the translucent walls and roof, and the entire temple lit up, not from electricity—there wasn't any—but only from the glow of the equatorial sunlight through the walls, and the thousands and thousands of candles. It was incredible. All at once, I felt I was in the presence of God. It was the most beautiful light I had ever seen—warm, enveloping, peaceful. The air smelled rich, and everything on the outside seemed to disappear. I had the hardest time pulling myself away.

The next day, we took a boat down the Nile River to the temples at Karnak. I wanted to see and touch this great river that is supposed to be the birthplace of humankind on this earth. As I floated slowly down the river and watched how the people lived along its banks, I was surprised at how it seemed as if time had just stood still on the Nile. There were families in mud huts tending to their animals, washing their clothes, and feeding their families. The tall reeds served as a curtain against the rest of the world.

Seeing the Karnak temples was amazing. The huge pillars and the layers of the city being rebuilt on top of each other throughout the centuries, and the enormous amount of manpower it had taken to create this, was overwhelming to contemplate. We headed out to the nearby Valley of the Kings. The tour passed the stone guards carved out of a single piece of rock, towering more than fifty feet overhead. It made me wonder how humans had ever mastered these monumental accomplishments.

Standing inside the actual tomb of King Tut was a once-in-a-lifetime experience. I was amazed by the paintings and reliefs depicting his life and was even more amazed by the images that looked like people wearing space suits and helmets. I didn't want to leave. I felt as if I was looking at family albums and I wanted to learn all that I could, but the tour was not long enough.

From Egypt, we went to Rome and then Athens. As awesome as the sights of Rome—such as the Roman Forum, the Colosseum, and Trevi Fountain—and the Acropolis in Athens were, nothing could touch the majesty and power of the pyramids. In hindsight, Egypt should have been the *last* visit on our trip, because everything after it paled in comparison.

After coming back from our trip, and realizing that nothing had changed in our marriage, it just seemed to show even more clearly how different Leon and I had become. How far apart we had grown. There was just so much distance between us.

Leon's constant calls back home just slowly became a subject that I didn't even care about anymore. At home I was swamped with work again. . . . Vacation time was over. I was asked to star in a two-hour *Love Boat* special that featured many of the top named models in the fashion industry. I had already done one show for them with John Amos. In this episode, I would be working with Halston and the famous Halstonettes (including Pat Cleveland), costumer Bob Mackie, Gloria Vanderbilt, and a slew of other famous actors.

Immediately after *Love Boat*, I was asked to return to *CHiPs*. I had previously only been a guest in an episode; this time I was hired to star in a television pilot for a series spin-off called *Mitchell and Woods*. Again, the network came back with "We want you, but we can't figure out whom to pair you up with." Eventually, the pilot was done, but after the show aired it never got off the ground.

Hollywood was so set on stereotypes, and its perceptions of ethnicity, that when they wanted to cast a Black actress, I oftentimes wasn't seen as Black enough. Despite these ongoing casting challenges, I continued to get work as an actress. I never fit anyone's mold, I never tried to follow the formula, and against all the odds my career was definitely on the rise. I was doing something that was extremely rare for a Black actress at that time: I was going from project to project. I had done it. The ten-year plan had worked; however, I had crossed the finish line by myself.

By early summer of 1981, other people had begun to notice that Leon and I were having serious relationship problems. A few tried to offer advice, and a few tried to drive the wedge even deeper.

The movie *Body and Soul* was scheduled for release in the fall of that year, and Leon and Hugh Hefner thought that I was now popular enough to do a cover for *Playboy* as part of the marketing and promotion of the film. I was *not* going to do a *Playboy* cover. So, as a compromise, the deal was that since I would not do a nude layout, there would be a few *Playboy* models thrown into the film and a *Playboy* magazine article as well. Again going against my wishes as he had with the MAPS, Leon booked the cover photo shoot anyway. I canceled it. He rebooked it, and I canceled it a second time. We argued about it, and he rebooked me a *third* time. Again, I canceled the shoot.

Leon decided to approach me differently after that.

He challenged me, saying he felt that during the entire ten years of our marriage, I had never *once* done anything for him. His list of my slights and his grievances was long and detailed.

In December of my last year with CBS, Leon's father had passed away from a long bout with cancer and Leon asked me to wear a black armband on the *NFL Today* set. I didn't, thinking that it was inappropriate, since I got so little time to speak on camera anyway, and it was always such a rush just to cover football. He said he felt I had not cared at all.

There was also the time when I was booked as a guest on *The Tonight Show Starring Johnny Carson*. Years before, in the early 1970s, I had appeared on the show as a product girl. Probably most of you don't even remember when that was a part of the show. A sexy girl would come onstage holding a sponsor's product so Johnny could talk about it, leading into the commercial break. This time it was the early 1980s and I was a guest who actually got to sit on the couch and talk with Johnny. This was a major coup for my career.

After arriving on set, I found out that Johnny was out and Bert Convy was sitting in for him. I sat in the green room waiting to go on, summarizing in my head what I needed to say. I kept thinking of how I had gotten there, all the shows I had done on the NBC soundstages, the years of shows with Bob Hope, Redd Foxx, Flip Wilson, Dean Martin, *Rowan & Martin's Laugh-In*, and many, many specials.

I thought about all the people at NBC who had believed in me and had helped along the way. I even thought about the wonderful old Black man who greeted me each and every day, with the biggest smile and the warmest heart, from his shoeshine stand in the NBC hallways. Every day, he was there shining shoes for the most amazing people in Hollywood. Every day, he was listening to the inner workings of a business that held the attention of the world. Every day, he took the time to truly connect with *everybody*, making that one moment in your life special. No one entered NBC without a respectful hello to him. Senior executives and major stars could often be seen sitting in his chair long after their shoeshine was done. And every day since the very first day I walked into the coveted NBC hallways, he'd tell me how special I was, how proud he was of me, and he'd simply glow as he smiled at me.

I also thought about my conversation with Leon the night before. Leon had asked me to talk about him and *his* projects, to take advantage of my moment on the *Tonight Show* to promote *him*. I just couldn't do that. It didn't feel right—this was an interview about me. I had earned this rare opportunity to appear on the *Tonight Show*, and more importantly, CBS had painted me as the villain who had breached our contract, and this was my first public chance to set that record straight.

My mind continued to race as the time to go onstage with Bert Convy got closer. *Speak Up, America* had been canceled that fall. And with MAPS, I had two new shows in the can that I was hoping had some potential.

I was very pleased with how I handled myself, but when I got home, Leon was furious. I couldn't believe my ears.

"Listen, Jayne, if our marriage is going to last, you must give in to three demands: One, have a baby; two, allow my girlfriend to move in as my second wife; and three, quit your career."

Obviously, I was doing none of those ridiculous demands. But I wasn't walking away. Yet. I decided to do the *Playboy* cover as the last thing I would do for him. Before I agreed to the photo shoot, however, I called my mom and asked her what she thought. She said, "As long as it doesn't show anything that a bathing suit wouldn't show, then it's all right."

When the July 1981 issue hit the stands, it nearly ruined my career . . . and my soul. I was the first Black actress to ever appear on the cover of *Playboy* and even though it was one of the biggest sellers for Hefner that year, many thought I'd sold out, even though I did not pose nude. I also did not do any solo photos, all were with Leon in various poses of embrace. I was no longer their *precious* Jayne. Newspaper headlines denounced me. Even my hometown papers that always referred to me as "our Jayne" were now just saying "Jayne Kennedy of Hollywood."

Our Bible-study group was producing our first Living Proof Gospel Music Festival in Washington, DC, at RFK Stadium. The group, comprised of notable artists and musicians, was scheduled to perform at the event with the goal of spreading "the Word of God" to a packed stadium audience. Shortly after the cover came out, even though I had been at odds with the Bible-study group since that retreat in San Bernardino, I was very much looking forward to attending.

Though they were very polite, the study group asked me not to attend. I was crushed. These were my best friends—or so I thought. I had been going to Bible study with these people and on numerous retreats with them for years. For the past few months, they had served as marriage counselors for Leon and me. But now they felt that the audience would be more focused on my appearance in *Playboy*, instead of my message. The purpose of the event was to bring people to Christ, and apparently my place in doing so was tainted, my personal witness no longer required.

I was devastated and alienated. I remember when I first started going to Bible class I felt so useless because I didn't have a message, a testimony. I prayed for something to share where I might be able to do some good. I had not been in touch with anyone, with *real* people, that is, over the years because I had spent so much time on the road. I was so out of sync with reality. My life was about going from one studio to another, one airport to another, and while it was wonderful professionally, spiritually I had lost any sense of the essence of life.

When I was on the road, I was by myself. When I was home, I was up there on top of that hill by myself. My family was three thousand miles away and I didn't really have a church home in LA either. I was praying every day for God to help me. I was so desperate for him to welcome me into his arms. I was so lonely and depressed. I was out of touch with God and I needed to share that. And I remember thinking: Be careful what you pray for. You just might get it.

Now here I was about to go in front of tens of thousands to share my testimony, without the support of the people I thought loved me for me, with all my faults, even with the *Playboy* cover. I had finally gotten my first national mainstream magazine cover, but this was what came with it.

Pastor E. V. Hill of Mount Zion Missionary Baptist Church, the church home of my supposed "friends," was the only one who believed in me and supported me through those times. He asked me if I believed in my heart that I had a message. I truly believed that I did. He encouraged me to go to DC, saying that no one could stand in my way if I felt I should be there. He said no one should ever stand in the way of someone who feels they have God's work to do.

I didn't have anywhere to turn. The people in the church had ostracized me, and my support system in my husband—or what I had believed was my support system—was gone. I lived so far away from everyone, and had worked so much, that I literally had no friends. I wouldn't dream of bringing this drama back home to Mom and Dad. I had always prided myself in being self-sufficient in their eyes. My marriage was beyond repair, I was in the middle of a divorce without even realizing it, and I was angry and hurt every day. I was losing weight, and I thought I was losing my mind too. By then I had repainted our house at least five times. . . . It was my way of blowing off steam.

The night before the event, I was staying in a quaint little bed-and-breakfast in Washington, DC, that served as a Christian retreat. I was in the attic bedroom all by myself and I couldn't sleep. I was so afraid of appearing on that stage the next day. The fear was worse this time than any other time in my life. I wanted to do the right thing, but I wasn't sure I knew what that was. I prayed to God to use me to do his work, in whatever way he wanted. I prayed to let him use me and give me strength and the words to say.

I prayed at the side of my bed for what seemed to be half the night, and He came to me. He promised me that He still loved me. A floodgate of emotions opened, and at the same time, I felt the greatest sense of calm. That's all I needed to hear. My eyes cleared, my head cleared, then my heart cleared, and I went to bed.

I stood on the stage at RFK Stadium with Billy Davis Jr. and Marilyn McCoo at my side, propping me up, and I professed my faith in God. I rededicated my life to pleasing only God. And I cried. I could not stop from crying. I felt God within me. I felt loved, and for the first time in years, I felt at peace. At that moment, standing on that stage, I remembered my Mom's words: *The only ones you have to please are yourself and God.*

# CHAPTER TWENTY-FIVE

# HOME
# IS WHERE
# THE HEART ISN'T

I f I tried to tell you all the things that went wrong in our relationship, it would surely be another book, and I don't believe it would do any good to rehash all of it. But I will say that I had lost all hope in the institution of marriage. I had lost trust in the one person outside of my family who I considered to be my safety net. I was always taught, and I believed, that marriage was forever—when I was growing up, I think I could count on one hand the people I knew who were divorced. Now I think I can count on one hand the number of people who are still married to their original partner.

Leon was so consumed with meeting the goals of our ten-year plan, which we both believed in and were committed to achieving, that he forgot that I was a person and not an object to place on top of a pedestal. That was always the way he saw me. He was at cross-purposes with himself and did not even realize it—until it was too late. Ironically, he was tearing apart the very thing that he was working so diligently to build . . . manufacturing the idealized embodiment of the Golden Couple (as we were once anointed in the press) that everyone wanted to believe was true.

He recently spoke to me regarding that very contentious time in our relationship.

"An elderly woman whom I had never met before walked up to me and said, 'Tell me it isn't true? You and Jayne are getting a divorce?'

"'Yes.'

"'Well, now I can just go home and die,' she replied."

By September 1981, I don't know what we had, but it wasn't a marriage. I started seeing other men, and Leon was still determined to get me to agree to his three demands. At that point, he was living full-time with the second woman he had selected to be his "second wife."

He had another apartment where he told everyone he lived, but it wasn't furnished. He told me that it was my fault he didn't live at home, because until *I* got *my* act together and accepted his terms, he only had an empty apartment as an alternative. Since he couldn't live in an empty apartment, and I was keeping him from coming home, he had no choice but to stay with his girlfriend.

Hearing that convoluted reasoning, I went shopping and bought everything he needed for his new place. I then went to his apartment manager, smiling, and told him that this apartment was where my husband stayed when he worked long nights, instead of driving home; that he wanted me to furnish it for him; and that I'd forgotten my key, so could he let me in, please? The apartment manager happily agreed. In four hours, the place was completely furnished, down to the silverware and napkins. I then called Leon.

"Jayne, I told you I—"

"Leon, you can go home now. I furnished it top to bottom for you. You have no more excuses. Pasadena isn't your home anymore."

In October 1981, we released *Body and Soul*. When the film premiered in Los Angeles, it was a major event. For me, it had literally taken a piece of *my* body and soul to bring it thus far. Leon was so focused on the production that

I don't think he even saw my pain. I don't believe he knew the hurt that came from his single-vision perspective. He was all about making a great film, no matter the personal cost. We were angry with each other, so much so that I don't even know how we ever got the film done.

Even though the shooting had been an emotional disaster, I wanted this, my first Los Angeles film premiere, to be very special. I dressed at Smokey and Claudette's, and we took a limo to the theatre in downtown Los Angeles, planning to arrive a little early because I had to stop at the box office to pick up my tickets. They had been previously delivered to my home—"Jayne Kennedy plus one"—but when I was leaving the house I couldn't find them. As I approached the red carpet the paparazzi began taking pictures and calling, "Jayne! Jayne! Look this way! Jayne, look over here! Jayne, whose dress are you wearing? Jayne, how about a smile over here?" It was a wonderful frenzy. This was going to be a night I would remember forever. I picked up my duplicate tickets at the box office and entered the theatre.

I was walking on air, smiling confidently, and I headed down to the front of the theatre to take my seat with the cast, then abruptly halted in utter disbelief: Leon's girlfriend, Evil Spirit, was in my seat. She was just sitting there, all full of herself, smiling away at me, seeming to enjoy my shock and dismay.

My heart sank. I felt like a mule had just kicked me in the gut. My whole body ached. I noticed people looking at me as if to say, *Uh-oh, what's she going to do now?* I was so humiliated—everybody knew, *everybody knew*. I had no idea what I was going to do. The usher looked at *her* ticket and acknowledged that she was in the right seat. She had taken my tickets from the house. I turned and walked toward the back of the theatre, and before I could collect my thoughts my longtime friend Glynn Turman gently took my arm in his. He looked right through me and into my soul. I guess I looked lost. Then he whispered, "You're going to sit with me."

I will forever be grateful to Glynn for his sensitivity and kindness that night. We walked to two seats in the back of the theatre, and I don't remember the rest of the night at all.

As far as our fans were concerned, we had the perfect marriage, and we agreed to maintain that image so it wouldn't hurt the success of the film. We opened on the road in Chicago. We had agreed to travel separately but appear to be together. When I arrived at the hotel, the desk clerk told me that Mr. Kennedy was already in our room. I was shocked. I had really hoped we could do this without the drama.

I went up to the room and there he was, in my hotel bed. I asked him what he was doing.

"Well, I thought about it, and you're right, we should be together."

"Leon, I'm done. I can't do this anymore. I'm completing this tour and I'm done. You have to go."

It was a pivotal day for me; I had really tried to make my marriage work, but I was through trying. I never looked back after that day.

I found out on October 27, 1981, that Leon had filed for divorce, ending our ten-year marriage. He announced it to everyone, including me—on a *call-in radio show*—on my thirtieth birthday. Most people think it was me who filed for divorce; not true.

We agreed that I would keep the house since he had already moved out, but every time I turned around, there he was, coming through the door—even when I changed the locks. Somehow, he always had a key. I couldn't take the mind games, the manipulation anymore, so I told him I was moving out. I had made it all possible once, I could do it again.

On Christmas Eve 1981, I moved out with three suitcases and two small boxes.

# CHAPTER TWENTY-SIX

# A NEW VIEW
# FROM A NEW HILL

I did it once, I can do it again.

Over and over, like a mantra, I said that to myself—it became my motto. I moved into a beautiful home right in the heart of the Hollywood Hills, at the top of Mulholland Drive. It was much too big for just me, but I wanted to feel as if I hadn't lost anything and was moving on. It was important to me that I feel no regrets for how the past ten years had ended. The house was contemporary Mediterranean and sat on stilts on the side of a hill over- looking the San Fernando Valley. I loved it—four bedrooms, three and a half baths, a formal dining room, a gourmet kitchen, two fireplaces, and four bal- conies. Everything was white with dark oak trim throughout, exposed beams, Spanish tile, and high ceilings.

As soon as I walked in the front door, I knew it was mine, even though I had no idea how I was going to pay the rent. It was just like moving into my first house. I had been looking all over the place and nothing had seemed like me. Without hesitation I rented the house for one year.

The week after, my thirteen-year-old cousin, Kenny, was helping me to unpack when there was a knock at the door. Kenny answered, and a man was standing there. Just behind him was a car—an incredibly beautiful Clénet roadster—parked in my driveway. Kenny just stood there, stunned, his eyes as big as saucers. As I walked past Kenny to greet the unexpected guest, a man I had gone out with a few times, the guy started smiling. He had heard I had left Leon and had tracked me down.

He offered to help me unpack, and I graciously declined. He then held out the keys to his car.

"I brought this for you."

I looked at him and gently pushed them away, smiling, but firmly saying, "No thanks" as I tried not to scream, taking in how gorgeous that car was. Again, he tried to convince me,

"Just for a while, then. You could even live in my house in Beverly Hills until you get on your feet, and you don't have to pay for this place. I'm still living at my place in New York, so you would be there by yourself."

I politely refused, a second time, and consciously did not ask him to come sit down, so we stood there in the entryway talking a bit awkwardly. Then I escorted him back to the car, kissed him on the cheek, and promised to call him the next day.

The door closed. Kenny ran to the window, gawking at the beautiful, shiny, custom-built car, then turned back to me, practically jumping up and down. "Are you *crazy*???"

I stepped up close to Kenny, brushed back his hair, and looked him right in the eyes. "Nothing comes for free. One way or another, I'd have to pay. I don't want to owe anyone anything, ever again. If I take that car now, he'll have expectations that I don't want to commit to right now. Do you understand?"

Kenny was still confused. "But he said it was just for a little while. Couldn't we just go for a ride?"

I had to smile at his innocence. "No, Kenny, I'd still owe him. And I'm not for sale."

I never wanted to be dependent on anyone else ever again. I was going to be on my own for the first time in my life. I was going to be fine . . . on my own.

At that moment, I only had enough money for two months' rent. It was going to take a year before the divorce was settled, and there was no money from our marriage until the paperwork was completed. I had no idea how I was going to pull this off. I had left behind almost everything I had. When I moved out, I had taken some personal things, my clothes, and my dignity, and that was about it. I even left behind all my beautiful wedding gifts, including my handmade lace place mats from France that were given to me by my mom's lifelong friend Mrs. Farr, my collectibles from around the world—everything.

So, there I was again, in a huge empty house, with no job, no money, and no furniture. Most of the credit cards were in my name because I had a pretty steady paycheck. However, I had no credit on my credit report because unbelievably, at that time credit was only in the husband's name. So when you divorced, that credit stayed with the husband, no matter who built the credit line. I had no one to depend on but me. It was the first time in my life that I was truly on my own. I was thirty years old.

At nineteen, I had gone from my parents' house to a house with my husband, and I admit, I was frightened of finally stepping out on my own. The house on Mulholland sat on the hill overlooking the city lights in the distance. Right out the window was the backyard, three stories straight down—no rolling slope like the hillside I used to sit on back home in Wickliffe wondering where I would go in the world, just straight down—and I was always afraid of heights. This next step was not going to be easy. If I failed it would be a long way down—literally and figuratively.

I signed up for drama class with Milton Katselas, a talented director, acting coach, writer, and painter . . . and my friend. He taught out of the prestigious Beverly Hills Playhouse for twenty years.

I began looking for work. I kept my secretary from before (she was Leon's cousin's wife), and I converted two of the bedrooms into office space. Thankfully, I still had Rudy Tellez as my manager. Together, we devised a plan for me to become more independent. I was not content to wait for the phone to ring; I *had* to make something happen. I formed my own production company, Jayne Kennedy Productions, and quickly set out to decide what project I wanted to develop first.

In 1976, I had been invited to present at the Black Filmmakers Hall of Fame Awards in Oakland, California. Backstage, I ran into a woman who grabbed me, shook me, and hugged me so tightly I could barely breathe. Then she gasped, "If anyone plays my sister, it's got to be you." It was Vivian Dandridge. I had been familiar with who Dorothy Dandridge was, but not her life story. I only knew that she had been the first Black woman nominated for an Academy Award for best actress; however, she didn't win, and as of 1981, no Black actress had. Combining the role of Dorothy Dandridge with my own personal goal to become the first Black woman to win the coveted award seemed the perfect vehicle for my new production company.

So, there I was, five years later, reading the biography that had been written in 1970 by Dorothy's manager, Earl Mills: *Dorothy Dandridge: A Portrait in Black*. It seemed that on every page, I was reading about my life. This story was so close—too close, even—to many secrets about my own feelings. There may have been different circumstances, but the feelings permeated my soul. I had to do this. I had to expose her shortcomings, so other young ladies wouldn't make the same mistakes.

I met with Earl and bought the rights to his book. I hired a writer. I wanted a female writer so I could incorporate all the subtle feminine issues and attitudes that men oftentimes don't seem to understand.

But despite that, I'd worked with a writer on *Body and Soul* and he convinced me to allow him to at least draft the first treatment to present to the studios because he really needed the money. I acquiesced. Eventually he tried to steal the property from me, and I had to take him to court, winning my own property back. But that's another story.

Apparently, Leon and Cannon Films had already planned to produce *The Dorothy Dandridge Story* starring me, as a follow-up to *Body and Soul*. Even though the deal had been done, partial funding had been raised, and they had even begun to shop the film . . . I was never told. Even Earl Mills, who had previously sold the rights to his book to Cannon and Leon, never told me that it was intended as a vehicle for me. I only found out years later when I happened upon their promotion advert that was created for presale financing: "The Cannon Group Inc. presents Jayne Kennedy in a Leon Isaac Kennedy production of a Michael Schultz Film: *The Dorothy Dandridge Story*."

This time it was me who shopped the project *everywhere*, but no one wanted to touch it. For whatever reasons, while I continued to pay the option fee for the rights, there were no takers. Once again, I was ahead of my time. Eighteen years later, Halle Berry ended up playing Dorothy in the Emmy- and Golden Globe–winning *Introducing Dorothy Dandridge*. But even two decades later her road was still not an easy one, I learned. I heard that when the original pitch was made to HBO, there wasn't an immediate awareness of who Dandridge even was. But they had taken a previous risk several years before on a little-known Black dancer by the name of Josephine Baker in *The Josephine Baker Story* starring Lynn Whitfield that was a huge success for the network . . . so they ultimately gave *Dandridge* the green light. Interestingly enough, the *Dandridge* script was cowritten by a then unknown scribe just getting her feet wet in Hollywood by the name of Shonda Rhimes.

Luckily, I didn't have to worry about making my rent. I got small jobs as a host on several TV shows. I was offered a syndicated series named the *Jayne Kennedy NFL Report* but then after two shows the executive producers ran out of money.

Rudy had quickly become my good friend in addition to him being my manager, and once we started banging our heads together a lot of energy was generated, and we found very little time to sit and ponder what to do next.

Rudy got a call from Charlie Fasch in Nashville. Charlie had an idea about my hosting a series of exercise records and tapes for his company, Complete Records. I agreed, but only if I also coproduced the project. A big ask, but I had to, and they agreed. Charlie and I hammered out the details, and we signed a record deal with Polygram Records for distribution.

I called the project *Love Your Body*. At that time, Jane Fonda had the only exercise video in the marketplace that was generating significant sales. Richard Simmons was beginning to make some headway, and the market was wide open for me. I basically took the concepts I had developed through my years of experience in dance and exercise and tied them in with sound exercise advice from professionals. I hired a staff of very talented individuals to assist in putting it together: Rudy, Tracey Wilson—who had become my new personal assistant and was so absolutely wonderful in every aspect of the job that I made her my associate producer—and Toy Gibson-Igus, my writer. I sent the list of the music I selected to Charlie Fasch, who began producing all the music for the exercise routines in Nashville. I hired Bruce Fisher, my then brother-in-law, who had written the Joe Cocker hit "You Are So Beautiful," to write and produce the title cut for the album, and Thomas McClary from the Commodores wrote and produced the single "Steam Room" for me. They were great. . . . I, on the other hand, as a singer, left a little to be desired.

Coincidentally, my friend Billy Davis Jr. from the 5th Dimension called and asked if I would be interested in hosting an exercise video he was producing with Jeff Tuckman and Chicago Teleproductions. I agreed, but again, only if I coproduced the project and we tied it in with my *Love Your Body* concept. We were able to make a distribution deal with RCA Columbia Home Video. *Love Your Body* received high praise from the critics and was well on its way to *Love Your Body & More* and its follow-up—*The Complete Love Your Body*.

The entire Love Your Body franchise was now in the top three in the country, along with Jane Fonda and my friend Richard Simmons. Then came the touring and once again I was on the road.

I lived at Mulholland Drive a year and a half.


Over the course of the next eighteen months my career began to diversify even more. Sports had remained a major part of my life, and I was signed to be the first female host in the thirty-year history of the longest-running syndicated sports series *Greatest Sports Legends*, a position I held for five years.

Usually, they would produce the show with a different host each year, but I had gained a substantial amount of support from the athletes and had the added value of being able to bring athletes who had previously turned down appearing on the show. It had become commonplace for the production office to run into a brick wall trying to book guests. But when the guests were told that I would be the host, no problem.

Bill Russell had turned down *GSL* several times throughout the years. But this time when they told him Jayne Kennedy would be the host, he readily agreed. Before we started taping I just had to ask him, "Why me? What made you do this for me?" And with all sincerity he said, "Because you are building a legacy, and I want to be a part of helping to make that happen for you." I was stunned and extremely honored.

(Many years later at the 2018 NBA Awards show in Santa Monica, I found myself making my way to the legends table so that I could give a very long overdue, gigantic hug to Mr. Russell, along with the other legends, Kareem Abdul-Jabbar and Oscar Robertson.)

This happened on other sports shows I hosted as well. *CBS Sports Spectacular* had tried to get an interview with Julius Erving and they wanted to shoot at his home. Julius and his then wife, Turquoise, had repeatedly denied any press access to their home. They told CBS that the only way they would allow filming in their home was if I were the interviewer. My personal friendships were added value to my professional life.

In addition to my sports-related work, I had been trying to get a spokesperson deal with Coca-Cola for years, but there was always something that seemed to get in the way. Back then I was legally represented by Edward Bell, an attorney I'd known since 1975. I met Ed in Chicago at a party for Muhammad Ali. We had become fast friends, and Ed was always there for me—not only as an attorney, but also as a truly good mentor and counsel through many of the obstacles in the entertainment industry.

Ed lived in Detroit. Whenever I went to visit him at his offices, it was quite common to run into any number of other notables—celebrities, attorneys, and businesspeople—including my good friend Jesse Jackson, who I campaigned for in his run for the presidency in 1984. After hours was a time to gather and hang out. Ed knew all the best restaurants and was always treated like royalty, and not just in Detroit. Everywhere we went—New Orleans, Seattle, New York, Philadelphia, San Diego—it was life on a grand scale. That was Ed Bell, my spiritual backup, my friend, and my lawyer.

One day in 1982, I got a call from Ed that I should get on the very next plane from Los Angeles to Detroit. Ed and I were going to a dinner party hosted by Stuart Geller, the Detroit Coca-Cola bottler. Stuart had told Ed that Roberto Crispulo Goizueta, chairman, director, and CEO of Coca-Cola, would be there, and that we should be there too. I ran out the door and caught the first flight, smoking to Detroit.

As soon as I arrived, I was picked up in a limo and rushed to Ed's office. By the time we got to the dinner the party had already started. It was a black-tie affair, and everyone was having a wonderful time. Ed introduced me to Mr. Goizueta. We chatted for no more than ten minutes and suddenly he asked, "Why aren't you working for Coca-Cola?"

Ed laughed and slapped him on the back. "That's exactly what we've been asking ourselves. Jayne would be a great asset to your company. Unfortunately, we've been encountering some internal holdups."

Roberto quickly said, "I'll take care of it. You don't have to worry about that anymore."

The very next morning Ed got a phone call from Coca-Cola's corporate headquarters in Atlanta with instructions to draw up the papers, and the deal was done. Just like that. I worked with Coca-Cola for the next six years.

My first assignment was for the introduction of Diet Coke to the world, beginning with a press conference in New York. Tab, another Coca-Cola product, was the number one diet soft drink in the world at that time, and the company wanted to make sure the bottlers understood there would be no cannibalism within the two brands. Diet Coke would not knock off Tab. I was going to be one of the models for the big Tab campaign once Diet Coke hit the shelves.

In the past, many of the spokesmodels that Coca-Cola had were merely poster models. But I was not just a pretty face; I had done my homework.

They began by introducing all the models one by one, with each girl taking a turn at the microphone to say a quick hello. When they finally got to me, I went to the podium, took the microphone, and went into a full description of the Coca-Cola marketing plan that I had found in the handout materials the day before, and how Tab and Diet Coke could survive in a common marketplace. They were quite surprised that I could talk at all, let alone pitch them on their own products. I was booked on Coca-Cola–sponsored events within a couple weeks, touring around the country as a *spokesperson* for both Tab and Diet Coke.

*Love Your Body* had just been released, and Coca-Cola wanted to tie in their campaign with my advertising campaign. Or should I say, they were going to allow me to tie in with them. The *Love Your Body* product was just what Coca-Cola had wanted. The natural tie-in with exercise was a great success for them, and we worked together in TV commercials, print ads, speaking engagements, and personal appearances all over the country in every kind of circumstance. It was a great opportunity for both of us.

Whenever you work for a corporate entity, you always maintain representation of the product wherever you go. I was great at that. I loved Coca-Cola anyway, so it was easy—wherever I went, I sang the praises of Coke, Diet Coke, and Tab. If I were in the middle of a meeting, I always had a can of Coca-Cola product in front of me. At any press conference, front and center I had my can of Diet Coke or Tab. At photo opportunities, I was never without my can of Tab.

Over the next two years, the deals kept coming. I signed a contract to produce and host a series of ten-minute exercise clips for American Airlines called *AAerobics*, the very first in-flight exercise program ever. I went on to produce and host *RadioRobics*, a daily five-minute morning exercise show, and sold it into radio syndication. I signed on to represent Fashion Fair cosmetics and was booked to do beauty, exercise, and makeup seminars around the country. I then signed to do radio commercials and print for Esoterica skin care products. I became a spokeswoman with Revlon in TV commercials and print. The cities began to all blend together once again, one airport, one city just like the next: Houston, Atlanta, Detroit, Cleveland, DC, Chicago, New Orleans, Dallas, Portland, Montgomery, Jackson, Las Vegas, Pittsburgh, Houston, Boston, New York, and on and on. I was never home.

But I was determined to also find time for my drama classes. I had continued taking classes with Milton Katselas. It was getting harder and harder to squeeze in the classes, but if I was going to develop and star in my own films, working toward that coveted Oscar, I needed to work on my craft. It was also my sanity in a world that often wasn't sane. Acting was my safe haven, my only escape. No drinking, no drugs, no smoking, just acting—that was my high.

In 1984, after working with Milton for nearly three years, I was doing a scene with Conroy Gedeon, my favorite acting partner. The scene was from *Lady Sings the Blues* where Billie Holiday has been on the road for months too long and is heavily into drugs. One night after the show, she returns to her dressing room to find Louis McKay waiting there. He'd been more than worried about her deterioration. It is an extremely emotional and dramatic scene as their love for each other clashes with Billie's drug-induced state of mind.

I knew this woman. I knew the road. I knew about love and the longing and the need to have that love. I decided to start the scene with Lenny Welch's song "Since I Fell for You."

I played the part from my soul. The pain of being alone day after day, the minutes that dragged begrudgingly into another tormented hour. Too many tears that even makeup couldn't cover. The pacing round and round in hotel rooms because I was too afraid to go outside.

The emotions welling up from the scene triggered memories, or was it the other way around? A floodgate of sentiments I had held back for far too long.

I remembered being on the road in the South, hearing the desk clerk say, "I wouldn't recommend that you go out for a walk, Miss Kennedy, not alone in this part of town. Not a lone Black woman."

I remembered the times on the road with the Ding-A-Ling Sisters when, after a show, I had to stay in the car while the other girls went into the restaurant to eat, and they had to bring my meal out to go . . . because I was the Black girl.

I remembered getting off work at two a.m. and not being able to call anyone because I would have woken them up.

I remembered calling Leon at two, three, four a.m., hoping that I *would* wake him up, and he was never there. I remembered all the pain, and then the anger came. It felt so good to finally release all that anger. It felt too good. After the scene was over, I practically collapsed in my chair.

It took me a while to come down after the scene. Jeffrey Tambor was sitting in for Milton that night and his critique was overwhelmingly positive. Then he asked me if I was crying backstage as I prepared before my entrance. As I had been outside in the alley behind the stage, I had thought no one could hear me, but I knew I had to find that place that gave me that life before I entered the stage. And the only thing I knew was hurt, pain, and tears. I only know that now because afterward, I listened to the cassette tape of his comments. But that night, I couldn't hear anything he said—that night the sound of the memories was far too deafening.

I went home and cried. Why was all this my life? What was my purpose? Somehow, I knew I had to find it. But I had no idea how.

# CHAPTER TWENTY-SEVEN

# BILL . . . WHEN I NEEDED HIM MOST

n 1973, while I was working as a Ding-A-Ling Sister, Bill Overton moved into the same apartments Leon and I had moved to in Burbank, California, a huge, brand-new complex that sat on the top of a hill overlooking the Universal Studios and the Warner Bros. back lots and was near NBC. It was a big complex and I was on the road a lot, so although he and Leon occasionally bumped into each other and worked out together while they talked about the industry, Bill and I never met.

Bill had been chosen to play the part of Apollo Creed in *Rocky* and had been in training for weeks. As Sylvester Stallone noted in a recent Instagram post with a photo of him and Bill, "Fate or just bad luck? Until Carl Weathers showed up, this fella was going to play Apollo Creed."

Before he actually moved to LA, Bill was commuting between Los

Angeles, where he was shooting the television series *Firehouse*, and New York, where he was in demand as a model.

Bill was born in Roxbury, Boston. An only child, he went to the prestigious Boston English High School, an all-boys school at the time, where he excelled in academics, student government, and sports. Though he was an all-around athlete, it was football that provided Bill scholarship opportunities for college. He ultimately chose a school as far away from the "fairer sex and potential distractions" as possible—a junior college in McCook, Nebraska, where he was the only Black person in town.

After two successful years at McCook, Bill received a full athletic scholarship to Wake Forest University in Winston-Salem, North Carolina, as a linebacker for the Demon Deacons, where he was one of the first Blacks to play in the phenomenal Atlantic Coast Conference (ACC). Bill's experiences in the Deep South playing in front of crowds that jeered, spit on him, and threw liquor at him as he entered the stadium were a constant reminder of the most important reason he was there—to get an education and get out.

After graduating, Bill was signed for the Dallas Cowboys and was eventually traded to Hank Stram's 1969 Kansas City Chiefs. After a year with Kansas City, Bill went on to play in the Canadian Football League with the Hamilton Tiger-Cats. If he had stayed in KC he would have earned a Super Bowl ring the very next year, but there he was in Canada. About to be traded again, he knew it was time to get out of professional football altogether.

New York became Bill's next objective. He moved to Manhattan in the early 1970s and began working with a sports marketing agency, where he traveled recruiting young athletes for professional representation while also working professionally as a model. But as it was for me, acting was his first love, and he began training in New York with the Lee Strasberg Institute. Bill soon found success in TV and film, which led to numerous roles: *Guess Who's Coming to Dinner*, where he played the lead against Leslie Charleson; the series *Firehouse*, which brought him to Los Angeles; the film *Grambling's White Tiger*, along with Caitlyn Jenner; and notably, the miniseries *Backstairs at the*

*White House*, as part of a stellar cast including Olivia Cole, Leslie Uggams, Louis Gossett Jr., Robert Hooks, Lee Grant, Leslie Nielsen, George Kennedy, Cloris Leachman, Paul Winfield, Robert Vaughn, and a host of others.

Fate tried to bring Bill Overton and me together many times. It took a minute to get it right. First, if I was not joining Wilhelmina, I had considered joining the Eileen Ford modeling agency. Bill was already signed, and we would definitely have met then.

Then we both moved to LA within two years of each other, and out of all the thousands of apartments in LA, we ended up living in the same apartment complex. But we didn't meet then either.

*Firehouse* was literally igniting his career, so again, the last thing he needed or wanted was to be distracted by females.

Bill decided he was taking a break from dating and was focusing on his career. One night he went to a club in Hollywood, and as he walked in the door, he immediately saw "two gorgeous women sitting at the bar . . ." Sounds like a joke. But these two women happened to be my sister and me. He took one look at us, shook his head, and consciously decided that I would be a *major* distraction, so he turned around, walked right back out. Too much temptation.

Fate must have been shaking its head. Three opportunities for our meeting now missed—the Ford agency, the apartment complex, and the bar—so a fourth opportunity came up, this time through my dear friend Lamonte McLemore.

Lamonte was, and is, my all-time favorite photographer. He always could see right through me, somehow managing to capture my thoughts and feelings in stills. He taught me everything I know about relating to the photographer when you're in front of the lens. We always had a natural ease with every session. He was that once-in-a-lifetime special connection that I had never had, my best friend from the moment we first met. Whenever I looked into the lens, I'd see his sparkling green eyes behind it; he has always brought me peace. So, whenever Lamonte wanted to do a shoot, I was there.

When Lamonte was starting a new magazine called *TWO*, he asked me if

I would be part of the couple he needed for the cover. I was more than happy and headed over to his studio. I came out of the dressing room wearing a nude bodysuit and nude heels, and who should I see . . . Bill Overton, model and former NFL player, already in place on the backdrop before the camera, wearing nothing but a simple pair of red briefs and a full beard. Even though he had a great body from his years of sports, for some reason I thought what was most handsome about him was the beard and the eyes.

The cover shoot was very simple, with several other shots for the inside of the magazine in full tux and evening gown. Bill was very professional and extremely quiet. After the shoot was over, he left Lamonte's studio quickly. Lamonte loved the photos, but the publication never got off the ground. It seemed like somewhere in the cosmos, the sole purpose—or should I say *soul* purpose?—for the shoot had been for Bill and me to finally meet.

A couple of years later, when Bill returned to LA and Leon and I had moved to Pasadena, Leon ran into Bill again and this time he invited him and his girl-friend over to our place for dinner. By that time, Bill had started dating our mutual friend Kathleen Bradley, abandoning his "no female distraction" rule.

Kathleen was a singer and dancer with the hot international 1970s pop group the Love Machine. Love Machine was a lot like the Ding-A-Ling Sisters and The Golddiggers, but they were *so* much better. More my kind of singing, my kind of dancing. In a nutshell . . . more *soulful.*

Kathleen, Sheila, Mary, Paulette, Bernice, Gwen, Sandra, and Renee—they were hot. Lots of leather, halter tops, hot pants, fringe, big Afros, and thigh-high platform go-go boots was their usual wardrobe. Bill and Kathleen soon became part of our circle of great friends.

Although we didn't have time to see Bill and Kathleen—or many of our friends—nearly as much as we'd have liked while we lived in Pasadena. It was a long drive from our home in the Kinneloa Ranch all the way into LA and Hollywood, and people couldn't just drop by for a visit. I didn't realize it at the time, but that distance seriously affected my life in terms of sustaining most of my friendships. But whenever Bill came to visit, he'd call and announce that he was on his way, giving me just enough time to bake my signature chocolate cake by the time he arrived. It became an ongoing joke between us—I always made the cake just for Bill, and he'd eat the whole thing.

Toward the end of the 1970s, when Leon and I were having marital problems on and off, we were still talking about how to celebrate our ten-year wedding anniversary on June 26, 1981, when we got an invitation to Bill and Kathleen's wedding, which was to be the day after.

Even though the announcement was addressed to the both of us, Leon decided to go to Texas with his girlfriend for our anniversary instead.

The weekend of Bill and Kathleen's wedding came. I really wasn't in a "wedding mood." I had already sent my gift, and I reasoned they probably wouldn't miss me anyway.

The night of my anniversary, the day before their wedding, I decided to stay home . . . and get drunk.

Bad decision. I don't drink. I have never been a drinker. I don't smoke. I don't do drugs. Although I had liked the taste of Kahlúa in hot chocolate one time at Christmas, so that Friday night, I decided to mix Kahlúa in hot tea. I fixed a whole mug of it, took a sip, and passed out.

The next morning, I woke up with the tea still on my nightstand and decided I was a fool to let Leon steal the joy of my sharing our friends' special day. I was going to that wedding, and I was going to have fun no matter how hard I had to work at it. I got dressed, jumped in my car, and raced all the way, hoping I hadn't missed it because I was so late.

Since I had never been where the ceremony was taking place, it took me some time to find the house. By the time I parked, I could hear the music starting. I ran up to the front steps but didn't see anyone inside. The door was open, so I raced through the empty house toward the music coming from the backyard. I ran out the back door just as the wedding march began. I was obviously not supposed to enter through *that* door at *that* exact moment, as that was where the bridal party was entering . . . at that exact moment.

I was absolutely mortified. All I could see was Bill's face looking at me from the other end of the aisle, standing there in his black tux, and that handsome full beard, slightly smiling and shaking his head. I quickly jumped aside and from behind me came the flower girl, the bridesmaids, and Kathleen. She looked stunning. But in all honesty, that was the first time I was struck by how truly handsome Bill was.

Everything about the wedding was beautiful. After the ceremony, I met Bill's parents, Hessie and Eugene, and we took a few pictures. But shortly thereafter, I decided I couldn't handle the wedding—the love, the commitment, the happiness. *Not today.* I was too emotionally fragile, fighting against the memories of my own wedding ten years before, even though I had really wanted to be there for my friends.

I went outside and waited in the car, and I cried. After a few minutes, a friend tapped on my window and told me where the reception was and encouraged me to go. I took a deep breath and cheered myself up, again, and headed out. Maybe that would be more fun, more relaxed, easier. My mistake, again. I left.

The *Playboy* magazine release, and all the devastation that came in its wake, was the next month, July 1981. Newspapers around the country were ready to slit my throat, when just the month before they had cheered when *Playboy* featured Bo Derek and her husband. But not with me. When I was photographed with Leon in my *Playboy* feature, I was attacked from all sides.

I had just finished reading a particularly disparaging article about the cover when the phone rang. "Can you meet me for lunch today? We need to talk." It was Bill. I told him I had a meeting at my manager's office, and he said he would meet me there afterward for lunch.

My meeting went long—two hours long—but Bill waited. We ate, and I smiled a lot. Then somehow the entire conversation did a 180, and he asked me about what was really on his mind . . . the whole reason we were even having lunch at all: "How are you dealing with the *Playboy* article?" No one had asked me that before. Yes, everyone seemed to have an opinion that they freely gave . . . but here he was, asking me *"How are you?"* I found myself talking openly and honestly about all the hurt I was feeling, and how I felt that my world was falling apart, how I was feeling pain that I never thought imaginable, my heart literally ached, my mind could not focus, my hands shook continuously, my stomach was always in knots . . . and my house was now a *sixth* color. Bill offered me comfort in his wisdom. I talked about betrayal, humiliation, abandonment, anger, and trust that I thought could never be rescued, and he responded with faith and hope. I admitted I was afraid, and he told me to smile. Then we talked about my standing on my own, and he showed me how I was strong. For the first time in years, I actually had someone to talk to. He said something in reference to *Playboy* that I have carried with me every day of my life since: "Be careful how you walk. You may be the only Bible someone will ever read."

Before he left, he hugged me, and I knew I would be all right. I didn't know how or when, but I knew I would be all right . . . in time.

My friend had caught me when I was dangerously on the verge of falling completely apart. I couldn't have made it through that year, or the next two, without Bill's friendship and support. He made me believe in myself again, and he healed my soul.

I remember praying a lot in those years. I remember asking God to fix my marriage. I asked him to make things work out, to take away the pain, to make Leon understand, to make *me* understand. I asked God for so many things that I finally was too confused to figure out if any of my prayers were being answered. Eventually, I realized that the only thing I really needed God to do was to make me happy. And if he granted me happiness, then it didn't matter what form it took, whether I was married or alone—if I were happy, then it wouldn't matter what I had or didn't have. In the end, that was all I really wanted from God. Happiness.

Three years later, in 1984, and after a few failed attempts at dating, when my life was finally silent enough for me to listen, when I was at peace again, I realized that he *had* already answered my prayers.

Eventually, I made a greeting card for Bill: *At a time in my life when I needed God most, He sent me you.* I was so nervous when I gave it to him. He was my best friend, and I could not risk losing his friendship, but I wanted him to know how grateful I was for him. He had changed my life; he had caught me, and he taught me to trust again. Something that I had never thought was possible.

Without saying anything and certainly not thinking romantically at all, just feeling embarrassed and awkward, I handed it to him, and after he read it, I mumbled to myself, "My lips are dry." And he leaned in and kissed them. And I knew.

His marriage to Kathleen had amicably ended long before then, but I still felt weird. She was my friend. So, without telling Bill, I called Kathleen. And the first thing she said through the laughter was "I knew you two should be together." We both decided that I should follow my heart and date Bill, and once we started officially dating, even though I don't recall what our first date was, our love blossomed quickly. It had been nearly ten years in the making. A love built on friendship is the strongest love of all. Finally, the fates had won.

# CHAPTER TWENTY-EIGHT

# BILL COSBY

After the *Lady Sings the Blues* incident in 1972, I was hired by Sidney Poitier for a part in his second feature with Bill Cosby. The trilogy of motion picture comedies where he directed and starred with Cosby were absolutely some of the best films starring Black talent of the time. After their first hit, *Uptown Saturday Night*, it proved that there was indeed a market for top-quality movies that just happened to feature performers of color. Moreover, Sidney made a point to hire as many behind-the-scenes Black craftspeople as possible, in order that their résumés might afford them the opportunity to join Hollywood's craft unions, which were then almost exclusively white and male and nearly impossible to enter.

The second film was *Let's Do It Again* in 1975. I was hired for just a bit part, no lines, and it was only one day's work. But the impact it had on my career was amazing! You all know how the business of filmmaking works: shooting scenes out of sequence, shooting one part of a scene and then the other, often acting when the actor you are supposed to be talking to isn't even there. Well, all I was told was that I would walk across the yard on a construction site in a tiny miniskirt and halter top, get some papers signed, and return to the office. That's it. I never saw a script and had no idea what the scene was about at all. So, I whipped out my trusty sewing machine, made the miniskirt and top in ninety minutes, and went to the Warner Bros. soundstage. I don't think there were any of the main actors on the set at all at that time. I was to imagine Bill Cosby's character driving a forklift and being so busy "eye-balling" me that he ran right into a huge pile of crates. And that was it. The camera would catch my reaction and then my day was over. Nothing special, just a bit part. But I never actually worked together with Cosby, or for that matter even with Sidney. My part was shot on a completely different day than Cosby's and directed by the second unit director.

When the film was released there was definitely a lot of "buzz" surrounding that scene, and before I realized what had happened, people everywhere were asking, "Aren't you the girl that Cosby was watching when he drove into those crates?" instead of "Aren't you that Ding-A-Ling girl?" Thank goodness. It was the first time I became a bona fide recognized entity in Hollywood.

Though we never met on that movie, I had worked with Cosby before when the Ding-A-Lings opened for him at a state fair in Arizona, or was it California? There were so many different shows and main acts that I've lost track. But we worked there for three days, and Helen and I would spend some of the time between shows just talking to Bill in his dressing room. He kindly offered to be available for *any* advice that I needed along the way. Throughout the years he had become somewhat of a godfather, a mentor. We were even frequent tennis partners in the annual *Jet* / American Airlines Tennis Classic, which at the time was the most exclusive celebrity invitational tennis tournament in Los Angeles.

Then one day in the early '80s he asked me to work with him on a project he had in mind. Every week for several months we met with four or five other "creative types" at his home in the Pacific Palisades and drafted the concept for a television series treatment where I was to costar as his wife in a family sitcom. It was so amazing working with a man I considered a comedic genius. Of course, I was also a big fan and was so honored and impressed that he had chosen me to help develop and costar with him in this exciting project. It was a blessing and such an education; I treasured every moment. It was like going to a master class every time we met.

When we finally felt it was pretty solid, he said he would meet with the network executives and their writers and let me know how the pitch was received. The next thing I knew, *The Cosby Show* was on NBC with Phylicia Rashad as his wife. I couldn't believe it! That was supposed to be me! I had worked for months on the development, and I knew that *he* knew I really wanted that role. I called Bill many times, with no response. I finally reached him and asked what had happened. According to him, NBC thought I was too young. That no one would believe that I was his wife. He was forty-seven and I was thirty-three. And therefore, the network *never* considered me.

Hollywood 101 . . . yet again. I was so angry. We all had worked to develop that show, and I know that they had far more production expertise than I had, but that did not take away from the fact that I had contributed toward its development. And just like that, there I was left out in the cold again. Not even a "Developed by" or "Created by" credit. No update phone call from Bill—nothing. It was me who had to call him. I just felt so betrayed and devastated! I didn't talk to Bill for years after that. I watched that show along with the millions of other viewers year after year, knowing that should have been me. To this day, I'm not certain if the network ever knew I was involved in the development of the show at all, and I never reached out because I knew it would just be my word against his.

Our paths have crossed several times over the years, and he always acted as though nothing had happened. Of course, more recently he has had his own issues with "betrayal," which it appears he misguidedly believes to be the case on the part of the women who have accused him of sexual abuse and assault. Like many, especially in Black Hollywood (but around the world as well), I am disappointed by the actions of many men in the industry, which are yet another example of the ugly legacy of male patriarchy and misogyny that has existed in Hollywood since the days of Louis B. Mayer, Darryl Zanuck, Jack Warner, and others.

But interestingly enough, Bill never once "came on" to me. There were many opportunities for him to do so and he did not. Not once.

I'm reminded of one of the last times I saw him—it was many years ago, when we were cohosting the Clio Awards in New York. Out of nowhere, he oddly suggested I cut my hair like his wife, Camille. He gave me the name of her salon and suggested I speak with them as soon as possible. Which I thought was kind of strange. Not that I didn't like Camille's short crop; as a matter of fact I loved the look for her—not me! Then he went on to tell me that I should "never wear that dress again!" Uhh, excuse me. I was wearing a gorgeous red beaded Jeran Couture dress with a plunging neckline that I loved. Still a bit chastened by the sitcom snub, I thought to myself . . . *Some advice you take in life and some you don't.* He never mentioned *The Cosby Show.*

# CHAPTER TWENTY-NINE

# OKAY, GOD, I HEAR YOU

In 1984, shortly after Bill Overton and I had started dating, he decided that I needed a getaway. Bill had a 140-acre, 125-year-old farm in Maine. His dream was to turn it into a summer camp for inner-city children.

He invited me to join him, offering peace, solace, and a chance to get away to a place where no one would recognize me. He promised me a real opportunity to let my hair down. He was going to spend the entire summer there and he left explicit directions for me since there was no phone. (The local corner store had the very last working hand-crank phone in America. It wasn't removed until the late 1990s.) If I decided to come, the door would be left open. I laughed at him. "You actually think I can go somewhere for two to three weeks and *no one* will recognize me? They're gonna ask me about the NFL." He said, "This is Maine we're talking about." We made a bet.

I flew five hours to Boston, changed planes, flew one hour to Portland, Maine, where I rented a car and drove an hour and a half to this small town, where I was instructed to turn east, go through town (which took two minutes), and turn left as the road continued north. When I got to the corner store 5 miles down the road I was to turn east again. Then I went 2.3 miles down this road, where I was supposed to see a mailbox with his name on it.

I didn't see the mailbox.

I drove back and forth five times until I finally saw this farmer in his front yard, so I stopped and asked where the Overton farm was. "Do you know Bill Overton?" He looked at me, and with his typical Maine accent said, "Aye yup." Then he squinted. "Hey, you're that gal on *The NFL Today*, aren't cha?"

I laughed so hard he must have thought I was crazy. The very first person I talked to, outside of the one who had rented me the car, and I was recognized. I immediately directed him, "You're going with me. Get in the car. We're going to collect a bet."

What do you know, Bill was his next-door neighbor. His mailbox was bigger than Bill's and was right in front of Bill's, and there was no way I could have seen it. I just happened to ask the right guy. So, there we were, Larry and me, trying to convince Bill that I didn't bribe Larry into saying he knew who I was. And of course, Larry wanted to know all about what I thought about the next game. . . . Of course he did!

A couple of hours later Bill and I went back down the 2.3 miles to the highway, then the 5 miles to town, then west 1 mile to the "corner market." We both went in and while Bill was shopping, I browsed through the magazines. I picked up one with Muhammad Ali on the cover and I started to read. The clerk looked at me. "Aren't cha that Jayne Kennedy from *The NFL Today*?"

I yelled over to Bill, "Get your butt over here." Then I asked the clerk to repeat his question.

"Hey, Bill, I meant no harm, it's just that she looks like the gal on *The NFL*."

Bill tried to deny it, but we were laughing so hard we had to fill the clerk in on the joke. And Bill never did make good on our bet.

That summer we totally renovated the actual house and cleared forty acres of fields surrounding it. And even though I found myself loaded with mosquito bites and broken nails, this was absolutely one of the best getaways I could ever have hoped for. For the next few months, we found ourselves back and forth between Maine and Trinidad, or Maine and Washington, DC, or Maine and New York. Maine had now become home base. By then we were beginning to bring busloads of kids from Boston's inner city to the camp-grounds at our Maine home for a cultural exchange program. One day we got a call from the highway patrol—it seemed that one busload of kids and their supervisor had pulled off to the side of the road. They were lost. They were also all Black. The officer said, "Hiya, Bill. We got a busload of Black kids here and we figured dey was coming to yo place. We can escot dem if you want." Mind you, this was a one-hour drive away from our home. Of all the people the officer could have called, he called the only Black man he knew. At the time, there were not many Black folks in that part of Maine. From that day on, Bill teased him relentlessly.

I realized we had succeeded in introducing these kids to a different way of life other than the inner-city streets when one of the girls said to me that she was refusing to drink water that came from out of the ground. I tried to explain that all water comes from the ground, lakes, or rivers, and since there was no lake or river nearby, we were drinking out of the ground. We had a freshwater well that produced the best-tasting water I have ever had. But she wanted a faucet. Our home had many faucets, but the whole idea of camping was that we did not live in the house. *AND* the water from the faucets was pumped up from the well. She demanded that she only have sodas for the rest of the week. Then she brought out her nail polish. . . . That's when I knew we were in trouble with this one.

But then out of nowhere an intervention happened in my life, and I knew I had to listen. I was working for Coca-Cola as cohost of their annual International Bottlers Convention in Atlanta, Georgia, with Julius Erving. They converted the brand-new convention center into a huge playground. One of the more impressive features was the "Room of the Future." Everything was silver, and it literally looked as if you had stepped through a time warp into the year 2500.

The convention went on for days, with bottlers arriving from around the world. One day was set aside for the display of Coca-Cola's new advertising campaigns, and Dr. J and I were hosting the onstage presentation. That afternoon I was sitting in Gladys Knight's hotel room, talking about the good old days, before her scheduled performance later that night. Suddenly, I had sharp pains in my lower abdomen, as if I had just been stabbed. They only worsened by the hour, but I had to do the show. I barely got through the program and off the stage before collapsing. I was taken back to my hotel and Clare Bisceglia, one of the Coca-Cola executives, called a doctor, who she assured me was one of the best in the country, and handed me the phone.

I told the doctor about the tiny pains that I had been getting for a month or so, but this was absolutely the worst, and totally different. I explained to him about the blackouts I'd had since the age of twelve, and about anything else I thought might be relevant. I waited to hear some reassurance and information that would guide me as to what my next step should be, but I was floored with his response—I couldn't believe my ears. He said, somewhat patronizingly, "This was nothing serious, nothing to worry about, and you should lie in the bathtub and let hot water run over your stomach." That was a surefire cure for what he called "female problems."

Angrily, I hung up the phone and immediately called my OB-GYN in LA, Dr. Lloyd Greig, who told me to get on the first flight back to Los Angeles and go straight from the airport to Cedars-Sinai Medical Center, where he would meet me. After three days of nonproductive procedures, treatments, and tests, he finally told me he was scheduling an ultrasound to check for endometriosis.

"Endo what?" I had no idea what endometriosis was; I had never even heard the word before, but it sounded ominous. Even worse, the test results confirmed Lloyd's suspicions.

I went into true "Jayne mode," reading everything I could get my hands on about the disease. I learned that endometriosis is a buildup of endometrial tissue that grows on the outside of the uterine wall, instead of inside the uterus. Even though the tissue is in the wrong place, it continues to function as it would if it were inside the uterus—thickening, breaking down, and bleeding. With nowhere for the displaced tissue to go, it becomes trapped, developing scar tissue and sometimes adhesions. The degree of pain is not related at all to the amount of scar tissue buildup. Some women can function normally, while others can't get out of bed because of the intense pain. Back in 1984, endometriosis was considered a "new disease," or a "career woman's disease," and no one really knew what caused it—but one thing was for sure, there was no cure.

The diagnosis came at a time when *Love Your Body* was at its peak of popularity. The exercise video was critically acclaimed; Jane Fonda, Richard Simmons, and Jayne Kennedy . . . we were the pioneers in a brand-new industry, and I was flying throughout the country doing seminars, clinics, publicity, and promotions. My contracts with Esoterica and Coca-Cola were due in large part to the success of the exercise program, since I mainly represented Esoterica's healthy skin and Coke's diet product, Tab. My line of exercise wear on Butterick patterns was also going great. I was scheduled to do the third follow-up video to *Love Your Body*, which would require public appearances, touring, and a demanding physical travel schedule—and I couldn't even do *one* sit-up. I couldn't believe it. Devastated, I had to leave it all behind.

I had three laser laparoscopic procedures—outpatient surgeries where an incision is made through the navel, and scar tissue is burned off with a laser beam—but it always came back. I tried newly invented medicines and went on continuous birth control pills, fooling the body into believing I was pregnant because the hormones developed during pregnancy eliminated the pain, and nothing worked.

I went to see specialists in Los Angeles, Chicago, New York, Atlanta, and Boston, toting the videos from my surgical procedures under my arm with the same passion and commitment as when I had auditioned for *The NFL Today*. They all had the same bleak answers that yielded no results. No matter what I tried, the endometriosis always came back. In desperation, I even tried to make an unholy alliance with the disease, taking pills to try to manage the pain so I could at least have my life back. It didn't work.

While endometriosis is not a life-threatening disease, it brought a different kind of death to me, an ending of the active life I had lived since childhood. All my life I had been healthy and fit. When I graduated high school, I had perfect attendance since the first grade, when I was out for two weeks with the chicken pox. I couldn't begin to imagine living without the level of physical activity and exercise that had been such a normal and integral part of my entire being. . . . It was part of who I was, part of my self-identity. When I couldn't even stand up straight without pains in my abdomen, it was a major blow to my spirit and my soul. It hurt to walk. It hurt to cough. It hurt to do everything.

The disease took from me personally as well. Bill and I had been dating not even a year when I received the somber diagnosis. He was so supportive that he even went with me to the various cities for treatments, making the appointments himself in Boston based on referrals and recommendations from his friends, especially those in the medical field. He cooked for me when I couldn't walk, he ran my bath, and he tucked me into bed with a jumble of heating pads.

In November of 1984, I went to see Dr. Greig for a checkup, and to review my medical situation after months of disappointing news. He finally looked at me and said in his thick Jamaican accent, "You know, Jayne, the best treatment for the pain and symptoms associated with endometriosis . . . is pregnancy."

I laughed at him and threw the drape at his head. Then with the biggest smile I simply said, "Okay." Lloyd Greig was my friend and all at once I knew he was onto something. It felt so right. But also, I was so sick and tired of being sick and tired I was willing to try *anything* . . . even if it meant a drastic change in my life.

As I drove home after the appointment, my thoughts drifted to the last few years. It seemed I had been on the road my entire adult life. And while I had always thought about having children, every time I seriously moved toward motherhood, a big career opportunity came up. I had put off having a family so many times because the timing was not right. So, I asked myself, when was it ever going to be right?

God had spoken. I was going to have a child, and he had made the way so I could not put it off anymore. No more excuses, no more waiting. I looked up and spoke to God: *Okay, God. I hear you. I got the message loud and clear. Thank you.* There is good in all things—you just have to look for the silver linings.

Now all I had to do was tell Bill that we needed to be pregnant.

# CHAPTER THIRTY

# TO THE SEVEN OF US

I left the doctor's office, went straight home, and as soon as Bill walked in the door that night, I told him: "The main way to alleviate endometriosis is . . . pregnancy." Bill laughed. And then stopped abruptly when he saw the look on my face.

"I'm serious."

Bill looked confused. I went upstairs, brought down my birth control pills, waved them in his face, and then threw them out.

"I want to have a baby. I want to have *your* baby," I said. "I'm *supposed* to have a baby—*right now*."

Bill smiled this time instead of laughing. "You're serious. . . . Are you sure?"

My giant smile was my only reply, the tears welling up in my eyes.

"Then let's get started," he whispered.

Oh my, I love it when he whispers.

It was exciting to think about having a baby, but in the back of my mind I also remembered that Dr. Greig had said one of the problems with having endometriosis was that for many women it made it very difficult to get pregnant. I didn't care how long it took—I was willing to give it a shot.

In April 1985, Dick Clark booked me to host *The Most Beautiful Girl in the World*, a beauty pageant in Sydney, Australia. I had done the show for him the year before in Hawaii.

Just before I left for Sydney, I went to see Dr. Greig for a pregnancy test.

"You're pregnant," said Bill. "Right now."

"Well . . . I still have to get a test."

"Test doesn't matter," Bill said. "You're pregnant."

The test was negative, but Bill insisted it was wrong—he was 100 percent sure that I was. He made another bet, this time with Dr. Greig: We would do the test again in two weeks when I returned, and the winner would be treated to dinner. We laughed and left the office, both Bill and Dr. Greig confident of having a paid dinner in just a few weeks. The next day we left for Sydney.

I left LA feeling pretty great. Especially since for the first time in a long time I was finally having no pain.

My cohost for *The Most Beautiful Girl in the World* was David Hasselhoff. It was always nice to work with someone tall like David because I could wear my highest heels. And it always made me feel less inhibited and freer to express myself. When I was taller than the other talent, I had to keep my movements limited, and I hated that.

There is a tremendous amount of work that has to be done in preparation for any live broadcast, and many live shows often have pretaped video packages somewhere in the broadcast. Beauty pageants have a lot of these packages in the openings that showcase the events the girls are involved in before the night of the actual pageant. All of these packages are edited and programmed, and the run times are allocated down to the split second. After doing *The NFL Today*, I felt I could handle just about any live broadcast. I was soon to find out that Dick Clark felt the same way.

About ten minutes before the show was going on the air, Dick came to my dressing room, and he didn't seem to be stopping by just to wish me luck.

"We've got a problem, but I'm sure you can handle it. This is exactly why I hired you. Of all the people I could have booked on this show, I have a great deal of confidence in your ability to handle live programming, just in case. You know? Well, I know you can get us out of this one. We'll do it together."

There had been a power failure that had caused the circuit boards to blow, and we had lost all of the programming. The opening of the show included a live parade of the girls introducing themselves, but after that there was supposed to be a large block of pretaped packages. So now we were facing ten minutes of dead air.

The production team had found our technician in Sydney, who was being shuttled by helicopter to our location twenty minutes north with a new computer board. He had to reprogram the entire motherboard, which was too large to fit inside, so he was literally dangling with it *below the chopper's cockpit*, in the cargo lift—no easy task.

The plan was that Dick would go onstage with David and me as we "filled" for the ten-minute gap. Now, ten minutes may not sound like a lot, but ten minutes of precious prime-time network is an expensive eternity. That's why it is so important when you do live TV that you familiarize yourself with every nuance of the production. My first day on *The NFL Today* had taught me that lesson.

The show opened, and before we even finished the introduction of the girls, the new board was in place and the show went on just as though all the preceding drama had never happened. Quite honestly, I was more worried about the programmer than I ever was about me. To this day, I don't know how he did that under those emergency conditions.

The rest of the show went smoothly and was a success—until the stage collapsed at the very end, when all the girls rushed to congratulate the winner. The throne and all the girls fell fifteen to twenty feet, right through the stage floor. Crew members were rushing to rescue the girls from the gaping hole amid all the screaming. And of all the pictures the newspapers could have run the next day, they chose the one with a girl being pulled to safety with half the front of her dress falling off her shoulders, leaving her exposed and horrified. Guarantee it was a guy who selected that photo.

I was exhausted when I got back to my hotel room. Bill had to return to the US earlier that day, so I planned to take a shower and go straight to bed, then get up early in the morning to pack my bags.

I walked to the bathroom and looked into the mirror, and there was a message for me written with a bar of soap. *LUV YA BOTH*. Then there was a strict note to the maid: *Do Not Touch*.

I smiled, and then I laughed, and then I cried. I was so hopeful, and he was so sure. But that was Bill, always so sure everything was going to be just fine.

The day after I returned to LA, Bill had already made my appointment to see Dr. Greig, but we learned I didn't need another test. There had been a mistake—the initial test was positive. We were going to have a baby in November, almost a year to the date from when we first planned it. Dr. Greig lost the bet, but instead of dinner he committed to caring for me over the span of three pregnancies, which was the best gift ever.

A couple of weeks later Bill asked me to dinner. He was pretty secretive about where we were going, and I could tell something was up. He told me to dress really nice and to do my makeup and hair. I just knew he was going to propose to me, and I was glowing inside and out. We had never actually talked about getting married or made any plans, but we knew that we would someday. Bill had always been a "no-frills" kind of guy, and he wasn't overly romantic—our favorite restaurant was always the beach with a sub sandwich under the stars—so for him to *ask* me to get dressed up meant something special was in the wind. Then when he had a limo pick us up, "Breathe, Jayne" I told myself . . . I *knew* this was it.

The limo took us out to a small, quiet restaurant in the San Fernando Valley that was brightly lit. My first thought was, This is very nice, but it's so bright—more romantic lighting would be nicer. We sat and talked quietly about nothing really, and as I began to glance around the room, I noticed all the people at the other tables were in full camera-ready makeup, and I thought, Maybe there's a movie shooting somewhere nearby and they're on dinner break. Then this guy started questioning us about whether we were interested in buying rare exotic birds on the black market. He kept trying to convince me that this was the thing to do: "It's illegal, so we would have to make sure everything was kept hush-hush." And Bill was interested? Really? What's wrong with this picture? Why would he be talking to him, when he's supposed to be proposing to me?

Then it hit me. *Wham.* All at once, it hit me like a ton of bricks, and I was so mad, I wanted to stand up and scream, but I didn't. I hardly said a word, even though I was fuming. The problem was, I didn't know *what* to do. I wasn't quite sure what I was expected to do. Because I wasn't quite sure what *show* I was on—but I absolutely knew that I had been set up.

Believe it or not, it was Dick Clark's *Super Bloopers and Practical Jokes.* I should have screamed; that would have made a great moment in the show. But I was the only one in the whole room who even had a remote inkling of a wedding proposal on their mind, including Bill—*especially* Bill. And I didn't think it was funny at all. I wanted to yell at the top of my lungs, *But I'm supposed to be getting married!* But no one else knew that; that was only in my mind.

I guess Dick thought I was a poor sport about it all, but actually I was just an angry sport. I couldn't even tell Bill why I was so upset, because I didn't want him to propose out of a sense of obligation. But the truth is, I had been ready to say yes whenever he asked—I was having our baby, and suddenly, the idea of getting married was important to me.

About a week later, I got up the nerve to say something about not wanting to have a big wedding, as I'd done that already. "I think the next time I get married, I'd like to be on the beach in Santa Monica, or Malibu, or Point Dume—somewhere with just my family."

Bill looked at me and said, "I was thinking the same thing. I've done the big-wedding thing and once was enough. But I was thinking Bermuda."

My eyebrows went straight up. "Bermuda would be great."

And that was it. He never actually proposed. Just like everything else in our lives, it was as if it was just supposed to happen, and we were destined to be together, so he never had to ask.

We really wanted it small and simple with just our parents. We rented a gorgeous four-bedroom estate on a cliff above the beach and told *no one* we were getting married.

My travel agent booked the flights to Bermuda for our parents and us, and then sent a bottle of champagne to my home with a note: *Are congratulations in order?* I didn't respond.

We told our parents we were inviting them on a "vacation." We sent them the tickets and told them we would pick them up at the airport when they arrived. We invited Bill's childhood friend Rashid Silvera, a very famous model in New York. Rashid has had many occupations, including one as an ordained minister, so he could do the ceremony—but we didn't tell him about the wedding, we just asked him to join us for a vacation. Two down, one to go.

Another friend from Boston, Ardis Graham, happened to be a photographer. We told him that we were location scouting for a movie and asked if he would come to take some shots for us. We sent him a ticket and said we would pick him up at the airport. Three down.

Everything was set. Then Mom called and said that Dad wasn't coming. He never liked flying and he'd be missing too much work. "Oh my God, Dad," I responded to her in exasperation, then played the guilt card that I wanted this to be a special gift to *both* of them—"Mom, you *have* to get him on that plane." I don't know how she did it, but she did.

My sister Brenda was living with me in Los Angeles at the time. Even with my buying a white dress and spending hours sewing crystals to it, I suppose she thought it was for a show or something and she never guessed what we were up to. She was so busy trying to launch her singing career that she had no idea a wedding was being secretly planned.

The day before we left, Bill thought we had better let Rashid in on the surprise, in case there was anything special or any documents he had to bring for the ceremony. It was a good thing we called, because to our surprise, Rashid had given up his license to the ministry a few years earlier. We asked Rashid to come anyway, he already had his ticket, and he happily agreed. We figured we could just find a minister in Bermuda, because we absolutely did not want to get married at city hall.

There we were in Bermuda with no minister. Bermuda is predominantly Catholic, and everywhere we went, they refused to marry us, on the grounds that both of us were divorced. We were shocked, and frantic, and out of time. We absolutely did *not* want a city hall wedding with a justice of the peace. We literally ran all over the island trying to find someone, anyone, to perform the ceremony. Finally, we found what was probably the only Baptist church on the island, where an elderly minister agreed to marry us, but only if we did premarital counseling for three days prior to the wedding. We sat for one day, because that's all we had, and finally he was convinced that we were the real deal and happily agreed. Blessings. Yes!

When both sets of parents arrived the next day, we picked them up from the airport in taxi cabs. After the introductions we brought them to the house and we showed them their rooms, where I had laid on their beds my hand-made invitations to the wedding, sprinkled with rose petals, and red and silver sparkling confetti. That's when the screaming started. Both moms were laughing and crying at the same time and the dads were trying to figure out where they could go buy cigars.

Then Rashid and Ardis arrived, and we were all set. Of course, everyone was in shock but there was so much love in the room, the house was grand and gorgeous with a flaming fireplace, the view out over the ocean was sublime, and the housekeeper had made a splendid supper. Nothing could have been better.

The next day we took off on those little moped scooters that everyone drives in Bermuda, and what a sight that was. Especially my big, six-foot-three, he-man dad on the tiny little moped.

Not taking any chances of anyone finding out we were getting married, we had ordered a bridal bouquet without ever saying it was for a wedding or a bride. We had ordered the traditional Bermuda wedding cake without ever telling anyone it was for a wedding. I just hinted that we had heard how good it was and wanted to try it. The next day our housekeeper showed up with the cake. Turns out it was something like a fruitcake. I inserted a bunch of exotic flowers from the garden into the cake along with slender toothpick candles, and it was perfect. We finally managed to get to the day of the wedding without anyone on the island finding out about our special day.

As I was getting dressed, my mom came to the door—seems the minister had arrived with several carloads of family and friends, all wanting to see Jayne Kennedy get married. Oh my God! The minister, who had no clue who we were, had mentioned the wedding to his deacon. The deacon had recognized me when we came in for the counseling the day before and filled him in on what was happening, and they all invited themselves and their families to our extremely private ceremony.

I had Dad go tell them, reluctantly and very politely, that my sisters and brother were not even here, so there was no way I was going to allow anyone else to attend. They would have to wait in their cars. Very sorry.

Finally, we were getting married. The day was perfect. The backyard ceremony began just before the sun bowed out over the ocean. The sky was gray-blue, and the water was the same. It had just rained that morning and the house was beautiful, filled with the smell of the exotic flowers in the backyard garden—but my white satin shoes were a disaster.

Only the minister came in. When we had been with him for the counseling, he was so calm, quiet, and confidant. But today, this poor little man was so overwhelmed by the circumstances that he lost his place three times, so we had to start the vows all over again . . . each time. But I have to admit, it wasn't all his fault. Bill is, unabashedly, always a practical joker. He teased him relentlessly. When we got to the part where Bill was to say "I do," he paused for an eternity, then asked the minister, "Now, am I supposed to say I do, or I will, or what?" The minister totally lost his place, *aaaand* we started all over again. Then, when we got to the part where Bill put the ring on my finger, because of Bill's teasing, the minister was trembling so bad, I gave him a giant hug.

We ate a truly delicious meal that our housekeeper had made, along with the Bermuda wedding cake, and then sat back, glowing in the warmth of the roaring fireplace. Rashid and Ardis had left to go hang out at the local clubs, and Bill decided we should do a toast. We all stood—Mom, Dad, Bill's mother and father, Bill and I—as we clicked our glasses, and Bill said, "To the *seven* of us." We all raised our glasses and sipped champagne, except me with my concealed sparkling apple juice. Bill's mom was the *only* one to look around, a bit confused as she began to count. Wondering if he'd had too much champagne, she leaned over to him and asked, "Seven?" That's when we announced the pending arrival of their grandchild.

In every way, Bermuda was fantastic, but I only have one regret. I really, really, really missed my sisters and my brother. I wanted them all to be there.

# CHAPTER THIRTY-ONE

# A LOVE LIKE NO OTHER

While I was pregnant, I kept working. I loved, loved, loved my work. When I was five months pregnant, I hosted another pageant in Mauritius, 11,440 miles away, nearly halfway around the world off the coast of southeastern Africa. There were stopovers in Switzerland and Kenya. At Dr. Greig's orders, my sister was to travel with me in case of an emergency. I could only manage to fly by positioning myself backward on my knees and leaning into the seat with my belly hanging below. But I was good.

After shooting the pageant, we were departing the next day. The entire cast and crew had boarded the plane when an announcement came that our flight was to be delayed. It seemed there were unclaimed bags on the plane, and we were not permitted to take off until the owner was found. Just a few days before, a bomb had exploded at an airport in Japan, so everyone was just being extra cautious. We sat on the tarmac for hours before finally it was uncovered that a passenger had changed her mind about leaving and did not have time to retrieve her luggage. They offloaded the bags, and we were finally on our way. Our flight plan was to stop in Paris, where a travel agent would greet us with all the connecting flight tickets. Then the plane would continue on to London. However, the delay had caused us to miss our no-fly window in Paris. Planes were not permitted to take off or land after a certain time of night because of the noise disrupting the surrounding neighborhoods. We would have to remain in Paris until morning.

However, the pilot had other plans. He locked the cockpit door and flew directly to London, causing our entire cast and crew and all the pageant contenders to miss their connection with the travel agent . . . who had *ALL* of the connecting flight tickets. Every last one. Except mine. I had had so many issues with organizations booking me for engagements and then in the end they had no return ticket for me. Or they would say, "We will reimburse you," which many times they never did. So, since my agreement with the producers was that round-trip tickets be provided before I left the USA, my sister and I were the only ones with return tickets home. When we landed in London, the police handcuffed and escorted the captain off the plane and left us stranded and sleeping on the floor for the remainder of the night. It was at the very same time as Wimbledon and there were no available lodgings anywhere. The next morning my sister and I left on a nonstop back to LA and the remainder of our troop had to wait three or four extra days before they could go home.

In Chicago, I cohosted a show with Lou Rawls, big belly and all. All the time I was pregnant there were no pains from the endometriosis. I was in heaven.

November 19, 1985, I woke up at five a.m. and thought I might be in labor. By early afternoon, I was *sure* I was in labor. I had my weekly doctor's appointment later that afternoon, and after checking me, Dr. Greig thought otherwise. He told me not to worry, so we went to Bill's scheduled acupuncture appointment, and the doctor said I looked like I could use a treatment myself. I couldn't imagine anybody poking me that day, so I passed.

Sitting there in the outer office, I knew I wouldn't make it through the night. We weren't home for five minutes before Bill was calling Dr. Greig again. This time he told us to go to the hospital and he'd meet us there. The drive down the never-ending curves of Sunset Boulevard, coming from the Pacific Ocean into Beverly Hills, is not recommended for a mother in labor. By the time I got to the hospital, I was so nauseous from all the twists and turns, I couldn't wait to get out of the car, and it didn't help that Bill's nerves got the best of him and he drove right past the hospital. I tried to laugh but I couldn't. It hurt too much.

Dr. Greig had been on his way to a black-tie dinner when we called, so when he walked in the door in his tuxedo I had to laugh, a belly-roll laugh. "All this just for *me*?"

I was in intense labor all that night, but I never dilated more than three centimeters, so at seven a.m. on the 20th he decided to perform a C-section. I was so disappointed. I cried as I held on to Bill. I had really wanted a natural childbirth. As they were wheeling me into the surgical room, one of the nurses noticed that Dr. Greig was my obstetrician and reassuringly whispered to me, "Girl, he's the best. Every nurse in this hospital thinks he's the best. You are so lucky." She had no idea how much those words meant to me. I smiled and was happy it wasn't another NFL fan asking me about the game that week.

It was a long day and night, and I was exhausted, but Bill was wonderful and Dr. Greig was just as great as his reputation.

Twenty-eight hours after my first signs of labor, Bill was telling me we had a girl. She was screaming bloody murder. Then as soon as they placed her on my chest, she stopped crying. I will never forget that feeling. She just lay there nestled under my chin. When they took her away and placed her in the baby tray, she began to cry all over again. All I could see were her little fingertips flailing above the sidewalls. They were so precious and I found myself experiencing a new kind of love.

She fared much better than me. I had a very difficult time in recovery and couldn't stop shaking for hours. They wouldn't let me hold her until I stopped, but I just couldn't. It is true what they say: You forget all that when that little baby is in your arms. By that time the word was out that I was in the hospital, and we had to change rooms several times because of all the fans' phone calls.

Savannah Ré Overton, my firstborn. SRO. Standing Room Only. Sold Out. Either way, her initials meant she would be a success. Bill had determined that a fair deal would be if I had the joy of carrying the baby, then he got to name her. Somehow, I still couldn't figure out how that was fair, but as long as I had veto rights, that was fine with me. When I got home there was a message from Johnson Publishing—*Ebony* magazine wanted an *exclusive* picture for their next cover. Mom and Dad had arrived from Cleveland and Mom went shopping to find her grandchild's perfect outfit. So, at one month old Savannah had her first magazine cover.

I just loved being a new mother. I rarely let anyone steer me away from any opportunity to be with my baby. It was enormously rewarding. I exercised with her. She worked with me. I cooked with her, and she read with me. We did everything together. She was so full of energy and charisma that I fell head over heels in love with motherhood. It was an easy decision to just be there for her. I got totally involved in her education, her wardrobe, and all the bragging rights that go along with being a new mother. My friends called her Imelda Marcos, since she had a different pair of shoes for every outfit. Oh yeah, I was totally into being a mother.

I think a lot of my joy in having a daughter had to do with Cheyenne—Bill and Kathleen's daughter, my stepdaughter. Cheyenne was just the prettiest, most precocious little thing you'd ever want to meet. When Cheyenne would start singing Stevie Wonder's "I Just Called to Say I Love You" (her favorite thing to do), I would just melt. Not that she did it only for me; she'd sing to everybody. She'd call and leave the message on the answering machine and then giggle and hang up.

One day when she was about two years old, she and I were out shopping for a computer part. We were walking across the parking lot, and she looked up at me and said, "Wait, Mommy . . ." I don't have the slightest idea what she asked me. All I heard was "Mommy," the first time she had called me Mommy.

The first time *anyone* had called me Mommy. I thought to myself, *I gotta get me one of these.*

Cheyenne was just instantly in love with Savannah when Savannah was born. And Savannah loved her big sister to no end. They were great together, whether it was destroying my dining room table or Savannah's crib with crayons and markers, or those precious moments when Cheyenne would teach her to read and then sing her to sleep.

Then three and a half years later, Kopper was born. Her birth was so unlike Savannah's. They say that the personality of the child is a lot like their birth experience. Savannah was just plowing ahead ready to take on the world, and Kopper was perfectly content to just take her time. Even today, Kopper's famous words are "Wait a minute" or "Hold on a second."

I was late by two weeks—or should I say, Kopper was late by two weeks. An ultrasound determined she was fully cooked, and we scheduled admittance to undergo Pitocin drops to induce labor. Three days of Pitocin went by and still nothing. Finally, we gave in and scheduled yet another C-section. Out came the baby and Bill announced, "Another girl."

Kopper Joi was *sooooo* cute. With golden hair and golden skin, she was just perfect for her name. She was so easy to care for, but she always had a scowl. An intense look that pierced right through you.

Savannah was born in November at nine a.m., and Kopper was born in May at nine p.m.—their birthdays six months apart exactly. My mother was born in November and my father born in May. Savannah has many characteristics and looks of my mother and Kopper has the looks and characteristics of my father. When my mother first saw Kopper she looked at Dad and teased, "If I had seen this baby out in the streets, I'd have to come home and slap you."

Savannah and Kopper are night and day in so many ways. Opposite ends of the year, opposite ends of the day, and opposite personalities. But the bond they have is magical.

When I was pregnant with Kopper, I realized that I would not be able to go on the road like I had with Savannah. That put a definite hold on my work schedule. By then Savannah was starting school and I pretty much had to settle down. I couldn't be dragging them all over the world and have them missing school.

So, we changed our approach. Bill and I decided that we were going to produce a musical stage play, *The Journey of the African American*, written and directed by Cepheus Jaxon, which would allow us to stay in Los Angeles. The musical chronicled the four-hundred-year history of the African American experience from the motherland, the Middle Passage, slavery, war, the Great Migration north, and the Civil Rights Movement of the 1960s, on into the present day. The finale was a tribute to the strength and endurance of the African American family.

We partnered with the city of Inglewood and Crozier Middle School for a six-week run. Our agreement with the city was that Crozier students would shadow any member of our staff—in the office, backstage, wardrobe, makeup, tech crew, sound, sales, in the box office, and all the other positions—as a learning experience. By the time Kopper was born we were up and running. It was perfect work. We were doing what we loved and were still with our kids, who loved it as much as we did.

Opening night everyone was on pins and needles. It was a star-studded event sponsored by my friends at Anheuser-Busch. Since 1983, the beginning of the Children's Miracle Network, I had hosted their annual telethon along with Marie Osmond, John Schneider, Marilyn McCoo, Merlin Olson, and Mary Hart, along with many others, supporting more than ten million children each year. CMN has raised more than seven *billion* dollars for children's hospitals across North America. So naturally, I called my friend from all those years of cohosting the telethon at Disneyland, Mary Hart. She brought her crew from *Entertainment Tonight* to cover the opening reception. With our promotions team along with Crozier Middle School and the City of Inglewood, it was standing room only.

By the end of the night, we were definitely a hit. From there on, word of mouth helped fill our theatre every weekend. The play was an instant success and there was no doubt we would run far beyond the six weeks. . . . We ran for the next ten months, with many in attendance bringing friends, sometimes seeing the show four or five times.

Cheyenne and Savannah loved to join the dancers in the show whenever there was a family scene. Kopper rode on my hip day in and day out. We just about lived at the theatre. All the cast loved the girls, and all the other kids played with Kopper while we worked. It was perfect.

Of all the productions I've done, it's the one I am still most proud of. Every performance had me crying . . . right along with all the people in the audience. When Nelson Mandela was released from prison on February 11, 1990, we changed the lyrics of the finale to include Mandela's struggle and the celebration around the world at the news of his release.

Four months later on June 30, 1990, with fifteen thousand admirers chanting Mandela's name, Mayor Tom Bradley welcomed Mandela to Los Angeles with a grand, star-studded ceremony on the steps of city hall and a command performance by our troupe of our finale, "The African American Family," as Nelson and Winnie Mandela exited the doors of Los Angeles City Hall to glorious applause. It was such an honor, not only for me but for our incredibly gifted cast.

By then we were nearing the end of our ten-month Los Angeles run and preparing to take the musical on the road, with our first stop being Atlanta, then on to Detroit and Houston. The cast and crew could not have been more excited and were looking forward to a successful tour.

And then . . . the phone call from Leon.

# CHAPTER THIRTY-TWO

# THE UNEXPECTED

When I initially began to write my memoir, I had a different picture in mind. I wanted to explore who I was—no longer solely looked upon as someone's daughter, girlfriend, wife, mother, or role model. My goal was to finally write about my personal journey of self-discovery and finding my true authentic self. Oprah had wisely advised me to wait until my youngest was a young adult and out of the house and I had the time and energy to devote to me. To allow myself the space to be as candid and self-critical about my life as I could possibly be. Which meant I would have to finish the part of my book that I dreaded the most. The part that would be the most difficult . . . the most agonizing . . . and the most devastating. My youngest, Zaïre, graduated university in 2017 and still I wasn't able to write this particular piece—the puzzle was still a mystery. However, I now think I have a complete understanding of what actually happened. And I find myself obligated to write this specific chapter.

After years of making the resolute decision not to publicly speak about my relationship with Leon and why we divorced, I came to realize that in doing so I had lost control of the narrative. I now understand that when you abdicate and relinquish that responsibility, that narrative will be taken on and written by others, and the resulting collateral damage can be irreparable. In order to attempt to repair some of that destruction, I need to address what happened EIGHT YEARS *AFTER* OUR DIVORCE when a privately recorded VHS tape of us engaging in consensual married intimacy was stolen from his home and leaked onto the then very nascent home video black market and became the very first female celebrity scandal of the video era. And once again, I was a pioneer. Except this time, being a pioneer was a position that I neither wanted nor was proud of. It destroyed my career and it destroyed a part of me in the process.

After thirty-five long, pensive, and introspective years, I am now officially going on the record.

When I look back at the events of my entertainment-industry career, I have many treasured memories of incredibly wonderful people, extravagant locations, opportunities to excel financially, and the love of many people around the world. There are so many great rewards that come with being a celebrated personality, and things that as a young girl I'd dreamed of but never ever in a million years thought would be even remotely possible.

Throughout the mid-1970s and early '80s, life had become glamorous for Leon and me. We were truly international jet-setters. We were A-list guests for many of the who's who of Hollywood's global footprint. The only thing we had to worry about was packing our suitcases. We flew all over the world to the various Ali fights; attended the Cannes Film Festival in the South of France and the Monte Carlo Grand Prix; filmed movies in foreign countries; toured the world with Bob Hope; went on photo safari in the Philippines; rode camels at the base of the pyramids in Cairo; drifted down the Nile on our way to visit the Karnak temples in Luxor, and the Valley of the Kings and the tomb of King Tut, with first-class accommodations everywhere we went.

We explored the Roman catacombs, the Colosseum, and the Forum; gazed out over the city of Athens, from the vantage point of the ancient Acropolis; snorkeled in Honolulu or off the Great Barrier Reef of Australia; played in tennis tournaments in the Caribbean's Jamaican islands; and dined in

Acapulco. We were truly citizens of the world. We were celebrated worldwide as "The Golden Couple."

When we went to Hong Kong in 1975 after the "Thrilla in Manila," we were picked up at the airport in the most beautiful Bentley that I had ever seen. Enrique Zobel, our friend who we had met in the Philippines at Muhammad's fight, gave us his car and driver for the entire time we stayed in Hong Kong.

Enrique had also made arrangements to connect us with his dear friend, Andrew Yu. Andrew was a major businessman not only in East Asia, but around the world. He owned television stations and was greatly respected for his international ventures in the film industry. His wife was considered one of the great beauties in the world.

Our first stop was Yu Castle. He introduced us to Nathan Road, Kowloon, and all the wonderful shopping. That's where I bought a black lacquer furniture set with inlaid mother-of-pearl and had it shipped back to the US, where I proudly displayed it in our Pasadena home that, after five years of pretty much an empty house, I had somehow managed to finally begin to decorate.

One night Andrew invited us to join his family for dinner and I had the most incredible seventeen-course meal ever. I was just amazed with all the entrées they placed before me. I tried to eat everything, not wanting to offend anyone, but I just had to call it quits at seventeen. Then Andrew told me that their custom was to keep feeding their guest until they said no more. You have no idea how much I wished I'd known that ten courses earlier, at least before they brought out the stuff I didn't recognize and was not going to ask what it was.

During that trip, Leon and I bought a video recorder. They were brand-new in the market and cost much more in the States, but we got a great deal by buying one while we were overseas. With all the film and television development work we were doing, it was a great tool to be able to tape the work as we went along, to try out dialogue as we wrote, and to make changes, and of course for scene study in drama classes or prepping for an audition. The video recorder was a big help with working toward our ambitious film goals.

On our fifth wedding anniversary, in 1976, Leon suggested that we use the video recorder for another reason—he wanted to make a memento of our love to share on our fiftieth wedding anniversary. He reasoned that we would certainly not look as good in fifty years, and it would be better than taking Polaroids like almost everybody else was doing—not many people had an expensive piece of video equipment like we had. This was early on, when things were truly going well in our marriage.

Leon was always keeping souvenirs, notes, and cards from different times in his life, so I wasn't surprised at how sentimental he was on our anniversary. It was something so completely innocent and private. We made the tape and then never looked at it. *Leon safely locked it away, for our golden anniversary.*


The series of events that followed *The Journey of the African American* could never have been forewarned in my wildest nightmares.

For the previous ten months, our weekends had been spent at the theatre, three shows on Saturdays and two shows on Sundays. At last, we had a whole Sunday afternoon to spend with the girls at the beach. It was a perfectly beautiful Sunday.


That's when we got the call.

It was 1990.

Nothing would ever be the same. . . .


It was Leon. I could tell immediately something was wrong. He was using his best practiced disc jockey voice, the one that confidently asserted, *Hear what I say, because this is important.* He wanted to come by to speak with Bill and me, the sooner the better. It had been eight years since we had divorced and nine years since we had separated, and over those years, I had gone from abject anger to receiving God's grace and just focusing on being happy. Eventually, after Bill and I had married, Leon and I were able to salvage our friendship. Leon had always had tremendous respect for Bill. Initially, I was uncomfortable reigniting any kind of relationship with him, but eventually that friendship became genuine. Leon never had children of his own and he had wanted to share a part of my girls' lives, even if it was minimal. He came to the hospital when they were born. He brought them birthday gifts. He and Smokey came to support us during the run of *The Journey of the African American*. So, it was not unusual that he would call, but the urgency in his voice this time was far from usual.

As soon as I opened the door, I realized how right I was. He was extremely nervous, and the underarms of his pressed shirt were soaking wet to the waist. We invited him into the living room, and we sent the girls to their rooms to play. As soon as he sat on the edge of the sofa, without hesitating at all, he said: "Jayne . . . THE TAPE IS OUT."

And there it was, just like that. He never averted his glance, looking me straight in my eyes. He knew this was a dagger that would strike me to my very core. I could see he wanted to hold me, but he did not. I could see that he never wanted to hurt me, but it did. And even though I hadn't thought about that tape for a single moment in the nearly fifteen years since it was made, I immediately knew exactly what he was talking about. I looked at Bill and told him that we had videotaped an intimate moment of ourselves to save as a keepsake until our fiftieth anniversary. It was not difficult to share this news with Bill, because I always shared everything with him. We had no secrets. He was my rock, and if there was ever a time that I needed him to be that rock . . . IT WAS TODAY. Leon and I had never even watched it and he had put it away in our safe. If I had not completely forgotten about it, I would have destroyed it when we got divorced eight years prior.

Then Leon went on to explain, "You know I always have people around the house. One day I was away and someone who I probably knew broke into the house and into the safe where I kept my watch that you bought for me in

Italy and my other valuables. The guy I'm thinking of most likely was intending to sell them to buy drugs. And in the process, he accidentally stumbled upon the video, and realizing that was more valuable than the jewelry, he grabbed it instead. The tape has ended up in Houston, Texas, at the National Radio Disc Jockey Convention."

Of all places, this was the worst.

After a beat, he asked: "What are we going to do? What do *you* want to do? I will honor whatever decision you and Bill make. You know I've always put you on a pedestal, Jayne. I've never in my life met someone like you and this hurts me to my heart to see you in this moment of pain. I would do anything to make this go away. But I think we should hold a press conference and let people know what actually happened instead of leaving it to speculation."

I can't honestly tell you what happened over the course of the next half hour, because I was in a state of total shock. I saw his pain. I saw Bill's pain as he was trying to comfort me and tell me how strong I was. I do, however, recall that Bill and I decided against the press conference, knowing that would be complete humiliation. In hindsight, it possibly would have been the best thing to do, but who can say? What I do know is that Leon was true to his word. Whatever I decided during the entire ordeal he honored, no matter the pain or consequences he personally suffered, and to this day, he's continued to do the same.

Once Bill and I decided against the press conference, we opted to meet with the FBI instead. And through all their investigation they could not find one single source of the crime. By then there was so much speculation from everyone and it became impossible to rein it all in.

And from that Houston convention the VHS tape—going "viral" (thankfully, there was no internet back then) throughout a wide distribution network—encircled the globe, as well as my neck, strangling my every breath.

When the video was released, it was an undeniable cultural marker. It was decades before the Paris Hilton, Pamela Anderson, Kim Kardashian, and other celebrity sex videos became commonplace. Decades before the Janet Jackson Super Bowl "wardrobe malfunction" incident. And decades before nude photos of celebrities routinely appeared in the media, and by design instantly put them in the cultural zeitgeist. When it happened to me, it wasn't just shocking—it was publicly scandalous. Which is why it held such power over me. The power to tear down my life. The power to blow up my career. Most devastating of all, the power to turn my happiness, self-confidence, and success into rock-hard humiliation.

Overnight, the tape became a huge seller on the black market. Bootleggers sold it at major events and on street corners. The press fed the furor with sensational headlines. And like with the *Playboy* cover, many in the African American community once again turned their backs on me. I was victim-shamed years before that phrase became accepted into the popular vernacular. Embarrassed and mortified beyond any ability to express, I retreated to the only place I felt safe . . . with my family inside our home. It would become both my sanctuary and my prison. Because inside my house was the only place I could be sure, sure that I wouldn't run into anyone—friend or foe— and have to ask myself the question that wouldn't stop playing over and over in my head: Have they seen the tape?

However, we were still committed to being on the road with the cast and crew with bookings in Atlanta, Detroit, and then Houston. We had just wrapped our final show in Atlanta when we got a call from our promoter that the balance of our tour was canceled. Both Detroit and Houston the-atres had been informed about the existence of the tape and they pulled the contracts. There we were, stranded, with thirty-five cast and crew members with no hotels and no flights back to LA. Bill had worked relentlessly to achieve the success the play had garnered, and because of me, it was all destroyed.

Overnight, I became persona non grata. So-called friends disappeared, or so I thought. One friend came to me in the dark shadows of the backstage drapes.

"Jayne, I can fix this for you. I used to be a Navy SEAL. I can fix this."

I'm not even sure what he meant, and I did not want to know. "Oh my God, has it come to this? NO. NO. NO. A thousand times NO."

But it had come to this. Important deals evaporated. I lost nearly everything. Most debilitating of all was losing belief in myself.

The career and financial consequences of the tape's unauthorized release were almost as devastating. Once I was wooed by everyone from advertisers to agents, but after the tape went public, my phone stopped ringing—except to cancel.

When we arrived back in LA, Bill and I were invited to a star-studded black-tie event that many of my peers were sure to attend. As we all filtered into the main lobby, I felt all the hot, glaring, blaming eyes.

Had they seen the tape?

I began to perspire, and my hands began to shake uncontrollably as I searched for the nearest corner to retreat. Actress and singer extraordinaire Cyndi Gossett (then wife of Lou Gossett Jr.) approached me, no judgment, just eyes filled with pure love. She put her hands on mine to stop the tremors. Then she put her arms around my shoulders to steady me. She stood face-to-face with me and looked deep into my eyes. Not a word was spoken. Then came the giant gentle hug that I will never ever forget. We both cried.

And with a wisp of air I said, "But I have to leave." I knew then that I couldn't stay. I just couldn't. And she knew too.

A few days after, I received a card from actress Sheila Frazier that I have kept to this day:

*Jayne,*

*Marriage is sacred, and love is sacred. God must have an incredible plan for your life, because Satan has tried and tried to defeat you. Hold on and hang in there. You are an absolutely beautiful lady inside and out. Trust God to work things out. He'll make the crooked ways straight. You're His, so don't worry. When you're not sure which way to turn, then stand still and rest in Him. It'll be OK. Call me if you need me.*

*Your FRIEND,*
*Sheila Frazier.*

Once the media picked up on the scandal, they came out of the wood-work. Geraldo Rivera and on and on . . . It was nothing short of pigs at the trough.

My family remained steadfast. However, I was never able to speak about this with my parents, who were always so proud of me. How could I ever face them to talk about THIS? I wondered what they were encountering within our own family, at church, with their friends and my dad's coworkers. My sisters and my brother also became victims. One of my sisters served on the protection detail for a collegiate football team bus. As soon as she stepped aboard, she saw that the team was watching the video on the bus's overhead monitor. Of course, they had no idea that she was my sister. To this day, I've never asked her what she did. The guilt I felt in placing her in that situation was overwhelming.

And on . . . and on . . . and on . . . It was everywhere. And unfortunately . . . never-ending.

Shutting down virtually all ties with my past, including the few close friends that I had, and my career, while desperately trying to stare down the shadows of depression, I completely immersed myself in my immediate family . . . my husband and my daughters. They were my lifeline, my salvation. Inside I had died. But with most deaths, you go through a period of mourning. Then you get back on your feet. Unfortunately, for me, that moment was nowhere to be found. For me, it was changing the entire focus for my life. Motherhood suddenly meant something entirely different, with a whole new direction and purpose.

The release of the tape had done so much damage not only to me . . . but to Leon as well. Everyone blamed him, thinking he had released it himself to sabotage my career. A misdirected blame that turned into unmitigated public hatred toward him. And truth be told, for a while, I was even one of those who believed that he had some part in it. My heart was so full of pain and anger that I retreated from everyone, and especially him. I never spoke to him again for the next ten years. I didn't speak with anyone, not even my best friend, Claudette Robinson (Smokey's ex-wife), for many, many years. I so wanted to be able to forgive Leon, to forgive anyone, but I didn't know how. I knew that my rage was only hurting myself and that I would never be able to go on unless I found a way to forgive, period. Throughout my entire life I had always believed that as a Scorpio I had issues learning how to forgive and forget, but this was something that I wanted so desperately to overcome. I prayed and prayed, and I just had no answers.

Many years later, after my youngest daughter was born, I was driving to the market one night and I happened to drive past a tiny one-room church with a bright golden light glowing warmly through its open doors. The music was like a siren call. In all the years we lived in that neighborhood, I had never noticed this church before, and we drove past it nearly every day. I could hear the sweet, soulful voices even from the street . . . inviting me in. I made a quick U-turn. There were maybe four rows of benches that likely held no more than forty people at maximum capacity. I sat in the back and waited for the choir practice to end, and that's when I found Pastor Jenkins.

Without hesitation, I told this complete stranger: "I need help, and I have no idea who can help me. I have prayed, I have cried, I have blamed others, I have given up. But I can't give up. I have four children and a husband, whom I cannot abandon. I am so torn. I don't know what to do. I hurt every day. A pain that goes so deep that it tears the life from my soul. I cry all the time. I don't want to see anybody, and I certainly don't want anyone to see me. And worst of all I canNOT continue like this with my children. I keep thinking how I'm hurting them by not giving them a hundred percent of me. My children are my whole life. I can't . . . I can't keep doing this. I can't."

He gave me a handkerchief and told me, "These things do come in handy sometimes."

And we both smiled.

After quite a while where we both just sat without saying a word, I could see a question lurking in his eyes. He wanted me to take the initiative . . . to go on.

I took a deep breath . . . and after a moment of analyzing the million questions in my mind, "I don't know how to forgive or who to forgive," I said.

"But I know forgiveness is the key that would set me free. I am constantly filled with so much pain and anger. I need to learn how to forgive, and I don't know where to start."

He listened to me pouring out thoughts that had been killing me in the recesses of my mind, that I had not shared with anyone. I was rambling on and on, but I needed this. Even if this was all there was that came from me being drawn to this little nondescript church that had called out to me, I was willing to play the game. But even in that moment, I knew who was calling out to me. . . . It was God.

"I open my heart to you, Lord God. Can you heal me, please? Please."

And even with Pastor Jenkins being a perfect stranger there was something there that told me he held, within, the power to guide me to all my answers. He was my doorway to God. Over the next several weeks, we met often. I felt safe. I knew that I was destined to find him.

After four or five weeks he asked, "Have you written down all these thoughts and feelings?"

"YES," I quickly exclaimed. I was so confident. At least I had done one thing right.

He continued, "Through the process of putting your life on the written page you will find a way to forgive YOURSELF."

I stopped breathing. That was a concept I had not engaged in. . . . I was desperately trying to forgive others when what I needed was to forgive myself. It didn't matter what for, I would eventually learn that, but on this day, I needed to learn self-forgiveness. And he showed me how. We prayed. My heart felt as if the weight of the world had been lifted off my shoulders. We said our goodbyes and planned to meet again the following week.

However, to my surprise, when I got there the church was boarded up— there were no signs that it had even been open before. I called Pastor many times, to no avail. I called his wife, and she said they had gone their separate ways, and she hadn't seen him in months. I never saw or spoke with him again. The church was demolished not that long after. God had put Pastor Jenkins in my life when I had no place else to turn. And I was healed.

Healed enough to finally go forward and face my demons.

It had been ten years.

Bill and my sister Brenda both had suggested that I begin to journal what I was experiencing. And now Pastor Jenkins as well. I had been putting words to paper just to exorcise all the memories, thoughts, and feelings through the years, without giving a thought that it would ever possibly become a book. I just needed to get them out of my head. And when I realized in my conversations with Pastor Jenkins that carrying such a burden was hurting me more than anyone, that's when I called Smokey, and went to see him at his home.

"I need to speak with Leon." I hadn't spoken to either of them in years.

As we sat in his living room, Smokey suggested I think twice about writing such a book: "You know, a book stays around long after you're gone. So, if you write a book, you better be sure." I just shook my head.

Finally, he gave me Leon's phone number. I told Leon I was writing this book, and it would cover our life experiences . . . some that may not be flattering to him. And with the greatest sincerity he told me, "You have my full support, Jayne. Whatever you need, I am here."


Writing this book has been the most cathartic awakening, and it has truly given me the power to move forward. And in Leon, I have found my friend again.

I began to rediscover my life as well. I began to reach out to others whom I had abandoned. But the best part was I found ME . . . a woman completely prepared to fill her children's lives with the mother they deserved—not only the half I had been reserving for them, but the half I had been hiding from the public as well . . . ALL of me. One hundred percent.

Many years had passed before I finally found the one most important reason to go forward.

What I have discovered is the art of forgiveness. Once I could forgive, it allowed me to grow. My daughters would have been denied the opportunity to know me in my wholeness had I not been able to forgive, and that would have been the ultimate waste of God's gift to me: my four amazing daughters. MY DAUGHTERS SAVED ME. In every possible way. They provided a world where Jayne Kennedy took a backseat to simply being "Mom." I didn't have time to be weak; I had to be strong for my girls. They needed me, and I found that I needed them even more.

Throughout these many years I have found a love beyond all measure. Bill has allowed me the space, time, and support to grow through the process of finding Jayne. God has blessed me even when I thought I would never again be worthy. All those years I spent searching for my purpose in life only to find that somehow, my purpose had found me.

Several years ago, I received an "anonymous" call, even though I definitely recognized her voice. Through deep, heaving cries, she begged me to forgive her, over and over again. She kept apologizing: "I'm so sorry. I'm so sorry." Then she abruptly hung up.

And now I have found my answer. I received a call from Leon's cousin, who had remained my sister-cousin all these years and with whom I maintained a relationship even though Leon and I were divorced. She told me that their cousin had passed away and that literally on his deathbed, he "confessed" to her that it was him who stole the video. The very same cousin who had stolen my mink coat in 1981, the very same cousin who was married to the woman on the other end of the anonymous call.

# CHAPTER THIRTY-THREE

# LEARNING TO EXHALE

For years I had struggled with how to tell my daughters. For years I had shielded them, but I knew that eventually I would need to tell them.

I never wanted to disparage Leon. I never wanted to berate him, rake him over the coals, make him pay. None of those things that so many people wanted me to do. The media dug endlessly for the gritty, salacious details on why we had divorced. In my opinion it was nobody's business. But so many felt that since our marriage was so public, why shouldn't our divorce be?

I rarely spoke publicly about our divorce, and not much privately either. But I just couldn't work through all the damage it had done to my spirit. Unless I was able to sort out and confront certain issues myself, I was never going to be able to go back to a life in front of the public.

Actually, it wasn't the issues around the divorce as much as it was what happened afterward. It was because of an unknown. Someone's hatred so great that there was no concern for the lives they had destroyed. A friend called it an *assassination attempt*. It was certainly a near miss.

I found myself hiding. After gaining weight people didn't recognize me as often as before. I once heard someone say, "Hey, that's Jayne Kennedy." And the other person said, "No, that can't be. Jayne's not that fat." I could function in the world of "Mommy" and not have to deal with all the faces that knew my history. I retreated. I loved being Mommy, showing up at every event for my kids, being there to support them and shape their characters. I would never trade that in, not for a hundred billion in gold. But I also found this to be an easy way out. I found myself lost . . . and then found . . . and lost again! At thirty-four when I gave birth to my firstborn, I did not know how much I would need them all at forty-one!

I felt I had been robbed of *one* of the things I truly loved . . . my career. But even worse, I felt I had been violated.

And once my daughters were at an age when there was a chance they'd hear it on "the streets," I couldn't hide it from them any longer.

When Mayor Bradley died in September of 1998, Savannah was thirteen. I had taken her with me to the memorial service at First AME Church, a church we frequented. How could I not go? Mr. Mayor was a dear friend whom I greatly respected. No matter what was going on with me internally, I had to say my last goodbye. Reverend Cecil "Chip" Murray spoke, Stevie Wonder sang. And Savannah watched as we were seated with state and federal politicians on both sides. It occurred to me, What if something happened to me? I would want her to know my struggle from my own lips.

Afterward, we went to eat at a quiet nearby restaurant. As the words came easily, I found myself wishing I had told her earlier.

She looked at me directly, putting her hands over mine, and said: "It's okay, Mom. We got you."

And that was it. No judgment. "WE got you."

Soon after, I told all the girls. I was so relieved to know that not once had they been judged by their outside world because of me.

But I had become such a recluse that I no longer participated in anything Hollywood related. Eventually, Bill just stopped telling me we were invited to anything, because he knew what my answer would be. Years went by, and one day we were invited to present the NAACP Theatre Award for best producer, an award we had previously won for producing *The Journey of the African American*. He was prepared to say no, but he decided he would ask me anyway.

"Jayne, we have been asked to present the Theatre Award for best producer. . . . I can call and decline."

I said nothing. . . .

"Jayne . . . did you hear me . . . Jayne?"

He was turning to go away and I meekly mustered up, "Yes. We can go."

In utter disbelief, he quickly turned back. "Are you sure?"

"Yes." I had been holding my breath . . . and I exhaled.

And that was it. I had made the commitment, and I'm not sure why. Perhaps I knew I could no longer go down this rabbit hole that had made my life pitch-black, devoid of any purpose other than family. I had told my girls; it was time to move on. So, it was about time that I actually did.

The day of the awards found me terrified. The getting dressed, the grand entrances, the paparazzi, all of it. What had I done? The mere thought of standing onstage in front of my peers was becoming more overwhelming with every passing minute. I tried to deep breathe but the breaths just kept coming faster and faster. My heart raced. . . . I could feel it pounding inside my chest. The evening went on and finally we were escorted backstage to prepare for our entrance. Celebrities were bristling; the typical backstage drama and excitement filled the entire space. While Bill was being given our speech, in my mind I was frantically disintegrating in an attempt to become as small as possible, trying to make myself invisible so no one could find me. My eyes were darting back and forth trying to find the nearest exit door, or any exit. Maybe there was a window through which I could escape. I kept telling myself: Come on, Jayne, there has to be an exit door. Nearly hyperventilating by now, I tried to hide in the stage curtain, when suddenly the makeup artist came for touch-ups, pat-pat-pat with the powder. Then someone grabbed my arm and pushed me toward the wings, where I found Bill. I tried to tell him . . . "I have to go. I can't do this." But he had already stepped onstage and was reaching back to me, prodding me to join him. And there she was again, pat-pat-pat.

I reached out to Bill's hand knowing that if I didn't, then surely, I would run. As we stepped up to the podium, he completely disregarded the speech he had been given, pulled me in close, and, taking the microphone, said, "I would like to thank the NAACP Theatre Awards for getting my wife out of the house." All I remember after that was a row-after-row standing ovation that seemed to last for an hour but was more likely less than a minute.

These were my friends, my peers, offering their unconditional love and support. The exact same people whom I had intentionally shut out of my life for far too long. Then once it was all over, Roger E. Mosley grabbed me and said, "Where the hell have you been?" And we laughed.

# CHAPTER THIRTY-FOUR

# NO MORE PAIN

During all of this, in 1995 Zaïre was born. My third and last biological child. Her birth was altogether different from either of the other two girls. When I found out I was pregnant with Zaïre, I told Dr. Greig, "I want a scheduled section and a total hysterectomy." I was through with suffering from endometriosis, and I wanted it to end. I knew I would not have more babies—I was forty-four, so I knew beyond any other reason that the hysterectomy was my answer to NO MORE PAIN. My life at that point already had enough pain. I had to start draining my body of whatever source of pain I could. He laughed and said it was much too early to think about that. I told him that I was so finished with endometriosis, that I wanted my life back. I wanted a total hysterectomy. About six months later I reminded Dr. Greig, "I want a section and a total hysterectomy." Again, he said I should wait, that I might change my mind. The day I went in for my ninth-month checkup I told him point-blank: "I want a scheduled section and a hysterectomy." I guess he finally took me seriously. With no labor pains I gave birth to my last little Overton, Zaïre, a perfectly healthy baby girl.

I had C-sections and epidurals with all my babies. Savannah and Kopper I remember quite well. But Zaïre was different. I was so doped up from the additional drugs for the anticipated hysterectomy that I don't remember much of her birth at all. I do remember my doctor asking me if I wanted to see my uterus. I couldn't believe him. Here I was expecting him to say "Do you want to see your girl?" and he says "Do you want to see your uterus?" I don't think I answered him, but I do remember him holding up this thing that looked like a huge basketball. That's the last thing I remember.

I wish someone had told me that I was out of my mind having a hysterectomy and a baby at the same time. I was thinking about "one less surgery." But I was way off base. There is no possible way I can describe how difficult it was with two kids at home, a brand-new baby, and the aftereffects of the procedure I had gone through. I was totally incapacitated. I was to stay in the hospital three days, but I wouldn't stop bleeding. At five days I went home. Two days later, my incision reopened, and I had to go back into surgery to open it completely *and* reclose.

When I got back home, I had epidural headaches from the fluid dripping into my spine and I couldn't elevate my body at all, and certainly not my head, from the tremendous pain. I didn't know what was wrong. I was at home alone with the kids, and my head felt like a knife was lodged into my brain. Every time I raised my head even an inch, I thought I would die. And when I went to the bathroom . . . I was screaming from the pain as I tried to crawl across the floor. Every inch forward hurt. My sweet babies were my angels that day. Seven-year-old Kopper was holding my head, trying to keep it horizontal as I struggled to cross the floor. Ten-year-old Savannah called Dr. Greig and described precisely my agony and he said, "I'm on my way right now! I'll have medication delivered immediately." She then called the pharmacy, which had just closed, and she told them my doctor would be calling. "It's an emergency!" They immediately made all the arrangements to have some medication delivered to the house. Kopper kept busy applying ice packs and pacing with Zaïre, who at that point was less than two weeks old, to keep her from crying. Bill arrived ten minutes after the medicine arrived. The girls were so proud that they had saved me . . . AGAIN.

I was a mess. Then, when I wasn't put on hormone replacement right away, I became an *angry* mess. . . . I took forever to heal. I was miserable. Months passed and I could not take walks or exercise, which meant that after giving birth at forty-four I was now faced with not being able to get rid of the weight I had gained during the pregnancy.

When Zaïre was nine months old, I was rushed to the hospital yet again in the early hours of dawn with kidney stones. I was still breastfeeding Zaïre and didn't have milk stored for her. I was so worried about who was going to take care of my children since Bill was taking me to the hospital. Kathleen—Bill's ex-wife—popped in before the sun came up to help with her usual all-hands-on-deck attitude, ready to fill in wherever she was needed. And again, my two angels came to the rescue. They were the only ones Zaïre would let touch her. Savannah and Kopper were Zaïre's sole providers for five days and Savannah totally weaned her. Me, on the other hand . . . I found myself thinking endometriosis wasn't so bad after all. It seemed that the entire year that I had hoped would be relief from eleven years of suffering was just a nightmare.

Zaïre is one of the old souls you hear people talk about. She has definitely been here before. I'd look into her eyes and see the entire universe. I recall the times I would look into Kopper's newborn eyes and recognize the similarity between her eyes and the eyes of an artist creating a masterpiece on canvas. You could see the sparking light of the creativity at work, but it was up to you to step back and assess what she was creating. There was always something going on in her mind that was like a huge secret that she treasured, and she was only willing to share her gifts with those who mattered most. The degree of sparkle equaled the degree of love and knowledge input. But with Zaïre it was as if I was learning from *her*. The questions and comments that have come out of her mouth have oftentimes made me stop and catch my breath. She is so intense and creative. I always thought she was going to be the one to follow in my footsteps. She loved to entertain, and she loved to make people laugh. One day when she was about five she had us on the floor laughing while she did this wild reenactment of a Chris Tucker scene from the movie *Rush Hour* with Jackie Chan. Then she came to a dead stop, put down her arms, looked at us with absolute seriousness, and exclaimed, "I should be doing this for a TV show." And she walked away, while we proceeded to pick up our chins from the floor.

When I was seven months pregnant with Zaïre, my family and I went back east for our summer vacation. The Harrison Family Reunion was scheduled for Philadelphia, so we planned to fly to Boston, rent a car, stay there to visit Bill's parents, drive to Philly, where we would meet up with my parents, sisters, and brother for the reunion, then drive back to Boston and stay for about another week.

Earlier that year Bill's dad had been diagnosed with cancer. He had undergone an extensive amount of treatment but had come through it pretty well. Whenever we went to Boston, we were so used to his dad, Papa Gino, picking us up at the airport. He had this gravelly voice and tough demeanor. He was an ex-military cop. But he was the kindest, most wonderful soul you'd ever want to meet. He didn't speak much, quite a contrast from my dad, and when he did it was always to the point. The kids loved him and couldn't wait to grab Papa Gino in a big bear hug.

This trip he met us as at the airport, and we all went to the house and had a blast. He was doing so well and was absolutely his old self. The next day he had a slight relapse and went into the hospital. We all visited him that afternoon, laughing and talking about how much we loved him. He seemed a little tired, so we left and went home. The next day we were meant to drive to Philly, but Bill wanted to stay in town with his father and he didn't want me driving at seven months pregnant. Savannah, Kopper, Cheyenne, and I took the train. The kids loved this even better. Uncle Harold picked us up from the station and took us to the hotel, and as usual it was swarming with Harrisons.

There was the usual Friday-night talent show. My Dad even modeled the official Harrison Family Reunion T-shirt and Kopper ran up onstage and modeled with him; she was such a cute little diva. Then came the Saturday-morning business meeting where we discussed the status of the planning committee, voted on the location of the next reunion, discussed family members in need, etc. And then came the afternoon events, culminating with the banquet on Saturday night. I was scheduled to be the guest speaker, and there was a special first-time event on the program because the Harrison family had established a collegiate scholarship fund available to any Harrison who wanted to seek a higher education. Applications would be provided ahead of each reunion. Sunday afternoon, Uncle Harold drove us to the train station and Bill picked us up in Boston. Right away I knew something was wrong. Just before we got to the house, he pulled over and told the kids and me that Papa Gino had died.

It's always very difficult dealing with the death of someone you love. But there were so many blessings with Papa Gino's passing. In the days before and after, we were there, and not three thousand miles away. Bill was there for his mom. The kids got to see Grandpa before he passed and Grandpa got to see them. He didn't suffer. There were so many blessings. The only thing missing was that Papa Gino didn't get a chance to see his last granddaughter, Zaïre.

Two years later, the whole family went back to Boston. On our first day we decided to visit Papa Gino. As soon as we parked at the gravesite, Zaïre jumped out of the car, ran over to the headstone, and fell on the ground, face down and spread-eagle. She yelled at the top of her voice, "Hey, Grandpa. Can you see me now?" Well . . . we were all shocked. No one had said anything about Papa Gino not getting to see her, not to her anyway. We hadn't even explained that he was in the ground. "Hey, Grandpa, I'm right here. Can you see me now?"

Sure, there are many more severe medical conditions than endometriosis. But endo attacked me and changed my life, turning it totally inside out.

Through all the tears, the devastation, and emotional trauma it caused, I have to still say *"THANK YOU, GOD."* Because of endometriosis, I have the most incredible blessings in my life in the form of motherhood: Cheyenne, Savannah, Kopper, and Zaïre. Cheyenne, the forever optimist and mother to my grandson Kingyari. Savannah, the ultimate in confidence and compassion with a heart of gold, and mother to my grandson Jaris II. Kopper, the quiet, smooth, steady, poetic, reserved rock: my *QUIET STORM*. And Zaïre, the sweetheart blast from the past ready to take on the world, forever my right hand.

# CHAPTER THIRTY-FIVE

# WHAT'S IN A NAME

When each of my girls reached the seventh grade, they were assigned to do a major project called "Who Am I?" It was a project that required them to work on all facets of their life. Over a five-month period they would utilize all the skills they had learned in the seventh grade. One particular essay required research on the meaning of their name: first, middle, and last.

When I initially saw this, I was angry because there was a major part of this assignment that was taken for granted by the teacher for many of the white students. It was assumed that there would be no problem in completing all the required interviews and research for all the background in the areas of family, family roots, family crest, history of the family name, the country of origin of ancestors, and cultural traditions passed on through the generations. However, for a Black child, their report could be greatly lacking in these areas. As an African American I found myself asking, Who am I?

My daughters and I spent many, many hours talking about the significance of this assignment and what we believed would be suitable for inclusion in the final report. We talked about the European connotations of our family names: Thompson, Overton, and Harrison. We even talked about how difficult it was for me with a last name that didn't belong to me, Kennedy.

When I divorced, no one knew who Jayne Harrison was, so I continued to use Jayne Kennedy. Changing my name to Jayne Kennedy Overton after getting married to Bill Overton seemed pretty stupid to me, but I really had no choice. Kennedy was not a part of what I had inherited. It's so amazing how you can lose your entire identity by losing your last name. And every time I reach a milestone in my life and my name is honored for whatever reason and all the fans remember Jayne Kennedy, I think: That is not who I am. I am Jayne Harrison. My family should not be left out just because I got married. Why do I have to give up an identity I shared with the people who brought me into this world, the people I love and lived with for the first nineteen years of my life?

After much discussion on this portion of the "Who Am I?" assignment, Savannah wrote an excellent paper acknowledging that the rubric was biased, and it did not allow for cultures other than European ancestry. She made her case by explaining how as an African American, she does not have the "luxury" to know her roots, her family crest, the significance of her name, what town she came from, what *country* she came from, what foods her ancestors ate; therefore, the school district *must* rethink this assignment. Her report came back with that essay section marked as A++++, accompanied by a note from the teacher: *Savannah, thank you.* You *have taught me something.*

There is value in a name. My children were taught to always keep their maiden name and to only *add on* their husband's name. If I had it to do all over again, I would prefer to work as Jayne Harrison and that's it.

And then I stopped to think . . . Was I really even Jayne Harrison? Harrison was only the name of our enslavers and not our FAMILY name. The Harrison family is huge. Since 1977 we have held the biennial Harrison Family Reunion. Each reunion committee had the job of adding onto the family tree, which goes back to Peter and Harriet Edmunds Harrison, my great-great-grandparents, and Peter's mother Rose, my great-great-great-grandmother.

We number well over seven thousand, and at least a thousand of us turn out for the reunions. Some of the other Harrison family notables include Wally Henry, previous punt-return specialist with the Philadelphia Eagles; Kenny

Harrison, 1996 United States Olympic gold medalist in the triple jump event in Atlanta; and my cousin Mariah Stackhouse, an LPGA Tour professional golfer. At only seventeen, Mariah was the youngest African American woman to play at the US Open, as well as the first African American woman on the Curtis Cup golf team. The printed program is a major part of the reunion celebration as it includes the family tree and many photos and writings of family members, as well as an autographed congratulations from Alex Haley: *From Kunta's family to yours.* And there is also the copy of the original Bill of Sale that shows John Harrison Sr., of Fairfield County, South Carolina, purchasing Harriet and her two children for $1,240 on January 1, 1856. That means somebody's family was torn apart on New Year's Day. But that somebody was not a Harrison. They only came to be a Harrison.

And so, Bill has given our children names that stand out on their first names alone. Hence, Cheyenne, Savannah, Kopper, and Zaïre.

# CHAPTER THIRTY-SIX

# FINDING
# A BALANCE

Savannah Ré and I traveled around the country quite a bit when she was first born. Wherever I went, I'd have my mom or Bill's mother meet us there. I used to take every opportunity on the road as a chance for some grandmother/granddaughter bonding. It was a perfect arrangement. I never ever would leave my child with a hotel babysitting service, so this was the ideal solution. Grandmas got a chance to travel and to know Savannah while I worked. My mom had never traveled like that before. Remember . . . her home was her entire world. Her traveling was limited to vacations back home to Virginia and with Dad's relatives in South Carolina. I believe it was very enlightening for her to be on the road traveling through airports on her own to various cities. I'd have a car meet her at the airport and bring her to the hotel. Mom and Hessie, Bill's mom, both loved it. It seemed this kid-on-the-road thing was going to work out just fine. Savannah was ecstatic, moms were in heaven, and I was finally on the road and not lonely.

When Mom was asked to be a guest on the Ed McMahon Mother's Day TV special to be shot in Las Vegas, I don't know who was beaming more broadly—Mom or me. That bold and audacious country tomboy, Ginny from Virginia, was going to be on TV! She and Dad had been interviewed many times before, but this was something truly unique and special. This was on a huge stage in VEGAS . . . solely paying tribute to mothers. This day was all about her. And the icing on the cake was that it was with Ed McMahon, whom, like the rest of America, they had watched on TV in their living rooms for so many years on *The Tonight Show Starring Johnny Carson*. That was something that I know she could have never, ever imagined in her lifetime!

My mother has left her thumbprints all throughout my life. There are so many moments that stand out, small, seemingly insignificant ones that linger because she always resides within my entire being. One day just a few years ago, I asked her if I could do her hair and makeup and shoot photos of her, just for fun. She laughed with her distinctive giggle, and the next thing I knew I had lights and camera all set up, and there she was just posing and beaming.

When Bill was hospitalized for a few days, I got a greeting card from her with a note that said, *Here's just a little help to get gas for back and forth to the hospital.* She had included a $20 bill. Mind you, I *was* working again by then . . . but that's just my beautiful mom!

At this point in my career, I started doing a lot of events that had to do with "family." In addition to hosting the Children's Miracle Network telethon for seventeen years, I became the spokeswoman for the National Council of Negro Women's Black Family Reunion celebration, and the spokeswoman for the American Lung Association's campaign to educate expectant, unwed teenagers on the dangers of smoking during pregnancy and breastfeeding. I was also the spokeswoman for the Endometriosis Association. All of these were a far cry from the many sports banquets I had been invited to where I was often the only female in the room.

Many times, I would take Savannah with me to the events. She'd sit in her high chair alongside me on the dais, laughing and shaking hands with everyone in the long line of fans, posing for the camera and trying to take the pens and bite them whenever I tried to sign an autograph or biting the microphone when I spoke. We really made a great team!

Once I ended up somewhere in the South for a banquet. When we disembarked from the plane there was a big crowd of people at the gate awaiting my arrival. Snapping pictures and shaking hands, Savannah and I worked our way to the airport entrance. A local high school band and choir had assembled in the median and struck up a song as we exited. Immediately Savannah, who was about eighteen months by then, ran forward with her arms outstretched as if all this pomp and circumstance was just for her. She always stole the spotlight 100 percent. And I loved that she enjoyed it so much.

When Savannah was born, I was the happiest woman in the entire world: I had an absolutely wonderful husband who worshipped the ground I walked on. I had a booming career. I had the most incredible little bundle of joy, and the endometriosis had gone away.

Bill and I would take Savannah out to jog and bike three to four days every week. We walked the beach. We were in love. Everything was great. I had started back to work by the time she was one month old. The house was loaded with gifts and flowers from well-wishers and fans and the people I worked with. Stuart Geller, the Detroit Coca-Cola bottler who was instrumental in securing my contract with Coke, even sent her a *mink teddy bear*. We had boxes, big boxes, of baby products from Coca-Cola. Savannah was a living, breathing, almost-walking, not-quite-talking billboard (which I'm sure they intended). She had Coca-Cola T-shirts, onesies, socks, booties, sweaters, sweatshirts, hats, toys, you name it, all emblazoned with their logo.

They even sent her a sleeping bag and a Coca-Cola river raft. It was so much fun. I was in a totally different and truly foreign world. Even with coming from a house full of kids, the world of baby merchandizing had changed so drastically since I was a child. We actually made our toys out of an empty spool of thread, a bobby pin, and a rubber band, or a drum out of an empty round box of grits, and we couldn't have been happier.

It actually seemed possible that I could work and still be with my baby. So much of the work that was coming my way had to do with being a mother. A whole new arena had opened. In 1986, when Savannah was only two months old, Muhammad Ali and I appeared at the Children's Peace Foundation fund-raiser in Beverly Hills along with John Travolta and Ted Lange (*Love Boat*), and Ali was carrying Savannah around for a while. The next thing I knew, the papers again had us "married" and ran a picture of Ali holding "his" baby—probably because Ali said it was his . . . a callback to our "wife" joke that began in the Philippines. I was never offended, as I knew Ali always had a heart of gold when it came to me and my family. But all practical jokes aside, Ali was always the consummate gentleman and never once crossed the line with me.

Coca-Cola also sponsored Hands Across America. It was a major, major campaign that most likely took years of planning: one continuous line of people crisscrossing the entire country, holding hands from coast-to-coast all at one specific moment in time. Coca-Cola asked Bill, Savannah, and me to participate in the line in front of the White House, where all the company executives were positioned. It was one of the most inspiring events of my life. You could actually feel the electricity when the time came for tens of millions of Americans to hold hands all at once. Bill held on to me, I held Savannah in my arms, and Savannah held the finger of the lady who stood next to me. At that point in time, I was particularly proud to be an American.

From there, we were off to Florida, Alabama, Detroit, New York, and Charlotte. It never seemed to stop. For about a year I was working and caring for my child simultaneously and seemingly effortlessly.

It only takes one disaster to totally make you rethink whether you're doing the right thing. Or not.

Bill, Cheyenne, Savannah, and I were traveling together for an event in the South, where I was to be the keynote speaker for the NAACP. From the minute we exited the aircraft, there seemed to be something wrong. No one mentioned a problem, but I could tell by all the whispering between Bill and the police officers who had escorted us from the airport that there was most definitely a serious issue. The girls and I were instructed to remain in our hotel room. I was supposed to be speaking at a banquet later that night. Apparently, CBS New York got a threat on my life, scheduled for the event that evening. They forwarded it to CBS Los Angeles. It just so happened a friend of ours worked in the CBS newsroom in LA and we had mentioned to him that we were headed to the event. He phoned ahead of us, notifying Bill of the potential problem. The police officers performed a thorough sweep of all the locations and found nothing. I went under police escort on a secret route to the banquet, and the evening went off without an incident. I was so afraid; I'm surprised I could speak at all.

Not that I was worried about me. I had many disturbing correspondences in the past. But this was the first time my kids were with me, and that took the wind out of me. Ever since that incident, I had to become a different person. If I was out with my kids, it was rare that I would give an autograph. I was always concerned about where they were and whom they were with. Whenever I left them at a day care, I insisted their cots and cubbies be put away from the front door. Of course, it's not so much of a concern now that they're adults. Savannah stands six foot two, Kopper stands at five eleven, and Zaïre and Cheyenne are trained in self defense. My friend told me just the other day, "Lighten up. I pity anyone that comes after Savannah." I pity anyone who comes after an Overton girl.

Another time, I got a letter from a guy in a psychiatric hospital who insisted I was his long-lost wife and that I had run away with his three kids: He was being released the next week and when he got out, he was coming for me. I called the FBI and they delayed his release.

On another occasion, I had a teenage white kid appear on my front door-steps one day at my home in Pasadena. He had done tons of research, tracked me down (mind you, this was pre-internet), and hitchhiked all the way across the country, just to meet me. Thank goodness all he wanted was an autograph.

I know that there would be no career without fans; however, it only takes one time to be wrong about someone.

When Savannah was maybe five, I took her to Hilton Head, South Carolina, for four days. We flew into Savannah, Georgia, the closest airport, and Savannah was thrilled, as she'd always talked about going there one day. As the plane approached the airport, the pilot announced his welcome to Savannah. Savannah yelled out to everyone onboard that *she* was Savannah and this was her city. She hit the airport gift shop first and made me buy one of everything that had her name on it.

I hosted a celebrity golf tournament for a couple days, but the rest of the time we just hung out. It was tourist off-season and the whole place was rather quiet. We spent the days in the ocean swimming with dolphins. We rode bikes on the beach. It was magnificent.

She'd take my face into her two little hands and shake my head back and forth and say, "I lub you so much, Mommy." Then with those big, pretty eyes she'd look deep into my eyes, touching the tip of her nose to my nose, and she'd whisper, "I so poud o' you." Even at five, she knew Mommy was doing something special.

I didn't need the approval and acceptance from the world. Just from this one little girl. And she was so proud of me. I never wondered what she thought of me. I only knew I could see through her eyes and see me as God made me. I opened my arms wide and embraced the warmth and solace. I opened my heart, inviting more, more, more.

Savannah Ré was born November 1985.

Kopper Joi was born May 1989.

Zaïre Ollyea was born September 1995.

And the precious little thing that first called me mommy, Cheyenne, was born August 1982.

The lights of my life.

# CHAPTER THIRTY-SEVEN

# CIRCLING THE FAMILY WAGON

had been traveling on the road so much during Savannah's first year of life, I hadn't had the opportunity to have her dedicated or baptized yet. I was speaking at the Southern Christian Leadership Conference, and Coretta Scott King was holding and playing with Savannah. What a moment that was for me. I mentioned to Dr. Joseph Lowery, then president of SCLC, that I felt really awful that I had not dedicated my baby to Christ.

He immediately picked Savannah up into his hands, holding her high up to God, gathering the other ministers into a tight circle as they all put hands on the shoulders of the minister in front of them until at the core was Dr. Lowery . . . holding my baby. I was witnessing an entire room filled with more than thirty ministers laying their hands on my little girl as they began to pray for her, just like the tribal ceremony in *Roots*. It was absolutely the most beautiful, most blessed experience I'd ever felt. I cried. Of course I cried. I had no idea how much *we* would need those prayers years later.

One Saturday night back at home we were all going to the market, when we passed the local recreation center. The door to the gym was open, and bright yellow light spilled out onto the parking lot, carrying with it the sounds of cheering and dribbling. We decided to pull over and check it out. To our amazement there was a coed basketball team kicking some serious butt against the all-boys team. And the four girls on the coed team were the stars of the show, and what a show it was. And they were only nine.

Bill has always been a strong advocate of physical fitness, and all my girls participated in some sport activity at young ages, starting with swimming at the age of one. By three they began soccer in the American Youth Soccer Organization program. Then in third grade they started basketball, volleyball, and track within the school system and the city's department of parks and recreation programs. As they advanced into high school, playing a myriad of sports continued to be their norm.

I am a firm believer that keeping kids interested and involved in athletic programs throughout their youth establishes healthy life patterns and self-discipline, and also keeps them out of trouble. The skills learned help lead to experiences that can be called upon in both their personal and professional lives in their adult years. And it is especially necessary for girls—my girls— because it is important for them to be raised to be independent. I want them to always know in their heart that if all else fails, they can make it on their own. I want them to be strong leaders of their community. I want them to be smart and compassionate. All this can be learned through sports.

Research has shown that:

Girls who play sports are more likely to graduate from high school.
Daily exercise can reduce mortality by 60 percent in breast cancer survivors.
In the *Fortune* 500 list, 80 percent of female executives played sports.

Savannah had shown a real love and talent for basketball, but I wasn't impressed with the level of play that was available to her. What we saw in the gym that night changed many things for us.

The coach, Dr. DeVaughn Peace, was starting a club team, the Westchester Starletts. Savannah signed up and I became a "gym rat mom." We were always at the gym for practice and constantly traveling the country to the different games and tournaments. Dr. Peace had this idea of "taking a team of beautiful young girls to any court in the country and takin' names." He had a vision of building a girls' team with a reputation for excellence.

Now I had always been used to my girls being physically head and shoulders above their classmates. Savannah was only average height on this team. She had her work cut out for her if she wanted to hang with these girls. At age ten, the Starletts won the California State Championship and went on to the AAU Nationals in Salt Lake City, bringing home the bronze medal. The very next week they were back at practice getting ready for next year. Again, as the state champions they went on to the nationals in Milwaukee and brought home the silver, losing out on the gold by only one bucket. By then Coach Peace had achieved his goal. This team was one of the best youth teams I had ever seen. They were awesome, defeating girls' and boys' teams alike. Then in their third year, also as state champs, they went to Orlando, Florida. Again, they came home with the silver. But Savannah wasn't there this time—she was home in a *wheelchair*.

Savannah loved basketball with her whole heart. She loved to control the floor when she was with her school teams, bringing to the team what she had learned in club ball. She talked about it all the time. She cried when they lost, and she cried when they won.

The team had a game in Las Vegas, the Nike Easter Classic, when Savannah went down from a jump shot, landing on her right knee. The bruising and swelling was pretty serious. A month later, I was walking behind her and one of the dads said, "What's wrong with Savannah's leg?" Her right leg was bent so badly below the knee that it looked like it belonged to someone else. We could still detect swelling, so we took her in for examination. That's when we found out that she had *adolescent Blount's disease* . . . a disorder of the growth plate under the knee. Instead of closing evenly as she grew, the plate converged on one end and spread open on the other, causing her leg to eventually bow out below the knee.

For several months, we went from one specialist to another in hopes of finding a solution. For many months there was a series of measurements as they tried to determine her rate of growth and how serious the problem was. As the time went by and I watched her leg bow more and more with each passing day, it just about broke my heart. I'd drop her off at school and watch her as she walked into the building. She had developed a severe limp, and with every step I felt a pang in my heart. She no longer played anything.

December 29, in her seventh-grade year, she went into surgery. They cut the tibia and the fibula, pulled them apart two inches, and adjusted them back and to the left under the kneecap two inches. Then they inserted eight titanium pins through the bones and into titanium steel rings around the leg to hold them in place while the bones grew back together. She would wear this for four months. With the use of a wheelchair, she would be able to return to school.

Her fourth-grade teacher, Mrs. Helen McCullough, came to visit her the same day as the surgery and stayed there holding her hand while she slept. I couldn't believe her. Most visitors just came with good wishes and left shortly after. This teacher who had not had Savannah in her class for three years thought enough of her to come and say hello while Savannah managed to open her eyes and quickly closed them again, falling asleep. Then Helen pulled up a chair and stayed until Savannah awoke again, six hours later, just holding her hand.

Savannah's team came to visit her as well. They gave her an official first-year WNBA basketball, autographed by the entire team. We didn't know it then, but that's the last time she would be with them as a teammate altogether.

She had a weeklong hospital stay and then she came home for a month before returning to school. There was a tremendous amount of at-home care necessary to prevent infection from setting into the bone. The hospital visits were three times a week. So that she didn't miss too much school, we scheduled the visits for the end of the day, which meant that she had to miss only her last-period class Mondays, Wednesdays, and Fridays. Which also meant we had to drive in rush hour LA traffic one hour to the hospital and one hour back. We had no other life during this period.

Every morning, we would get up early to do the cleansing routine and change the sponges at the pin sites. The nurses had trained Kopper how to do this so that she felt part of the healing process. Then we'd try to get Savannah dressed and into the car comfortably; load the wheelchair, backpacks, lunches, and violin; drop Kopper to school; drop Zaïre to preschool; and then take my time to get Savannah to school. We were so lucky that because her first-period class was PE, they allowed her to arrive at her leisure. But Savannah hated being late. She wanted to be there to help the teacher. She was such a trouper throughout all this. All of her teachers commented on how well she handled the entire episode. She never missed a class, other than for doctor appointments, and never allowed one grade to slip. I, on the other hand, was exhausted—I think mostly from the emotional stress.

Four months later, the doctors allowed her to use a walker and crutches, and it is a day I will always remember. We came home from the hospital and she slipped on a throw rug in the kitchen. I don't think anyone can imagine having a cage around your leg with titanium pins going through the leg and having that leg fly up in the air and land down on a marble floor—right on the cage. I'm sure my heart skipped a beat, but I didn't panic. I felt so helpless. She was in such pain. It was late but I called her doctor, and he told me to give her enough medication to manage the pain and that there was no way the fall could have done any damage to the leg.

The next morning, she was fine, as fine as could be, and it was raining. When Bill walked her through the doors of the school there was a puddle of rainwater. She hit it and the crutches went flying out from under her again and she screamed so loud when she hit the floor the whole school came out into the hallways.

I would have gladly taken her pain.

Then months later she had to have a second surgery to remove the steel pins, and the physical rehabilitation (three days a week) seemed to go on forever. I never could figure out why a hospital that catered to children and offered services that required frequent visits never offered hours outside of the school day. The only times a child could get an appointment were between nine and four and never on Saturday. Schools let out up until three fifteen. If you were lucky, you could get to the hospital by four p.m. in rush hour traffic, but the last appointments were mostly taken and began before four o'clock. It was always a challenge. And because I would never be able to get back in time to pick up Kopper and Zaïre, they had to go with me each and every time.

Several months after the physical therapy ended, I realized Savannah was limping again. I took her back to the doctor and asked that they measure her legs. They refused. I insisted one leg was longer than the other. After much arguing with the superiors, they finally measured her again, and that's when they realized that indeed, her left leg had continued to grow, leaving her right leg one and three-quarter inches shorter than the other. They had spent six months estimating her rate of growth; *how* did this happen? I truly believe their projections were off because it was a children's hospital and Savannah was already taller than anyone in her school. Unbelievable! Eventually her back could not handle the differential. Again, we were back and forth from the school to the clinic two to three times a week. She then had to wear lifts in her shoes to balance out her hips. The smiles were few and far between.

She was now in high school. By the summer leading into eleventh grade, Savannah was in so much discomfort, and after about ten different doctors we still didn't know the origin of the pain that had caused her to miss the last month and a half of school. I had developed a plan with the school and the teachers where I would go every day to get her assignments and class-work. We would do the work together at home, and then I'd take it in the next day. With all the meetings with the teachers and staff I felt like I was back in school myself. We knew we had to find out what was causing her pain or she would be held back in the fall.

We revisited her orthopedic doctor at Children's Hospital LA. And waited in the outer office for three hours . . . again. After the numerous doctors we had visited before him and all the MRIs, bone scans, and other tests, this doctor looked at her for all of three minutes and determined that she had

*fibromyalgia.* He immediately sent her to the children's rheumatology department, where they confirmed the diagnosis. I had no idea what that was.
Apparently, there is no one-size-fits-all treatment.

I spent the rest of the year trying to find out what to do for Savannah. She
spent the rest of the year trying to smile. Pain every day. Missed classes every
week. She couldn't sit long in class, she couldn't read long, she couldn't write
long—everything hurt. But fibromyalgia creates a sensitized response to pain
and the pain meds didn't work, so we took her off the meds completely. This
led to pain management classes. No sports, few friends, no social life, but a
whole lot of heart. She never quit. So I couldn't either.

She learned to manage the pain . . . somewhat. One of her many doctors
informed us that the pain was actually caused by stress and is a sleep disorder.
We immediately learned ways to make life a little less stressful. But looking
ahead, how would she be able to do that in her senior year? Her GPA had
dropped by this point from all the work she had missed.

When I finally had time to sit and wonder when *I* could get enough time
to get back in shape and resurrect my career, I just went blank. But I couldn't
think about that. Not now. Not only was I on pause, but so was the entire
family. In my heart, I *knew* the time for me would come . . . eventually.

And Savannah, with the help of her principal, who graciously spent
the entire summer with her so that she could enter her senior year, worked
so hard to graduate on time with her classmates in 2003. And from there
she graduated from Pepperdine University with two majors, worked at Fox
Broadcasting, then went back for her master's at Syracuse University, graduating with honors.

Throughout all of this, I have never been so proud of anything else as when
I witness how my family has somehow become a single unit. My girls would
do literally anything to support and love every moment of each other's lives.

When Cheyenne gave birth to Kingyari, Savannah and Kopper were right
there in the delivery room rooting her on. Kopper helped Savannah heal, both
when she was sick as a child and now as she transitions into motherhood
and is raising her own son, Jaris II. Cheyenne sat outside of the hospital for

hours and hours praying and waiting for updates on Zaïre following her rup-tured aneurysm during the covid pandemic, with all of us wondering if she would survive. Savannah and Kopper flew across the country to be at her bedside as soon as she came out of surgery and stayed the entire seventeen days while she was in the intensive care unit. When Zaïre was studying abroad in Brazil for five months, all of them flew out to visit and travel with her for ten days during Thanksgiving, bringing her a sense of family when she felt all alone in a foreign country. Savannah stood by Kopper, my sensitive, creative, poetic genius, throughout her journey of self-discovery, and then moved to Texas so they could be closer, and she also served as the officiant at Kopper's wedding in Costa Rica. Zaïre flew to DC to pack up Savannah's entire house when Savannah was six months pregnant with two giant dogs in tow, while her husband was settling into his new job and their new house making sure everything was ready once they all arrived.

If I said I was blessed a million times to have them as my children, it would still not be enough. I'm not bragging just because they are mine. There is just something special about their bond that makes it worth every single second that I've been out of touch with my career.

# CHAPTER THIRTY-EIGHT

# GONE BUT NOT FORGOTTEN

I t was 2017; Zaïre had just graduated from the University of Southern California, Kopper had graduated from Pepperdine University in 2011, and Savannah had graduated from Pepperdine as well, before attaining her master's at Syracuse University. I had finally achieved my goal by ensuring that they all had a college degree. Something that I never had but was determined they would.

And then from out of the blue, I got another call, but this time it was great news!

Earl "Butch" Graves Jr., president and CEO of *Black Enterprise* magazine, had personally called to inform me that I had been chosen to receive the 2018 Legacy Award at the Black Enterprise Women of Power Summit, an annual event composed of the most powerful and influential Black women in the corporate, political, entertainment, education, and arts realms. But he felt it would not be complete unless all four of my daughters were there to witness the honor. Especially since it was one of the most significant acknowledgments of my career, he wanted them all to experience the moment.

My daughters and I arrived late in the evening the night before the awards and the next morning, I awoke with the biggest smile on my face, feeling truly blessed as I spent a few minutes contemplating my acceptance speech that I'd be giving later that evening. I turned over to pick up my phone to check messages and clicked on my Instagram page: The very first image that popped up was a little girl with a cardboard cutout frame that had "Jayne Kennedy" emblazoned around the edges. She was wearing a giant smile, a crown, and a banner across her chest that read "Miss Ohio 1970," and she was holding a football in her hand, resting it on her shoulder, just like my iconic red-silk-shirt-NFL football photograph. Her teacher had asked her class to create a project that would be a part of the classroom's "living museum." She clearly understood the assignment. That little six-year-old Black girl named *Faith* never could have imagined how much she inspired and motivated *me*. My spirits could not have been higher going into that evening's celebration.

That very same night women of all ages, from all parts of America and all walks of life, were sharing stories about their journeys. My daughters soaked in every moment. The energy in the room was beyond amazing, but I happened to see a young lady who looked to be in her mid-twenties standing a few feet away watching me intently. I walked over to meet her, she told me her name was Arielle, and she began her story.

Immediately after graduating from college, she had been hired by Apple and left her home and family to live in Silicon Valley. Her life had become one of isolation as one of the few women and certainly few Black women working in her field. She missed her family. She had no friends. She had begun to question her purpose and life choices. But, as she went on to say through the tears streaming down her face, "Listening to you tonight, about how you overcame the challenges of everything you faced in your career, made me realize that I could never give up." By then she was shaking so hard I had to hold her in my arms. Kopper, who has seen her parents assist those in need her entire life, then stepped to the young woman and gave her *her* business card, saying, "If and when you ever feel like that again, you just call me." I was so proud of my baby girl at that moment, and by the way, she has remained friends with Arielle to this day.

Then, as if that wasn't enough, in March of 2020 I was invited to attend the fifteenth anniversary of the Women of Power Legacy Award Summit in Las Vegas, celebrating past Legacy Award honorees along with my long-time friend Debbie Allen and her sister, Phylicia Rashad. And who should approach me immediately after the ceremony with the biggest hug? Arielle: "I did it. I stayed. I endured. THANK YOU. I came here this year in hopes that you would be here as well just so I could say THANK YOU."

A few years ago, I received a call from a woman who had been an adviser for my daughter Zaïre at USC. She had left after Zaïre's freshman year due to medical issues and we had not heard from her since. She asked me to be their family's guest at her father's funeral. He had been a very prominent Black doctor in Los Angeles for many, many years. She and her two sisters had grown to become very successful in their respective fields. Then she went on to tell me that when she was young one of the long-standing traditions in her household every Sunday was that her father would sit his three daughters down in front of the television to watch Jayne Kennedy on *The NFL Today* on CBS. And every Sunday the message was always the same . . . "Look at her, the first Black woman doing a man's job in sports broadcasting. I want you to see that and know that you can do anything you want to do. Blaze your own path." And of course, I humbly accepted the invitation to the funeral.

So many stories and so many hearts and minds touched over my lifetime. I had no idea back then what I represented to so many people. Today, I realize I was indeed part of that continuum of "anointed" Black women who were purposely placed on this earth to serve a greater purpose . . . much greater than my own personal goals and aspirations. I represented hope, a deeper need for self-worth, and a sense of pride to millions of Americans who saw something in me through their own individual prisms.

Clearly, my immense media presence resonated with legions of people of color, and I also represented ideas of empowerment to white women who were similarly looking to be validated, both personally and professionally.

I know that I opened doors and smashed ceilings for female talent and executives of all races during a time that was believed to be the beginning of the end of the white male patriarchy in business, entertainment, and certainly politics. Well, we were all certainly naively optimistic, and ultimately rumors of its demise were premature. . . . Cue the #MeToo movement.

I was front and center of the American "media dream" for twenty-five years as a film and TV actress, television sports anchor, host of the longest-running syndicated sports show in history, spokeswoman for *Fortune* 50 corporations, guest on dozens of daytime game shows, talk shows, and prime-time series, entrepreneur behind the third-bestselling fitness video that launched a new media platform, and host of two of the very first national infomercials; I launched the first syndicated radio exercise show, and created the first exercise-in-the-sky platform on American Airlines—did all of that really happen?

I had to question myself: Did I make a mistake walking away from it all? Even in spite of all the whirlwind of controversy, should I have hung in there and fought? It was a very different era and a very different time.

# CHAPTER THIRTY-NINE

# FINDING THE JAYNE THAT NO ONE KNEW— NOT EVEN ME

*I lived apart in a world of pain*

*Pain held within leaving nothin' to gain*

*From the eyes of the world and everyone I'd meet*

*The pain closed in as I went through life with my eyes on my feet*

*Losing all touch with reality, a life left behind*

*Creating a whole different world in a whole different time*

*But still each day I'd try to find the key*

*Not to my head or my heart*

*But to my soul that it would someday set me free*

*Hiding inside with my head to the ground*
*Can't look up from the weight of looking down*
*Hiding inside with my head to the ground*
*Under a river of tears my soul's sure to drown*

*Then I heard someone say ~ Look Up*
*Hold your head up high*
*On the wings of an angel, you can fly*
*Look someone in the eye and stop dangling your life by a thread,*
*Bury that pain . . . instead of your head*

*The eyes are the windows to the soul it's true*
*Couldn't bring myself to fix my eyes upon you*
*Couldn't bring myself to fix my eyes upon me*

*And I heard someone saying ~ Look Up*
*Hold your head up high*
*On the wings of angels, you can fly*
*When it seems there is nothing good for you to see ~ Look Up*
*And fix your eyes on me*

*And I heard God saying ~*
*And fix your eyes on me*

—JAYNE HARRISON KENNEDY OVERTON

When I decided to stay home with my family instead of continuing on with my career, I always knew that I would eventually return to the entertainment industry. I knew it would be difficult. It might even be impossible . . . but I have never let impossible stand in my way.

When you've been around, trying, and you've never achieved the success you had hoped for despite what it might have looked like from the outside . . . and there's that *one* acting role that you knew you could really sink your teeth into—but you never did, and you're my age . . . what is the likelihood that that role will find you?

Hollywood rarely allows a leading woman to age gracefully like it does with leading men. But not only did I have the challenge of coming back as a woman, I would also have the burden of returning as a Black woman. Since the roles available to Black actresses are few and far between even today, some fifty years later, I knew it was going to be overwhelming. I knew I had to have a master plan.

Even with the celebrity status I had once enjoyed, many of the people in hiring positions would be millennials or younger and were just babies or maybe not even born when I first came to Hollywood. Perhaps this would be one of those times when a few would look at me with awe in their eyes and gleefully state, "Oh my gosh. I used to watch you when I was a little kid," or "My parents used to watch you and they made us watch too." Or "Jayne, when you were in your prime, I couldn't turn on the TV and not see you. You were everywhere!"

I'd been having conversations with some of the people I had previously worked with in the 1970s and 1980s as I had made up my mind to reenter the business. I was looking for an opportunity to get some feedback and maybe an avenue that I could pursue.

Strangely enough, I got questions like "What about becoming an event coordinator? You'd be good at that." "Maybe you should attend a conference I'm hosting with personnel managers who might be able to find some office work for you?" Someone even said, "Maybe you should go to a department store and apply for a job at the makeup counter?"

It was very clear that they didn't expect me to have any presence in television and film. But I thought to myself, That's not at all what I had in mind. They clearly did not know me. But that begs the question: What *does* an actress do after Hollywood?

Thank God that there has been *some* degree of change in attitudes within the industry and the culture at large over the past few decades since I've been away. My heart soars with pride when I see Angela Bassett, Marla Gibbs, Sheryl Lee Ralph, and the throngs of other magnificent Black women gracing the marquees of the entertainment industry—many of whom I had the opportunity to work with in my past. A past where there were only a handful of Black women who became successes despite the odds: Diahann Carroll, Cicely Tyson, and Ruby Dee, just to name a few. I believed with all my heart that I could still do this given the opportunity. I believed with all my soul that I was supposed to do this. I believed that it was a part of God's plan for me.

*God, I'm ready to do your work. Whatever lessons I had to learn let me learn them now, and let me learn from those I have already lived through. I am ready to move on. Teach me what to do. Show me how to use the talents that you have given me so that I can do your work. Forgive me for the sins I have done and help me to forgive myself and to forgive others. Help me to succeed at this so that I can be a better mother and provider for my children, so that I can be a better partner for my husband, so that I can make life better in any way for others, so that I can be a better child of God. In Jesus's name I pray. Amen.*

I got off my knees and went to work.

There I was as I began to formulate my plan to rediscover myself. I knew it would take a long time. I knew it was a process. Then it dawned on me I didn't even remember what kind of makeup I used to wear or even where it was sold. I used to do all of my own makeup; now I didn't even know what makeup to buy. And now, I needed glasses to put it on, along with a magnifying mirror. I used to proudly boast about doing my makeup on the airplane just looking into the window. I knew my face and its contours so well and it was ridiculously easy.

How much had the new technology changed, the way the filming process was done? Would I be outdated when I set foot in the studio? How was

I going to be able to still be the best mom I knew, and do the best work I knew? Was I even doing the right thing by jumping back in? So many questions.

I began working out with a trainer. I needed the motivation from an outside source. I had resurrected my *Love Your Body* workout tape and begun the long process . . . but OMG. I had no idea before how difficult that workout routine actually was. I had developed a program to effectively get in shape and I used to do it sometimes twice a day, but it's a long road to travel when you can't even do one sit-up. *I needed motivation.*

My kids and I were in the car at peak traffic hours on Wilshire Boulevard coming home from school in the midst of the usual traffic jam, and I was wearing my standard-issue baggy sweats and ponytail with no makeup in the hot LA sun. The kids were arguing about having a sleepover when I heard a line on the radio.

*"Yo, honey was so blazin'. She was just . . ."*

"What?"

*"Yo, she looked like Jayne Kennedy, word bond, to my mother, man."*

*"She was that ill, man."*

I slammed on the brakes.

The song was "Ms. Fat Booty" by rapper Yasiin "Mos Def" Bey. It was 1999, twenty-eight years since I woke up in Leon's car and saw that HOPE STREET sign in downtown LA.

I looked in the rearview mirror at the girls. Startled, Zaïre said, "Um, Mom, did he just say your name?"

Then Kopper, looking shocked, chimed in: "Why is Mos Def saying your name?"

"Mom, you're in a rap song," Savannah said. "You got street cred."

The next day I went to the gym and right in the middle of trying to do my upper body workout, I heard over the radio, *"Yo, honey was so blazin' . . . she looked like Jayne Kennedy."*

That was it. That's all I needed to hear. That was when I came to the decision that *I* was going to look like Jayne Kennedy too. Thanks, Yasiin!

It was mid-December 1999 and I was in the supermarket when I noticed this woman staring at me. Then she finally came over and apologized: "I'm so sorry to bother you. I have seen you in here many times and I never wanted to intrude on your private time, especially when you were so wrapped up with the kids. But have you seen the new *Ebony*? The millennium edition? You have to see it. It's wonderful, the honor that they gave you. It's on the front shelf right now." And as she turned to leave, she repeated, "You have to see it. Don't forget."

I rounded up the kids, quickly finishing our shopping, and I grabbed the *Ebony* and went straight to the car. They were all huddled over my shoulder as I thumbed through the pages, and there it was. They had several categories of the "Twenty Most (whatever)" people of the twentieth century.

In the category of the "Twenty Greatest Sex Symbols," along with Lena Horne, Naomi Campbell, Billy Dee Williams, Dorothy Dandridge, Joe Louis, Josephine Baker, Eartha Kitt, Billy Eckstine, Harry Belafonte, Tina Turner, Marvin Gaye, Pam Grier, Richard Roundtree, Vanessa Williams, Denzel Washington, Halle Berry, Michael Jordan, Alek Wek, and Tyra Banks, was *Jayne Kennedy*. The kids started screaming, "Mommy, look at you. I like that swimsuit. Is that you, Mommy? What is that from? Mommy, you're right next to Richard." (They knew Richard Roundtree from the times we spent at his ranch for his annual Easter egg hunt.)

As the tears welled up, I thought about Bob Johnson, the late senior editor of *Jet* magazine, who was always in my corner. He believed in me to no end, and he was my friend. I had known him since I first came to Hollywood. Whatever I did, Bob covered it. *Jet* was born the same year I was, and Bob and I would always call each other to say happy birthday.

I had always thought of John Johnson as my *silent partner*. As the founder of Johnson Publishing Company, *Jet* and *Ebony*'s parent company, this is the man who held the power to shape Black images in this country for over fifty years. This man—who had maintained the highest level of integrity in a world that, I'm sure, had attempted to make it nearly impossible for him to succeed—had sat silently in my corner from the time I was seventeen years old. Before Bob Johnson died, he told me about a picture that was sent to him about a year after Leon and I divorced. Whoever sent it in had hoped Johnson Publishing would run it. The picture was of Leon escorting a woman, and Bob later told me, "John said not to use it. We're not going to run anything that would hurt 'our' Jayne."

In August of 2005 John Johnson passed away. One of my biggest mentors, gone.

A writer by the name of Daryl Middlebrook was compiling interviews for a book he hoped to publish entitled *Sepia Cinderellas*. We met over coffee one morning and the first question out of his mouth was "Not meaning to slight you, but how did you manage to get so many *Jet* covers without ever having a hit television show, song, movie, or anything?" I laughed. He was right. I couldn't even remember how many times I was featured in *Jet* and how many times in *Ebony*. For the first six years I was in Hollywood, Bob was always calling me to schedule a shoot or interview.

(Many years later, I was asked to shoot a sizzle reel for former actress and now very hot Hollywood director Salli Richardson-Whitfield for a project she was pitching about the *Jet* "Beauties of the Week" and she had a box full of all the *Jet* covers I had been featured on, and I think we counted close to twenty.)

I thought about how John and Bob Johnson had single-handedly invited me into the living rooms of millions of African American households over a couple of decades. I smiled at Daryl, and I replied, "I guess the Johnsons just liked me. That's all." And I'm sure they sold a lot of issues whenever I was on the cover of either magazine.

In 1996 it was so hard, having a baby at forty-four after eleven years of endometriosis, taking drugs like Prempro as a result of the hysterectomy— hormones that had a tendency to make me gain weight, and being overweight to begin with. But I had to lose weight. Not only for my public image, but also for my self-confidence and for my family. The lifestyle I wanted to share with them was not the lifestyle I was living.

After Zaïre was born, Savannah and Kopper bought a Walkman for me (the new gadget of the moment) and Tina Turner's 1991 *Simply the Best* greatest hits CD. Every morning, I would hit the beach with Zaïre in the jogging stroller that Claudette Robinson had gifted me, and I had Tina blasting in my ears. Beating out the rhythm in the sand, matching the music in my headset, I attacked the beach with unforgiving grace. It was my soul savior, my breath of sanity, and my motivation. Tina was my shero. It was Tina who made me persevere. I played her anthem "The Best" until I literally wore it out . . . *several* times. I do believe that at one time or another every interviewer has asked me "Who is your role model?" I always said I didn't have one. But at that time in my life, after Zaïre, I would have answered beyond the shadow of a doubt that it was Tina Turner. But it was more than Tina. It was that one collection of songs. The instrumentation, the drive and aggression. There was nothing else like it for me. I was very depressed, with my many complications after the delivery. Tina's music and messaging kept me strong. Depression is an evil monster that sucks the lifeblood from its victims. Tina was my transfusion.

I admit it. I was also a true Beatles fan. As much as I loved all things Motown, I was addicted to both Motown *and* Philadelphia International (Kenny Gamble and Leon Huff's hit-making machine). But I was truly engulfed in Beatlemania. I bought Beatles bubble gum and records, right along with their other millions of fans. I loved George Harrison just because we shared the same last name, so that was good enough for me. I sang every lyric of every song and watched them invade America, like a swarm of locusts, in the mid-'60s.

Forty years later, I found myself sitting in front of my television anticipating the performance of my shero . . . Tina. I couldn't make it to her last show here in Los Angeles, so I eagerly awaited the broadcast of her special *Tina, One Last Time: Live in Concert.*

Oh my gosh. I just looked at the woman. She was still so beautiful and sang better than ever. She never missed a beat, nor a step with those fabulous legs. She was a *survivor* in every sense of the word. I sat there waiting for my inspirational theme song, "The Best." Tina and the orchestration blew me away . . . again. It's so powerful that I know now why I looked at it as my personal anthem. It has pulled me through so many rough spots. Sitting there watching her on TV that night was like being reborn. And then she unexpectedly sang the Beatles' "Help!" . . . *as a ballad*. It was as if I had never heard the lyrics before. How many times had I heard that song, and I had never really listened to it like this. Not like this. It hit home. My heart cried out.

As long as I was in the world of my incredible husband and my four blessings-from-God daughters, there was nothing in the world greater. It was when I was alone that something inside me fell apart.

Sometimes we need—*I* need—to reach out to someone. When I can't seem to hold on one more second, when I seem lost and I don't know which way to turn, when I feel that I haven't proven to myself what my real purpose is in life, when I think it's too late to make a change, when I believe it's supposed to be better than this—I need to reach out. And I have found solace. In people I don't know, total strangers, people who have said, "Jayne, we believe in you. We need you." And I find that I can finally . . . finally . . . look them in the eye and not be afraid anymore.

And in my mind, I fall back on Tina's words. Because what those strangers didn't realize was that I needed them *more*.

On May 3 of the year 2000, we celebrated my parent's fiftieth wedding anniversary and I finally began to write *Plain Jayne*.

I was never a product of "image makers" and press agents. I was always just me. I was inching closer to turning fifty, and I was faced with figuring out just what my image would be in this new decade. Who would I be at fifty, sixty, seventy? I really didn't know. I kept thinking I needed some downtime to be able to get to know myself. Thing is . . . I had no downtime. I only had Mom time. Writing this book became even more important.

But how was I going to get back to *ME*?

I walked around each day with my notebook, jotting down notes about myself. I'd take it to bed, and in that consciousness between sleep and awake,

I'd jot down whatever popped into my head. I felt like I was putting together a giant jigsaw puzzle. *Today I will work on this color and this design pattern. Tomorrow it will be the edges. Then in the end, I will see all the nuances of who I really am.* Sometimes the interlocking pieces were easy to find. But others seemed as if the manufacturer had misplaced them. These linking pieces were so hard to find, obscured under that pile of rubble that day-to-day life had just dumped, burying my treasures. How will all these pieces of my life come together? What is the picture I'm trying to build? When you put the jigsaw puzzle pieces together from the box, you have the picture on the cover to guide you. I had no final picture. I had to remember what it looked like myself, and so much of it seemed so far away.

Life is about the missing pieces. And I felt that there was something missing in mine. The one piece that completed the puzzle. Nothing was ever perfect. When it felt like perfection was lying in my arms or just around the corner, something new and challenging would appear, and the drive would begin all over again.

Eventually I would have to face the demon. The demon that had been dumping garbage on top of my puzzle pieces, on top of me, for over ten years.

Finally, my fiftieth birthday arrived, and I didn't want to think about all that.

I told myself: I'll start again tomorrow. It can wait another day. I've waited ten years already.

# CHAPTER FORTY

# REPRESENTATION MATTERS

On Martin Luther King Day 2022, while blending my green juice, I sat down at my computer to check my email. And there it was, a Google Alert for "Jayne Kennedy Overton." I am usually so hesitant to open unknown content, especially anything with my full name. Usually, it just says "Jayne Kennedy." But something about this one seemed okay. One of my Instagram followers was being interviewed regarding her podcast and was asked, "How is what you're doing through your podcast uplifting the legacy of Dr. Martin Luther King?" Her answer was two words: "Representation matters."

She then went on to say, "I want young Black girls and women my age that think that they do not have a chance, or it's too late for them, to know—it's not too late. Black women, we need to know that we have a voice, and we can use it for good. And that's what Dr. King did. He used his voice for good, for justice, for people to be free, to be equal. With my platform I want to inspire people, I want to inspire women. . . . I can give you a quick story of who inspired me, and yes, Oprah was part of it, but back in the day when this young girl was watching sports on TV, and everything else, there was an amazing woman on who was named Jayne Kennedy. And I follow her on IG, and she was the first Black woman I saw that had a microphone and she was talking sports. Well, I was already in love with sports, but you got a Sistah on here . . . that's talking about football??? And surrounded by a majority at that time of white men. Back in the day you didn't see a person of color let alone a woman holding a microphone and talking about sports. I was hooked, I was like—OMG she looks just like me. And then fast-forward four years later, you had Oprah that came on in 1986 with her own show. . . . Wait a minute. A Black woman got her own show . . . her own audience. . . . Are you kidding me? And then in the early nineties, you had Robin Roberts on ESPN's *SportsCenter*. So, it was just like things that I loved as a young girl going into her preteens and teens and seeing that someone that looks like me—my color, my lips, my nose, my shade, the coarse hair . . . all of that—and seeing that on TV . . . I said, 'Oh my gosh . . . I can do that.'"

And I thought, WOW . . . I did all THAT?

Within the whirlwind of my meteoric ascent to fame and celebrity, I was completely oblivious to the impact I was having on millions of people who looked up to me as a beacon of Black excellence and achievement at a time when those images were few and far between . . . at least in the general media. As the years have gone by, I've come to understand and appreciate all that I have represented to the culture and to women specifically.

The very first year that the WNBA was established, Rhonda Windham, former general manager of the Los Angeles Sparks, informed me that she never would have had the opportunity to do what she was doing had it not been for me. Women from nearly every sector of sports have shared with me their stories of how I made it possible for them over the years. A field producer for MSNBC's *Headliners & Legends* attributed her decision to go into her first job in sports production solely to seeing me on television when she was a little girl.

There have been so many kids who have said, "I want to grow up to be like you." I'd tell them, "Never settle for being like me or anyone else. Be better than me! You might grow up to find the cure for cancer while I am just an actress, someone who just happens to be on TV."

I have always hoped that people would see me just for me—I never really wanted to be a "celebrity," I only wanted to be considered good at what I did and good enough for it to withstand time.

But more recently, that impact has come full circle as a result of the social unrest of 2020 and the acknowledgment of contributions made by unsung people of color as attempts have been made to "whitewash" and marginalize pivotal aspects of American history and culture, reminding me daily with examples that illustrate that reality.

✦ My manager and I were finishing lunch at a restaurant in Beverly Hills, and as we were waiting at the curbside valet, I was approached by a young lady who looked to be in her late twenties, waiting for her car as well. She politely asked, "Excuse me, are you Jayne Kennedy?" When I smiled and reached out to shake her hand she began to cry. "I can't believe this, I am such a fan. You have no idea what you mean to me as a Black woman trying to find her way in life." She went on to say that she always looked up to me as her North Star of how a proud Black woman should present herself. She told me that because of me, she knew she was beautiful, despite the fact that she had suffered rejection as an actress and model due to her dark complexion. We could see she really needed to have that "release," so we just let her talk as she trembled, and it ended with us both in tears and a long, warm, heart-filled hug.

✦ When I was presented with the Black Enterprise Women of Power Legacy Award, one woman asked my daughter Kopper, "Were you aware of who your mom was growing up?" Kopper replied that yes, she knew about my career, she knew that I was a pioneer, but basically, I was just Mom to her. I wasn't really a celebrity at all . . . rather a soccer mom, pick-me-up-from-school mom, can-you-review-my-college-applications mom. It wasn't until that very night in the main ballroom at that event that Kopper actually saw, with her jaw dropped, the powerful impact of my career on the thousands of Black women who were there to honor her mother. All of whom were amazing trailblazers in their own right. Kopper could only say, "Now I know what y'all been talking about."

✦ I recently received a message on Facebook from a middle school teacher requesting I visit the school and autograph a giant portrait of me that she had made for her students. She was mounting it in their main hallway under the banner IF YOU SEE IT—YOU CAN ACHIEVE IT. She told me that I represented intelligence, beauty, strength, and grace to her as she was becoming a young woman and that she wanted her students, both male and female, to know the proud legacy that I left behind for them to emulate in their own lives.

✦ One day when I worked at NBC, the shoeshine guy—the one who had worked the hallowed halls of NBC for decades prior to my arrival—asked to lunch with me. "I see you," he said. "I see you today and fifty years from now. You will be the one." There was an element of great pride that I could see in his eyes as he watched me navigate the corridors of NBC . . . job after job after job. I could see that same element of pride years later as Black airport baggage handlers would clamor to greet me curbside and take my luggage coming and going. I saw it everywhere . . . wherever I went . . . it wasn't so much my celebrity . . . I was the one they could claim as their OWN.

✦ In the process of researching for my book, I went to Las Vegas in late 2019 to meet with Brent Musburger, who was my co-anchor on *The NFL Today*. He currently owns a very popular sports-betting radio and streaming network (VSIN), with the studio located on the ground floor of a major casino. I had not seen nor spoken to Brent since I was summarily fired from CBS some forty years prior. Somehow the press got wind of our meeting and the area outside of the studio was packed with reporters and curious bystanders. I recall specifically one of the female reporters (a white woman in her fifties) coming to me and saying how it was because of me that she had wanted to start a career in sports broadcasting and how she had always wanted to meet me in person to thank me for showing her it was possible. Again, more tears, and I had to do everything under the sun to prevent myself from crying as well because I was minutes away from going on-air for Brent's show, and photographers were everywhere. Of course, women in sports broadcasting are now the norm, not the exception. You can't watch a single game on television these days without seeing women in the studio, on the sidelines, even as play-by-play announcers. Super Bowl LVI opened its February 13, 2022, pregame broadcast with *two* females on the desk.

✦ When Zaïre was in kindergarten, I was asked to deliver a Kwanzaa presentation one day during student assembly for Black History Month and absolutely shocked the principal when I said no. Then I followed up with "But I *will* produce a multicultural festival for an entire week. They won't learn this in thirty minutes. I need a week." That week turned into an annual event for the next five years, winning awards from the students, the school, and the California PTA.

✦ One day, I went to pick up Savannah from basketball practice at her middle school. She was playing at the ultimate level for the Westchester Starletts AAU basketball traveling team, winning bronze/silver/silver, consecutively, three years at the AAU Nationals. But this was middle school. Basketball practice typically was outdoors. On this particular day it was raining hard, and when I arrived, Savannah was sitting on the steps to the gymnasium soaking wet. "What happened to practice?" As she raised her head I could see the tears in her eyes. "They canceled the girls practice and the boys got the gym instead." Well . . . need I say more? That was the day I became an advocate for girls in sports. I now had my marching orders. Since then, I've scouted, recruited, coached, and managed dozens of young girls in basketball and soccer. Many of whom have gone on to earn scholarships to play in Division 1 collegiate programs.

One of the many joys I have been blessed with in mentoring these young girls from age nine to twenty-two is when they finally realize that "Momma Jayne" is actually Jayne Kennedy.

\* \* \*

Then BLM happened. And I knew at that point I was on the right path. There were many conversations being had about important and influential people of the 1970s and '80s who had made a difference in the acceptance and recognition of Black people in a society that didn't want to acknowledge our undeniable contributions. It was a sign that my story indeed needed to be told.

I'd been writing this book on and off for over twenty years. I needed this "social reckoning" as much as America needed it, but especially Black America. The enormous responsibility that was entrusted to me was something that I surely didn't comprehend in the moment when my career was at its apex. But now in the quiet of my solitary moments, I know I was never alone.

# CHAPTER FORTY-ONE

# REFLECTIONS

All of my life people have had certain expectations of me. As a child I abided by the rules of my parents and other family members. My parents wanted me to be a good girl, to be strong, and to make the most of whatever opportunities came my way. I left home at the age of nineteen and became the wife of a man who had very high expectations for who he wanted me to be. He put me high on a pedestal, which meant I had to be perfect, and I wasn't. I didn't even want to be. I soon came to believe that I couldn't live up to the expectations of others. I could never be happy, truly happy, until I learned who I really was as a person. It was then and only then that I would be whole.

When I left Ohio, I vowed I would never change. I would never become the product of some marketing executive or public relations firm. I liked who I was. I only wanted to explore my horizons and dare to dream. That really had nothing to do with becoming rich and famous. I never wanted to become a celebrity; I just loved the work.

People always asked me, "How does it feel to be so beautiful and to have people stare at you wherever you go?" I told them that I was used to having people stare at me. Ever since I was twelve, I've been just about the tallest kid in the room, and I grew up as one of the only Blacks in a mostly white community—I got stared at all the time. Today it may be for a different reason, but I had become totally unaware of the glances. I never thought of myself as beautiful. It was an uncomfortable thought.

Oh yes, I understood the effect of hair and makeup and a certain gait when I walked, but for the most part that wasn't really me—that was just part of a costume. But when everything is working right, the hair, the makeup, the wardrobe, it *feels* beautiful. . . . That's different. I was always more at ease in jeans, a baggy sweater or sweatshirt, and sneaks. I always wore lots of makeup when I worked on camera though, thinking that I needed it.

Many years ago, I got a call from *Essence* magazine for a cover shoot. I had dreamed of the idea of a glamour magazine with me on the cover. The wardrobe, and professional stylists, and please don't forget the airbrushing. This was a dream come true. When I got to the shoot, there was none of that there. The makeup artist smeared on a hint of blush, some mascara, and lip gloss. That was it. "But what happened to all the glamour makeup and wardrobe?" I asked. How could they miss the boat with this no-makeup look?

Apparently, *Essence* had been looking for an opportunity to portray the beauty of a Black woman who needed none of those accoutrements. The concept for the shoot was that they wanted to take advantage of an opportunity they had sought out for many years . . . to put someone on their cover who needed absolutely no hair . . . no makeup . . . and no wardrobe. They wanted everything to be as "natural" as possible. They even wanted me to wear a simple white men's undershirt.

And they had chosen me. I was honored. But jokingly, I told them, "You owe me one."

I was very upset but tried not to let it show. I had always had different opinions about how to apply my makeup. From the very beginning, with *The Dean Martin Show*, the makeup artist finished, and I looked like he had no idea how to apply a look for anyone of color, forcing me run back to my dressing room to wash it all off and reapply it *my* way. But I totally expected this shoot for *Essence* to go without a hitch.

I was crushed but I gave in after convincing them to give me a little color on the lips rather than plain gloss. There I was, on the beach with the wind tossing my wet hair every which way. My first big shot at a glamour cover looked like a typical day at the beach.

But when I saw the cover, I absolutely loved it. It was so me, Plain Jayne.

It just costs too much to try to carry around the burden of expectations. Always wondering what others are thinking of me. Why hadn't I realized this long ago? Even when I traveled on the road so much during the 1970s and '80s I had a standard policy for any short trip: If I can't carry it on my back, it's not going. Why hadn't I learned from that in my personal life as well? I was tired of waiting on baggage claim and losing it. Well, I'm tired of waiting for someone to claim this excess emotional baggage I've been carrying around for far too long. I don't want to worry about what people think. I want to like me again.

I had gone into hiding. I gained more weight. A lot of weight. I stopped working. Not only did I drop out of the business, but I dropped out of society as well. I had lost my raison d'être, my reason for being. I functioned totally in the realm of my children. I had given up all that I fought and sacrificed for and spent my days lovingly chauffeuring my four kids back and forth from school to doctors appointments, to soccer, basketball, hair appointments, grocery stores, and libraries. I had even dropped out of the church. But I had not lost faith in God. He was my very thin string that I desperately, secretly, held on to. And I had done exactly what my father always said not to do. *I had quit.*

I have so much love and hope in my heart; maybe that's why I cry at the drop of a hat. I cry at basketball games, at TV commercials, and at shows and movies before they're even ten minutes along. My kids laugh at me and say, "Already, Mom?" But it's not the content. It's what it reminds me of. Just like in drama class with sense-memory techniques used to place you emotionally in a scene. One incident, one touch, one word can bring back an avalanche of emotion. I had a drama instructor, Gail Kobe, who did many years of acting before teaching. She had lost a child once. Whenever she needed to cry in a scene, she would place her baby's bootie in the pocket of her wardrobe. During the scene she would hold and rub the bootie in her hand and the tears would flow freely.

Life, for me, is that way. I see a car and I'm transported to an emotion. I hear a note, just one note of a song, and the memories flood my mind. I see a flower and the smell alone will take me back to times that I have long since forgotten and even to my dreams of things in my future that have not yet happened.

I love being sensitive. I love being loved. I love having a purpose so that I can do something with all these feelings. My children filled that gap for me. But as far as my career was concerned, I felt so lost that I hadn't found the next step in my destiny. Yes, I do believe in destiny.

# CHAPTER FORTY-TWO

# PRETTY IS
# AS PRETTY DOES

At this point I find myself reminiscing again about a conversation I had with Oprah Winfrey in 2010. Now, fifteen years later, a question she asked that day . . . a question that I had no answer for . . . came to mind. It had been ten years since I first began to put pen to paper after a conversation with Alex Haley got me thinking. But the question they both had dangled in front of me was . . . in essence the same.

Shifting to sit on the very front edge of the sofa, Oprah had looked at me and said, "Jayne. Yours will be a great book, and the story needs to be told, but you know what book I would go out and buy in a heartbeat? I want to know what it was like to walk into a room and know that you are the most beautiful woman there. To walk in and all eyes are on you. Gayle and I used to watch you and think, Oh my God, she is so beautiful. We used to call you a nickname that we made up for different women and you were The Ultimate. So, I want to know . . . how does that feel to walk into a room and know that every eye is on you because you are so beautiful?"

As she continued on and on, I had to interrupt her: "Oprah, I could never write that book, because I would have no idea what I would write about. I have never ever walked into a room and thought, Damn, I am all that. Every single time I have ever entered a room I am constantly thinking: But my hair, is it frizzing up, did I wear the right dress, is my lipstick still on evenly, did I wear the right shoes? And: I wish I had money to buy couture, am I going to say the right thing, do the right thing?"

And she sat there shocked. "I don't believe you. No way. But what about when people stare at you?"

I had to laugh—there was that question again. "Oprah, ever since I was twelve and shot up to five foot ten, people have stared at me because I towered above the girls *and* the boys. Ever since my family moved to a nearly all-white community people have stared at me because I was the little Black girl in a sea of Italians. That is what I grew up with. I became accustomed to being stared at."

"But, Jayne," Oprah said, "you are the only one who can write that book. If you wrote about it at your age now, then people would believe you and not condemn you. If Halle or J. Lo or Beyoncé wrote it people would just say they are bragging. But you would be talking from the perspective of your present age looking back some thirty years ago and what that was like."

Caught in a moment of silence, I flashed back to the conversation I had with Alex Haley. He was the first one to put the thought of writing a book in my mind.

I was speaking at the 1982 World's Fair in Knoxville, Tennessee, when I found myself on the dais with him. I was one of the millions who had sat glued to the tube following the heartbreak, agony, joy, humiliation, rage, and exhilaration of the landmark miniseries *Roots*. Kunta Kinte's struggle brought about so many emotions and levels of self-evaluation for me and my place in this land I called home. To actually meet Mr. Haley was like meeting the Great Enlightened One. His stature belied the strength within. His words were so powerful, yet he seemed so meek and gentle in person.

It wasn't until after the event when we found a few moments away from the crowd that he sent shock waves through my body. I greatly admired his ability to tell a story and yet there he was telling me, "I would like to work with you to write the story of your life." I knew I must have heard him incorrectly. Again, he spoke gently and directly: "I would be fascinated to reveal the plight of being beautiful and Black in America today. I can imagine it all. I've been thinking of it for quite some time and here we are . . . together . . . tonight. Jayne, we have to work together."

I couldn't imagine what he was talking about. Laughingly, I asked him, "Are you sure you have the right girl?"

And he smiled. "Absolutely. It would be a huge success. Think about it."

He wanted us to collaborate on how it is to live daily in the struggle of being a beautiful woman of color and how the world sees us. To tell my story about what it was like to look the way I do. Something I never felt comfortable with. He wanted to tell the story of how men see beautiful women and how they see women in general. How men dominated women, fighting to maintain their positions of power. He would say: "Every role model helps us to dream. . . . We help them dream out of the ghetto. If you are successful you can count on the fact that there will be people who will detract you, but if you deserve to be successful, you will endure.

"You could help so many women," he told me, "particularly young women. We'll talk."

But before we got around to it . . . he was gone.

I would have loved to tell the story as he saw it, but I felt so inadequate trying to do it alone. I felt like I was a hammer with no arm to swing it with. And I've been waiting to strike for a long time.

Oprah's perplexing question loomed heavily over my head, and I had no immediate answer for her.

Over the years, I have tried to analyze my thoughts on the paradox of "pretty."

I've never been comfortable talking about my looks. Never. I always found pride in looking my best, but it was never my sole motivation that I had to be the most attractive woman wherever I went. It wasn't important to me, most likely because everyone in my family on both sides was physically beautiful. . . . That's what I grew up with. In my mind, I never stood out as the pretty one, because everyone around me was "easy on the eye."

Dad's home in South Carolina was always bursting with cute boys. One summer I remember very clearly. We had just arrived in Winnsboro, South Carolina, and Dad's first stop was Harrison's Truck Stop. I was thirteen. Harrison's was the gathering spot for almost all of the local youth. The jukebox was blasting "Under the Boardwalk" by the Drifters while my sisters and I peeked out the truck's window, and there were young guys everywhere. Well, we started primping and smiling as we jumped out of the back of the truck. These were some of the cutest boys I had ever seen. This was going to be a great vacation, until Dad started with "Hey, ain't you so-and-so's boy? And you're so-and-so's boy." Yep . . . each and every one of them was our cousin.

And not just on the Harrison side. My mother's side is even larger, with a host of beautiful men and women running up and down the family tree. Mom was the most beautiful woman I'd ever seen when I was a child. She was proud and wanted to be sure all of her girls always looked their very best. With six children, five of them being girls with long hair, she took the time to wash, dry, and curl our hair all the time. No easy task at all. I remember that we would dry our hair with the vacuum cleaner by removing the dust bag, cleaning the insides, and reversing the flow of air in the hose—a makeshift blow-dryer, which didn't exist at that time, at least not in our home. I would never be able to estimate how many dresses she made for us over the span of our childhood years. As we became older, we were able to manage our own hair, often setting it in giant beer-can rollers. Mom took great pride in her beautiful little girls. She made sure to instill within us that we would be beautiful outside *only* if we were beautiful inside . . . and that has stayed with me to this day.

Yes, I always wanted to look pretty (what little girl doesn't?), but that was never the primary thought on my mind.

Inside . . . I was always the proverbial "tomboy" with scabby knees and elbows.

Yes, I enjoyed and took great pride in making my own clothing, because I knew how to make it fit just right for my statuesque frame, instead of buying off the rack. And because of that, I made sure to be the best seamstress I could be. I didn't want to wear sloppily sewn dresses. I loved learning the ins and outs of makeup, creating a look that worked for me. And as my career blossomed, I thoroughly enjoyed showing up in the perfect dress that I had designed and created with my own hands. I knew I had an *aura*, but I never once thought it made me a better person. It was all a part of the facade of Jayne Kennedy. Inside, I was still that rough-and-tumble tomboy who wore denim jeans and tank tops, which was a staple from my 1960s hippie-flower-child days.

In hindsight, now recognizing the influence and not-so-subtle nuances of colorism in both mainstream and Black culture throughout our history, I do understand the fact that I was "fair-skinned" with so-called "good hair" made my prominence, especially to White America, more palatable.

When I did *The Dean Martin Show*, I recall being told by the NBC publicity department that letters were pouring into the network inquiring as to my ethnicity. That's when I decided to wear the Afro wig on the show to tell all the doubters that I was indeed a *sister* and proud of it. Even though the producers never urged me to do so, I think they were very pleased that I took that initiative. Ironically, for both parties it was done for very different reasons: They wanted to score cultural diversity points for placing a Black female in prime time, and I wanted to let America know that *we* were being "seen" on prime-time TV.

I was consciously aware of the legacy of the "mulatto" Black female in film, going back to the 1920s with the Oscar Micheaux films, through Josephine Baker, Lena Horne, Eartha Kitt, and Dorothy Dandridge. It was a constant (and aggravating) bone of contention with my fans and the media, that I just *had* to be mixed with something else, with the inference being I was *too pretty* just to be a Black female, which of course I found as insulting then as I do now. I remember being a guest on a national talk show and the white male host asking me what I was "mixed with." When I answered, "I'm Black," he absolutely refused to believe that I was African American. By the third time of pressuring me to admit that I was "mixed," my mind was asking me, What is wrong with this man? Although I knew exactly what he was trying to say, I refused to let him win. I had become angry, so I said, "I'm Black. And isn't it you who said that if I had one drop of Black blood in me—then I was Black?" The show abruptly went to a commercial.

Hollywood has always had an uncomfortable and complicated relationship with African American women outside of the standard roles offered to them as maids and hypersexualized concubines to white male leads—a ridiculous legacy that has impacted the image of Black women, and as a result the global psyche of how Black women in film have been projected and perceived over the years. Which also speaks to how Hollywood chose to tell stories about Black love, something that is still problematic to this very day.

It didn't help that because of my height I wasn't cast in more roles as the love interest, since a lot of leading men are under five foot ten, and God knows Hollywood was certainly not comfortable with "interracial" love stories, as it was still echoing from 1967's *Guess Who's Coming to Dinner*. But I always wanted more substantial character roles that weren't centered solely around my appearance. And aside from a couple of television shows that alluded to me having a romantic partner, the only time I was offered a significant dramatic role as a fully realized Black woman in a normative relationship was in the film self-produced by Leon and me, *Body and Soul*, in 1981.

Don't get me wrong, I'm not saying that the way I looked did not allow me certain advantages. It's just that I always believed rightly or wrongly that I was hired because I worked *hard*, and I made certain to never give anyone a reason to say, *Oh, she only got that job because she is pretty.*

I knew there was an abundance of beautiful Black female actresses in Hollywood when I arrived (e.g., Vonetta McGee, Lonette McKee, Judy Pace, Tracy Reed), so I was determined to persuade Hollywood to focus on my *talent* and not my looks. Unfortunately, because there just weren't enough lead roles written for Black actresses back then, I realized very early on that I wouldn't have a career at all if I just sat by the phone and waited for it to ring.

I recently heard a podcast interview—*Corner Table Talk* with Brad Johnson—where Billy Dee Williams was the guest, and it was so reaffirming to hear Billy Dee also echo that same sentiment about *his* physical appearance. He said he had no idea at the time, early in his career, of the impact he was having by providing Black males a role model and someone positive to look up to. When those images in film and television were so few and far between, his only objective was that he wanted to simply find dignified work as an actor, and everything else was what *other* people projected onto him. I almost cried when he said that, as it mirrored my exact experience and perspective.

People forget that in my prime during the 1970s through the 1990s, there was no social media or TMZ and therefore no constant 24-7 feedback loop for an actor/performer, so you really didn't know how you were being received by the general public until you went out and were recognized. And in my case, first, because I was constantly traveling, and second, because I was never really on the party circuit, I didn't know the impact I was having. I found myself somewhat alienated due to my experiences of being on the road alone for so many, many years. It's still amazing to me today when people of all ages approach me in public and tell me stories about how seeing me in film or TV profoundly affected them in ways that I could have never imagined at the time.

Knowing that I can possibly be in the same cultural conversations as the legacies of Josephine, Lena, Eartha, and Dorothy is beyond my wildest dreams, heartwarming, and very humbling.

When I received recognition—such as "The Most Hypnotic Eyes in the World" or *Ebony*'s "Twenty Greatest Sex Symbols" of the twentieth century—I really didn't know what to say. I was eternally grateful when it happened, but it always came as a surprise.

But the whole "pretty" culture was also different at that time. If you compare glamour celebrity shots from the 1970s to present-day imagery, you will find a myriad of conflicting messaging today that begins with girls who are not yet even ten years old—the overwhelming desire for plastic surgery, Botox, the artificial filtering of photos. . . . I could go on and on.

I do admit to having a side of me that wants to be seen as "pretty," that hopes that there are no new wrinkles, that doesn't want to stand on the scale, that wants to be recognized as "glamorous." I cringe when I see unflattering photos of myself in the media, I sigh when certain clothes don't fit anymore. I regret the years I lost before age set in when I was just trying to survive. I lost a LOT.

I had been dyeing my hair since it first started turning gray in my fifties. But when covid hit and everyone was in lockdown in their homes, I decided to let it grow out and see what it was that God had given me. Never would I have expected to embrace a crown of silver gray. Now I wear it as a rite of passage.

Today I find myself looking in the mirror and saying "There she is," the Jayne that I liked on the outside. I'm perfectly comfortable with the one in development on the inside.

# CHAPTER FORTY-THREE

# CIRCLE OF LIFE

April 28, 2014: I saw Kopper's caller ID. With my cheeriest "Good morning, Kopper," my whole world changed. "Mommy"—she sobbed heavily.

It was 8:24 a.m. and immediately I thought she was on her way to work, so she must have been in a car accident. Her voice told my heart to stop beating. Then she pulled herself together, but only for a split second.

"Mommy, Grandpa died."

All I remember is crying and screaming with the phone still in my hand, and I could not stop. Bill ran in and I cried out loud, "Daddy died," and hearing those words coming out of my mouth for the first time, I collapsed to the floor. Kopper was still on the phone and I knew I had to say something for her . . . but nothing would come.

I wanted so much to comfort her. I could hear her crying and yelling to me, "Mommy! Mommy!" All I could think of was I had just written a memo to myself the day before—*Call Dad tomorrow*. Then Bill took the phone; I was heaving and crying a gut-wrenching cry that radiated from within my body that I had never heard before. Then only minutes later Savannah called from Boston. Then Kopper called again and said it was all over Facebook, and

Zaïre was in class. Kopper did not want Zaïre to find out on social media, so she raced to USC to bring her home. By the end of the week, we were all in Ohio.

He had come into the house from his usual hanging outside in the garage fiddling with stuff, waving to the neighbors as they drove off to work, and he asked Mom to fix him a cup of coffee. He told her to sit on his knee, which she did, and he said, "You know, Momma, if anything ever happened to me, the kids would take care of you."

And she kissed him, turned to get the coffee . . . and he was gone. . . .

On the day of the wake so many of Dad's friends and family came from all over the country to pay their respects. People he worked with, people we went to school with who I didn't even realize he knew very well. They all remembered him. So many neighbors and coworkers came to the wake from reading about it in the local paper. And then Mr. Lenenski—the Wickliffe High School choir director phenom who we all loved because he was *that* teacher, the one who changed your life, the one who you will never forget. He walked into the wake at the funeral home with his wife, greeted us all, and proceeded to approach Dad, place his hand gently on Dad's heart, and pray. Then with that rich baritone voice of his he began to sing.

*May the Lord bless you and keep you.*

And like magic, because there were so many of his former students in the room from the span of decades that the Harrison family attended Wickliffe High, the sopranos, the altos, the tenors, and the basses, they all began to join in. . . .

*The Lord lift his countenance upon you. And give you peace . . .*

The *amens* were certainly filling every crevice of my heart, with a moment that I will never ever forget. Our family was being wrapped in total love. I was experiencing a different Wickliffe than the one I recalled from 1970 when they couldn't accept that a Black girl was their new Miss Ohio, or the Wickliffe father who said "Who invited the nigger?" Thank you, Mr. L, for your gift.

Thank you to all of Wickliffe. Thank you to all the friends who not only loved Mom and Dad but loved what our community stood for and what our family stood for. This was spectacular, because it was from the hearts of our friends to Dad's heart, which had finally given out after so many years of caring for others before he cared for himself. And because his heart was filled with so much love, God saw fit to take him mercifully. No suffering. His heart failed and he was gone before he hit the floor.

Out of the ten children in Dad's family, his only surviving siblings were Janet, Mable, Ruth, and Elizabeth. Throughout the years these ladies *always* had something to say, but on that day, they sat stoically in silence, in utter disbelief, with nothing to say. There *was* nothing to say. Their eyes said it all. All of their lives, without parents to raise them, he was their protector. He was the family patriarch, the brother, the adviser, and the provider. And he was gone. As I left the wake the director reached out to hold on to my arm and said, "You know, Herb had time for everyone. Just a few weeks ago I saw his red truck and waved, but then he pulled over to shake my hand and greet me." A wave just was not enough.

As I had ridden around town in Dad's red truck that week, I couldn't figure out why so many people were always waving. Now I knew: They thought I was Dad.

Covenant Baptist Church of Wickliffe was our church home. In 1971 Reverend Ronald Kelder performed my wedding there. Ever since it first opened its doors in 1957 under the pastoral guidance of Reverend Otto Loverude, the Harrison family took care of Covenant Baptist. We grew up painting, building, cleaning, and repairing that church *every* weekend. In 1962 a second section of the church was added with additional rooms that the board of education rented as classrooms. It was in one of those classrooms in 1963 that I sat listening as the public address system was interrupted with a flash bulletin announcement—President John F. Kennedy had been assassinated.

Covenant Baptist was our home away from home. But in 2014 it was up for sale. The church had long been vacated, the flooring was torn up, many of the pews had been sold, and all the decorative finery was gone. The four-and-a-half-acre lawn was now ten inches high. Covenant's membership had been dwindling and the church had been closed while the members looked for a smaller church home.

Only the cross affixed above the pulpit remained. But Covenant's newest pastor, Reverend Christine A. Smith (Covenant's first female pastor), thought it would only be fitting to reopen the doors of Covenant one last time for Dad's homegoing service. The last service at Covenant Baptist on Johnnycake Ridge Road was Dad's.

And the ten-inch grass was because it hadn't been cut since the rains that fell when Dad died: Year after year Dad mowed that lawn, and now the lawn was missing him too. We filed in and sat opposite of how we did every Sunday fifty years before . . . Mom and then youngest to oldest. This time it was Mom and then oldest to youngest.

His final resting place was a hilltop on a country estate beneath a row of pine trees. He had picked it out himself. Just six months earlier he drove my niece India to the spot, pointed to the hilltop, and said, "That's where I want to be buried, India. Remember this."

So, when my sisters Lisa and Brenda and my brother Herb were making Dad's final arrangements, they were looking through his papers but couldn't find any reference to his final plans. Overhearing the conversation, Brenda's daughter, India, told them that he once showed her where he wanted to be laid to rest. Since they were at a loss, Brenda asked, "Do you know the name?"

India said, "No."

They were disheartened.

Then she chimed in, "But I know where it is." Running out the door to Dad's truck, she called back over her shoulder, "I put it in Grandpa's GPS."

Just like Dad . . . he never left things undone.

He passed April 28, 2014. His sage words stay with me to this very day. . . .

"You spend so much time holding on to things. You don't have the ability to grab on to the blessings coming your way. You can't hold on. You have to let go. They're only things that just happened to come your way. When my mother died in February 1940, I was ten. I lost everything. My mother had given me everything I ever wanted. I had so much. But then she was gone. I ran into the woods, and I cried, 'Why me, God? Why me?' Why at ten I had to pull myself together and start life all over again. Sometimes people have to start *more than once* in life. It can't be done unless you release the past, the things. Sometimes you have to start all over again, and again, and again. But each time you have to release all that you had. There are always blessings that await you if you can release and start over strong. Failure comes from weak beginnings. It doesn't matter how many times you start over. Just open your hands and let go . . . and grab onto that new blessing that awaits you."

Life is cyclical. There is no universe where we exist in a vacuum. I am not *just* my father's daughter. I am not *just* my husband's wife. I am not *just* my children's mother. I am *all* of those things.

And we are now all caretakers of the woman who brought us into this world.

My mother has dementia, such a cruel disease. All that you have lived is slowly eaten away. The glorious memories of the things you hold most dear just melt away like they never existed. Dad had kept this away from us while he struggled with caring for her on his own. Now the six of us understand even more about the love he had for this woman.

Following Dad's funeral, I stayed with her for six weeks. And every night she prayed, mixed with the Bengay, Icy Hot, and ibuprofen she needed to manage the pain in her hip. Sometimes the pain was accompanied by spasms in her thigh, requiring deep tissue massage. She was devastated, which brought on a whole other level of total anxiety. (Over the months and years that have followed she has left that devastation behind as well. She manages happily, and knowing that my two sisters are there for her assuages the guilt I feel in living three thousand miles away. Every night she prays before bed just like she did with Dad. And she always ends with . . . *and God bless America.* But when she goes to bed, she has to know that *everyone* is tucked in. She has to check the doors, turn out the lights, and check every room before she retires.)

So, there I was, fully awake, in the dark, lying in bed in the room I grew up in, and listening to new thoughts rumbling through my mind. I had been on this *Plain Jayne* journey to find myself for fourteen years and suddenly I was realizing that I was wrong. All this time I had thought I was onto something . . . being my true self, finding my identity. But lying in that bed it had become so clear: We must live in unity. It was my father teaching me from beyond the grave that life is about family . . . once again. I had fallen into this new era of independence, of technology alienating us day by day . . . when instead we are all our brother's keeper and should never try to avoid that. I have complained endlessly that society's members have lost their compassion for one another, that common decency has become a thing of the past . . . and all the while I had been falling into the *me, me, me* trap myself.

What was I thinking?

My father's death brought together my mother, my four sisters, my only brother, and me all in the same room for the first time in twenty-five years.

Sitting in my bed, in the same bedroom where my teenage self had cried many nights asking God to help her find an answer, I found myself this time talking to Bill, from under the blanket with a pillow over my head so Mom wouldn't hear that I was on the phone. I told him I was keeping a journal of the last month, what I had observed, and what I'd learned. Then he said the most amazing thing: "Jayne, this is your last chapter." Instantly I knew what he meant. That night I couldn't get it out of my head. I started writing again, a reawakening, with new words. I tightened the bed covers as I furiously jotted down my thoughts with only the light from my cell phone on into the early morning hours.

*When I came to Cleveland four weeks prior, the trees were bare and brown but today, I awake to emerald city. Life has been rejuvenated.* That was the last thing I wrote that day.

The B&O train whistled in the distance just as it has since I first heard it as a five-year-old. My dreams as a child of all the far-off places that train would go inspired me to see the world . . . and I did. But there I was again, writing in my old room, and the B&O was still going—it never stops, life never stops. Endings only become new beginnings.

# CHAPTER FORTY-FOUR

# THE LINE IS NEVER BROKEN

I n all those years I had not seen *Amistad* (produced by my friend Debbie
Allen). And when I finally did, as I contemplated these last chapters, I realized, or shall I say I was reminded, that there is no Plain Jayne. There is no me
without all the others. I am the sum of all parts: Overton, Kennedy, Thompson,
Harrison, and all my ancestors I will never know. The pivotal scene in the movie
is when Cinque (played by Djimon Hounsou) says to John Quincy Adams
(Anthony Hopkins) just days before his case is argued before the Supreme
Court: "We won't be going there alone. I will call into the past. Far back to the
beginning of time and beg them to come and help me at the judgment. I will
reach back and draw them to me and they must come. For at this moment,
I am the whole reason they have existed at all. . . . We understand now, we've
been made to understand, and to embrace the understanding . . . that who we
are *is* who we were."

My friend Isaac Belai always talked about the richness of the red
soil of his homeland in Eritrea, Africa. He spoke so spiritually about how

it made him feel and how its color showed up in the skin of the Eritrean people.

In *Roots* Alex Haley wrote of the significance the land held for his family, for all African American families alike.

I recall the feeling of empowerment and belonging when my feet first touched African soil.

It was Mother Earth, the power of Mother Earth.

I have always thought of the world as a whole whenever I heard the phrase *Mother Earth*, putting the emphasis on *Earth* with a capital *E*. But I have come to learn how wrong I was with that as well. It's not Earth; not the planet, it's the soil, the dirt . . . and it's the title *Mother* because we are all birthed from its womb.

The soil. The dirt.

I look at it in its many forms, igneous rock, sedimentary, and metamorphic. I see all colors of dirt from the rich red of the savannas of northern Africa and Georgia to the fine black dirt of Orange County, New York, to the incredible white sand of Tahiti and the Maldives. I see geological plates of all kinds making up the Earth's crust. I see layer upon layer of molten rock, lava, and mantle, until finally at the center of it all it melts down to only one form, the core. Mother Earth, soil from which we were born.

Humankind and the Earth are the same, all colors, all shapes of geological plates, all forms of bodies, like the layers of the Earth. But in the end, we are all the same. In the "core" of our existence we are all the same.

And in the end, isn't it to the dirt that we return?

But as I reflect again on that *Amistad* line, "Who we are *is* who we were," I find myself looking into the future, a future where all people form a melting pot. Where all people have traits of their ancestors that have combined to make one beautiful multicultural blend of people who love one another unconditionally in their sameness as well as in their differences . . . an evolution of race, if you will. And as I have found that Plain Jayne is the fulfillment of all the Jaynes, it is only a truth that the human race is a fulfillment of all races.

Perhaps it is true that my purpose is to forge a path for someone else.

I've thought about that question of purpose for years. . . . What was it that I was supposed to do? . . . And then I thought: Maybe all I am here for is to open a door. And if we can see that—instead of thinking we are some extraordinary end result but rather just simply a way, a passage—then we will be better people preparing for a brighter future. And our future is the whole reason we have existed at all.

We are never plain. We are supreme. We are the culmination of all our combined experiences to make a *gift* to our children, our future. We *are* sons and daughters. We *are* husbands and wives. We *are* mothers and fathers. We *are* grandchildren . . . and great-grandchildren. We are our family. Our collective lives have intersected at this particular time in the universe for a reason. And my family is your family.


Every time I go home, I visit Dad's grave. I take with me a blanket and a cup of coffee that I pick up from the quaint convenience store down the street from where he rests. Dad loved his coffee. I sit with him and pour a sip on the headstone, and we share. Then I talk. Usually quite a lot. Two years after he passed, I found myself again at his graveside sharing coffee. It was a beautiful fall day, and it just reminded me how much I miss Ohio and the changing of the leaves. The view from his hilltop is majestic, and so I spent quite a lot of time enjoying just being there and telling Dad about my new direction and what I'd been doing over the last two years and how I had so many questions yet unanswered about how to relaunch my career, and all kinds of "stuff," for which I truly didn't expect answers.

Then I remembered the very last words he ever said to me, when he dropped me off at the airport after Savannah's graduation from Syracuse University, whispering in my ear, *Jayne, you're better than this, you need to lose weight,* as he hugged me and sent me off to catch my flight.

So, I sat there beaming as I told him that I had kept my last promise to him, to lose weight, and was down more than sixty pounds and losing more. I just needed to vent. And when I was done, I sat quietly . . . for a long time: listening to the cars whisk by on the lonely, picturesque country road filled with the brilliance of the autumn leaves. Basking in the sunlight with the crisp wind in my hair, I was truly having a beautifully serene moment . . . when suddenly I heard Dad's big booming voice.

"What the hell are you waiting for? I've already given you all that you need to know. JUST DO IT."

That was 2016. I began writing this chapter in 2014 and I kept telling myself, and everyone else, that I hadn't written the final chapter. Oprah had suggested I should wait to publish the book until my youngest was out of university. So that was my excuse, I was waiting, on Oprah's timeline. Well, in May of 2017 Zaïre graduated from college. My last excuse was now gone.

As I am finally finishing, May 2025, eight years later, I realize I didn't want it to be Dad's death that was my final chapter. Why is this so hard? But as Cinque argued, it is not final—because he is standing beside me.

Plain Jayne is finished . . . time to begin again.

# CHAPTER FORTY-FIVE

# THE QUEEN OF INFINITE WINS

According to my daughter Zaïre when she researched the etymology of the origin and meaning of my name, it turns out that *Jayne* is defined as "the queen of infinite wins." Believing this and actually accepting it presents a stark dichotomy. At times in my life, I wondered why I was so blessed. Yes, it was a massive struggle to succeed, with the many sacrifices that led to *Jayne Kennedy* becoming a household name. In 1985 Coca-Cola named me the "Most Admired Black Woman in America." *Ebony* wrote, "Jayne Kennedy was one of the most popular names in America." BET featured me—along with others, from Audrey Pulvar to Oprah Winfrey—in a list of the "Ten Black Females Firsts in TV Journalism Around the World," women who helped to break color barriers across the globe. *Essence* magazine listed me in its "10 Black Women News Anchors Who Paved the Way in Broadcast Journalism," and there were numerous other accolades.

Along with Mayor Tom Bradley, I welcomed Queen Elizabeth II to the city of Los Angeles. I campaigned for Senator Ted Kennedy. I worked on congressional committees with Ron Brown and Congressman Ron Dellums. I stood beside "Auntie" Maxine Waters, Mayor Karen Bass, Congresswoman Diane Watson, and on many occasions Reverend Jesse Jackson, including during his 1984 run for the Oval Office. I led initiatives with Dr. Dorothy Height's National Council of Negro Women and the Southern Christian Leadership Conference.

Fast-forward thirty-plus years later and it's almost as if I *never* existed. When the Obamas were in office, I was hoping to offer my services to FLOTUS, Michelle Obama, on one of her many programs to assist young girls and spread awareness about her global education initiative Let Girls Learn. I reached out to her office in advance of a trip to Washington, DC, to visit my daughter, and we were scheduled to meet in First Lady Mrs. Obama's office at the White House. After a very long wait, Savannah, Zaïre, and I ended up having a brief and seemingly gratuitous meeting with her senior policy adviser instead, since the First Lady was preparing for her trip to Cuba. The adviser was polite and asked that we spread the word about FLOTUS's agenda items . . . but that was it. The staffer had no idea who I was and did not respond to my request to join the other celebrities who had been recruited to promote the program nationally.

My point is not to air "sour grapes" or demonstrate resentment toward anyone, especially women whom I deeply admire, but I must consistently weigh the costs of my sacrifice. If you could see in my heart the battle each and every day to stay strong . . . you would know the excruciating pain of my darkness even after so many years of being in the *light*.

A few years ago, I met with an agent at one of the top talent agencies in LA. Well, let's say I *requested* a meeting. An industry acquaintance recommended someone who they thought would be the best possible agent for me to work with to jump-start my career. After about a month of "gentle" reminders to my friend, she finally gave me a name and I called to set up the meeting. The agent's assistant set the date when I should *call in* to take the meeting. Wait. What? It would only be a phoner? And this was way before Zoom calls became a thing. I wanted to come in to meet the agent in person the way I was accustomed to in my "previous" life. How do you sign talent without even having face time with the artist? But I acquiesced. I called in. Even though by then I had a sinking feeling what the outcome would be.

After some ten minutes he condescendingly said, "We only represent stars." I was, of course, already very familiar with their talent list and I knew that already. So, basically, he was telling me that I was not a star—not anymore. I guess it didn't matter to him that without me and other women like me who in the 1950s, '60s, and '70s broke down barriers for African American women in Hollywood today, the path for actresses like Halle, Viola, Kerry, Taraji, and so many others would arguably not have been so accessible. And there certainly wouldn't be a Black "superagent" telling me I was no longer relevant and not even good enough for him to spend thirty minutes of his time with me face-to-face . . . if for no other reason than out of respect for what I had accomplished.

Yes, there was a huge cost to pay—and it hurt. Today's Black actresses continue to assert how difficult it is and how much further Hollywood must go before there is a sense of equity and balance in how they are hired, perceived, and "valued" by the powers that be . . . and they are 100 percent correct. But if they only knew the pain of those before them who truly suffered. The Hollywood Queens who opened the doors and paid the price. Some will never be given their due respect and some whose careers have been completely forgotten will never be acknowledged or duly chronicled. For all of those who fought tooth and nail for their talents and voices to be seen and heard, I bow down: Judy Pace, Vonetta McGee, Teresa Graves, Lynne Moody, Lonette McKee, BernNadette Stanis, Kathleen Bradley, Tracy Reed, Gloria Hendry, Trina Parks, Nichelle Nichols, Irene Cara, Tamara Dobson, Rosalind Cash, Paula Kelly, Madge Sinclair, Lee Chamberlin, Brenda Sykes, Joan Pringle, Denise Nicholas, Jeannie Bell, Jonelle Allen, Sheila Frazier, Akosua Busia, Rosanne Katon, Diana Sands, Shirley Washington, Lola Falana, Juanita Moore, Marki Bey, Esther Rolle, Gail Fisher, Ja'Net DuBois, Nell Carter, Isabel Sanford, and so many more.

You may think that I'm bitter, but I am not. Not in the least. I had my shot . . . my day in the sun . . . and I celebrate my contemporaries who are still in the game and thriving: Sheryl Lee Ralph, Vanessa Williams, Debbie Allen, Marla Gibbs, Phylicia Rashad, Margaret Avery, Jackée Harry, Leslie Uggams, Vanessa Bell Calloway, Debbi Morgan, Dawnn Lewis, Shari Belafonte, and others. However, there are still these persistent feelings that keep me awake at night. Voices in my head and in my heart that say the *queen of infinite wins* is not done yet . . . not just yet.

# CHAPTER FORTY-SIX

# HOLLYWOOD'S PARADOX

Despite the manner in which film and television over the decades has depicted Los Angeles as a city with a prominent Black population, the percentage of African Americans has rarely been in the double digits. There was, of course, the Great Migration from the South beginning at the early part of the twentieth century up until about 1970, when Blacks were escaping bigotry and racial violence and Los Angeles became the most populated city for Blacks on the West Coast—but those numbers started to decline by 1980. Today, the percentage of Blacks in Los Angeles is teetering around 8 percent.

So, when Leon and I arrived in LA in 1971, I'm pretty certain we thought there would be a vibrant and robust Black community, intertwined throughout the city, that would embrace us, much like the cities we were raised in back East (e.g., Cleveland; Washington, DC; Detroit). In fact, what we actually discovered was quite the opposite. The majority of Blacks in LA were pretty much redlined into two enclaves: South Central and Baldwin Hills / Ladera Heights. Both seemed to be doing relatively well (albeit on opposite ends of the economic spectrum), and Black culture was indeed thriving. But while geographically in mere miles they were not that far from Hollywood, by every other measure that distance might as well have been as wide as the Grand Canyon—and that became obvious to us very quickly.

We both intuitively knew that because of the times we would probably not be welcomed with open arms by mainstream Hollywood, but we were young and ambitious, and despite the fact that it was literally just a few short years after the Watts Riots in 1965 and the assassinations of Martin Luther King Jr. and Bobby Kennedy—resulting in fiery social rebellions that upended cities across the country—we were not daunted in the least. We knew we had Leon's uncle and aunt's household as our temporary home base. Moreover, we came to LA with a syndicated TV show in hand, having already been sold into several cities, so we were not exactly complete neophytes in regard to the business. Instead, we anticipated we would be able to impress Hollywood enough to at least get us up and running fairly soon.

Fortunately, meeting Lamonte McLemore of the 5th Dimension was a significant foot in the door, as it seemed he knew almost everyone Black in LA's entertainment industry (not exactly a huge number at that time). Not only did Lamonte assist on numerous occasions by notifying me of potential job opportunities, but his Encino home was "Grand Central Station" for Hollywood's African American entertainers, who flocked to his door. However, other doors began to open for us as well. Despite the fact that there weren't that many Blacks in LA to begin with—you can now imagine what the subset of that universe looked like for Blacks in Hollywood—there were a few industry nightclubs Blacks were comfortable patronizing, most notably Maverick's Flat on Crenshaw Boulevard. There, on any given night familiar faces from TV and film, as well as R&B hitmakers, would all be present to celebrate LA's festive nightlife. For Leon and me, *the* place to be seen and to network was the coveted house parties of our good friend Sammy Davis Jr. We had the incredible opportunity there to mingle with the "true" Hollywood elite, the *real* dealmakers and executives who called the shots in town—most of whom were *not* Black.

The early 1970s was also a very challenging time for the film industry in general, as the legacy studios were having a problem transitioning from the middle-of-the-road fare of the 1950s and '60s (i.e., John Wayne Westerns and Doris Day and Rock Hudson rom-coms) and trying to figure out how to attract a younger, more rebellious audience seeking entertainment that reflected their own experience—not that of the fifty- and sixty-year-old white executives who were green-lighting the seemingly irrelevant films of the day. So that presented a very unique (and unfortunately short-lived) opportunity for Blacks in Hollywood who had been struggling for years to get a toehold inside Tinseltown . . . and Blaxploitation was born.

Melvin Van Peebles opened Hollywood's eyes to an entire new "urban" audience it had been neglecting when in 1971 he independently produced and starred in *Sweet Sweetback's Badasssss Song*. The film *was* made on a shoestring budget and went on to gross over $15 million (that's nearly $120 million today). Leon and I knew due to unforeseen industry circumstances (and our good fortune) that our timing could not have been better.

It was around this time in the mid-1970s that a burgeoning Hollywood film industry was taking shape in, of all places . . . the Philippines! Filipino producer, director, and writer Cirio H. Santiago, who had established himself as an accomplished filmmaker in the 1950s and '60s, wanted to expand his reach into international markets with international talent and began a collaboration with B-movie producer Roger Corman and his New World Pictures company in Hollywood. They had a modest success in 1971 with *The Big Doll House*, which starred a then unknown young actress by the name of Pam Grier. *The Big Doll House*'s release, coupled with the off-the-charts success of *Shaft* later that year, caused Hollywood to recognize the monetization opportunity of Black media, and they couldn't produce Black-themed action films fast enough. In retrospect, it is commonly acknowledged by film industry historians that Blaxploitation literally saved Hollywood's bottom line during those years, as many of the major studios were struggling to find stories that resonated with more diverse audiences.

I auditioned for and was cast as one of the leads in Cirio's 1976 film

*The Muthers* and, as a result, was his choice for the lead in his follow-up film *Death Force* in 1978, along with Leon, James Iglehart, and Carmen Argenziano. Leon and I were successful in negotiating a producer's credit on *Death Force*, which expanded our résumé beyond simply being "talent." Years later, Quentin Tarantino has cited these two films among his all-time favorites from that era!

With the advance of B-films, the small community of Black actors, directors, producers, and writers in LA were finding legitimate employment in their respective crafts—many for the very first time. And just a few years prior to this, in 1967, the NAACP (which had been putting pressure on Hollywood for decades, going all the way back to *Birth of a Nation* and *Amos 'n' Andy*) had launched its own Image Awards to recognize Black achievement and excellence in the business. Those early years of the awards show were akin to the painful birthing of a child, compared to the joy and pride of what it has become today. But the few of us who were managing to make a living in the industry did everything we could in those nascent years to ensure that the show went on. We were family, and the NAACP Image Awards was like a family reunion. We were all there to support each other, to celebrate our achievements—even if mainstream Hollywood did not. We all turned up and showed out to make sure our collective dreams became a reality.

In my research for this book, I unearthed archival records that I hadn't looked at in over forty years. Personally, I had six huge plastic bins (each two to three feet deep) full of magazine cover stories, newspaper clippings, photographs, and miscellaneous materials dating back to the mid-'60s. And that was only the tip of the iceberg. Leon also had a cargo container full of the same for both of us that would no doubt require the assistance of a professional archivist because of the sheer volume of memorabilia that we had generated. What was most incredible about rediscovering these materials was, number one: how accurate my memory had been as I compared my manuscript against articles written decades ago; and number two: what I didn't remember because of the whirlwind vortex we were both in for so many years. There were scores of interviews and cover editions of magazines and photo sessions that I didn't even recall participating in or conducting. And while there were the occasional general market articles in *People*, *TV Guide*, and *Us* magazines (rarely if ever the cover though), the vast majority of the materials were from the Black press—and my God, I could not believe how *much* had been written about me and later about the both of us and then again about me after our divorce. Even before I met Leon there were tons of newspaper articles about the "young Negro girl" who was modeling at the May Company, winning scholastic awards, representing her high school at Girls State / Girls Nation, and any number of accolades. How did I find time to do all of this? What made me such an overachiever? And the later articles once I landed in Hollywood, in now-defunct Black magazines like *Right On!*, *SOUL*, *Sepia*, *Focus*, and so many others—not to mention the dozens of articles and covers for *Ebony* and *Jet*—where my face (and oftentimes *our* faces) appeared on the cover, along with expansive four-to-six-page spread articles examining every possible aspect of our public lives, with quotes credited to me that I'm certain I never actually said.

Then in the magazines from the mid-'80s, I noticed a dynamic shift to more general market periodicals, including publications like *Good Housekeeping*, *American Baby*, and even *Vogue*. That was a clear sign that something truly positive was definitely happening for me career-wise—that I was becoming a household name . . . not only on the coasts, but in middle America as well.

So . . . all of this leads me to ask the question: Did I *really* impact the culture in any significant way or was I just a novelty of the times? This question resurfaces in my mind when there are times that I feel "erased" or omitted when conversations about public figures in contemporary media are discussed or chronicled. CNN produced a multipart documentary series in 2023 entitled *See It Loud: The History of Black Television*, and I was nowhere to be found despite having appeared in tens of dozens of television shows, most of them in *prime time*—not even a footnote. On June 23, 2014, *Jet* magazine released its final printed issue, entitled *An American Icon*, with thirty-eight of their past covers on the front, and the entire issue was permeated with significant stories in all categories of Black life and the people behind those stories. Reading through the pages, one cannot help but be inspired by our legacy as a people and the hundreds and hundreds of significant people who made those stories a reality. Yet, as I read through every page, there was no mention of me at all. I have been told that I had the most *Jet* covers ever . . . roughly twenty in total. But in 2014, where was I?

And then out of the blue in 2022, I received a call from a representative of Quentin Tarantino. He said he was a huge fan and that *The Muthers* was highly influential in shaping his directorial style. He had completely restored the film at immense personal expense (I was told mid–six figures) and was having a premiere screening at the LA theatre that he owned . . . and wanted to know, would I please be his guest of honor along with two other actresses in the film? Are you kidding me??? Of course I said YES. It was a sold-out red-carpet event with tons of fans, media, and paparazzi. So, for that brief moment, I knew my work had reached a mass audience and captured the attention of a world-class director—but still it has not been sustained.

Perhaps I have to take some of that blame myself. After the videotape was released, I hid from *everyone* for many, many years. It was during this time that I became very involved with my daughters' academic activities, including elite sports programs, coaching, and managing their club soccer and AAU basketball teams—and even then, most of the other parents never recognized who I was because of my weight gain. In my mind, the Jayne Kennedy that the world knew had literally disappeared. So yes, I do have to take some personal responsibility for the lack of recognition by today's Hollywood (Black or otherwise) in what I had accomplished over my career, my contributions, and my legacy to the entertainment industry and the culture in general.

Fortunately, there was a New York City agent, Murray Weiss, who believed in my story, and after nearly eighteen months of pitching to almost every major publishing house, we landed with Aliya King Neil at Andscape, which has allowed me, in the words of Auntie Maxine, to finally "reclaim my time," and I could not be more grateful to the both of them for finally *seeing me* when so many others chose not to.

All that said, I cannot in all honesty say I have been completely forgotten, as organizations over the past few years have made a point to acknowledge my hard-fought victories as a pioneer for all women, a word that as a young lady in my twenties, I would have never thought would be used to describe me.

There have also been a couple of NFL-related documentaries that I was asked to participate in, one being the *History of the Black Quarterback*, a story near and dear to my heart due to my relationships with Doug Williams, James "Shack" Harris, and other players who broke long-standing barriers in the league. Only in hindsight can I appreciate how key my role was. In 1978, there was only one Black quarterback in the NFL, Doug Williams. The first Black quarterback was Fritz Pollard in 1920. He became the first African American head coach in the NFL in 1921. In 1920, he and Bobby Marshall were the first African American NFL players in the entire league, and they won the 1920 championship. James "Shack" Harris became the first Black quarterback to start an NFL game, in 1969. There were zero Black head coaches in the modern era until 1989, when Art Shell came on board with the Oakland Raiders, and certainly no Black team owners. However, more recently Magic Johnson (Washington Commanders), Mellody Hobson and Condoleezza Rice (Denver Broncos), and Venus and Serena Williams (Miami Dolphins) are thankfully making strides to change that.

Being asked to be a part of these projects has indeed taken a little bit of the "sting" out of my sense of feeling *sidelined* (sorry for the pun). My hope is that the ensuing years of my career will be as impactful as the years that have preceded them and that my passion and authenticity will continue to motivate and inspire generations for years to come.

# CHAPTER FORTY-SEVEN

# IN MY OWN SKIN

've often wondered how different my career would have been had it been a few decades later: a time when women in the entertainment industry, especially Black women, are experiencing greater acceptance and more agency and options regarding their chosen profession. A time now when women are taken more seriously as entrepreneurs and thought leaders and have the ability to speak their minds and express themselves on issues that matter to them without fear of "stepping out of their lane."

Being a product of the 1960s, I was fascinated and gripped by all of the social unrest and upheavals of that era, and I had very pointed opinions about nearly everything in my youth. Perhaps that was why I made every effort to be active in as many high school activities as I could, including student government. With the Kent State uprising, I was determined to do my part to take a stand and be involved, even if that only meant being a part of Girls Nation—I was going to *do something*. God knows there was no way on earth that my parents would have ever allowed me to be in harm's way and actually participate in any student sit-ins or demonstrations.

Make no mistake though, I challenged and pushed wherever and whenever I could if I saw something that wasn't right. In hindsight, I probably could have applied a bit more of that chutzpah in certain aspects of my career, but I was paving my own path without any real role model or mentor who could point out the proverbial land mines. As the saying goes, I was building the plane while we were flying. No full-time management team, no sisterhood of like-minded young women who I could lean on when times were hard. I specifically recall that it was Marla Gibbs who intentionally made herself available when it came to me seeking advice. I would have so loved to have had just a small network of female friends who I could have been close to through that part of my life. But I wasn't ever that girl. I think friends close to me were waiting on me to make the first move, but being on the road had turned me into a lone wolf.

Yes, there were a few friends that I have held close to my heart throughout my lifetime. But to be honest, particularly after the videotape incident, I pushed everyone away—everyone. Even Claudette, my best friend since I was nineteen. So, I must accept my role in not maintaining the few close female bonds that I had established. Of course, there were my four sisters, whom to this day I love with all my heart.

Which brings me to my little brother, Herb Jr. Because there was such a gap in age between us (nearly fourteen years), we really did not get to know each other that well until we were both adults. I took *every* opportunity to include him in my life. I rerouted my travel plans to make it home to see his baseball games. I took him with me to the Indy 500 so he could sit in the lead car with me and wave to the hundreds and hundreds of thousands waving back and calling my name. . . . He just beamed with overwhelming joy. Then there was also the jazz cruise to Mexico. And when he turned twenty-one, I threw a small birthday party for him, but what he remembers the most is that I gave him the keys to my Mercedes so he could drive around town and visit his friends. But I think the highlight was when I introduced him to Magic Johnson, who invited him to participate in his summer basketball camps for the next four years. My six-foot-nine basketball-powerhouse brother couldn't have been prouder . . . that is, until Magic decided to play a pickup game and asked him if he could borrow his sneaks.

Of all of my siblings, I always thought that Herb was the one who may have been the proudest of me. There was always a special connection between us. So, it absolutely broke my heart when, in 2020, he had a freak accident at his home, damaging several vertebrae, resulting in him being paralyzed from the neck down. Needless to say, the entire family was devastated. Herb's wife, Sandy, has been an absolute godsend and has been with Herb every step of the way—literally though thick and thin. Fortunately, he has stabilized and appears to be handling it with as much grace as could be expected.

Family has always been the *essence* of my strength. It gave me my value system, my sense of being, and the confidence to conquer anything I set my mind upon. Family indelibly informed me and made me who I am today. How else would a small-town Midwestern girl who grew up picking tobacco on her uncle's farm in the summers ever find the courage to embark on such an improbable journey? Now as a mother myself to four beautiful young women, I have been so conscious of ensuring that I have given them everything that I had—and more. That "more" being a university education, something that I had always dreamed about and planned for . . . but life had a different direction and mission for me. My girls have provided me so much joy and appreciation for life. I'm not sure how I could have survived without them. They are each so unique in their own way and yet so much alike. Bill and I are so fortunate to see them all now as self-sustaining adults, with full lives and successful careers.

There is one day that I will remember forever. My daughters know how much I desired to graduate college. I had instilled in them the value of a college degree since they were in kindergarten. So, when Zaïre, my last little Overton, graduated from USC, they had a graduation robe and hat specially designed for me. On the back of the robe was embroidered "Class of '07, '11, and '17," indicating that I had in fact graduated three times with all the time

I put into supporting every aspect of their collegiate journey. They had all graduated from Santa Monica High School, Home of the Vikings, so the cap read MOTHER OF VIKINGS. I couldn't have been prouder!

The last several years as I have tried to understand the meaning of my life, existentially speaking, I've begun to see myself and all that I have accomplished ironically through *other people's eyes*. During the whirlwind days of my career, I never had time for introspection or even contemplated what impact I was having on the culture. It did not cross my mind, not even once. There was no internet or social media, so there was no feedback loop; all I knew was that I was continuing to be booked for films and television shows and magazine covers and interviews—so I *must* have been doing something right.

It really hadn't hit me until these last few years as I've been thinking about the final chapters of my memoir and how to put my life into some kind of context, not only for you, the reader, but also for me. Fortunately, things started to come into focus in 2018 when one of my social media followers sent me a photo from the Smithsonian National Museum of African American History & Culture of me on the wall next to Nat King Cole, Diahann Carroll, Nichelle Nichols, Don Cornelius, and Diana Ross and the Supreme. It was part of the Television and the Media Landscape gallery, a subsection of the *Watching Oprah* exhibit, which celebrates media pioneers. I was completely speechless—surely it was a mistake. I messaged him back immediately: "OH MY GOSH, when did you do this? You gotta be kidding me. This is unbelievable. Too bad you didn't get it from the other angle so I could actually see that it was really me." The very next day I got another message from him. He had gone back and taken another photo from the other angle—and there I was right next to Nat King Cole. Pinch me.

I called Savannah, who lived in Washington, DC, at the time, and told her I was booking a flight the following week and that we had to go see this in person. I cannot describe the feeling of finally being "seen" that I had that day when we entered the museum and saw the exhibition. All the years of busting my butt . . . every *no* . . . every *you're too tall* . . . every *you're too light* or *too dark* . . . every *you're too* . . . every *we don't feature Black women on magazines because they don't sell . . .* every *Black people don't buy posters, so we aren't interested in creating one for you. . . .* None of that mattered now—the Smithsonian's Museum of African American History & Culture knew what I meant to them. I've never felt so humbled in all my life. My mind quickly flashed back to Girls Nation, when I stood at the giant Foucault pendulum in the floor of the Smithsonian's Museum of History and Technology (now the National Museum of Natural History). The pendulum seemed to be moving, but in actuality, it was the earth that was moving—leaving me to ponder what that pendulum saw for me in my future.

When CBS fired me, without even knowing it they had not only swung a sledgehammer at me, but also sounded a wake-up call to Black America. *What happened to Jayne Kennedy?* was uttered in Black beauty salons and barbershops across the country. And while CBS did not see nor appreciate my value to the culture—especially *to* the Black community—now, four decades later, the Smithsonian's Museum of African American History & Culture *did*. And guess which photo was selected out of the thousands of images taken of me over the years? . . . Yep, my publicity photo from *The NFL Today*.

A few years later, in 2022, I received an invitation from the venerable National Sports Media Association, a long-standing organization that up until recently had consisted mainly of the white male sports journalists who dominated print and broadcasting media across the country—many of whom, back then, had very unfavorable and misogynistic things to say about my days as a co-anchor on *The NFL Today*. The NSMA wanted to present me with their Roone Arledge Award for Innovation. This was the *last* organization I had ever expected to receive any recognition from, yet here they were inviting me to be their keynote speaker and recipient of their highest award for sports journalism. It was a wonderful evening, and I was so pleased to see so many *female* journalists in the audience, something that certainly did not exist when I was shattering the glass ceiling on the Emmy Award–winning *NFL Today* back in 1978.

And speaking of *The NFL Today*, NFL Films was commissioned in 2023 by CBS to produce a documentary on the groundbreaking show, which had premiered in 1975 and which completely changed the rules of pregame football programming forevermore. Brent Musburger and I, as the only two hosts still alive, were asked by NFL Films to be the featured subjects of the documentary, *You Are Looking Live!*, which ran on CBS right before the 2024 Super Bowl. I was leery of a bittersweet experience, since I did not leave the show of my own volition. Before they hired me, I did tell the documentary's producers that I would speak my truth, thinking they would just edit what they wanted to out of it. However, *The NFL Today* still and will forever hold a place in my heart. The walk down memory lane with Brent was amazing; then, at the end of the show, the producers showed me a clip they had filmed of Thomas "Hollywood" Henderson (the famous Dallas Cowboys linebacker) when he had appeared on the New York desk at CBS the season after I left, saying directly to Brent on air: "We miss our queen . . . Jayne Kennedy . . . we miss our queen." I had never seen that clip before. A multitude of emotions welled up within and I lost it right then and there on the set. I couldn't speak. I'd always known how much the athletes respected and supported me, especially the Black players, but to hear one of them verbalize that on the show the season after I had been so unceremoniously fired brought me to tears. Thankfully, the NFL Films producers let me tell my side of what *really* happened and how CBS had lied at the time about my departure, and unbelievably it was *not* edited out of the final cut that aired on the network that Super Bowl Sunday. I have felt a sense of calm that I've never felt before about that entire fiasco since the airing of the documentary, which ultimately won a coveted Sports Emmy later that year. Vindicated at last.

In the spring of 2024, during the annual television and film awards season here in LA and just before the NAACP Image Awards, I was invited by the Hollywood chapter of the NAACP to participate in a panel discussion about the disparity in pay for people of color, especially women, in front of and behind the camera in the entertainment industry—a controversial issue that Taraji P. Henson boldly spotlighted earlier in the year around the release of the reimagined version of *The Color Purple*. Sadly, much of that identical conversation had been had by me and my peers within the business some forty years ago. While I know some progress has been made over the intervening years, we still obviously have a long way to go.

The Image Awards were built and developed by so many of us Black actors and actresses who were denied recognition at the Oscars and other awards ceremonies. So we celebrated, and supported, ourselves. It was a challenge indeed, and no matter how long it took, no matter how we struggled to finance the awards, no matter if we had no airtime . . . we stuck together through all those early years because we were family.

In 1982, I had won the Image Award for best actress in a motion picture for my performance as Julie Winters in *Body and Soul*, sharing the stage that night with the incredible Louis Gossett Jr., who won best actor in a motion picture for *An Officer and a Gentleman*. That trophy had been stolen from me thirty years before and was my crowning achievement as an actress. For me, the Image Award was everything. And when it was gone it took a part of me as well.

But what made that night in 2024 truly special was that my manager secretly arranged to have a new Image Award Best Actress trophy made for me. So, after the panel discussion was over, they surprised me with the new award, and I was stunned, shocked, *and* astonished. You have no idea how much this meant to me. The standing-room-only auditorium audience was surprised as well, and they gave me a standing ovation that seemingly went on forever. What an incredible moment, and one that I will always cherish.

So . . . I guess all of this is to say that—despite personally not feeling as though I achieved and accomplished everything that I set out to—maybe I did in my own way make a difference after all. Maybe people did notice that I pushed myself every day to represent women and *my culture* in the most positive light that I possibly could, knowing what obstacles were being collectively placed in our way at every turn.

I know I wasn't perfect—in fact, far from it. But there was something deep inside me that compelled me to keep my eyes on the prize and hopefully open the door for those coming behind me with a similar dream.

Now at this stage in my life, I think I'm finally okay with some of the superlatives that have been attached to my name over the years. *Legend. Icon. Pioneer. Trailblazer. Shero. Boss Woman. Badass.*

Personally, for me, I'm now quite comfortable in my own skin and . . . *Plain Jayne* will do just fine.

# EPILOGUE

n late fall of 2024 as I found myself putting together the final pieces of the *Plain Jayne* puzzle, it dawned on me that literally up to the delivery date of my memoir, Mother Earth was still shaking the ground under my feet, and every day a new puzzle piece emerged. I have now realized that my puzzle has no edges at all. I suppose that is not necessarily a bad thing, as life is ever evolving and as an artist I thrive on *change*.

In October of 2024, I was asked by the family of the incredible actress Juanita Moore if I would speak at her posthumous award ceremony for her long-overdue "star" on the Hollywood Walk of Fame. Of course I said, "Yes, I'd be extremely honored."

I knew Juanita Moore's amazing legacy, as my mother had sat us down in front of the television when we were very young and made us watch her in *Imitation of Life*, which earned her an Oscar nomination in 1960 for Best Actress in a Supporting Role. It became one of my favorites. The film, starring Lana Turner, was groundbreaking. Juanita's character was a Black single mother who was a "domestic" with a daughter who was "passing" for white.

Juanita just knew that with the Academy Award nomination, more fully realized roles would be presented to her—so she vowed to never take any more job offers where she had to enter a scene "carrying a serving tray." Needless to say, the offers stopped coming in and she didn't work again for nearly two years!

When I heard that Debbie Allen and Margaret Avery had also agreed to be guest speakers, there was no way that I would miss this. Debbie, Margaret, and

I are dear friends and go way back to the early 1970s as determined actresses doing everything we could to make a mark in our craft. And we succeeded. My love for these two women is beyond words, and the opportunity to see them again in this setting, recognizing a true pioneer in Juanita Moore, whose shoulders we all collectively stood on, was a full-circle moment . . . perfect kismet and poetic symmetry.

It is still very humbling to receive unsolicited requests and invitations like this, as it reminds and "reconnects" me to the long continuum of Black women in Hollywood going back to Hattie McDaniel, most of whom have had to endure and sacrifice so much to stake their place and to just be seen in a business that only saw them primarily as "props"!

The Hollywood Walk of Fame ceremony for Juanita was warm and beautiful, and I had the opportunity to hug Debbie and Margaret and tell them how much I missed and loved them. There is an unspoken language that we all have when we encounter one another. It is one of acknowledgment and appreciation for still being here—and even more so for *surviving*. Knowing that we have all had our individual battles to fight in this industry, but that the greater *war* we fought was exactly the same; and with understanding that the generations of Black actresses who have come behind us, just as we had come behind Juanita, are still in the trenches today.

In November 2024, I found myself reflecting on the direction our country is taking. My formative years were in the 1960s when the Civil Rights Act had just been passed and the early 1970s when women and members of the LGBTQ+ community were just asserting their own push for equality under the law. It now breaks my heart to know that my four adult daughters will not have the same hard-won rights afforded to them as to me and previous generations of women, the right to have agency over our own bodies. I *am* proud to live in a country where a difference of opinion is respected, and everyone has the right to vote for whom they choose. However, in 2025 as a person of color in America, this is not what I had hoped to see as our future.

I was so proud to see Vice President Kamala Harris, a Black woman, rise to the level of a presidential candidate. It stirred the politically ambitious young girl in me who idolized Shirley Chisholm and was motivated to participate in Girls Nation. And while I would never dare to compare myself with the former vice president, we both no doubt made a mark on tens of thousands of young, aspiring girls of every race, creed, and color who have dreams of becoming leaders and trailblazers in their own right!

Through my message in *Plain Jayne*, I can only hope that our strength and resilience as a people and as a country will sustain the progress that generations before us have fought and died for. That we keep in mind that the only limits that hold us back are the ones that we place on ourselves. This journey began with a prayer that I would find the light of self-discovery. However, as I look at the times and the issues, we face an unknown. An unknown of what America promises. I see with clear eyes that my work is not done yet.

# ACKNOWLEDGMENTS AND HEARTFELT APPRECIATION

William Allen Overton

Savannah Ré Overton

Kopper Joi Overton

Zaïre Ollyea Overton

Cheyenne Maree Overton

Herbert H. Harrison Sr.

Virginia Mary Thompson Harrison

Grandma Jane Jannie Harrison

Grandpa William K. Setzer

Grandma Lois Dawson Thompson

Grandpa Percy George Washington
    "Turk" Thompson

Hessie Sinnery Waterhouse

Eugene Waterhouse

Brenda Harrison

Christine Harrison Chapweske

Herbert H. Harrison Jr.

Alise Harrison Waytes

Shirley Harrison

Kathleen Bradley Redd

Oprah Winfrey

Robin Roberts

Aliya King Neil

Sherri Shepherd

Murray Weiss

Marie Dutton Brown

Leslie Conliffe

Oz Scott

Frank Wheaton

Alex Haley

Claudette Robinson

Lamonte McLemore

Mieko McLemore

Leon Isaac Kennedy

Smokey Robinson

Laura Randolph

Ron Allen

Brent Musburger

Isaac Belai

Kenny Kingston

Judy Pezdir

Dalene Arndt

Sam Militello

Michael Ajakwe

Buster Laney

Sheila Frazier

Cyndi Gossett

Rich Podolsky

Nan O'Brian

Maureen Kennedy

Brent Musburger

Katie Able

Deborah DuCre

Linda Turner

Sherri Rose

Leonard Caldwell

Christopher Caldwell

Ruby Thompson Houston

Pearl Thompson

Dr. Janet Harrison Mason

Deborah Roberts

Bob Costas

George Schlautter

Ernie Johnson

Tamron Hall

Jemele Hill

Lesley Visser

Tavis Smiley

Robert Fishman

Jin Park

Cassandra Normil

Rebecca Lux

Byron Nickleberry

Rheba Fancher

Hank Fancher

Jason Winters

Amy King

Kelly Forsythe

Daneen Goodwin

Belviana Todmann

Olivia Zavitson

Jennifer Levesque

SPECIAL ACKNOWLEDGMENT

# GREGORY AMERSON

couldn't have crossed the finish line to the full realization of *Plain Jayne* without you. Over the last seven years since we first met and you soon after became my manager, the countless months, the exhaustive working sessions, and your ever-present search for clarity helped me to see my thoughts well enough to put to paper when I found myself stuck in "brain fog," trying to recall and compare materials covered over the many iterations of this twenty-five-year journey.

I immediately sensed a simpatico bond with you that I rarely feel with people who have not earned my friendship and trust over decades. There was a calmness in your demeanor, and obvious intellect, but there was something else much more intangible.

You truly *saw* me, parts of myself that I had not even seen—or had refused to acknowledge. Always candid and straightforward, yet thoughtful and sensitive in your critique. I could always count on you for the honest truth. And for that I cannot thank you enough, for your undying support and belief in me . . . and my story.

You helped to light the path at the end of the tunnel I began to construct so many years ago, and for that, I am forever grateful.

Thank you, my friend . . . my ride or die.

Jayne